DIRECTORY

OF

INTERNATIONAL

BUSINESS

DIRECTORY
OF
INTERNATIONAL
BUSINESS

2
Lebanon–Zimbabwe

Jack A. Gottschalk

Salem Press

Pasadena, California   Englewood Cliffs, New Jersey

ISBN 0-89356-822-8 (set)
ISBN 0-89356-824-4 (volume 2)

∞ The paper used in these volumes conforms to the American National Standard for Permanence of Paper for Printed Library Materials, Z39.48-1984.

This publication is designed to provide accurate and authoritative information in regard to the subject matter covered. It is sold with the understanding that the author and the publisher are not engaged in rendering legal, accounting, or other professional service.

Maps provided by Moritz Design

First Printing, Library Edition

Printed in the United States of America

Table of Contents, Volume 2

LEBANON, REPUBLIC OF

■ POLITICAL ENVIRONMENT

For many years this nation was in a state of chaos resulting from a civil war. Until recently, there was no semblance of any functioning government, much less any stability that would be conducive to foreign investment, except perhaps in the financial services sector.

Historically, Lebanon's principal economic activities have been directly or indirectly tied to the provisions of services, particularly financial services, e.g., insurance, offshore banking, and holding companies. These activities continued to function effectively throughout the violent period that embraced the nation.

Inflation is a major problem that faces the country. Unemployment is another, with some estimates placing the percentage of those willing and able to work but unable to locate jobs at over 50 percent.

The nation's external public debt is well within manageable limits, a key consideration with reference to Lebanon's economic future. The government has embarked on a needed program to rehabilitate the country with special emphasis being placed on rebuilding of the national infrastructure, specifically housing and transportation.

Private foreign investment is actively being sought by the government. Foreign monetary assistance in the form of major loans is also desired and, because of the country's relatively low public debt, should be available.

■ SUMMARY OF FOREIGN INVESTMENT POLICY

The principal government agency responsible for the country's program to acquire foreign investment is the Ministry of Economy and Trade.

There are no restrictions on the economic areas in which foreign investors may participate.

Firms that are established as industrial facilities are required to file a plan with the Ministry of Economy and Trade setting out details of the industrial activity.

No requirements exist with regard to managerial participation by the Lebanese government or individuals from the private sector except in the cases of holding companies and offshore companies.

Certain tax incentives are provided, particularly in the form of tax holidays for newly established industrial firms, for periods that can range up to ten years. Eligibility for the holiday requires that the enterprise be established in an area that the government wishes to have developed and that the products manufactured are not already being produced in the country.

■ FORMATION AND TYPES OF PERMITTED BUSINESS ORGANIZATIONS

Foreign investors may participate in the economy of the country through the creation of a public corporation, a limited liability company (i.e., a closed corporation), a general partnership, a special partnership, or a special partnership by actions.

Subsidiaries and branch offices of foreign corporations may be established. Joint ventures may be created between foreign and domestic investors. Foreign corporations must register with the Court of First Instance.

LEBANON

Special partnerships by action are governed by the laws pertaining to corporations and limited liability companies.

Corporations, including limited liability companies, subsidiaries of foreign corporations, and special partnerships by action are considered to be legal entities.

Holding companies may also be established to carry out limited activities in Lebanon. Holding companies need not have an office in the country, but must appoint a resident agent. Offshore companies may be established for the purpose of engaging in activities other than sales and marketing, e.g., leasing operations, ownership of real property, etc. Holding companies and offshore companies are required to appoint at least two Lebanese nationals to the board of directors.

■ ENVIRONMENTAL PROTECTION

The interest of the government in the subject of environmental protection is difficult to discern given the recent war. However, there is a high level office that has been given responsibility in this area, i.e., the Ministry of State for the Environment. Potential foreign investors are advised to contact this agency for complete and current information pertaining to current or projected laws and regulations on the subject of environmental protection.

■ RIGHTS AND OBLIGATIONS OF FOREIGN INVESTORS

The government guarantees that foreign and domestic investors will receive equal treatment under the law and with respect to investment and business opportunities.

Foreign investors may obtain financing from local banking sources.

Real property may be held by foreign businesses that are properly registered with the Court of First Instance.

Foreign investments and all income derived from such investments may be freely repatriated or remitted abroad. In the event of liquidation of any foreign investment, the proper share of such foreign investor may be repatriated or remitted abroad.

Nationalization or expropriation cannot occur under the law. Any taking of property by the government that is required for the benefit of the public must occur under the processes of the law and must involve fair and prompt compensation.

■ LABOR

There is a complete body of laws in existence with regard to employment and working conditions.

Foreign nationals employed in Lebanon must possess work permits and residence permits.

■ ACCOUNTING REQUIREMENTS

All businesses established in Lebanon must maintain complete and accurate accounting, statistical, and other records as required by the government. The law provides that a failure to maintain accounting records that are used for tax purposes can result in a fine that is equal to 50 percent of the tax involved.

Accounting records must be maintained in accord with internationally recognized standards. Public corporations and, depending on their size, limited liability companies must be audited on a yearly basis by an independent auditor.

■ CURRENCY CONTROLS

The Banque du Liban is the nation's central bank, and it has the major responsibility for all matters relevant to foreign exchange.

Foreign businesses and individuals may open and maintain bank accounts in foreign currencies.

Foreign exchange restrictions are quite liberal. There are no restrictions on the amount of foreign currency that may be moved into or from the country.

■ TAXATION

The major tax is that assessed on income, both corporate and personal.

Holding companies and offshore companies are exempt from the income tax, although the latterl are taxed on capital gains realized in Lebanon.

In addition to the income tax, there are other taxes levied to include those on real property, documents, dividends, customs charges, and certain license and registration fees, among other assessments.

Deductions and allowances are available to include depreciation, legitimate expenses, losses, and remuneration of personnel. Individual taxpayers are entitled to certain deductions to include costs of dependents, and educational, medical, business and other legitimate expenses and allowances.

Public corporations, limited liability companies, and special partnerships by action are considered taxable entities. General partnership and limited partnership income is taxed to the partners as individuals.

■ LEGAL SYSTEM

The court system includes the Criminal and Civil Courts of First Instance and the Courts of Cassation, which hear appeals from the Courts of First Instance and which may retry cases heard by those courts. Appeals from the Courts of Cassation are taken to the Courts of Appeal, which sit at Beirut.

■ CUSTOMS AND DUTIES

All goods entering the country are subject to customs duties that are charged either on an ad valorem or weight basis, depending on the nature of the imported goods.

■ PROTECTION OF INTELLECTUAL PROPERTY

Lebanon is a member of the World Intellectual Property Organization as well as accepting the provisions of the Berne, Paris, Brussels, and Washington conventions, the Hague Convention, and the London Conventions dealing with copyrights, patents, tradenames, and industrial property protection. In addition, Lebanon has enacted domestic laws on copyright, patent, industrial property (designs), and trademark and tradename protection.

■ IMMIGRATION AND RESIDENCE

Visas are normally required to visit the country. Potential foreign investors are advised to contact the Ministry of Economy and Trade for complete and current information on requirements and procedures for visas, work permits, and residence permits.

■ FOREIGN INVESTMENT ASSISTANCE DIRECTORY

Sources that can provide further information about foreign investment in Lebanon include:

Ministry of Economy and Trade
Government Offices
Beirut, Lebanon
Ministry of State for the Environment
Government Offices
Beirut, Lebanon

Central Bank of Lebanon
P.O. Box 11-5544
Beirut, Lebanon
Telephone: (0) 865303
Telex: 20744

Persons interested in obtaining additional information about foreign investment are advised to contact the closest Lebanese embassy or consular office.

Lebanon maintains diplomatic relations with Algeria, Argentina, Australia, Austria, Bahrain, Bangladesh, Belgium, Bolivia, Brazil, Bulgaria, Chad, People's Republic of China, Colombia, Cuba, Egypt, Finland, France, Germany, Greece, Haiti, Holy See, Hungary, India, Iran, Iraq, Ireland, Italy, Japan, Jordan, Democratic People's Republic of Korea, Republic of Korea, Kuwait, Liberia, Libya, Mexico, Morocco, Nigeria, Norway, Oman, Pakistan, Paraguay, Poland, Portugal, Qatar, Romania, Russia, Saudi Arabia, Spain, Sweden, Switzerland, Tunisia, Turkey, United Arab Emirates, United Kingdom, United States, Uruguay, Venezuela, and Yemen.

LESOTHO, KINGDOM OF

■ POLITICAL ENVIRONMENT

This nation has been torn by political strife that has continued over a period of many years.

A successful coup d'etat occurred in April 1991. Civil unrest, marked by widespread rioting which resulted in numerous deaths and extensive property damage, took place soon after. Another coup attempt, this one unsuccessful, took place in June 1991.

Lesotho is highly dependent on the Republic of South Africa although relations with that country cannot be described as friendly. The nation is largely agricultural and thus the economy is extremely vulnerable to weather.

The country is underdeveloped. Its annual inflation rate is high and unemployment is staggering.

■ SUMMARY OF FOREIGN INVESTMENT POLICY

The government is attempting to obtain increased levels of foreign investment. It has created the Lesotho National Development Corporation, which has the primary responsibility for promoting foreign investment. The governing law is the Foreign Investment Code of 1989.

There is a strong desire to increase the nation's industrial base, chiefly in the areas of small and medium manufacturing, particularly for export.

Foreign investment is accepted in all areas. However, in activities considered as strategically important to the nation's economic development, the government (in the form of the National Development Corporation) will be a joint venture partner. Such activities principally involve those where local raw materials are used.

Lesotho is a signatory to the Multilateral Investment Guarantee Agency Agreement and is a member of the International Center for the Settlement of Investment Disputes.

Areas of the economy where the government specifically is seeking foreign investment are in export oriented manufacturing, and in activities that are labor intensive thus reducing the currently high level of unemployment.

Additionally, the government is seeking to promote vertical integration in the textile manufacturing industry, and import substitution, particularly in connection with the construction of the Lesotho Water Project.

A variety of incentives has been created for foreign investors to include tax holidays, the establishment of industrial estates and factories, and the availability of low-cost financing.

■ FORMATION AND TYPES OF PERMITTED BUSINESS ORGANIZATIONS

Foreign investors may operate as private companies, external companies, or as companies limited either by shares or by guarantee.

Private companies are limited to the number of shareholders and cannot solicit public invitations to participate in the company. An external company is one that has been formed in another country.

Any company with share capital must be registered with the Registrar of Companies before establishing operations.

Companies limited either by shares or by guarantee are unincorporated enterprises.

LESOTHO

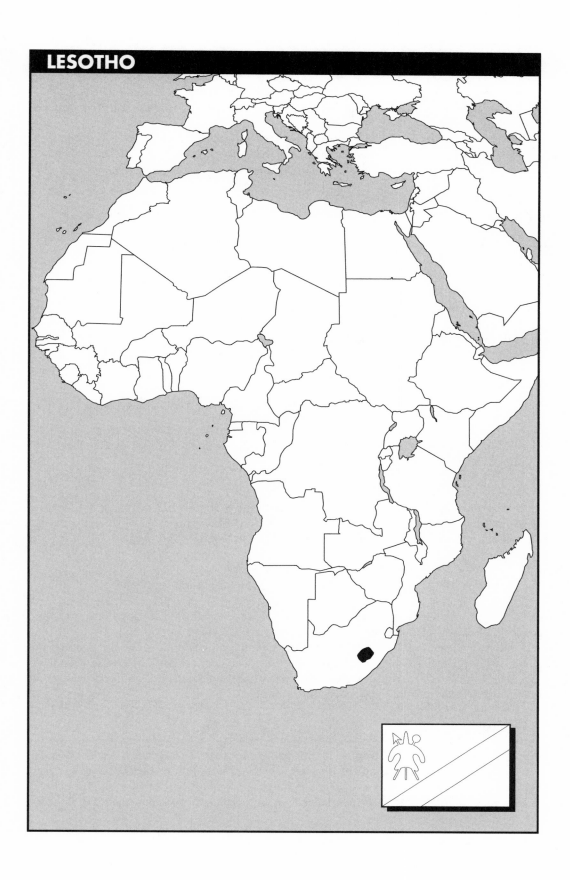

In the former, firm liabilities are limited to the extent of the members' shares. In the latter, the liability of the firm's members is that guaranteed by them in the event of dissolution.

There is no requirement for domestic participation except with respect to joint ventures that may be required between a foreign investor and the National Development Corporation in an enterprise involving strategic economic interests.

■ ENVIRONMENTAL PROTECTION

There is a high level of interest in protection of the environment. Potential foreign investors are advised to contact the National Development Corporation for complete information pertaining to laws and regulations on this subject.

■ RIGHTS AND OBLIGATIONS OF FOREIGN INVESTORS

In terms of investment opportunities, the government guarantees that there will be no discrimination between domestic and foreign investors.

Foreign companies cannot own land. However, the right to land use can be obtained through the National Development Corporation.

Financing may be obtained through the National Development Corporation.

■ LABOR

There is an extensive body of law regarding employment, industrial relations, working conditions, minimum wages, and other relevant matters.

A requirement exists to hire local labor on a preferred basis except in those cases where required technological or other skills are not available. Foreign nationals must obtain a work permit for employment.

■ ACCOUNTING REQUIREMENTS

Public companies must file annual accounts with the Registrar of Companies. All businesses must maintain complete records for tax and other purposes. Financial records must be maintained in accord with internationally accepted standards.

■ CURRENCY CONTROLS

The Central Bank of Lesotho has the responsibility for monetary matters including exchange controls.

The country is a member of the Common Monetary Area with Swaziland and the Republic of South Africa. There are no currency controls within that area.

Because of the changing financial situation, potential foreign investors are advised to contact the National Development Corporation or the Central Bank of Lesotho regarding current information on rules governing repatriation or remittance abroad of investments and income derived from such investments.

■ TAXATION

Lesotho is a party to numerous bilateral agreements on the subject of double taxation.

Foreign companies and individuals are subject to income and other taxes. There is no capital gains tax. There are numerous tax incentives for foreign companies that include tax holidays of up to ten years with a possible extension of five years if classified as in a pioneer status. Other incentives for which companies may be eligible depending on their fields of activity include special tax write-offs on machinery, equipment, and buildings; reduced rates for electricity, water, and sewerage services; and tax allowances for training of local labor and for wages paid to local labor.

■ LEGAL SYSTEM

The court system includes Central and Local Courts, which hear petty criminal and civil cases. The Central Courts may also act as appellate courts on decisions of the Local Courts. Appeals are taken to the Judicial Commissioners' Courts.

The High Court hears major criminal and civil cases and also functions in an appellate role relevant to cases from all lower courts. Final appeals are taken to the Court of Appeal, which sits in Maseru.

■ CUSTOMS AND DUTIES

The country is a signatory to the Lome Convention, which gives its products free entry to the EC, and is a member of the Southern African Customs Union.

Numerous incentives, including rebates of duties designed to protect foreign investors engaged in production for domestic consumption, and rebates of duties on imported equipment and raw materials used by companies in production for export, are available.

■ PROTECTION OF INTELLECTUAL PROPERTY

Lesotho subscribes to internationally accepted standards for protection of copyrights, patents, and trademarks.

■ IMMIGRATION AND RESIDENCE

Visas are usually required for entry into the country. Potential foreign investors are advised to contact the National Development Corporation for complete information regarding requirements for visas, work permits, and residence permits.

■ FOREIGN INVESTMENT ASSISTANCE DIRECTORY

Sources that can provide further information about foreign investment in Lesotho include:

Lesotho National Development Corporation
Private Bag A96
Maseru 100, Lesotho
Telephone: (0) 312012
Telex: 4341 LO
Fax: (0) 310038

Ministry of Trade and Industry
P.O. Box 747
Maseru 100, Lesotho
Telephone: (0) 322802
Telex: 43840
Fax: (0) 310121

Central Bank of Lesotho
P.O. Box 1184
Maseru 100, Lesotho
Telephone: (0) 324281
Telex: 4367
Fax: (0) 310051

Persons interested in obtaining further information about foreign investment in Lesotho also are advised to contact the country's closest embassy or consular office.

Lesotho maintains diplomatic relations with Belgium, Canada, People's Republic of China, Denmark, Germany, Italy, Kenya, Mozambique, United Kingdom, and United States.

LIBERIA, REPUBLIC OF

■ POLITICAL ENVIRONMENT

This country's recent history has been replete with military takeovers, widespread corruption on the part of high level government officials, and a prolonged civil war. There is a significant question as to whether the present government can retain control. Politically, democracy has ceased to be an operative principle in Liberia for many years.

The economy is a fragile one that is essentially based on agriculture. Rubber, along with coffee and cocoa, are the main exports. "Flag of convenience" shipping remains a major source of income.

The nation's infrastructure has been severely damaged by the civil war. Inflation has been rising. Unemployment has, however, remained low. The public external debt is moderate but growing, as international assistance is provided to the country in the form of loans.

■ SUMMARY OF FOREIGN INVESTMENT POLICY

The principal law with regard to foreign investment is the Investment Incentive Code of 1966. Foreign investment priorities are established by the National Planning Agency. The National Investment Commission, composed of high level representatives of the Departments of Commerce and Industry, Treasury, Agriculture, and the National Planning Agency, is the principal government department charged with the development of foreign investment.

No incentives are available to foreign investors except as provided under the Investment Code.

The areas of economic activity to which the Investment Code is directed are the processing, fabrication, and assembly of raw materials into commercial products; agriculture, fishing, and logging activities; and investment in all of the above areas. Incentives are only available to enterprises that agree to create new projects in any of the above economic activities, or to substantially expand existing activities in these areas of the economy.

All foreign investments must be proposed to the government and approved by it before any activities can commence and before any incentives are provided. A principle standard used by the government to determine the value of any foreign investment is whether the project will contribute to the overall economic growth and development of the country.

The application for approval must contain complete information on the background of the foreign investors to include banking references and a detailed description of the proposed investment including expected creation of local employment opportunities and materials and services that may be locally obtained.

Upon approval of the foreign investment proposal, the government will issue, through the offices of the Investment Commission, an Investment Incentives Contract.

Approved foreign investors are entitled to certain customs exemptions on raw materials, equipment, tools, and other items necessary to carry out the project. The customs exemption does not apply to materials or goods that are produced in Liberia and are of equal price and quality to the materials and goods to be imported.

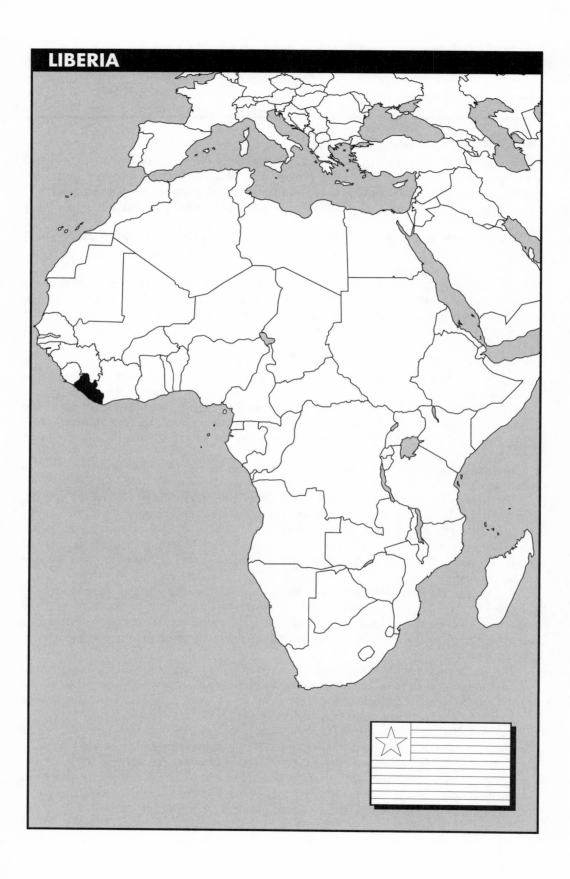

LIBERIA

The customs exemptions on raw materials are valid for a period of five years.

Approved foreign investment projects are entitled to a holiday of from five to ten years on the income tax with the understanding that the net tax exemption will not exceed 150 percent of the capital investment.

Additional incentives include necessary tariff protection; long-term, low-interest government loans; and long-term leases on industrial land.

■ FORMATION AND TYPES OF PERMITTED BUSINESS ORGANIZATIONS

Foreign investors may participate in the Liberian economy through the creation of corporations, general or limited partnerships, or sole proprietorships.

Subsidiaries of foreign corporations may be established.

Joint ventures may be created between foreign and domestic investors.

Corporations, to include foreign owned corporate subsidiaries, are considered to be legal entities and to enjoy juridical person status.

■ ENVIRONMENTAL PROTECTION

Potential foreign investors are advised to contact the Investment Commission with regard to the status of any existing or projected laws or regulations pertaining to environmental protection.

■ RIGHTS AND OBLIGATIONS OF FOREIGN INVESTORS

There is no requirement for domestic participation in the management of any enterprise owned to any extent by foreign investors.

Enterprises may be wholly owned by foreign investors.

Foreign enterprises and foreign nationals are not permitted to own land.

Any taking of private property must be on the grounds of public necessity and must be accomplished through proper legal means and be accompanied by just compensation.

Bilateral investment guarantees exist between Liberia and both the United States and Germany.

Foreign investments and any income derived from such investments may be repatriated.

Financing is available to foreign investors through government agencies.

In cases of disputes arising under any Investment Incentives Contract, the parties may elect to have the matter resolved either in the Liberian courts or through arbitration.

Personal effects of foreign nationals employed in the country may be imported exempt from customs charges and may be repatriated upon termination of employment and departure from the country.

■ LABOR

A complete body of laws exists with reference to both employment and working conditions.

Any approved foreign investor must agree to both employ and train Liberian workers.

All foreign nationals employed in Liberia must possess work permits.

■ ACCOUNTING REQUIREMENTS

All companies established in Liberia must maintain complete and accurate accounting and related financial records for tax and other purposes. Accounting records must be maintained in accordance with internationally accepted standards and are subject to periodic government audits.

■ CURRENCY CONTROLS

The National Bank of Liberia is the country's central bank.

Foreign exchange controls are stringently enforced.

Neither foreign enterprises nor foreign nationals are permitted to open and maintain bank accounts in any foreign currencies.

■ TAXATION

The principal tax is that imposed on both business and personal income. Other taxes include those assessed on real property, sales, customs, and various registration and license fees.

Deductions and allowances are permitted to include legitimate business and personal expenses, depreciation on assets, and charitable contributions, among others.

■ LEGAL SYSTEM

The court system includes Magistrates' Courts that are responsible for deciding minor criminal cases, and Circuit Courts that have a trial function with regard to more serious criminal cases and civil matters, as well as acting in an appellate capacity relevant to decisions of the Magistrates' Courts that are referred to them.

Final appeals are taken to the People's Supreme Court, which sits at Monrovia.

■ CUSTOMS AND DUTIES

Liberia, through its membership in the Mano River Union and the Economic Community of West African States, is involved with regional trading activities.

The country imposes customs duties on most imports.

When considered necessary, Liberia has imposed protective tariffs.

■ PROTECTION OF INTELLECTUAL PROPERTY

Liberia is a member of the World Intellectual Property Organization. Potential foreign investors are advised to contact the Investment Commission to determine the status of previous or current laws on the protection of copyrights, patents, trademarks, and technology transfer.

■ IMMIGRATION AND RESIDENCE

Visas are required to enter the country. Potential foreign investors are advised to contact the Investment Commission with regard to information concerning visa, work permit, and residence permit requirements.

■ FOREIGN INVESTMENT ASSISTANCE DIRECTORY

Sources that can provide further information about foreign investment in Liberia include:

Investment Commission
P.O. Box 9043
Executive Mansion Building
Monrovia, Liberia
Telephone: (231) 225163

National Bank of Liberia
P.O. Box 2048
Broad Street
Monrovia, Liberia
Telephone: (231) 222497

Department of Commerce and Industry
P.O. Box 9041
Monrovia, Liberia
Telephone: (231) 222141
Telex: 44331

Persons interested in obtaining additional information about foreign investment in Liberia are advised to contact the closest Liberian embassy or consular office.

Liberia maintains diplomatic relations with Algeria, Cameroon, Republic of China (Taiwan), Côte d'Ivoire, Cuba, Egypt, Germany, Ghana, Guinea, Holy See, Israel, Italy, Republic of Korea, Lebanon, Libya, Morocco, Nigeria, Poland, Romania, Russia, Sierra Leone, Spain, Sweden, Switzerland, United Kingdom, and United States.

LIECHTENSTEIN, PRINCIPALITY OF

■ POLITICAL ENVIRONMENT

The government is very stable. There are no internal or external threats to national sovereignty. Inflation and unemployment are virtually nonexistent. Most of the economic activity carried on in the country relates to banking and finance.

■ SUMMARY OF FOREIGN INVESTMENT POLICY

The government has no specific policy or program that is designed to attract foreign investment. Liechtenstein has an established reputation as a center for financial management enterprises.

There are no special incentives offered to the foreign investor. Advantages to financial management or holding companies that are established in the country are chiefly found in the tax considerations vis-a-vis the taxes that must be paid in other locations.

Foreign investments do not require approval except with regard to the operation of insurance companies or banks. There are virtually no opportunities for the establishment, by foreigners, of manufacturing enterprises. In those rare situations where such an opportunity may arise, government approval will be required.

Foreign participation, in terms of ownership of existing enterprises, is not limited, nor are there any restrictions on foreign investment in terms of mergers or acquisitions.

■ FORMATION AND TYPES OF PERMITTED BUSINESS ORGANIZATIONS

There are no restrictions on the percentage of ownership of any firm that may be held by foreign investors except in the insurance and banking areas.

Foreign investors usually tend to operate as either a corporation or an establishment.

In Liechtenstein, a holding company is organized and registered in that country and has as its essential purpose, the management of financial assets. Foreign investors may form such entities.

Foreign investors may also establish subsidiaries of branch offices of a foreign-based corporation and be characterized as a domiciliary company. Such a firm cannot carry on business, except for the management of financial assets.

Most foreign interests are represented through a corporation. However, some businesses are organized as either establishments or business trusts. The former is a type of corporation with attendant limits on liability. The latter is also, in most cases, created as a corporation and, as a fiduciary, carries on business interests as a trustee.

Foreign interests may, but usually do not, form or operate in general and limited partnerships, as sole proprietors, or in joint ventures.

There is no requirement for domestic participation in terms of either equity or management of enterprises formed with foreign investment.

Companies, including branches of foreign businesses, must be on file with the Register of Commerce.

■ ENVIRONMENTAL PROTECTION

Potential foreign investors are advised to contact the Office of Environmental Protection for complete information on this subject.

LIECHTENSTEIN

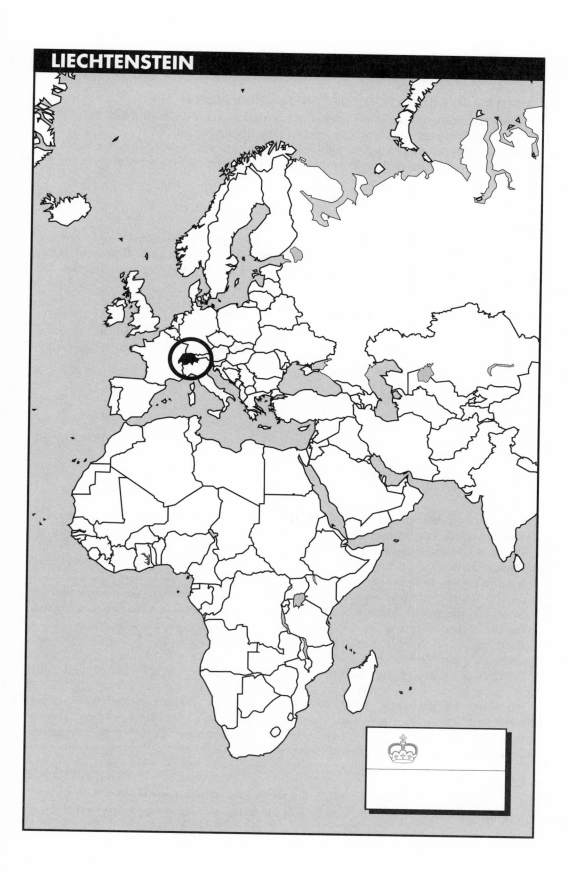

■ RIGHTS AND OBLIGATIONS OF FOREIGN INVESTORS

There is a government guarantee against nationalization and expropriation.

Foreign and domestic investors are treated equally under the law.

Invested capital and all income generated from such investment may be freely remitted abroad or expatriated. Income is subject to tax before such repatriation or remittance.

Foreign investors may obtain financing from local sources.

■ LABOR

There is a complete body of laws with regard to the rights of employees and working conditions. Labor, while very well qualified and motivated, is also in short supply. Despite this fact, work permits, which are required for all foreign personnel, may be difficult to obtain.

■ ACCOUNTING REQUIREMENTS

There are stringent laws relevant to the maintenance of financial and other records. Businesses must appoint qualified auditors and must undergo annual financial examinations.

■ CURRENCY CONTROLS

The Swiss National is the central banking authority.

No foreign exchange controls exist.

Foreign businesses and individuals may open and maintain bank accounts in foreign currencies.

The country is a party, with Switzerland, in a currency union.

■ TAXATION

Foreign businesses and foreign individuals are subject to tax. The tax year covers a 12-month period. Taxpayers may use the calendar year or another 12-month period.

The major taxes levied are those on corporate and personal income. There are numerous other taxes including those levied on real estate profits, documents, and those on wealth, estate, inheritance, and gifts.

Companies that are registered in the country are subject to taxes on income earned anywhere in the world. Income of foreign branch offices and subsidiaries is not taxed unless the parent company is established as a Liechtenstein based organization.

There are a variety of deductions to include those for legitimate business expenses, depreciation, and other taxes.

Partnerships are considered as taxable entities. However, in the case of joint ventures, the members of the venture are taxable as contrasted to the joint venture itself.

Individual taxpayers are subject to tax depending on whether they are resident or non-resident. The former are taxed on worldwide income, the latter only on income earned in the country. As in the case of businesses, there are allowable deductions to include certain business and personal expenses.

■ LEGAL SYSTEM

The court system includes County (or local) Courts, which hear minor criminal and civil cases; the Criminal Courts, which sit at the trial level; Superior Courts, which hear both criminal appeals and decide major civil cases; and the Supreme Court, which sits at Vaduz and is the final appellate authority.

■ CUSTOMS AND DUTIES

Liechtenstein and Switzerland are linked together in a customs union. As a result of that union, Liechtenstein is a member of all trade organizations to which Switzerland is a party to include the European Community (EC) and the European Free Trade Association.

The country is a major supporter of free trade and thus duties are generally quite low. Trade with other members of the EC is virtually duty free.

■ PROTECTION OF INTELLECTUAL PROPERTY

Liechtenstein is a member of the World Intellectual Property Organization. Domestic laws on copyrights, trademarks, and patents mirror those enacted by Switzerland on the subject.

■ IMMIGRATION AND RESIDENCE

In many cases, visas are not required to enter the country, however, that does depend on the individual's nationality. Potential foreign investors are advised to contact the Liechtenstein government, or the most convenient representative of Liechtenstein regarding current visa, work permit, and residence permit requirements.

■ FOREIGN INVESTMENT ASSISTANCE DIRECTORY

Sources that can provide information about foreign investment in Liechtenstein include:

Liechtenstein Bank
Städtle 44
Post Box 384
9490 Vaduz, Liechtenstein
Telephone: (41) (75) 68811
Telex: 889400
Fax: (41) (75) 68358

Department of Environmental Protection
9490 Vaduz, Liechtenstein
Telephone: (41) (75) 66111

Liechtenstein Chamber of Commerce and Industry
Josef-Rheinberger Str. 11
Post Box 232
9490 Vaduz, Liechtenstein
Telephone: (41) (75) 22744
Fax: (41) (75) 81503

Persons interested in obtaining additional information about foreign investment in Liechtenstein are advised to contact either the country's embassy offices in Switzerland, Austria, or at the Holy See.

Liechtenstein's diplomatic interests are represented by Switzerland and thus information may also be obtained from any Swiss embassy or consular office.

Switzerland maintains diplomatic relations with Algeria, Argentina, Australia, Austria, Belgium, Brazil, Bulgaria, Cameroon, Canada, Chile, People's Republic of China, Colombia, Costa Rica, Côte d'Ivoire, Cuba, Czechoslovakia, Denmark, Ecuador, Egypt, Finland, France, Germany, Ghana, Greece, Holy See, Hungary, India, Indonesia, Iran, Iraq, Ireland, Israel, Italy, Japan, Democratic People's Republic of Luxembourg, Malaysia, Mexico, Monaco, Morocco, Netherlands, Nigeria, Norway, Pakistan, Peru, Philippines, Poland, Portugal, Romania, Russia, Rwanda, Saudi Arabia, Senegal, South Africa, Spain, Sweden, Thailand, Tunisia, Turkey, United Kingdom, United States, Uruguay, Venezuela, Yemen, and Zaire.

LITHUANIA, REPUBLIC OF

■ POLITICAL ENVIRONMENT

Lithuania is one of the reestablished sovereign states that has emerged from what was formerly the Soviet Union. The nation had been forcibly annexed by the U.S.S.R. in 1940.

The government is caught between the desire to achieve a functioning market economy in the long term and its short-term inability to create and sustain a viable economic base without considerable foreign assistance.

In order to achieve its ultimate free market goals, the government has undertaken a number of actions, most notably an ongoing program of privatization of what were government-owned enterprises, and a movement to acquire substantial levels of foreign investment.

■ SUMMARY OF FOREIGN INVESTMENT POLICY

The government's interest in the acquisition of foreign investment as part of its ongoing program to achieve a free market economy is set out in its principal law on the subject, i.e., the Law on Foreign Investment in the Republic of Lithuania, which was enacted in 1992, as amended.

Under the law, foreign investment may take the form of capital, materials, equipment, or intellectual property rights.

There are requirements that must be met under the law relevant to foreign control of Lithuanian entities. In general, whenever a foreign investor obtains more than a 50 percent interest in a domestic firm, the firm must be restructured as a joint venture. In other cases, depending on the area of economic activity in which the acquired firm is engaged, it may be necessary to obtain a license from the government when a foreign interest exceeds 50 percent.

There are several government agencies, functioning at the ministry level, that may be involved in reviewing foreign investment proposals. The three ministries are the Ministry of Economics, the Ministry of International Economic Relations, and the Ministry of Trade. The Commercial Trade Department of the Ministry of International Economic Relations is the principal contact point for potential foreign investors.

Certain areas of economic activity are closed to foreign investment, principally those dealing with national defense. Firms that are less than 51 percent controlled by Lithuanian interests may not participate in such areas as telecommunications, air, rail or other surface transportation, oil and gas pipeline operation, and the generation and distribution of electric power.

■ FORMATION AND TYPES OF PERMITTED BUSINESS ORGANIZATIONS

Foreign investors may participate in the Lithuanian economy through the creation of public or private companies (i.e., corporations), partnerships, or as sole proprietorships. Foreign investors may also form joint ventures with domestic investors, including the Lithuanian government.

Subsidiaries of foreign domiciled corporations may be established.

There are no time limits on the existence of either a joint venture or of any enterprise that is formed wholly or partially with foreign capital.

LITHUANIA

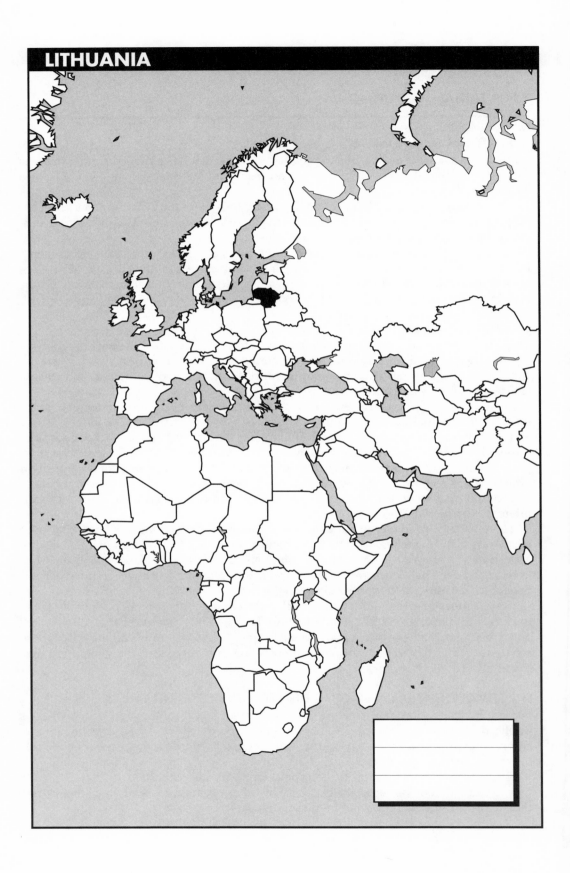

The shares of any joint venture must be transferrable to third parties unless the agreement under which the enterprise is formed prevents such transfer.

■ ENVIRONMENTAL PROTECTION

There is a high degree of interest on the part of the Lithuanian government in the protection of the environment. The investment law provides that any joint venture, or any other firm in which foreign capital has been invested and has been formed in the country, which fails to conform to the requirements of the environmental laws, may be enjoined from continuing its operations.

Potential foreign investors are advised to contact the Ministry of Health, which has the principal responsibility for overseeing the environmental protection area, to determine current laws and regulations on this subject.

■ RIGHTS AND OBLIGATIONS OF FOREIGN INVESTORS

Property held by joint ventures and other enterprises owned by foreign investors must be covered by insurance provided through insurance agencies located in Lithuania.

Foreign investors may not own property. However, commercial and industrial properties may be leased for periods of up to 99 years at the same rental unless the lease itself otherwise provides. There may be a provision for extension of such a long-term lease.

There are no prohibitions on the right of foreign investors to acquire shares in companies that have been established in Lithuania.

Foreign investments may be repatriated or remitted abroad or reinvested in the country. Income derived from foreign investment and that is repatriated is exempt from tax.

Foreign and domestic investors are generally considered to have equal standing under the law.

■ LABOR

The labor force is considered to be motivated and highly skilled. There is a substantial body of laws regarding employment and working conditions.

Lithuanian workers must be given preference in hiring by foreign employers. Foreign workers may be hired in cases where necessary skills are not locally available. All foreign workers must obtain work permits.

■ ACCOUNTING REQUIREMENTS

All companies operating in Lithuania must maintain complete and accurate financial and other relevant records for tax and other purposes. Accounting records must be maintained in accordance with accepted international standards.

■ CURRENCY CONTROLS

The Bank of Lithuania is the nation's central bank and it has the major operational responsibility for management of foreign exchange matters.

At present, foreign investors may not maintain bank accounts in any currency except that of Lithuania.

■ TAXATION

Foreign businesses and individuals are subject to the tax laws.

The major tax is that levied on income, both of business enterprises and individuals. There are a variety of minor taxes to include those on documents and imports.

Major tax concessions include a provision that profits generated as a result of foreign investment made in Lithuania before December 31, 1993, will be subject to a 70 percent tax reduction for five years, and a 50 percent reduction for a subsequent three-year period.

The tax year is generally considered to run from January 1 to December 31, although businesses may request permission to file annual tax returns on the basis of the fiscal year used by such businesses.

The law provides that any dividends received by foreign investors are exempt from Lithuanian taxation, as well as any profits generated as a result of foreign investment in the country.

■ LEGAL SYSTEM

The judicial system consists primarily of city or district courts, which have first instance jurisdiction in most civil and criminal matters. Appeals from the decisions of these courts are filed with the Supreme Court, which sits at Vilnius.

■ CUSTOMS AND DUTIES

Lithuania is a member of the newly created Council of the Baltic Sea State, which is seeking to achieve a program of regional economic cooperation and development that may include certain trade advantages and considerations.

Import duties are waived with respect to any forms of capital received in Lithuania for use by foreign investors to include raw materials, goods, equipment, and other imports required to establish and maintain a functioning enterprise.

■ PROTECTION OF INTELLECTUAL PROPERTY

The government has enacted domestic statutes with regard to the protection of copyright, trademark, and patent interests.

■ IMMIGRATION AND RESIDENCE

Visas are generally required to enter the country. Potential foreign investors are advised to contact the Commercial Trade Department of the Ministry of International Economic Relations for complete and current information on the requirements for visas, work permits, and residence permits.

■ FOREIGN INVESTMENT ASSISTANCE DIRECTORY

Sources that may provide further information about foreign investment in Lithuania include:

Commercial Trade Department
Ministry of International Economic Relations
Gedimino Pr. 30/1
2695 Vilnius, Lithuania
Telephone: (122) 226411 / (122) 226917 / (122) 226808
Fax: (122) 625432

Ministry of Economics
Gedimino Pr. 38/2
2326 Vilnius, Lithuania
Telephone: (122) 622416
Fax: (122) 625604

Ministry of Trade
Gedimino Pr. 27
2326 Vilnius, Lithuania
Telephone: (122) 621625
Fax: (122) 224601

Bank of Lithuania
Gedimino Pr. 6
2320 Vilnius, Lithuania
Telephone: (122) 622079
Telex: 261246
Fax: (122) 221501

Chamber of Commerce and Industry of Lithuania
Algirdo 31
2326 Vilnius, Lithuania
Telephone: (122) 661450
Telex: 261114
Fax: (122) 661550

Persons interested in obtaining further information about foreign investment in Lithuania are advised to contact the closest Lithuanian embassy or consular office.

Lithuania maintains diplomatic relations with France, Holy See, Italy, United Kingdom, and United States.

LUXEMBOURG, GRAND DUCHY OF

■ POLITICAL ENVIRONMENT

The government of Luxembourg and the political climate that exists there have been noted for the levels of stability for many years.

Annual inflation rates have remained at a consistently low level. Unemployment is extremely low.

Luxembourg is a major supporter of the European Community (EC) and since 1951 has favored increased levels of European economic integration.

A major government interest is that of attempting to diversify the national economy while, at the same time, assuring that Luxembourg remains a leading international financial center.

■ SUMMARY OF FOREIGN INVESTMENT POLICY

The government is interested in the acquisition of foreign investment and has charged the Ministry of Foreign Affairs, Foreign Trade and Cooperation with the responsibility for its promotion and, to some extent, with its regulation.

Special government priorities relevant to the use of foreign investment lie in the promotion of the overall growth of the economy and the maintenance of employment opportunities.

While desiring a general diversification of the national economic base, the government continues to offer incentives to banks, insurance firms, and holding companies to establish operations.

Foreign investors may participate in virtually all of the nation's economic activities.

Business activities, both foreign and domestic, must obtain a permit that is issued by the Ministry of the Economy. Banks and other financial enterprises must be licensed by the Ministry of the Treasury. The Ministry of Finance is the licensing authority for insurance activities.

Regional development is an important government interest and assistance is available to foreign and domestic investors to become established in such areas as the government deems desirable in order to expand economic activities throughout the nation.

Incentives are particularly available to those economic activities that are new to the nation, are productive, and involve a high level of technology. These incentives include government offers of tax holidays of differing lengths and reduced taxes, as well as non-tax incentives that take the form of direct government financial grants or guarantees.

Additional incentives are offered to enterprises that employ new equipment, technologies, methods of distribution, and transportation in virtually any economic area and that fit the classification of small and medium-sized enterprises.

Foreign enterprises may merge with, or acquire, domestic firms.

■ FORMATION AND TYPES OF PERMITTED BUSINESS ORGANIZATIONS

Foreign investors may participate in the economy through the creation of a societe anonyme-SA, or public corporation; a limited liability company; a general or limited partnership; or through the formation of a sole proprietorship.

Joint ventures may be created with either domestic or other foreign partners. Branch offices of foreign companies may be opened and subsidiaries of foreign corporations may be formed.

Articles of incorporation of all companies must be filed with the Tribunal de Commerce. Corporations, including public and private companies and foreign subsidiaries, are considered to be legal entities with juridical person status.

Special rules pertain to the creation of holding companies in Luxembourg. A holding company need not be formed as a corporation. It must restrict its activities to investment and management of foreign and domestic corporations, cannot do business with the public generally, and cannot directly engage in any business activities beyond those permitted by law, i.e., managerial, investment, and administrative functions.

■ ENVIRONMENTAL PROTECTION

There is a strong and continuing interest on the part of the government in protecting the environment. The Ministry of the Environment is the government agency with primary responsibility for developing and enforcing programs and policies relevant to environmental protection. Potential foreign investors are urged to contact that ministry for complete and current information pertaining to this subject.

■ RIGHTS AND OBLIGATIONS OF FOREIGN INVESTORS

Foreign investors are considered to have equal rights with domestic ones.

Investments made in Luxembourg may be remitted abroad or repatriated without restriction. Unrepatriated earnings from foreign investments may be reinvested.

Foreign employees may repatriate wages and salaries without limitation.

There are no restrictions with regard to foreign investors seeking and obtaining financing from local sources.

■ LABOR

Luxembourg has a substantial body of laws on the subjects of employment and working conditions. The work force is highly skilled at all levels. Foreign nationals of other than European Community (EC) countries must obtain work permits from the Ministry of Labor to be employed in Luxembourg. Such permits are issued only in cases where required skills are not available locally.

■ ACCOUNTING REQUIREMENTS

Companies, including limited partnerships and holding companies, must maintain complete and accurate financial records in accordance with international accounting standards.

■ CURRENCY CONTROLS

The Banque Nationale de Belgique functions as the central bank for Luxembourg.

There are no restrictions on the movement of foreign currency into or out of Luxembourg, nor any requirements concerning foreign capital registration.

Bank accounts may be opened and maintained in any foreign currency.

■ TAXATION

The principal tax levied in Luxembourg is that on corporate and individual income.

Among other taxes assessed are those on documents, land, and a value added tax. There are, in addition, a variety of minor taxes.

The tax year is the calendar year, i.e., January 1 to December 31. Companies may elect to file tax returns on the basis of their corporate fiscal year.

Deductions include business expenses, depreciation, bad debts, income to employees, insurance premiums, interest on loans, and credits to include a percentage of investment in new and depreciable fixed assets. The tax law also allows the government, at its discretion, to grant tax holidays or tax reductions to taxpayers based on a general criteria of the investment's value to the country.

Partnerships, for most purposes, are not considered to be taxable entities. Joint ventures are not considered to be taxable entities unless organized in the corporate form.

Individual taxpayers are taxed on income and capital gains. Deductions include those related to legitimate business and personal expenses.

Luxembourg is a party to bilateral treaties with numerous nations on the subject of double taxation.

■ LEGAL SYSTEM

The judicial system includes Courts of the Justices of the Peace, which hear petty criminal and civil cases. The District Courts decide more important civil and criminal matters. Appeals are taken to the Superior Court of Justice.

■ CUSTOMS AND DUTIES

Luxembourg is a founding member of the European Community and is a party to the General Agreement on Tariffs and Trade (GATT). The government is a major supporter of free trade. There are no customs duties levied on trade between members of the EC. Other customs charges are based on the ad valorem principle.

■ PROTECTION OF INTELLECTUAL PROPERTY

Luxembourg is a member of the World Intellectual Property Organization, the Berne Convention, the Paris Convention, and the Stockholm Act and thus fully supports internationally accepted standards of protection relevant to copyrights, trademarks, patents, and technology transfer. In addition, Luxembourg has enacted domestic laws for the protection of such forms of intellectual property.

■ IMMIGRATION AND RESIDENCE

Visas may be required for entry depending on an individual's nationality. Potential foreign investors are advised to contact the Ministry of Foreign Affairs, Foreign Trade and Cooperation for complete information regarding visa, work permit, and residence permit requirements.

■ FOREIGN INVESTMENT ASSISTANCE DIRECTORY

Sources that can provide additional information about foreign investment in Luxembourg include:

Board of Economic Development
19-21 Boulevard Royal
2910 Luxembourg
Telephone: (352) 4794-231

Ministry of the Economy
19-21 Boulevard Royal
2910 Luxembourg
Telephone: (352) 4794-231
Telex: 3464
Fax: (352) 460448

Ministry of Foreign Affairs, Foreign Trade & Cooperation
5 Rue Notre Dame
2911 Luxembourg
Telephone: (352) 478611
Telex: 3405
Fax: (352) 223144

Ministry of the Environment
5 Rue de Prague
2918 Luxembourg
Telephone: (352) 478870
Telex: 2536
Fax: (352) 400410

Ministry of Labor
26 Rue Zithe
2939 Luxembourg
Telephone: (352) 499211
Telex: 2958
Fax: (352) 499212

Chamber of Commerce of Luxembourg
7 Rue Alcide de Gasperi
2981 Luxembourg
Telephone: (352) 435853
Telex: 60174
Fax: (352) 438326

Persons interested in obtaining further information about foreign investment in Luxembourg are advised to contact the country's closest embassy or consular office.

Luxembourg maintains diplomatic relations with Austria, Belgium, Denmark, France, Germany, Greece, Ireland, Italy, Japan, Netherlands, Portugal, Russia, Spain, Switzerland, Turkey, United Kingdom, and United States.

Madagascar, Democratic Republic of

■ POLITICAL ENVIRONMENT

This government should be considered highly unstable. During the last five years the nation has suffered general strikes, political fragmentation, suspension of the constitution, riots, and almost constant incipient revolution.

Madagascar's inflation rate and its unemployment are both high and rising. There is a severe shortage of foreign exchange. Some of the country's external public debt has been rescheduled in order to prevent default.

■ SUMMARY OF FOREIGN INVESTMENT POLICY

The government is interested in acquiring foreign investment. In December 1989, the Investment Code was enacted. Key responsibilities for the promotion and development of foreign investment have been assigned to the Ministry of Finance. Other ministry level departments have responsibilities in cases where businesses will require their involvement, e.g., the Ministry of Industry, Energy and Mining.

Numerous incentives are available to foreign investors. Eligibility for such incentives requires a foreign investor to register with the Ministry of Finance.

Among the incentives are exemptions from a variety of taxes including those on imports, transactions, real estate, and income. Income tax exemptions are available for periods of up to five years. Subsequent to that period, eligible firms may enjoy significant tax reductions for another three-year period.

In addition to tax incentives, Madagascar has established numerous industrial free zones. Companies operating in such zones are free from all customs and related charges, in addition to receiving favorable tax considerations. Firms established in the free zones may be eligible for tax holidays for periods of up to ten years. However, firms operating in these zones must manufacture only for export markets.

The government is particularly interested in foreign investment to create increased manufacturing related to domestic consumption and to provide additional employment opportunities for local labor.

Madagascar is a party to the Multilateral Investment Guarantee Agency Agreement.

■ FORMATION AND TYPES OF PERMITTED BUSINESS ORGANIZATIONS

Foreign investors may participate in the economy through the creation of private and limited liability companies (i.e., corporations), or partnerships.

Companies must receive the approval of the Ministry of Finance to acquire more than a 20 percent interest in any existing domestic company or to form a new entity with foreign capital.

Any foreign businesses intending to obtain approval for operation in the industrial free zones must be formed as a corporation within one year after receiving approval of the government to operate in such a zone.

■ ENVIRONMENTAL PROTECTION

There is a high level of government interest in the protection of the environment. In particular, any companies operating within the industrial free zones are charged with a specific responsibility for environmental protection. Potential foreign investors are

MADAGASCAR

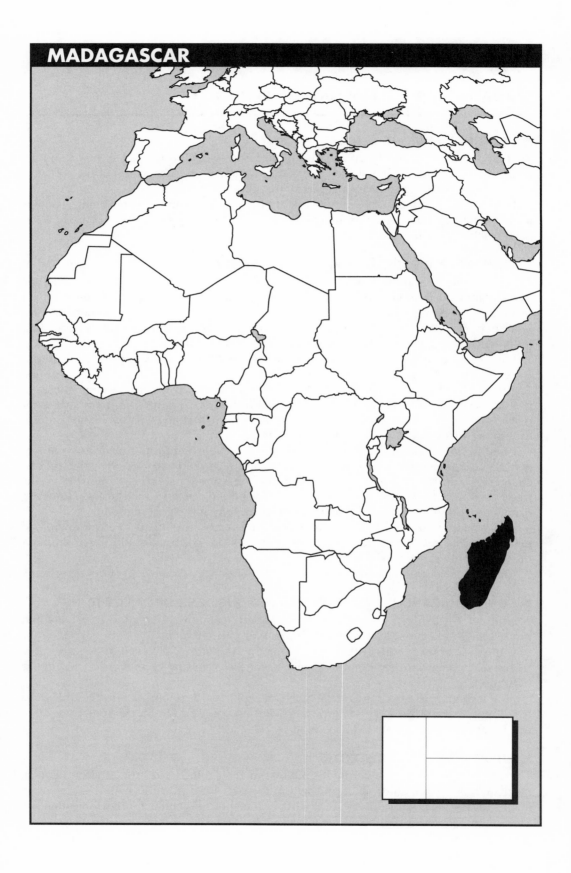

advised to contact the Ministry of Finance for complete information concerning this subject.

■ RIGHTS AND OBLIGATIONS OF FOREIGN INVESTORS

In general, foreign and domestic investors, and foreign and domestic corporations are accorded equal opportunities and rights.

The Investment Code specifically guarantees the right of individual and collective property. While nationalization, expropriation, or requisition are not eliminated as possibilities under the law, fair compensation is to be provided.

Investments and income derived from such investments, including in the case of liquidation, may be remitted abroad or repatriated, subject to payment of all due taxes.

Local financing from the National Bank for Industrial Development and other approved sources may be available to foreign investors.

Foreign nationals may remit abroad or repatriate between 35 percent and 60 percent of their net salaries or wages after taxes, depending on whether the employee's family resides in Madagascar or abroad.

■ LABOR

Madagascar has enacted an extensive body of laws regarding employment and working conditions. The labor force is highly motivated.

Foreign employers must give hiring preference to local workers except in those cases where special skills are required that are not locally available.

All foreign nationals employed in Madagascar, including those working in the industrial free zones, must obtain work permits.

■ ACCOUNTING REQUIREMENTS

All companies operating in Madagascar must maintain accurate and complete financial records. Annual statements must be provided to the government's Office of Administrative Coordination for distribution to all concerned departments on a yearly basis.

■ CURRENCY CONTROLS

The Central Bank of the Republic of Madagascar has the responsibility for operational management of the foreign exchange system.

Companies operating in the industrial free zones may open and maintain foreign currency accounts for the purpose of settling all outstanding accounts for goods and materials received from abroad.

Foreign loans may be obtained directly by firms operating within the industrial free zones.

Firms within the industrial free zones must open and maintain a local bank account in Malagasy currency.

■ TAXATION

Foreign businesses and individuals are subject to the tax laws.

The major tax is assessed on business and personal income. There are a variety of other taxes including those on transactions, professional assessments, real estate, imports, documents, and capital investments.

The tax year is the calendar year, i.e., January 1 to December 31, unless a business obtains approval from the Ministry of Finance to file on a basis of another 12-month period.

In addition to the incentives permitted under the various foreign investment programs, businesses are allowed a variety of deductions to include those for depreciation of plant and equipment.

■ LEGAL SYSTEM

A variety of courts exist within the judicial system. There are special courts that deal with economic crime and with robbery and associated criminal activities. General courts of the First Instance have been established to hear civil and criminal matters. Appeals are first taken to the Court of Appeal. Final appeals may be filed with the Supreme Court, which sits at Antananarivo.

■ CUSTOMS AND DUTIES

Madagascar is highly interested in the liberalization of its foreign trade program, of which the establishment of the industrial free zones is an integral part.

In accordance with this program, all raw materials and equipment, including that used for office operations, imported to the industrial free zones are exempt from customs duties and taxes levied on import and consumption.

All goods and services that are exported by companies operating from within the industrial free zones are exempt from export charges.

Customs exemptions are, in addition, available to firms that are eligible under the classification of small or medium-sized business.

■ PROTECTION OF INTELLECTUAL PROPERTY

Madagascar is a member of the World Intellectual Property Organization and accepts internationally agreed-upon standards for the protection of patents, trademarks, copyrights, and technology transfer.

■ IMMIGRATION AND RESIDENCE

Entry visas are generally required. Visas may be issued for periods of from one to three months and may be renewed. Multiple entry visas may be issued.

Residence visas, issued together with work permits, are valid for the length of the permit.

■ FOREIGN INVESTMENT ASSISTANCE DIRECTORY

Sources that can provide further information about foreign investment in Madagascar include:

Ministry of Finance
P.O. Box 268
Antaninarenina
101 Antananarivo, Madagascar
Telephone: (261) (2) 21632
Telex: 22489

Central Bank of the Republic of Madagascar
P.O. Box 550
101 Antananarivo, Madagascar
Telephone: (261) (2) 21751
Telex: 22329
Fax: (261) (2) 34552

Chamber of Commerce of Madagascar
P.O. Box 166
20 Rue Colbert
101 Antananarivo, Madagascar
Telephone: (261) (2) 21567

Persons interested in obtaining further information about foreign investment in Madagascar are advised to contact the country's closest embassy or consular office.

Madagascar maintains diplomatic relations with Algeria, People's Republic of China, Egypt, France, Germany, Holy See, India, Indonesia, Iran, Italy, Japan, Democratic People's Republic of Korea, Libya, Russia, Switzerland, Thailand, United Kingdom, and United States.

Malawi, Republic of

■ POLITICAL ENVIRONMENT

The country has experienced terrorism by factions that do not support its policies with regard to South Africa. These difficulties, coupled with a largely agricultural economy that is highly dependent on favorable weather conditions, have created economic problems.

The nation's currency has been devalued on two recent occasions. Payments on the country's external public debt were rescheduled in 1988.

There is an ongoing program of privatization of former state-owned industries.

There is a relatively high annual rate of inflation.

■ SUMMARY OF FOREIGN INVESTMENT POLICY

The government is seeking foreign investment. It has enacted the Investment Promotion Act and created the Malawi Investment Promotion Agency as the principal organization responsible for generating foreign investment.

There is a specific determination on the part of the government that the private sector should be the leading force in the development of the nation's economy.

The principal application of foreign investment is desired in the areas of small- and medium-scale manufacturing and in the development of export-based industries.

In terms of priority, the government seeks foreign investment in manufacturing, agriculture, mining, fisheries, and tourism.

There are no restrictions on foreign investment. All foreign companies, however, must file with the Registrar of Companies and with the Reserve Bank of Malawi. Licenses are required when a firm is engaged in the production of firearms, ammunition, or chemical or biological weapons, explosives, or any manufacturing involving hazardous waste or radioactive materials.

Malawi is a signatory to the Multilateral Investment Guarantee Agency Agreement and is a member of the International Center for the Settlement of Investment Disputes.

A variety of incentives has been made available for foreign investors including special tax and customs considerations.

■ FORMATION AND TYPES OF PERMITTED BUSINESS ORGANIZATIONS

Foreign investors may form corporations or partnerships, or operate as sole proprietors. Subsidiaries and branch offices may also be established.

Foreign investors are encouraged to join domestic ones in joint ventures.

There is no restriction as to the amount of foreign ownership that may be obtained in any business firm.

There is no requirement for domestic participation in the management of any firm funded by foreign capital.

■ ENVIRONMENTAL PROTECTION

There is a high level of interest in environmental protection. Foreign investors are advised to contact the Investment Promotion Agency for complete information on laws and regulations pertaining to the protection of the environment.

MALAWI

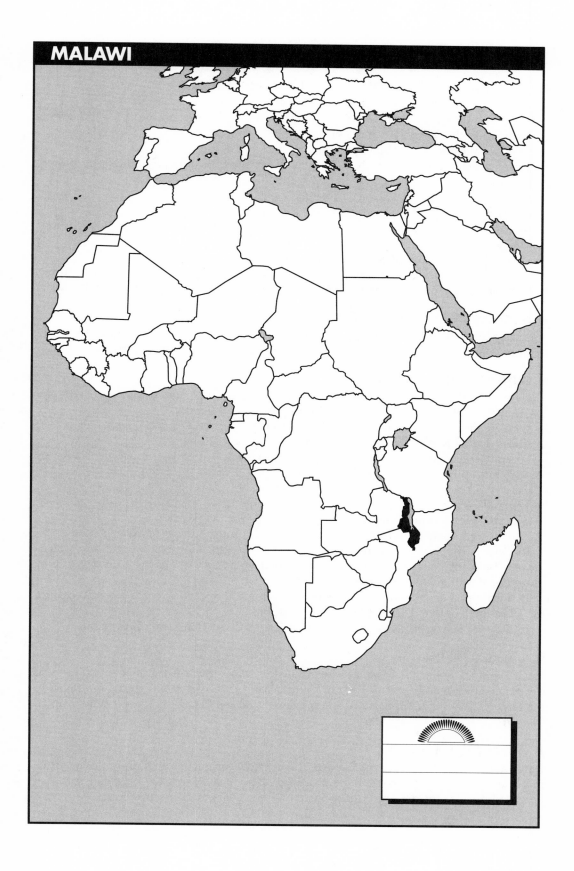

■ RIGHTS AND OBLIGATIONS OF FOREIGN INVESTORS

There is a constitutional guarantee against nationalization or expropriation.

Land may be acquired on a long-term lease basis for foreign investors for industrial, tourism, and other commercial purposes.

Foreign investors may obtain local financing.

Investments and income derived from such investments may be remitted abroad or repatriated.

■ LABOR

There is an existing body of law that regulates aspects of employment and sets working conditions.

There is no requirement to hire local personnel on a preferential basis.

The government will issue Temporary Employment Residence Permits to foreign nationals whenever it can be shown that required employment skills are not locally available.

■ ACCOUNTING REQUIREMENTS

All companies must maintain complete financial and other records. Financial records must be maintained in accordance with internationally accepted standards.

■ CURRENCY CONTROLS

The Reserve Bank of Malawi is the nation's central bank and is charged with the responsibility of monetary matters including foreign exchange.

Foreign investors may obtain foreign currency from commercial banks for use in business transactions where such foreign currency is required.

Foreign employees may remit abroad or repatriate up to two-thirds of wages or salaries after payment of taxes.

■ TAXATION

Foreign businesses and foreign nationals are liable for tax payments.

Malawi is a party to numerous bilateral treaties on the subject of double taxation.

Incentives that have been made available for foreign investors include allowances for new building construction; for operation in designated areas of the country; and for training costs relevant to employees.

In addition, a tax allowance is permitted relevant to operating costs incurred during the 18 months before actual start-up of operations.

Individual taxpayers are eligible for a variety of deductions and allowances.

■ LEGAL SYSTEM

Petty criminal and civil cases are heard in the Magistrates' Courts. The Traditional Courts are trial level courts for major criminal and civil matters. Appeals are taken to the High Court. Final appeals are taken to the Supreme Court of Appeal, which sits in Blantyre.

■ CUSTOMS AND DUTIES

Raw materials and equipment needed for manufacturing or other purposes may be imported without duty payment or, in some cases, may be eligible for a full rebate of any paid duty or for deferred duties for up to two years after importation.

Companies established in the export processing zones are entitled to special incentives including, in addition to those noted above, exemption from excise taxes and the value added tax (VAT).

■ PROTECTION OF INTELLECTUAL PROPERTY

Malawi is a member of the World Intellectual Property Organization and thus subscribes to internationally accepted standards of protection for copyrights, patents, and trademarks.

■ IMMIGRATION AND RESIDENCE

Visas are normally required to enter Malawi. Potential foreign investors are advised to contact the Investment Promotion Agency for complete information on requirements for visas, work permits, and residence permits.

■ FOREIGN INVESTMENT ASSISTANCE DIRECTORY

Sources that will be able to provide further information about foreign investment in Malawi include:

Malawi Investment Promotion Agency
Plaza House
Private Bag 302
Capital City
Lilongwe 3, Malawi
Telephone: (265) 780 800
Telex: 44944
Fax: (265) 781 781

Reserve Bank of Malawi
P.O. Box 30063
Capital City
Lilongwe 3, Malawi
Telephone: (265) 732 488
Telex: 44788
Fax: (265) 731 145

Associated Chambers of Commerce and Industry
Chichiri Trade Fair Grounds
P.O. Box 258
Blantyre, Malawi
Telephone: (265) 671 988
Telex: 43992
Fax: (265) 671 147

Persons interested in obtaining further information about foreign investment in Malawi also are advised to contact the country's closest embassy or consular office.

Malawi maintains diplomatic relations with Republic of China (Taiwan), Egypt, France, Germany, Israel, Republic of Korea, Mozambique, South Africa, United Kingdom, United States, Zambia, and Zimbabwe.

MALAYSIA, FEDERATION OF

■ POLITICAL ENVIRONMENT

Malaysia has been troubled by internal political issues for many years. Economically, however, the nation has enjoyed considerable success. Inflation and unemployment levels are both very low. There is an ongoing program of privatization.

■ SUMMARY OF FOREIGN INVESTMENT POLICY

The government is actively seeking foreign investment. The principal agency responsible for the promotion of such investment is the Malaysian Industrial Development Authority (MIDA). Laws that form the basis for foreign investment promotion are the Promotion of Investments Act of 1986 and the Income Tax Act of 1967.

There are provisions relevant to the degree of ownership of various projects that are permitted to foreign investors. In export-oriented enterprises, foreign ownership may be 100 percent depending on the size of the investment, technology, raw materials used, and other factors. In the majority of cases, however, the percentages of ownership will be between 51 and 80 percent.

Foreign ownership of firms engaged in domestic-oriented projects will range between 30 and 51 percent.

In projects involving non-renewable resources, i.e., mining and mineral ore processing, complete foreign ownership is possible depending on several factors including the size of the investment.

Malaysia is a party to numerous bilateral investment guarantee agreements.

All foreign investments involving manufacturing activities must be licensed by the Ministry of Trade and Industry.

The government offers numerous incentives to foreign investment to include export credit refinancing, tax deductions for research and development, tax allowances for firms engaged in the agribusiness and tourist industries, and local financing to firms engaged in manufacturing, tourism, and agribusiness.

Free trade zones and licensed manufacturing warehouses have been established to assist in the promotion of exports, and over 100 industrial estates have been created throughout the country to meet the needs of industrial producers.

■ FORMATION AND TYPES OF PERMITTED BUSINESS ORGANIZATIONS

Foreign investment may be in the form of a corporation, partnership, or sole proprietorship. However, it is the government's preference that business activities be in the nature of a joint venture between a foreign investor and a domestic business enterprise.

■ ENVIRONMENTAL PROTECTION

There is a strong interest in environmental protection. Potential foreign investors are advised to contact the Malaysian Industrial Development Authority for complete and current information regarding laws and regulations about the protection of the environment in the country.

■ RIGHTS AND OBLIGATIONS OF FOREIGN INVESTORS

Foreign businesses and individuals must file tax returns.

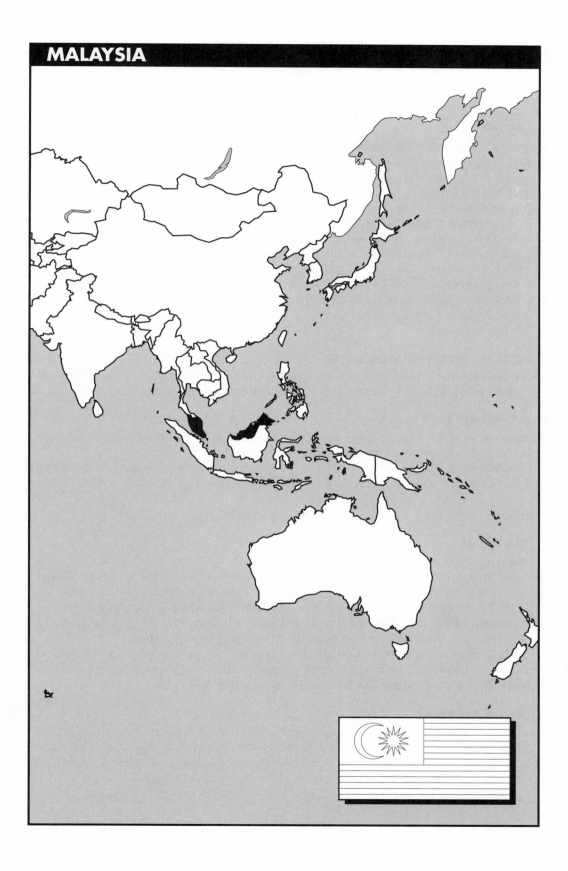

Investment capital and any income, including profits, royalties, fees, dividends, and commissions, may be freely remitted abroad or repatriated.

■ LABOR

There is a complete and extensive body of existing laws relevant to working conditions, wages, and other employment considerations.

In general, Malaysian workers must be accorded preference in hiring by foreign investors. This condition is waived in cases where there is a shortage or unavailability of trained Malaysian personnel.

In enterprises where foreign capital investment is equal to at least $500,000 (U.S.), key positions can be filled by foreign nationals for an indefinite period. Other executive, but not "key," positions can be held by foreign personnel up to a maximum of ten years but Malaysians must be trained to eventually hold the positions. Non-executive technical posts can be held by foreign personnel for a maximum of five years if Malaysians will be trained to eventually hold these positions.

All enterprises must strive to maintain a work force that reflects all of the races that comprise the country.

■ ACCOUNTING REQUIREMENTS

All businesses must maintain accurate financial records. Accounting and auditing records must be maintained in accord with internationally accepted standards.

■ CURRENCY CONTROLS

Foreign companies or individuals are not required to seek permission from the Controller of Foreign Exchange before making any investment(s) in Malaysia.

Remittances to other nations may be made in foreign currency except those of Israel and South Africa. Payments made within Malaysia must be made in domestic currency.

Foreign firms may maintain intercompany accounts.

■ TAXATION

Foreign companies are eligible for a variety of tax incentives to include significant exemptions from the income tax, the development tax, and the excess profits tax. Other tax incentives are available to eligible companies either in the form of a five-year tax holiday (when classified as being in the pioneer status) or an investment tax allowance for a period of five years. The determination between pioneer and non-pioneer status is made by the government based on prevailing economic requirements.

Additional tax incentives include abatements of the adjusted income tax, accelerated depreciation allowances, reinvestment allowances, and industrial building allowances.

Malaysia is a party to numerous bilateral agreements on double taxation.

■ LEGAL SYSTEM

The court system includes, at the lowest level, Magistrates' Courts, which hear minor criminal and civil cases, and Sessions Courts, which are at the trial level and hear and decide criminal and civil issues of more significance. Appeals are taken to the High Courts and then to the Supreme Court, which sits in Kuala Lumpur.

■ CUSTOMS AND DUTIES

Malaysia will provide tariff protection to industries that are major and quality suppliers to the domestic market. Import restrictions may also be granted as a means of additional protection.

Enterprises that are manufacturing finished products for export are eligible for full exemptions on imported raw materials, equipment, and other items necessary for local production. Enterprises that manufacture locally for the domestic market may be eligible for certain other customs exemptions.

Goods on which duties are paid and which are later used in the production of other items that are then exported will be eligible for a drawback of customs duties.

All proceeds generated from exports must be repatriated to Malaysia within six months from date of export. Necessary documents must be filed with Customs officials at the time of shipment.

Firms established in the Free Trade Zones are not liable for the payment of any customs duties and generally enjoy a minimum of customs controls.

■ PROTECTION OF INTELLECTUAL PROPERTY

Malaysia is a member of the World Intellectual Property Organization and thus accepts internationally agreed-upon standards relevant to the protection of copyrights, trademarks, and patents. Domestic statutes, e.g., the Patents Act of 1983, and the Trade Marks Act of 1976, are also in effect.

■ IMMIGRATION AND RESIDENCE

Visas are generally required to visit Malaysia. The type of visa, if one is required, and the duration of permitted visits, are dependent upon the country of origin. In most cases, a visit pass for business purposes is valid for a period of three months and may be renewed for an additional month.

Potential foreign investors are advised to contact the Malaysian Industrial Development Authority for complete information regarding the various types of visas, employment passes, dependent's passes, and resident permits.

■ FOREIGN INVESTMENT ASSISTANCE DIRECTORY

There are numerous sources that can provide information about investing in Malaysia and they include:

Malaysian Industrial Development Authority (MIDA)
3rd-6th Floor
Wisma Damansara, Jalan Semantan
P.O. Box 10618
50720 Kuala Lumpur, Malaysia
Telephone: (60) (3) 2543633
Telex: MIDA MA 30752
Cable: FIDAMAL

MIDA maintains offices in Sydney, Austrialia; Hong Kong, Tokyo; Seoul, Korea; Singapore; Paris, France; Berlin, Germany; Zurich, Switzerland; London, United Kingdom; and Chicago, Los Angeles, and New York City, United States.

Malaysian Trade Missions have been established in Sydney, Australia; Vienna, Austria; Brussels, Belgium; Sao Paulo, Brazil; Toronto, Canada; Deira, Dubai; Berlin, Germany; Paris, France; Hong Kong; Jakarta, Indonesia; The Hague, Netherlands; Beijing, China; Manila, Philippines; Bucharest, Romania; Jeddah, Saudi Arabia; Singapore; Seoul, Korea; Stockholm, Sweden; Bangkok, Thailand; London, United Kingdom; New York City, Washington, DC, and Los Angeles, United States; Moscow, Russia; and Belgrade, Yugoslavia.

Chamber of Commerce and Industry of Malaysia
Bangunan Angkass Raya, 13th Floor
Jalan Ampang
Kuala Lumpur, Malaysia
Telephone: (60) (3) 433090

Persons interested in obtaining further information about foreign investment in Malaysia also are advised to contact the closest Malaysian embassy or consular office.

Malaysia maintains diplomatic relations with Argentina, Australia, Austria, Bangladesh, Belgium, Bolivia, Brazil, Brunei, Canada, People's Republic of China, Czechoslovakia, Denmark, Egypt, Finland, France, Germany, India, Indonesia, Iran, Iraq, Italy, Japan, Democratic People's Republic of Korea, Republic of Korea, Libya, Myanmar, Netherlands, New Zealand, Nigeria, Pakistan, Philippines, Sri Lanka, Sweden, Switzerland, Thailand, Turkey, United Kingdom, United States, and Vietnam.

MALDIVES, REPUBLIC OF

■ POLITICAL ENVIRONMENT

Despite several attempts to overthrow the government that took place during the last decade, it appears that the nation is now internally secure.

The Maldives is basically dependent on four revenue sources: tourism, commercial fishing, marine products, and agriculture. Tuna fishing constitutes a major part of the fishing sector.

Tourism has been and continues to be a growth industry.

The annual rate of inflation is low and unemployment is minimal.

There is a strong interest on the part of the government, because of the country's narrow economic base, to both diversify and expand economic activities.

■ SUMMARY OF FOREIGN INVESTMENT POLICY

The government is interested in acquiring substantial foreign investment as part of its program to improve the nation's standard of living and generally increase revenues. Investors who can establish industrial facilities and modern technology are of particular interest.

The Foreign Investment Act of 1979, as amended, is the nation's primary law relevant to this subject. The Ministry of Trade and Industries is charged with major responsibilities for promotion and regulation of foreign investment. Another act, the Law on Tourism in Maldives of 1979, as amended, includes special foreign investor provisions as related to that industry. A third act bearing on the subject is the Law on Foreign Nationals Conducting Business in the Republic of Maldives of 1979.

All foreign investments must be approved by the government, i.e., by the Ministry of Trade and Industries. The information that must be submitted to the government includes complete financial backgrounds on the foreign investor; a reference from the Chamber of Commerce of the investor's home country regarding the investor's business activities; a feasibility study that has been conducted with regard to the proposed investment; a statement of the capital required in terms of cash and capital equipment needs; and a copy of the firm's Articles of Association.

If the proposal is accepted, the government will issue a Letter of Intent. It is usually anticipated that the project will commence within six months of the government's notice of approval.

The government will, in evaluating any foreign investment proposal, generally accord priority to those projects that will employ and train Maldive nationals for skilled, technical, and management positions; use locally available raw material and services; supply the local market with manufactured products; and introduce modern technology, expertise, and capital to the economy.

All foreign investors are required, subsequent to approval by the government, to deposit 10 percent of the proposed capital requirements with a local bank before the actual commencement of the project. Within one year of the date that operations begin, the percentage should be increased to 25 percent of the proposed capital or, in the alternative, the investor must provide a bank guarantee for the additional 15 percent.

The law requires that no less than 75 percent of the capital invested in the project be of foreign origin.

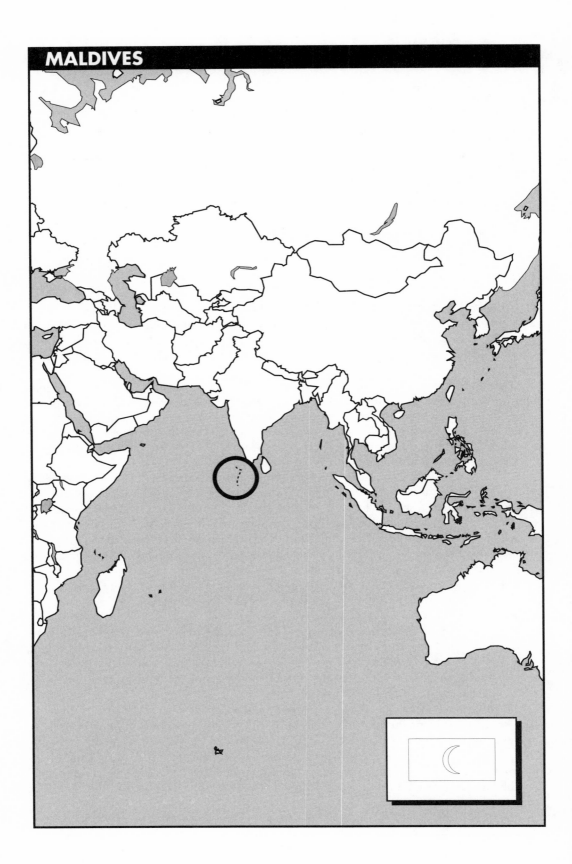

All tourism facilities, i.e., resorts and hotels, which are wholly or partially owned by foreign investors, are required to be registered with the Ministry of Trade and Industries.

Among the incentives that the government offers to foreign investors are a long-term tax holiday of up to ten years on duties and taxes; free currency conversion; and customs duty exemptions on materials and equipment imported for use in business operations.

In addition to specific incentives, the Maldives has developed a modern infrastructure capable of supporting substantial foreign investment to include a modern international airport and an Export Processing Zone.

■ FORMATION AND TYPES OF PERMITTED BUSINESS ORGANIZATIONS

Foreign investors may participate in the Maldives economy through the creation of partnerships with domestic investors or as sole proprietors. All businesses with foreign investor participation must be registered with the Ministry of Finance.

■ ENVIRONMENTAL PROTECTION

The government is highly interested in the protection of the environment, largely based on its national experience with weather and its economic dependence on agriculture and commercial fishing activities.

A high level government agency, the Ministry of Planning and the Environment, is charged with the continuing responsibility of developing policy and formulating draft legislation relevant to protecting the environment.

Potential foreign investors are advised to contact the Ministry of Planning and the Environment for complete and current information pertaining to laws and regulations on this subject.

■ RIGHTS AND OBLIGATIONS OF FOREIGN INVESTORS

In the event that any investment activity or area is closed by the government subsequent to foreign investments having been approved and operations commenced, such investment will be permitted to continue until its completion.

Upon expiration of such an investment, all foreign property may be removed from the country.

Income generated from foreign investments may be remitted or repatriated abroad subject to payment of due taxes. Investments may be repatriated or remitted abroad in cases of liquidation.

Any disputes that may arise between the foreign investor and the government must be settled pursuant to the provisions of the Maldives law.

The Law on Tourism specifically provides that no resort or hotel may be nationalized or expropriated (except for purposes of national defense) without notice of at least two years being provided to the facility operators.

■ LABOR

There is a complete body of laws with regard to employment and working conditions.

In general, foreign investors must provide hiring preferences to Maldive nationals except in those cases where required skills or expertise are not locally available. Foreign personnel may only be employed with the permission of the Ministry of Finance. All foreign nationals employed in the Maldives must acquire work permits.

■ ACCOUNTING REQUIREMENTS

All companies established in the country must maintain complete and accurate financial and other records. Accounting records must be maintained in accordance with internationally accepted standards.

■ CURRENCY CONTROLS

The Maldives Monetary Authority functions as the nation's central bank and is responsible for management of the country's foreign exchange policy and related matters.

Foreign businesses or individuals are permitted to open and maintain foreign currency bank accounts. Foreign nationals may freely move foreign currency into and from the country. A free conversion of currency is permitted to meet financial obligations necessary to carrying on commercial activities.

■ TAXATION

The major tax assessed is on business profits. There is no individual income tax. In addition to the business profits tax, other taxes levied include those on customs, tourism facilities, and certain registration and license taxes.

Depreciation is permitted on plant and equipment and deductions may be taken for expenses and losses, as well as deductions and exemptions offered as incentives to eligible foreign investors.

■ LEGAL SYSTEM

The basic court system is comprised of Courts of Summary Jurisdiction that are established throughout the country and handle all general criminal and civil cases. Appeals from decisions of these courts are taken to the Maldives High Court, which sits at Male.

■ CUSTOMS AND DUTIES

The government desires an expansion of its trade activities, particularly as they relate to exports. An Export Processing Zone exists on the country's Gan Island.

Licenses are required to both import and export, and such activities must be registered with the Ministry of Trade and Industries. Depending on the particular items, import duties can range from 5 percent to 200 percent of value.

■ PROTECTION OF INTELLECTUAL PROPERTY

The Maldives is a member of the World Intellectual Property Organization with regard to the protection of copyrights, tradenames, technology transfer, and patents. Potential foreign investors are advised to contact the Ministry of Trade and Industries for complete and current information on the status of domestic laws relevant to the protection of intellectual property.

■ IMMIGRATION AND RESIDENCE

Visas, valid for 30 days, are required to visit Maldives. The visas may be extended upon application to the Ministry of Immigration and Emigration.

Potential foreign investors are advised to contact the Ministry of Trade and Industries for complete information on the current requirements for visas, work permits, and residence permits.

■ FOREIGN INVESTMENT ASSISTANCE DIRECTORY

Sources that can provide further information about foreign investment in the Maldives include:

Ministry of Trade and Industries
Ghaazee Building
Ameer Ahmed Magu
Male, Republic of Maldives
Telephone: (0) (0) 323668
Telex: 77076 TRADIND MF
Fax: (0) (0) 323756

Ministry of Planning and the Environment
Ghaazee Building
Ameer Ahmed Magu
Male, Republic of Maldives
Telephone: (0) (0) 322965
Telex: 66110
Fax: (0) (0) 327351

Maldives Monetary Authority
Majeedhee Building
Marine Drive
Male, Republic of Maldives
Telephone: (0) (0) 322290
Telex: 66055
Fax: (0) (0) 323862

Ministry of Finance
Ghaazee Building
Ameer Ahmed Magu
Male, Republic of Maldives
Telephone: (0) (0) 324345
Telex: 66032
Fax: (0) (0) 324432

Persons interested in obtaining additional information about foreign investment in the Maldives are advised to contact the country's closest embassy or consular office.
The Maldives maintains diplomatic relations with India, Pakistan, and Sri Lanka.

Malta, Republic of

■ POLITICAL ENVIRONMENT

The island nation enjoys a very stable government under a functioning representative democracy.

There is a government desire to reduce its high level of dependence on tourism and to expand its economic base.

Inflation and unemployment percentages are low and there is a major trend toward privatization of the economy.

■ SUMMARY OF FOREIGN INVESTMENT POLICY

The Malta Development Corporation has been created to promote and acquire foreign investment. A principal law that was enacted to generate foreign investment is the Industrial Development Act of 1988.

A number of incentives are offered to foreign investors to include long-term tax holidays, industrial estates, government grants, low-cost loans, and customs exemptions. Incentives are only available to limited liability companies that are newly formed in the country.

The government is particularly interested in acquiring foreign investment that will provide the economy with modern technology and will increase the export manufacturing base. Offshore activities are also welcomed. There are some differences in the exemptions available between offshore trading and non-trading companies with the latter being eligible for a greater variety of incentives including income tax exemption.

Foreign investment is permitted in all areas of the economy except those that are provided by the public sector to include telephone, water, and similar services.

There are no limits on the amount of equity in any domestic company that is permitted to be held by foreign investors.

Malta is a party to the Multilateral Investment Guarantee Agency Agreement.

■ FORMATION AND TYPES OF PERMITTED BUSINESS ORGANIZATIONS

Foreign investors may participate in the economy through the establishment of public and private companies (which are known as partnerships anonyme and which are the equivalent of a corporation), general and limited partnerships, and sole proprietorships. In addition, the law provides for the establishment of branch offices and subsidiaries of foreign domiciled corporations. Trusts may also be formed for the management of offshore entities.

There is no requirement for domestic participation in the management of a company established with foreign investment.

Corporations, including subsidiaries of foreign firms and partnerships, must be registered with the Registrar of Partnerships.

Public and private companies and general partnerships are considered to have juridical person status.

Foreign investors may form joint ventures with domestic partners. Joint ventures, because of their temporary character, are not registered with any agency of government.

MALTA

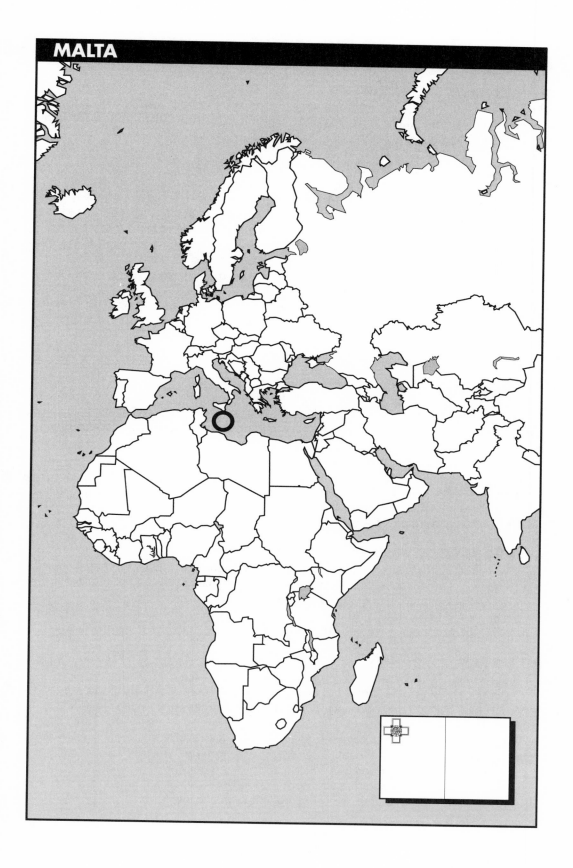

■ ENVIRONMENTAL PROTECTION

There is a major interest in environmental protection. Potential foreign investors are advised to contact the Malta Development Corporation or the Ministry of the Environment for complete information on this subject.

■ RIGHTS AND OBLIGATIONS OF FOREIGN INVESTORS

Foreign investors are guaranteed equality with domestic ones.

Local financing may be obtained by foreign investors both from government sources and from commercial banks. Firms domiciled in Malta in which foreign equity exceeds 20 percent must obtain approval of the Central Bank of Malta before loans may be made.

Foreign investment and income derived from such investments, as well as income derived from ongoing business activities, may be repatriated or remitted abroad.

All foreign investment activities must be approved by the Malta Development Corporation.

Firms that are established in the free trade zones are eligible for long-term exemptions from most taxes as well as customs and related charges under a 15-year benefit guarantee.

■ LABOR

There is a large and skilled labor force.

Malta has a complete body of laws regarding employment and working conditions.

Foreign labor may be hired only where required skills are not locally available. Training must be provided to domestic personnel for the purpose of replacing foreign employees.

All foreign employees must obtain work permits.

■ ACCOUNTING REQUIREMENTS

All companies must maintain complete and current financial records. Companies must be independently audited on a yearly basis.

■ CURRENCY CONTROLS

The Central Bank of Malta is responsible for foreign exchange policy and management.

Foreign investments are subject to approval by the central bank, as referred to it from the Malta Development Corporation and Ministry of Trade.

Foreign businesses and individuals considered as non-residents may open and maintain bank accounts in foreign currencies but deposits must be generated abroad.

■ TAXATION

Foreign businesses and individuals are subject to the tax laws.

The major taxes assessed are those on income of both companies and individuals.

Minor taxes include those on documents and sales, motor vehicles, and customs and excise levies.

The tax year runs with the calendar year, i.e., January 1 to December 31. Companies may request approval from the tax authority, the Commissioner of Inland Revenue, to use a different 12-month period.

Joint ventures and partnerships are not taxed as entities. Participants in these business forms are taxed on their shares of income in such organizations.

There is no capital gains tax relevant to business taxes.

There are various deductions to include business expenses and allowances for investments, research and development, training, and, where applicable, on export profits. In some cases, notably for those firms engaged in manufacturing, there is a tax provision relevant to accelerated depreciation of plant, equipment, and buildings.

Individual taxpayers are also entitled to deductions incurred relevant to business.

■ LEGAL SYSTEM

The court system includes Magistrates' Court, which hears petty criminal cases; Commercial, Civil, and Criminal Courts at the trial level; and Criminal and Civil Courts of Appeal. The highest appellate court is the Court of Appeal, which sits at Valletta. A separate Constitutional Court decides issues concerning the constitutionality of the nation's law.

■ CUSTOMS AND DUTIES

Goods and materials imported for use in manufacturing are exempt from customs charges.

Customs free zones, or free ports, have been created. Firms established in those zones are eligible for exemptions from currency controls, income and document taxes, and customs related charges.

All companies and individuals engaged in importing must obtain a license. In addition, all payments for imported goods and materials must be approved by the central bank.

Goods and materials imported for purposes of reexport are not subject to customs or related charges.

■ PROTECTION OF INTELLECTUAL PROPERTY

Malta is a member of the World Intellectual Property Organization. In addition, the country has enacted domestic statutes for the protection of copyrights, patents, and trademarks.

■ IMMIGRATION AND RESIDENCE

Visas may be required to enter Malta, depending on the visitor's country of nationality. Potential foreign investors are advised to contact the Malta Development Corporation for complete information regarding visas, work permits, and residence permits.

■ FOREIGN INVESTMENT ASSISTANCE DIRECTORY

Sources that can provide further information about foreign investment in Malta include:

Malta Development Corporation
P.O. Box 571
House of Catalunya
Marsamxewtto Road
Valletta, Malta
Telephone: (356) 221431 / (356) 222691
Telex: 1275
Fax: (356) 606407

The Malta Development Corporation also has offices in Bonn, Germany; Hong Kong; Milan, Italy; London, United Kingdom; and Washington, D.C., United States.

Central Bank of Malta
Castille Place
Valletta, Malta
Telephone: (356) 247480
Telex: 1262
Fax: (356) 243051

Ministry of the Environment
Floriana, Valletta
Telephone: (356) 222378
Telex: 1861
Fax: (356) 231293

Persons interested in obtaining further information about foreign investment in Malta are advised to contact the country's closest embassy or consular office.

Malta maintains diplomatic relations with Australia, People's Republic of China, Czechoslovakia, Egypt, France, Germany, Holy See, India, Italy, Libya, Russia, Spain, Tunisia, United Kingdom, and United States.

MAURITANIA, ISLAMIC REPUBLIC OF

■ POLITICAL ENVIRONMENT

This is one of the poorest countries in the world. The stability of the government is questionable. The economy is in disarray.

Mauritania possesses very few natural resources. The economy is based on agriculture (which provides employment for the majority of the nation's workers), commercial fishing, and mining activities.

Fishing represents the nation's principal source of foreign exchange. The government is hoping to increase the share of foreign exchange earned by agricultural output.

There is virtually no industry. The country must import the majority of its consumer and commercial requirements.

The economic problems faced by Mauritania are partially a result of the inability of the current infrastructure to sustain a modern economy. There are few roads, a limited single line railroad, and a poorly functioning telecommunications system.

For years, Mauritania has suffered from almost constant ethnic unrest that has resulted in violent confrontations between factions and sometimes with government forces. There has been sporadic disorder within the government that has resulted in the jailing of government leaders who displayed sympathy with views other than those espoused by the ruling political officials.

While inflation remains at a moderate level, the public external debt is a major problem, and there is a severe shortage of skilled labor. In order to obtain international financing, the government has agreed, upon the urging of the International Monetary Fund (IMF), to embark on a new economic program that includes at least a partial degree of privatization, more liberal foreign trade rules, and promotion of the country in terms of acquiring increased foreign investment.

■ SUMMARY OF FOREIGN INVESTMENT POLICY

The principal law relevant to foreign investment is the Investment Code of 1989. Under the provisions of this law, the National Commission of Investment has been charged with the responsibility of reviewing all proposals for foreign investment. The agency is composed of representatives from various ministries to include Finance, Industry and Mines, the central bank, and, in each case, the specific ministry with primary responsibility for the investment area affected by the proposal.

Other laws that are applicable to the foreign investment area include the Maritime Fisheries Code of 1986 and the Hydrocarbons Code of 1988.

Foreign investment proposals that are approved by the National Commission of Investment are then submitted by the commission to the Council of Ministers for further review. The council then forwards the proposal to the central bank for final approval or rejection.

There are a number of areas that the government considers as priority ones for foreign investment. Among those areas are the promotion of small and medium-sized enterprises; the development of manufacturing for export; and the improvement, creation, and expansion of activities that provide increased employment opportunities and the exploitation and use of the country's natural resources.

Information that must be provided to the National Commission of Investment by a

MAURITANIA

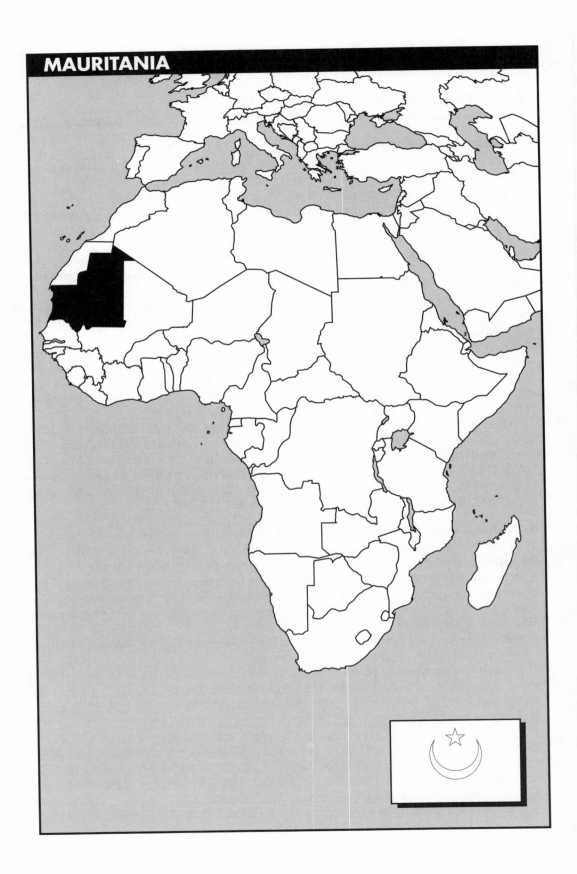

potential foreign investor includes the amount of capital to be invested; plans for the use of equipment and operations; procedures for arbitration in case of dispute; the opportunities provided for employment and the use of natural resources; and the expected financial return.

A variety of incentives are offered to foreign investors to include a six-year holiday regarding the industrial and commercial profits tax; a 50 percent reduction on the service tax beginning with the seventh year of enterprise operation; assistance from the government in the acquisition of lands and buildings for enterprise operations; reductions in customs duties on materials and equipment required for enterprise activities; and enjoyment of a stabilized tax schedule, i.e., that any new direct taxes that are enacted during the initial ten years of enterprise operation will not be imposed on the enterprise during that time period. Additional incentives are available to enterprises established in the interior regions of the nation.

The purchase of Mauritanian raw materials and the hiring of local personnel is highly encouraged and may be linked to available incentives.

Approved investments may request the assistance of the government in the form of tariff surtax to help protect the investment from those goods that are dumped on the domestic market and thus are able to achieve an unfair competitive advantage.

■ FORMATION AND TYPES OF PERMITTED BUSINESS ORGANIZATIONS

Foreign investors may form corporations in the country or operate as individuals. Subsidiaries of foreign corporations may be established. Joint ventures may be created between foreign and domestic investors, including the government.

■ ENVIRONMENTAL PROTECTION

The government has a strong interest in the issue of environmental protection. Potential foreign investors are advised to contact either the National Commission of Investment, the Ministry of Fisheries and Marine Economy, or the Ministry of Rural Development and the Environment for complete and current information on laws and regulations pertaining to environmental protection.

■ RIGHTS AND OBLIGATIONS OF FOREIGN INVESTORS

Mauritania adopts the position that there will be no discrimination directed against foreign investors relevant to commercial activities.

Any approved foreign investment may be freely repatriated or remitted abroad. Investors are cautioned, however, that any such transfers, including in the event of liquidation of an investment, may involve delays because of the nation's lack of foreign exchange.

Profits earned from foreign investments may be reinvested in Mauritania.

Nationalization or expropriation issues have not been a recent problem in Mauritania. The law provides that in the event of nationalization or expropriation, fair value of the property so taken will be provided and will be exempt from any taxes or other government charges.

In the event of any dispute between the government and an investor, resolution will be accomplished through existing treaties, through agreement between the parties, or through the provisions of international law to which Mauritania is a party.

Foreign investors may obtain local financing, including low-cost loans provided by

Mauritanian financial institutions to assist enterprises engaged in manufacturing for export.

Foreign workers may remit abroad or repatriate their salaries or wages under procedures established by the central bank.

■ LABOR

Mauritania has a substantial body of laws covering the subject of employment and working conditions. There is a large labor force, most of which is unskilled. There is a high level of illiteracy.

Foreign employers are encouraged to employ Mauritanian workers and this is of particular force relevant to boat crews engaged in commercial fishing.

All foreign nationals employed in Mauritania must obtain work permits that are renewable every two years.

Incentives may be linked to a requirement that a foreign enterprise provide training at the managerial, technical, and skilled worker levels to Mauritanian employees.

■ ACCOUNTING REQUIREMENTS

Companies that are established in Mauritania are required to maintain books and records that satisfy the regulatory needs of the government. A complete annual accounting record must be provided to the government within four months of the close of the fiscal year and must be certified by a chartered accountant.

■ CURRENCY CONTROLS

The Banque Central de Mauritanie is the nation's central bank and has responsibility for the management of the foreign exchange system.

The nation's unit of currency, the Ouguiya, is not freely convertible. The central bank must approve of all capital transfers abroad.

Foreign enterprises may obtain hard currency from the central bank to import necessary raw materials, equipment, or other goods, as well as for the purpose of repaying foreign loans that have been obtained for the purpose of investment in Mauritania.

Firms that are engaged in manufacturing for export may obtain permission from the central bank to open and maintain bank accounts in a foreign hard currency up to a maximum of 25 percent of the value of realized turnover in products manufactured in the country.

■ TAXATION

The major tax assessed is that on business income. In addition to the deductions and exemptions permitted through incentives available to approved enterprises, allowances are permitted regarding depreciation, losses, and legitimate expenses.

There are a variety of minor taxes to include those on documents, property, customs charges, and certain licenses and registration fees.

■ LEGAL SYSTEM

The principal courts include the Magistrates' Courts that hear and decide various levels of criminal cases; and civil courts that are established throughout the country. Appeals from these judicial levels are taken to the Supreme Court, which sits at Nouakchott.

■ CUSTOMS AND DUTIES

The government is highly interested in the development of foreign trade. Mauritania is a signatory to the Lome Convention, which permits preferential treatment of imports to the EC; of the U.S.-sponsored Generalized System of Preferences; and is a member of both the Mahgreb Union and the Economic Community of West African States. Both of these organizations intend to develop regional common markets.

Approved foreign enterprises, as noted, may benefit from customs exemptions or reductions on raw materials and goods necessary for their operations.

■ PROTECTION OF INTELLECTUAL PROPERTY

Mauritania is a member of the World Intellectual Property Organization and has enacted domestic provisions for the protection of interests in copyrights, patents, tradenames, and technology transfer. In addition, Mauritania is a member of the African Organization of Intellectual Property and thus agrees to support the provisions of the Berne Convention for the Protection of Literary and Artistic Works; the Hague Convention for the Registration of Designs and Industrial Models; the Lisbon Convention for the Protection of International Registration of Original Tradenames; the Washington Patent Cooperation Treaty; and the Vienna Treaty on the Registration of Tradenames.

■ IMMIGRATION AND RESIDENCE

Visas are required to enter the country. Potential foreign investors are advised to contact the National Commission of Investment for complete and current information regarding procedures for obtaining visas, work permits, and residence permits.

■ FOREIGN INVESTMENT ASSISTANCE DIRECTORY

Sources that can provide additional incentives about foreign investment in Mauritania include:

National Commission of Investment
P.O. Box 223
Government Offices
Nouakchott, Mauritania
Telephone: (0) 52935

Ministry of Fisheries and Marine Economy
P.O. Box 137
Nouakchott, Mauritania
Telephone: (0) 52476
Telex: 595

Ministry of Industries and Mines
P.O. Box 183
Nouakchott, Mauritania
Telephone: (0) 51318

Ministry of Rural Development and the Environment
P.O. Box 366
Nouakchott, Mauritania
Telephone: (0) 52020

Banque Central de Mauritanie
P.O. Box 623
Avenue de l'Independence
Telephone: (0) 52206
Telex: 532

Persons interested in obtaining further information about foreign investment in Mauritania are advised to contact the country's closest embassy or consular office.

Mauritania maintains diplomatic relations with Algeria, People's Republic of China, Egypt, France, Gabon, Germany, Republic of Korea, Libya, Morocco, Nigeria, Russia, Saudi Arabia, Senegal, Spain, Tunisia, United States, and Zaire.

MAURITIUS, REPUBLIC OF

■ POLITICAL ENVIRONMENT

The country has a relatively stable government. There is a very low inflation rate coupled with an extremely low rate of unemployment.

Over the past decade, the government has markedly reduced the inflation rate and has developed the outline of a program to limit the country's dependence on sugar, the nation's principal export.

There is a strong desire on the part of the government to develop the country into an offshore business center.

■ SUMMARY OF FOREIGN INVESTMENT POLICY

The promotion and development of foreign investment is the responsibility of several government departments to include the Export Development and Investment Agency, the Offshore Business Activities Authority, and the Bank of Mauritius.

Mauritius is a signatory to the Multilateral Investment Guarantee Agency Agreement.

There are numerous bilateral trade agreements now in force.

Export processing constitutes the largest industrial area for foreign investment. Tourism and offshore banking are other major areas that the government is particularly interested in expanding.

Incentives that are offered to offshore companies include freedom from exchange controls and numerous tax considerations.

All banks, insurance companies, and other offshore companies as well as those directly established to manufacture or operate in any other economic sector must register with the Registrar of Companies.

■ FORMATION AND TYPES OF PERMITTED BUSINESS ORGANIZATIONS

While foreign investors may participate in the economy through partnerships or as sole proprietors, the most common form of business organization, in view of the types of activities in which most firms will be engaged, is the corporation.

Companies may be incorporated on Mauritius under the provisions of The Companies Act of 1984, or foreign companies may establish branches. Branch offices must have a place of business.

There is no requirement for domestic participation in any foreign enterprise.

Offshore banks must be licensed by the Bank of Mauritius.

Offshore insurance companies, upon registration with the government, may conduct operations there either as a foreign entity, through a subsidiary, or as a locally incorporated firm.

Ship owners desiring to operate under Mauritius registry must file appropriate documents with the government's Register of Ships.

■ ENVIRONMENTAL PROTECTION

There is a high level of interest in protecting the environment. All new industrial and construction projects are required to meet environmental protection standards. Potential foreign investors are advised to contact the Export Development and Investment

MAURITIUS

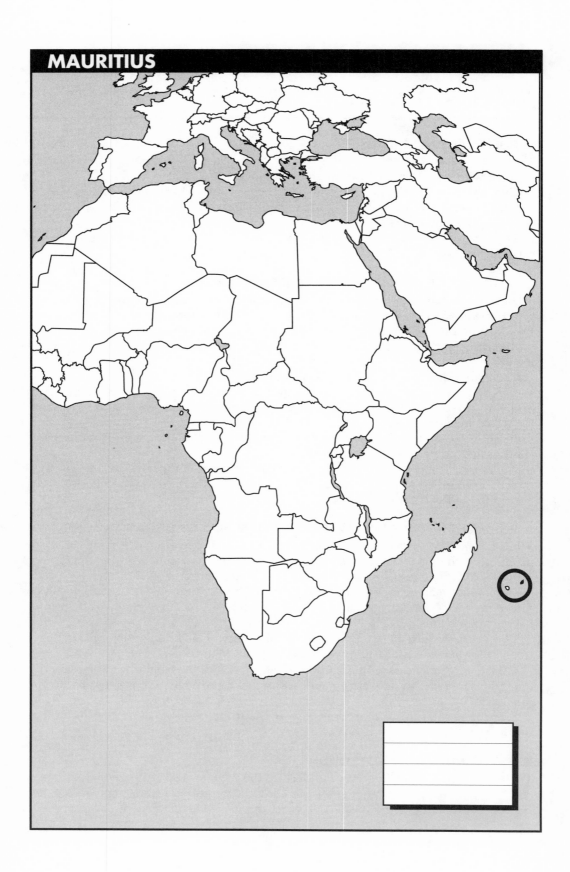

Agency or Ministry of the Environment and Quality of Life for complete and current information on laws and regulations pertaining to environmental protection.

■ RIGHTS AND OBLIGATIONS OF FOREIGN INVESTORS

Foreign and domestic investors are guaranteed equality of treatment.

Investments and profits derived from investments may be freely repatriated.

■ LABOR

There is a large and highly qualified work force at all levels to include executives and professionals. However, there is no requirement to hire local personnel.

Mauritius has enacted a body of laws regarding employment and working conditions.

■ ACCOUNTING REQUIREMENTS

All business enterprises must maintain accurate financial records in accordance with internationally accepted standards.

■ CURRENCY CONTROLS

The Bank of Mauritius is the central bank and is responsible for exchange controls and related matters.

Minimal currency controls are imposed on offshore companies.

Foreign nationals employed in Mauritius may repatriate or remit abroad salaries and wages.

■ TAXATION

Offshore tax incentives provided to offshore entities include a zero tax rate on net profits, various customs exemptions, and exemptions from stamp taxes.

Individual foreign taxpayers are taxed at half the usual income tax rate.

There is no capital gains tax in Mauritius.

Firms that may become established in the Export Processing Zone will generally be eligible for the same tax incentives made available to offshore entities.

Mauritius is a party to numerous bilateral agreements on double taxation.

■ LEGAL SYSTEM

There are numerous District Courts and Intermediate Courts from which appeals are taken to the Courts of Civil and Criminal Appeals. Final appeals are taken to the Supreme Court, which sits in Port Louis.

■ CUSTOMS AND DUTIES

Office equipment, cars, and household equipment of foreign personnel are admitted duty free.

Raw materials and equipment for use in manufacturing for export by firms established in the Export Processing Zone will be exempt from customs charges.

Mauritius is a signatory of the General Agreement on Tariffs and Trade (GATT), the Lome IV Convention, the African Caribes Pacific Group, and the Preferential Trade Areas for Eastern and Southern African States.

■ PROTECTION OF INTELLECTUAL PROPERTY

Mauritius is a member of the World Intellectual Property Organization and subscribes to the internationally accepted standards for the protection of copyrights, patents, tradenames, and trademarks.

■ IMMIGRATION AND RESIDENCE

Visas are normally required to enter Mauritius. Potential foreign investors are advised to contact the Export Development and Investment Agency for complete information as to requirements for visas, residence permits, and work permits.

■ FOREIGN INVESTMENT ASSISTANCE DIRECTORY

Sources that can provide further assistance on foreign investment in Mauritius include:

Mauritius Export Development and Investment Agency
PAI Building, 2nd Floor
Pope Hennessy Floor
Port Louis, Mauritius
Telephone: (230) 208-7750
Fax: (230) 208-5965

Mauritius Offshore Business Activities Authority
Government House
Port Louis, Mauritius
Telephone: (230) 201-2557 / (230) 201-1840 / (230) 201-1146
Telex: 4249 EXTERN IW
Fax: (230) 208-8622

Ministry of the Environment and Quality of Life
Barracks Street
Port Louis, Mauritius
Telephone: (230) 208-2831
Fax: (230) 208-6579

Bank of Mauritius
Sir William Newton Street
Port Louis, Mauritius
Telephone: (230) 208-4164
Fax: (230) 208-9204

Mauritius Chamber of Commerce and Industry
Royal Road
Port Louis, Mauritius
Telephone: (230) 208-3301
Fax: (230) 208-0076

Persons interested in obtaining further information about investing in Mauritius are advised to contact the country's closest embassy or consular office.

Mauritius maintains diplomatic relations with Australia, People's Republic of China, Egypt, France, India, Republic of Korea, Madagascar, Pakistan, Russia, United Kingdom, and United States.

MEXICO (UNITED MEXICAN STATES)

■ POLITICAL ENVIRONMENT

Mexico is facing difficult economic times. The country has a large public external debt and a major debt service. Inflation and unemployment rates are both high.

Key factors in Mexico's economic distress have been the soft global markets for the country's two major exports, oil and coffee. Payments of the foreign debt have been rescheduled.

In order to stabilize the economy, the government has embarked on an austerity program that has not been politically popular. Ongoing privatization, coupled with attempts to increase foreign investment, form salient parts of the government's program to spark economic improvement.

■ SUMMARY OF FOREIGN INVESTMENT POLICY

The government's desire for increased foreign investment is set out in the Law to Promote Mexican Investment and Regulate Foreign Investment. The National Commission on Foreign Investment is named in the law as the principal government agency responsible for the management of this area of activity. The commission, which is responsible to the President, is composed of key government ministers.

In addition, the law created the Committee for the Promotion of Investment in Mexico, which, as the name implies, is responsible for actively seeking foreign investment in the country.

Principal interests of the government with regard to the use of acquired foreign investment are to improve the nation's general technological level, create manufacturing for export opportunities, increase employment, and promote overall productivity.

Foreign investment is prohibited in several industries, notably petroleum and hydrocarbons, petrochemicals, railroads, telecommunications, nuclear energy, and electric power.

The law contains a reference to an "exclusion of foreigners clause" that must be present in the bylaws of a company investing in Mexico in order to gain general access to investment opportunities in the country. Essentially, the clause provides that the company in question will consent to be considered as Mexican in terms of company rights and obligations.

Companies formed with foreign investment and that operate under bylaws containing an exclusion of foreigners clause are permitted to participate in such economic activities as radio and television broadcasting, mass surface transportation, water and air transportation, forest exploitation, and gas distribution.

Foreign investment in any kind of economic activity is limited to no more than 34 percent in the field of mineral use and exploitation. In all other areas, the maximum percentage of invested capital by foreign interests cannot exceed 49 percent. Exceptions to this requirement and that permit 100 percent foreign acquisition of capital stock exist in cases where a Mexican firm is already owned by foreign interests to a greater extent than 49 percent of the capital stock.

Government approval, following application to the National Commission on Foreign Investment, is required for any foreign investment. Additional approval is required from the ministry involved in the relevant economic activity when foreign

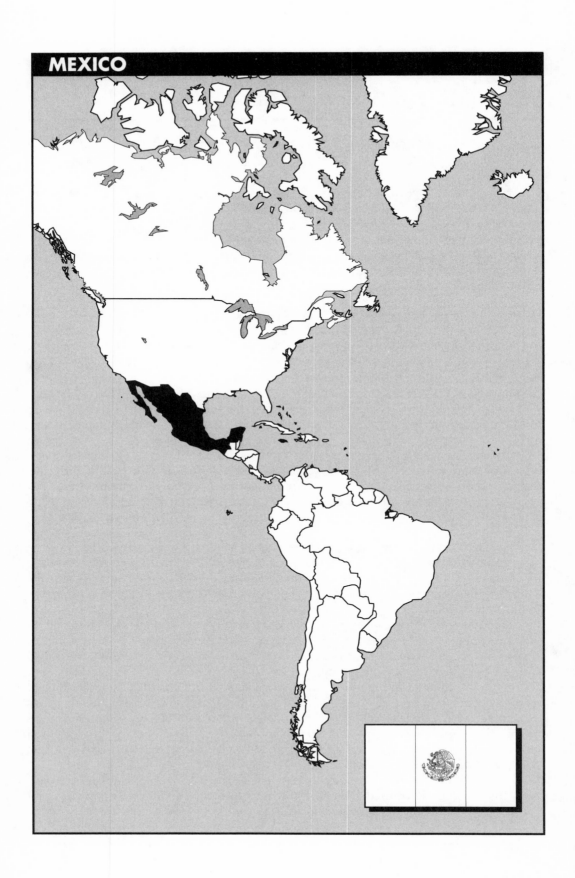

MEXICO

interests obtain more than 40 percent of the fixed assets of any existing business.

The essential guidelines for approval of a foreign investment are based on the contribution that such investment will make to the overall national economic development.

All foreign investments must be registered with the National Registry of Foreign Investments, which operates under the general direction of the Ministry of Industry and Commerce. Registered companies and individuals must provide such financial information as may be required by law to the Registry on an annual basis.

Foreign companies and individuals may obtain certificates of participation issued by trust institutions and that represent shares in public companies.

■ FORMATION AND TYPES OF PERMITTED BUSINESS ORGANIZATIONS

Foreign investors may participate in the Mexican economy as corporations, partnerships, or as sole proprietorships. Subsidiaries of foreign corporations may also be established.

All corporations, including foreign corporations that agree to be considered as Mexican nationals, are considered to be juridical persons.

Corporations can only be formed with the approval of the Ministry of Foreign Affairs. All corporations formed with any percentage of foreign capital must include, within the bylaws, a clause that excludes foreigners. In the absence of such clause in the corporate bylaws, an agreement must be filed with the Ministry of Foreign Affairs stating that the corporation agrees to be treated as a Mexican national and will not seek the protection of its own government. A failure to effect such a filing or agreement may, under the law, result in forfeiture of the foreign investment.

■ ENVIRONMENTAL PROTECTION

The foreign investment law provides that any corporation will follow all Mexican laws on ecology. Potential foreign investors are advised to contact the National Commission on Foreign Investment for complete information about Mexican laws on environmental protection.

■ RIGHTS AND OBLIGATIONS OF FOREIGN INVESTORS

Companies that have a clause excluding foreigners may obtain real property without seeking permission from the Ministry of Foreign Affairs.

Manufacturing corporations are required to locate their facilities outside of the areas that are considered as being industrially concentrated.

All foreign investors, whether business entities or individuals, must be registered with the National Registry of Foreign Investments in order to engage in any economic activities. Exceptions to this requirement include news organizations and certain representative offices such as foreign banks and reinsurance companies.

All corporations must, during the first three years of operation, establish and maintain a balanced foreign currency budget.

■ LABOR

Mexico has a functioning body of laws regarding employment and working conditions.

Foreign employers must give hiring preference to Mexican labor except in those cases where special skills are not locally available. Companies must provide such training to Mexican personnel as will enable them to perform such special skills within a reasonable period of time.

Foreign personnel must obtain work permits.

■ ACCOUNTING REQUIREMENTS

All companies must maintain complete and accurate accounting and other records. Accounting information must be maintained in accordance with internationally accepted standards. Independent audits must be conducted annually of all public companies.

■ CURRENCY CONTROLS

The Bank of Mexico is the central bank, and it is responsible for the control of the nation's monetary policy, including foreign exchange control.

Bank accounts in foreign currencies may not be maintained.

■ TAXATION

The major tax is that on corporate and individual income. Other taxes include those on real estate and assets. There is a value added tax (VAT).

Deductions are available to include depreciation and business expenses. Individual taxpayers may claim business expenses, medical and hospital expenses, and charitable contributions as deductions, among others.

Tax incentives available to eligible companies include those for establishing operations in certain geographic areas as well as for those business enterprises that are established in the free zones or perimeters.

■ LEGAL SYSTEM

The judicial system functions at both the state and federal levels. The state courts include those at the local or magistrates' level and at the circuit level, where more serious criminal and civil matters are heard. The circuit courts also exercise appellate jurisdiction.

At the federal level, there are district courts, or circuit courts, that exercise appellate powers, and the Supreme Court, which is the final appellate authority. The Supreme Court sits in Mexico City.

■ CUSTOMS AND DUTIES

Mexico is a party to the General Agreement on Tariffs and Trade (GATT) and has embarked on a more liberal trade policy.

Raw materials, goods requiring assembly, parts, and equipment necessary for operations may be imported without customs charges into the free ports. Finished goods moved into the country for sale will require payment of import taxes.

■ PROTECTION OF INTELLECTUAL PROPERTY

Mexico is a member of the World Intellectual Property Organization and subscribes to the internationally accepted standards of protection to be accorded to copyrights, patents, trademarks, and technology transfer. In addition, Mexico has enacted domestic laws that are designed to provide protection to copyrights, trademarks, and patents.

■ IMMIGRATION AND RESIDENCE

Visas may be required to enter the country. Potential foreign investors are advised to contact the National Commission on Foreign Investment for complete information about visas, work permits, and residence permits.

■ FOREIGN INVESTMENT ASSISTANCE DIRECTORY

Sources that can provide more information about foreign investment in Mexico include:

National Commission on Foreign Investment
Office of the President
Los Pinos
Mexico City, Mexico
Telephone: (52) (5) 5153353
Telex: 1760010

Secretariat of State for Commerce and Industrial Development
Alfonso Reyes 30
Mexico City, Mexico
Telephone: (52) (5) 2861823
Telex: 1775718

Secretary of State for Foreign Affairs
Ricardo Flores Magón 1
Tiatelolco 06995
Mexico City, Mexico
Telephone: (52) (5) 2775470
Telex: 1763478

Bank of Mexico
Avda 5 de Mayo 2
Mexico City, Mexico
Telephone: (52) (5) 7090044
Telex: 1772669
Fax: (52) (5) 6251557

Persons interested in obtaining further information about foreign investment in Mexico are advised to contact the closest Mexican embassy or consular office.

Mexico maintains diplomatic relations with Albania, Algeria, Argentina, Australia, Austria, Belgium, Belize, Bolivia, Brazil, Canada, Chile, People's Republic of China, Colombia, Costa Rica, Côte d'Ivoire, Cuba, Cyprus, Czechoslovakia, Denmark, Dominican Republic, Ecuador, Egypt, El Salvador, Ethiopia, Finland, France, Germany, Greece, Guatemala, Haiti, Honduras, Hungary, India, Indonesia, Iran, Iraq, Israel, Italy, Jamaica, Japan, Republic of Korea, Lebanon, Netherlands, New Zealand, Nicaragua, Norway, Pakistan, Panama, Paraguay, Peru, Philippines, Poland, Portugal, Romania, Russia, Saudi Arabia, Spain, Suriname, Sweden, Switzerland, Thailand, Turkey, United Kingdom, United States, Uruguay, Venezuela, and Vietnam.

MONGOLIA, PEOPLE'S REPUBLIC OF

■ POLITICAL ENVIRONMENT

The government is currently stable. However, a major reason for that stability may be the nation's geographic isolation. The changes that have swept over Mongolia's chief political and economic role model, the former Soviet Union, have just begun to be felt in Ulan Bator.

As a result of an increased imbalance between the prices that Mongolia can charge for its limited exports and the rising costs of imports, a large public external debt now exists. No official government information is available on the annual inflation rate or the percentage of unemployment. A degree of government interest has been shown with regard to the creation of a free market economy as a result of these negative economic facts.

■ SUMMARY OF FOREIGN INVESTMENT POLICY

The government is interested in acquiring foreign investment. A step toward this goal was the enactment of the Foreign Investment Law of Mongolia, which became effective in 1990.

Under the law, foreign investors may participate in any economic activity unless precluded from such activity by other laws. Effectively, this provision restricts foreign investment in such areas of defense, telecommunications, mass communications, and such services as commonly provided by public sector agencies.

Priority areas in which foreign investment is of particular interest include manufacturing for export or import substitution; production involving modern equipment; methods and advanced technology levels; modern agriculture; exploration and processing of mineral and other resources; development and modernization of the nation's infrastructure to include energy production, highways, and mass transportation; and development of the tourism industry.

Incentives relevant to foreign investment include customs exemptions and tax holidays.

Investments can take the form of capital, buildings, machinery, or other equipment, patents, skill, technical services, and other forms that may be negotiated between the investor and the government.

A separate act, the Petroleum Act of Mongolia, sets out the regulation of both foreign and domestic activities relevant to any aspect of the hydrocarbons industry from exploration through marketing and transportation.

The principal government agency involved with the promotion and control of foreign investment is the Ministry of Trade and Industry. Final decisions regarding activities of foreign investors may, however, be referred to the Council of Ministers for approval.

■ FORMATION AND TYPES OF PERMITTED BUSINESS ORGANIZATIONS

There may still be some lack of clarity regarding the powers of different business forms. Potential foreign investors are advised to contact the Ministry of Trade and Industry or the Mongolian Chamber of Commerce and Industry for more specific guidance on this subject.

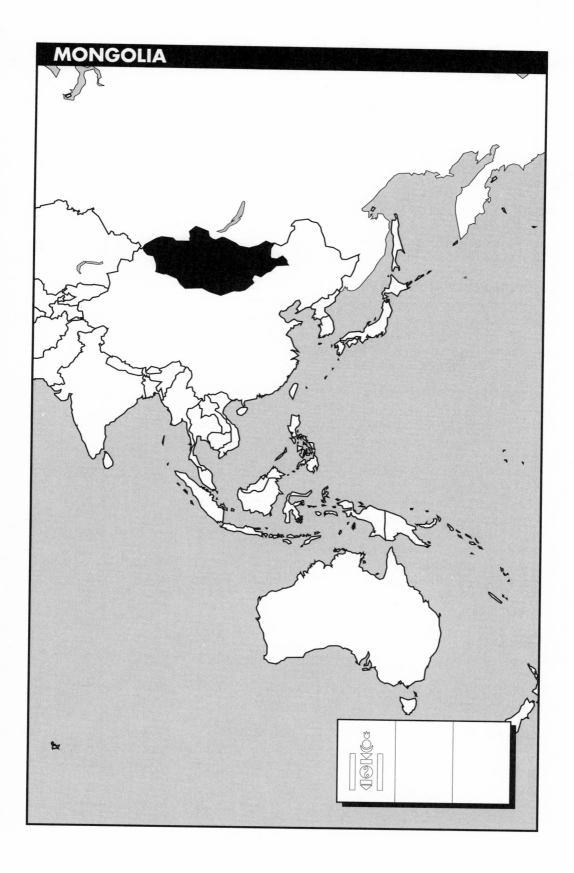

In general, however, both foreign and domestic companies or individuals may be established to do business. The law provides for enterprises with full or partial foreign participation.

"Foundation papers" must be filed with the government that reflect the amount and type of capital being provided and the charter of the organization.

Enterprises with foreign capital must be registered with the Ministry of Finance.

All entities with foreign capital must submit an application to the Council of Ministers for approval. The law provides that a decision on such an application must be made by the Council within 60 days of its receipt.

Enterprises are expected to have a specific period of existence set out in the foundation documents. Any desired extension of time of such existence must be contained in the foundation documents.

■ ENVIRONMENTAL PROTECTION

The government, through the State Committee for Environmental Control, maintains a continuing interest in this area. Potential foreign investors are advised to contact the Ministry of Trade and Industry for current information regarding government regulations pertaining to environmental protection.

Foreign investors must guarantee that they will protect the environment.

■ RIGHTS AND OBLIGATIONS OF FOREIGN INVESTORS

The government will provide assistance to any entity in which there is foreign participation with regard to obtaining raw materials and equipment.

Foreign investors may transfer their rights and obligations to either Mongolian or other foreign investors.

There are no limitations on foreign management in any entity involving foreign capital participation.

There is a government guarantee against nationalization.

Foreign investors are protected with regard to any change in the present investment law, i.e., if the present law should be amended, the entity may elect to continue under the present law or under the amended statute.

Investments and income derived from such investments may be remitted abroad or repatriated and such repatriated income will be exempt from Mongolian taxation.

A license fee must be paid to the government for the use of any water, land, forest, or other natural resources.

■ LABOR

Mongolia has a substantial body of laws regarding employment and working conditions.

Hiring preference should be accorded to Mongolian workers unless required managerial and technical skills are not locally available.

■ ACCOUNTING REQUIREMENTS

All companies must maintain financial records for tax and other purposes. Accounting records must be maintained in accordance with internationally accepted standards.

■ CURRENCY CONTROLS

The State Bank of the Mongolian People's Republic, now known as Mongolbank, is the central bank. It has overall responsibility for management of foreign exchange requirements.

Business entities may open and maintain bank accounts in foreign, as well as Mongolian, currencies.

Foreign nationals employed by organizations funded with foreign investment may remit abroad or repatriate, without limit, their after-tax income.

■ TAXATION

Foreign investments and foreign nationals are subject to Mongolian tax laws.

The major tax levied is that on income. Foreign entities must pay a differentiated tax on profits, which shall not exceed 40 percent of such profits.

Certain deductions and allowances are permitted. In addition, enterprises funded with foreign capital may be exempt from profit taxes for a period of three years from the start-up date.

Individuals must pay an income tax.

■ LEGAL SYSTEM

The court system includes the local (or district) courts to include the City Court of Ulan Bator, and the trial level (provincial) courts. Appeals are taken to the Supreme Court which sits at Ulan Bator.

■ CUSTOMS AND DUTIES

Mongolia is attempting to expand its foreign trade that, until recently, was directed primarily to what was the Soviet bloc.

Raw materials, machinery, tools, spare parts, and other items necessary for production by activities with foreign participation are exempt from customs charges.

■ PROTECTION OF INTELLECTUAL PROPERTY

Mongolia is a member of the World Intellectual Property Organization and thus supports internationally recognized standards of protection for copyrights, patents, trademarks, and technology transfer.

■ IMMIGRATION AND RESIDENCE

Visas are normally required to enter Mongolia. Potential foreign investors are advised to contact the Ministry of Trade and Industry with regard to information about visa and residence permit requirements.

■ FOREIGN INVESTMENT ASSISTANCE DIRECTORY

Sources that can provide further information about foreign investment in Mongolia include:

Ministry of Trade and Industry
Ulan Bator 11, Mongolia
Telephone: (0) (0) 706143
Telex: 221

Mongolbank
Ulan Bator 6, Mongolia
Telephone: (0) (0) 22847
Telex: 241

Mongolian Chamber of Commerce and Industry
Ulan Bator 11, Mongolia
Telephone: (0) (0) 24620
Telex: 79336

Persons interested in obtaining further information about foreign investment in Mongolia are advised to contact the closest Mongolian embassy or consular office.

Mongolia maintains diplomatic relations with Afghanistan, Bulgaria, People's Republic of China, Cuba, Czechoslovakia, Germany, Hungary, India, Japan, Democratic People's Republic of Korea, Poland, Romania, Russia, United Kingdom, United States, and Vietnam.

MONTSERRAT

■ POLITICAL ENVIRONMENT

Montserrat is a British Dependent Territory. It is ruled by a functioning, democratic government.

The Montserrat economy is heavily oriented toward tourism. The inflow of money from this activity has permitted the government to maintain, improve, and expand the infrastructure.

Inflation and unemployment levels are very low. Light industry generates most of Montserrat's exports. A high percentage of industry is devoted to the production of electronic components.

■ SUMMARY OF FOREIGN INVESTMENT POLICY

The government has a high level of interest in the acquisition of foreign investment. The key law relevant to this subject is the Fiscal Incentives Ordinance of 1975. Another important law, with more specific objectives, is the Hotel Aids Ordinance.

The government agencies charged with major responsibilities with regard to the promotion and regulation of foreign investment are the Ministry of Trade and the Economic Development Unit.

Foreign investments that will be entitled to incentives must be approved by the government. Among the general incentives offered are long-term tax holidays that are based on the amount of value added that an enterprise can provide. Tax holidays of 15 years are available to Group I enterprises that will generate a value added of 50 percent or more; Group II enterprises that will generate a value added of 25-49 percent; and Group III enterprises that will generate a value added of 10-24 percent.

Enclave enterprises, i.e., those that will produce exclusively for export beyond the CARICOM region, are entitled to tax holidays of 15 years. Capital intensive enterprises, i.e., those involving not less than $9.25 million (U.S.) are also entitled to 15-year tax holidays. Neither enclave nor capital intensive enterprises are required to meet a value added standard.

Foreign investment projects receiving incentive benefits are subject to performance reviews by the government. The first review normally occurs after the passage of three years and then at two-year intervals until the granted tax holiday period has elapsed.

Hotel investors are granted customs duties exemptions on materials and equipment needed for both hotel construction and operation. Tax holidays of up to five years may be granted. For five years out of the subsequent eight years following the expiration of the initial tax holiday, hotel investors may set off 20 percent of their incurred capital expenses against future income.

The government has created numerous factory shells or industrial parks that are designed to accommodate light industry.

There are no requirements relevant to the participation by Montserrat investors or the government in the management or equity of foreign firms.

Foreign investments must be registered with the government through the Ministry of Trade.

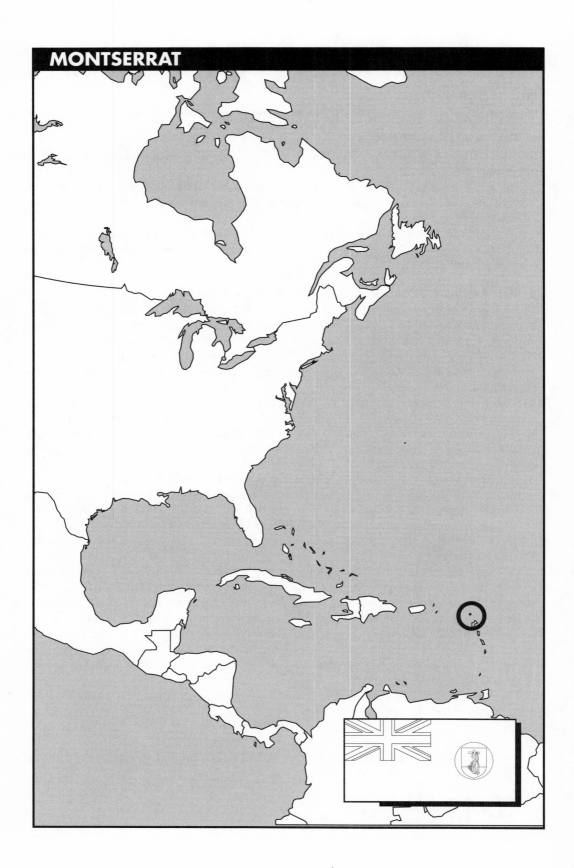

■ FORMATION AND TYPES OF PERMITTED BUSINESS ORGANIZATIONS

Foreign investors may participate in the national economy through the creation of public or private corporations, general or limited partnerships, or sole proprietorships. Subsidiaries and branch offices of foreign corporations may be established in Montserrat. Joint ventures may be created between foreign and Montserrat investors.

Corporations acquire juridical person status.

■ ENVIRONMENTAL PROTECTION

The government maintains a continuing interest in the environment. Potential foreign investors are advised to contact either the Ministry of Trade or the Economic Development Unit for complete information pertaining to current or pending environmental laws and regulations.

■ RIGHTS AND OBLIGATIONS OF FOREIGN INVESTORS

Foreign and domestic investors are guaranteed equality of opportunity and protection of the laws.

Registered investments and any income, including profits, dividends, royalties, and fees generated from such investments, may be freely remitted abroad or repatriated, to include the proper share of a foreign investor in the event of liquidation of a foreign investment.

Foreign investors may obtain local financing.

■ LABOR

There is a complete body of laws in existence with regard to employment and working conditions.

The labor force is well educated and highly motivated. There is a shortage of indigenous labor that requires the employment of foreign personnel at all levels of employment. Foreign nationals employed in Montserrat must have work permits.

■ ACCOUNTING REQUIREMENTS

All companies operating in Montserrat must maintain complete and accurate financial and other records. Accounting records must be maintained in accordance with internationally recognized standards. Public corporations must submit to yearly audits by a chartered accountant.

■ CURRENCY CONTROLS

The Eastern Caribbean Central Bank, with its head office in St. Christopher, is the central bank.

Foreign enterprises and personnel may maintain foreign currency accounts.

Foreign exchange controls are limited.

■ TAXATION

Foreign businesses and individuals are subject to the tax laws.

The major tax is that assessed on business income. In addition to the tax incentives provided, companies may file for a capital expenditure allowance upon the expiration of the granted tax holiday, which cannot be greater than the firm's total expenditures on plant, machinery, and equipment during the tax holiday.

In general, losses that are incurred during granted tax holidays cannot be carried forward against future income.

Companies that export beyond the CARICOM area may claim a tax rebate of from 25-50 percent, depending on the percentage of export profits to total profits.

Montserrat is a party to bilateral treaties on the subject of double tax relief with several nations.

The government has generally attempted to keep business taxes low in order to remain attractive to foreign investment.

■ LEGAL SYSTEM

The court system is composed of three essential levels, i.e., the Magistrates' Court that hears and decides petty criminal issues; the Court of Summary Jurisdiction, which is the trial level court that hears more serious criminal and civil matters; and the East Caribbean Supreme Court, which is the final appellate authority. The Supreme Court sits in St. Lucia.

■ CUSTOMS AND DUTIES

Montserrat is a member of CARICOM, a group of Caribbean states that has created a regional common market. As a British Dependent Territory, exports from Montserrat to Europe are covered under the trade provisions of the EC.

■ PROTECTION OF INTELLECTUAL PROPERTY

Montserrat is a British Dependent Territory and thus the laws of the United Kingdom relevant to copyright, patent, trademark, and technology transfer protection are provided under the laws of the United Kingdom.

■ IMMIGRATION AND RESIDENCE

In most cases, visas are required to enter Montserrat. Potential foreign investors are advised to contact either the Ministry of Trade or the Economic Development Unit for complete and current information pertaining to the requirements for visas, work permits and residence permits.

■ FOREIGN INVESTMENT ASSISTANCE DIRECTORY

Sources that can provide additional information about foreign investment in Montserrat include:

Ministry of Trade
P.O. Box 272
Plymouth, Montserrat
Telephone: (809) 491-2546 / (809) 491-2075
Fax: (809) 491-2367

Economic Development Unit
Government of Montserrat
P.O. Box 292
Plymouth, Montserrat
Telephone: (809) 491-2066
Fax: (809) 491-4632

Montserrat Chamber of Commerce
P.O. Box 384
Marine Drive
Plymouth, Montserrat
Telephone: (809) 491-3640
Fax: (809) 491-4660

MOROCCO, KINGDOM OF

■ POLITICAL ENVIRONMENT

Serious questions can be raised as to the stability of the nation. There is considerable tension caused by internal factions that were opposed to Morocco's participation in the Gulf War. This opposition emanates from groups that clearly support Iraq's policies. In addition, the nation suffers from a general unrest caused by long-standing economic problems.

■ SUMMARY OF FOREIGN INVESTMENT POLICY

Morocco has announced a policy of privatization of many areas of the economy although government participation in the overall economy remains a factor.

Foreign investment is high on the list of Moroccan interests particularly in the mining, industrial, tourist, real estate, and fishing areas where specific investment codes have been issued.

The Office of Industrial Development and the Ministry of Trade and Industry are the principal sources of guidance to potential foreign investors.

The government has established a free trade zone and has adopted various tax concessions to assist in the promotion of foreign investment.

Depending on the investment code, (i.e., mining, industry, tourism, maritime, or property) incentives to foreign investors include exemptions from corporate taxes, value added tax (VAT), certain business taxes, and exemptions from customs duties.

Some areas of the economy are closed to private investment, whether foreign or domestic. These areas include railroads and airline operations, and public utilities, i.e., water and power, which are operated by the government.

■ FORMATION AND TYPES OF PERMITTED BUSINESS ORGANIZATIONS

Foreign investment activities may be conducted by business organizations that include corporations, limited liability companies, general and limited partnerships, and joint ventures. Individuals may also operate sole proprietorships.

Corporations acquire a juridical person status upon formation. Subsequent to formation, a corporation must register with the government.

Limited liability companies, partnerships, joint ventures, and sole proprietorships do not acquire juridical person status. Joint ventures, which are formed for a specific project, may be formed between or among any type of business organization, including sole proprietorship.

No requirement exists for Moroccan ownership or management in any type of business organization formed by foreign investment.

■ ENVIRONMENTAL PROTECTION

Potential foreign investors are advised to make inquiries of the Office of Industrial Development relevant to any applicable environmental protection regulations.

■ RIGHTS AND OBLIGATIONS OF FOREIGN INVESTORS

Foreign and domestic investors have the same opportunities to participate in the Moroccan economy. Foreign companies and individuals cannot purchase land that is used

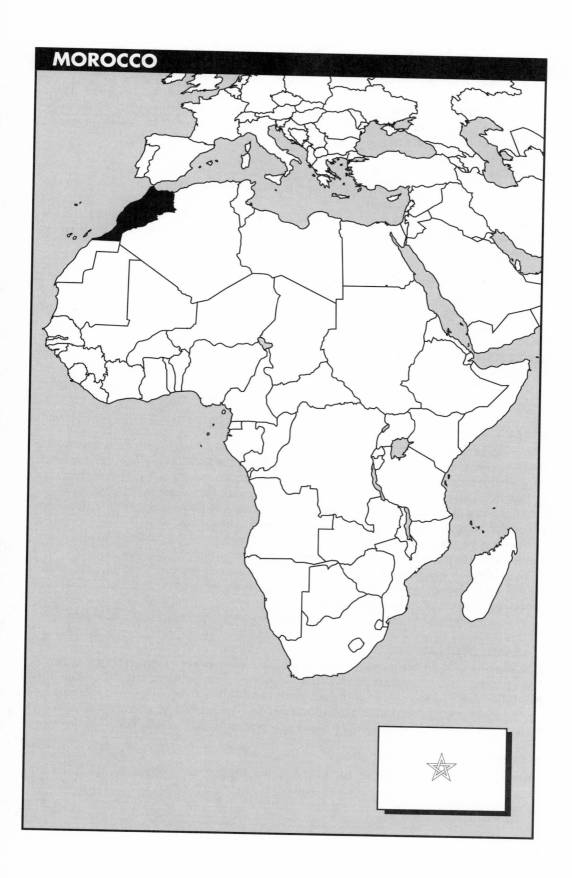

for agriculture. Agricultural land may, however, be leased by foreign investors. There are no restrictions as to foreign ownership of land that is used for industrial purposes.

There are no restrictions on the availability of credit and loans that may be provided by Moroccan sources to foreign investors.

■ LABOR

Morocco has a qualified labor force. Moroccan workers must be given priority consideration relevant to employment.

Working conditions, salaries, wages, and fringe benefits must be satisfactory and are often contractual. The government has an interest in the maintenance of positive labor-management relations.

■ ACCOUNTING REQUIREMENTS

All corporations and limited liability companies must maintain an orderly system of books and records. Corporations must undergo annual audits and every business must supply yearly income data to the Ministry of Finance.

■ CURRENCY CONTROLS

Morocco has an extensive system of regulations regarding currency controls.

In general, once the required procedures have been followed, profits and other income derived from foreign investment can be remitted abroad without limitation.

■ TAXATION

A corporation may select any 12-month period as its fiscal year for tax purposes. The taxation considerations for corporations and limited liability companies are similar. A partnership or a joint venture may voluntarily elect to be taxed as a corporation.

Individuals and partnerships are taxed on income obtained in the calendar year.

All income is taxable, including royalties and interest. Taxes also include those imposed for doing business, registration, and by local authorities.

There is an allowable depletion allowance relevant to oil and mining investments. Deductions are permitted for depreciation and other business expenses.

An extensive system of tax incentives exists to include tax holidays (i.e., tax abatement), VAT, stamp, business, registration, and certain other tax exemptions. These are contained in the various investment codes.

Morocco is a party to many bilateral agreements relevant to issues of double taxation.

■ LEGAL SYSTEM

A system of trial courts located throughout the nation hears cases involving criminal and civil matters. A separate court system has been established to hear labor-management disputes and to provide conciliation and arbitration relevant to such matters.

Appellate courts are located around the nation. The highest Moroccan judicial body is the Supreme Court, which sits at Rabat and primarily exercises appellate review.

■ CUSTOMS AND DUTIES

Foreign investors operating in the free zone of Tangier are exempt from all import duties and export duties on goods produced. Elsewhere, customs duties must be paid up to 45 percent of value.

■ PROTECTION OF INTELLECTUAL PROPERTY

Morocco is a member of the World Intellectual Property Organization and is a party to various international agreements concerning the protection of intellectual property to include patents, trademarks, and copyrights.

■ IMMIGRATION AND RESIDENCE

Potential foreign investors may apply for visas that are valid for 90 days and renewable for another 90 days. Residence permits are issued for one year and renewable for that period without limit. The Ministry of the Interior has general authority relevant to visa and residence permit issuance.

■ FOREIGN INVESTMENT ASSISTANCE DIRECTORY

There are numerous sources that can provide further information about foreign investment in Morocco. They include:

Office of Industrial Development (ODI)
10 Rue Ghandi
P.O. Box 211
Rabat, Morocco
Telephone: (212) (7) 708460
Telex: 36053
Fax: (212) (7) 707695

Moroccan Center for Export Promotion (CMPE)
23 Boulevard Girardot
Casablanca, Morocco
Telephone: (212) (7) 302210
Telex: 27847
Fax: (212) (7) 301793

La Fédération des Chambres du Commerce et d'Industries du Maroc
56 Avenue de France
Rabat, Maroc
Telephone: (212) (7) 765230
Telex: 31884

Persons interested in obtaining further information about investing in Morocco are also advised to contact the closest Moroccan embassy or consular office.

Morocco maintains diplomatic relations with Algeria, Argentina, Austria, Belgium, Brazil, Bulgaria, Cameroon, Canada, Central African Republic, People's Republic of China, Côte d'Ivoire, Czechoslovakia, Denmark, Egypt, Equatorial Guinea, Finland, France, Gabon, Germany, Greece, Guinea, Holy See, Hungary, Indonesia, Iraq, Italy, Japan, Jordan, Republic of Korea, Kuwait, Lebanon, Libya, Mauritania, Mexico, Netherlands, Nigeria, Norway, Oman, Pakistan, Peru, Poland, Portugal, Qatar, Romania, Saudi Arabia, Senegal, Spain, Sudan, Sweden, Switzerland, Tunisia, Turkey, Russia, United Arab Emirates, United Kingdom, United States, Yemen, and Zaire.

MOZAMBIQUE, REPUBLIC OF

■ POLITICAL ENVIRONMENT

This country possesses immense natural resources to include potential petroleum reserves and numerous mineral deposits to include beryllium, nickel, cobalt, manganese, chromium, platinum, bauxite, fluorspar, and coal, among others.

The nation is also rich in hydroelectric power potential, as well as in marine resources. Shrimp is, in fact, the nation's major export.

Despite the continuing armed conflict waged by the RENAMO terrorist guerilla group, the government appears to be strong. However, the conflict has taken a major toll on the economy and has created doubts among potential foreign investors as to personnel and asset security.

The RENAMO problem has exacerbated Mozambique's economic difficulties that were present from the nation's first day of independence in 1975. In addition, persistent drought has resulted in the country being dependent on external aid to meet the population's basic food requirements.

The government, in its attempts to meet the needs of its people and to generate a viable economy, has taken a number of steps to include currency devaluation and attempts to obtain foreign direct investment. Inflation is high and rising.

Despite the country's inability to feed its population, agriculture is the principal economic sector. Mozambique is the world's foremost exporter of nuts, principally cashews. Approximately 80 percent of the country's labor is employed in agricultural activities.

The continuing conflict has made it extremely difficult to create interest on the part of foreign investors in establishing industrial operations in the country. Domestic or foreign investors will find it difficult, at best, to import necessary raw materials.

A major effort has been carried out, despite the civil war, to develop and maintain a modern infrastructure, particularly in terms of rail and highway transportation. Most of the financing for this effort has been supplied by foreign countries on a bilateral aid basis or by the World Bank. An effective rail network is difficult to maintain because of the lack of skilled personnel, to include supervisory level workers, and insufficient rolling stock and locomotives.

The government, despite the enormity of these various problems, is pushing forward with its attempts to modernize and privatize the economy. The steps taken by the government, while economically necessary, are not politically popular and have resulted in widespread worker strikes and violence. These actions, of course, do not help to ensure the stability of the government. The essential, and as yet unanswered, question is whether the government's much heralded Economic Recovery Program, which is designed to move the country to a free market economy and improve the lot of the entire nation and its people, will move quickly enough to avoid increased civil war, increased lack of popular confidence, and complete structural breakdown.

■ SUMMARY OF FOREIGN INVESTMENT POLICY

The government, as part of its continuing attempt to attract foreign investment, has established the Office for Foreign Investment Promotion, which functions within the National Planning Commission and comprises representatives from the Ministry of

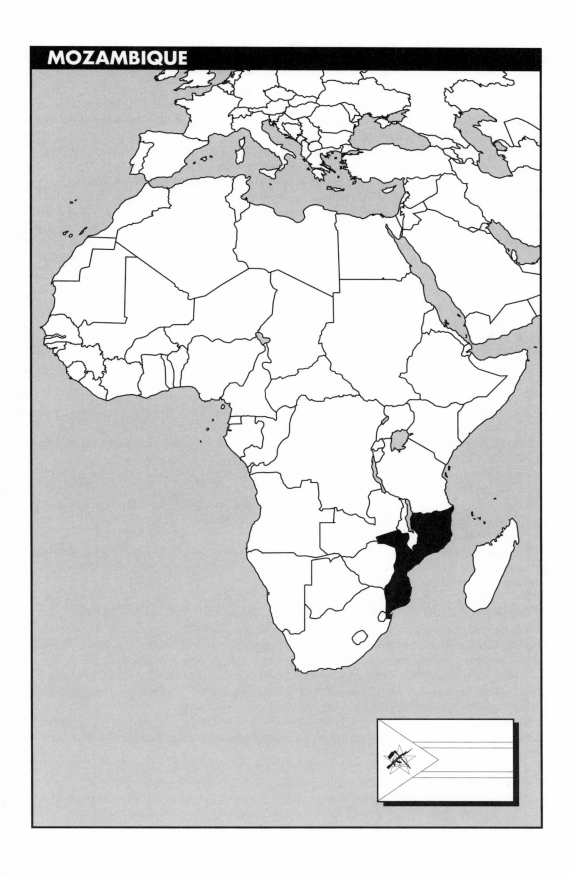

MOZAMBIQUE

Trade, the Ministry of Finance, and the Bank of Mozambique.

The primary statute relevant to foreign investment is the Foreign Investment Law of 1984. Other laws that impact foreign investment in specific areas are the Mining Law of 1986 and the Petroleum Law of 1981.

Priority areas that the government has determined for foreign investment are agriculture, livestock, agriculturally-oriented industry, mining, and forestry.

Foreign investment, under the law, may include equipment, capital, and technology transfer. Foreign investment in mining exploration and extraction projects may take any form. However, title to the mining sites remains with the government. The provisions of the Petroleum Law are similar in that monopoly rights are guaranteed to the government while providing contractual rights to foreign investors who find and develop hydrocarbon activities. Both the mining and petroleum laws provide incentives to foreign investors, principally in the form of tax concessions.

All foreign investments must be approved by the government's Evaluation Commission, which contains representatives from the Office for Foreign Investment Promotion.

The proposals generally include a request for approval of the project; backgrounds of the investors involved; technical and financial information about the proposal; management and marketing concepts to be employed; draft articles on the corporation (if that is the business form to be used); a copy of any proposed joint venture agreement involved; and any contracts relevant to the transfer of technology.

Essentially, the project will be evaluated based on its overall value to the national economy; the prospects for the success of the proposed project; the potential impact on the nation's balance of payments situation; uses of national resources; the level of technology to be provided and used; and the employment opportunities that will be provided to Mozambique personnel.

There are no existing rules or laws with regard to the acquisition of a Mozambique company by foreign investors.

Incentives to foreign investors as contained in the Foreign Investment Law include tax holidays for periods of up to ten years and tax deductions that are granted for the training of Mozambique workers.

No restrictions exist as to the percentage of any firm that may be held by foreign investors. Additionally, there are no requirements for management participation by Mozambique personnel.

■ FORMATION AND TYPES OF PERMITTED BUSINESS ORGANIZATIONS

Foreign investors may participate in the Mozambique economy through the creation of publicly held or privately held corporations, general or limited partnerships, or as sole proprietorships. Subsidiaries of foreign corporations may be established.

There are no rules with regard to the creation of joint ventures, which may involve only foreign partners or both foreign and domestic parties. Joint ventures are usually formed by the involved parties as privately held corporations.

Corporations, whether private (i.e., a private limited liability company), or public (i.e., a public limited liability company), are considered as legal entities and acquire juridical person status.

■ ENVIRONMENTAL PROTECTION

In view of Mozambique's current economic and political situation, there has been little government action taken with regard to environmental protection efforts. It is suggested, however, that potential foreign investors contact the Office for Foreign Investment Promotion to determine the government's position in this area.

■ RIGHTS AND OBLIGATIONS OF FOREIGN INVESTORS

Foreign investments and all income created as a result of such investments may be repatriated or remitted abroad subject to payment of due taxes and to the requirement that firms partially held by Mozambicans must prove convertible earnings or show a positive balance with regard to import substitution. Loan principal and interest payments may also be transferred outside of Mozambique where such loans were taken in connection with Mozambique activities and were authorized by the government.

According to the government, nationalization or expropriation of foreign investments would occur only under exceptional conditions and compensation would be provided.

Local financing sources are available to foreign investors. However, the current government policy is to restrict the supply of credit.

■ LABOR

Mozambique's labor force is large but mostly unskilled. The government requires any enterprise involving foreign investment to provide training to Mozambican employees. The Petroleum Law contains that requirement.

Any newly established company must submit a work force plan to the government, i.e., to the specific ministry involved with the economic activity in which the firm is engaged. After approval of the plan, which includes salaries to be paid along with classifications and numbers of workers, the firm may recruit personnel as needed.

The government has enacted a complete body of laws regarding employment and working conditions. Labor unions are common in Mozambique and there may be a tendency, in certain confrontations between management and labor, for the government to favor the latter.

The relevant government ministry must approve the employment of foreign personnel. Work permits are required of all foreign nationals employed in Mozambique.

■ ACCOUNTING REQUIREMENTS

All companies established in Mozambique must maintain complete records for both tax and other government purposes. Accounting records should be maintained in accordance with internationally accepted standards.

■ CURRENCY CONTROLS

The Banco de Moçambique is the nation's central bank, and it is responsible for management of the country's foreign exchange and related policies.

Foreign investors may open foreign currency accounts in either the central bank (which also operates as a commercial bank) or in Banco Standard Totta de Mocambique.

■ TAXATION

Foreign companies and individuals are subject to the tax laws. There is no difference in the application of the tax laws as between foreign and domestic companies.

All foreign nationals employed in Mozambique for a period of more than 30 days are subject to personal taxation. The personal tax rates in the country are high. Tax holidays may be negotiated for employees. Individual income is taxed at the source through a withholding system. Employees must also pay a National Reconstruction Tax along with a yearly Complementary Tax.

Tax deductions includes costs of personnel training, employee medical programs and other benefits, and the depreciation of physical assets. Tax incentives include long-term (up to ten years) exemptions for eligible firms.

The Industrial Contribution Tax is the major one assessed. Other taxes on business include the Consumer Tax and the Circulation (or transactions) Tax.

■ LEGAL SYSTEM

The Supreme Court is organized into sections, each with specific responsibilities. One part of the court functions as a trial section, which hears both civil and criminal cases. Appeals are taken to the appellate section of the Supreme Court, which sits at Maputo.

■ CUSTOMS AND DUTIES

Mozambique is a member of the Preferential Trade Areas for Eastern and Southern African States. The nation imposes no import price control and no protective tariffs. Customs duties are levied on most imports. Any foreign company importing raw materials or equipment should negotiate customs exemptions before shipment and arrival of the necessary items.

The government is considering the establishment of export processing zones. Bonded production facilities already exist.

■ PROTECTION OF INTELLECTUAL PROPERTY

Mozambique is not a member of the World Intellectual Property Organization, and the government has not enacted any specific laws with regard to the protection of copyrights, patents, tradenames, or technology transfer.

■ IMMIGRATION AND RESIDENCE

Visas are required to enter Mozambique. Potential foreign investors are advised to contact the Office for Foreign Investment Promotion for complete and current information concerning requirements for visas, work permits, and residence permits.

■ FOREIGN INVESTMENT ASSISTANCE DIRECTORY

Sources that can provide additional information about foreign investment in Mozambique include:

Office for Foreign Investment Promotion
P.O. Box 4635
Maputo, Mozambique
Telephone: (0) (0) 422456
Tex: 6876

Ministry of Trade
Praca 25 de Junho
Maputo, Mozambique
Telephone: (0) (0) 426091
Telex: 6374

Banco de Moçambique
Avda 25 de Setembro 1695
Maputo, Mozambique
Telephone: (0) (0) 428151
Telex: 6244
Fax: (0) (0) 429718

Chamber of Commerce of Mozambique
Rua Mateus Sansao Mutema 452
Maputo, Mozambique
Telephone: (0) (0) 491970
Telex: 6498

Persons interested in obtaining additional information about foreign investment in Mozambique are advised to contact the nation's closest embassy or consular office.

Mozambique maintains diplomatic relations with Algeria, Belgium, Brazil, Bulgaria, People's Republic of China, Congo, Cuba, Czechoslovakia, Denmark, Egypt, France, Germany, Greece, Guinea, Holy See, Hungary, India, Iran, Italy, Democratic People's Republic of Korea, Lesotho, Libya, Malawi, Netherlands, Nicaragua, Nigeria, Norway, Pakistan, Poland, Portugal, Romania, Russia, Somalia, Spain, Swaziland, Sweden, Switzerland, Tanzania, United Kingdom, United States, Zaire, Zambia, and Zimbabwe.

Myanmar, Union of

■ POLITICAL ENVIRONMENT

The nation has been confronted with political problems for many years. These issues have generally not been resolved by democratic measures but, instead, by often brutal government action. Stability, if it can be so described, has been achieved by the almost unbridled use of state power.

Agriculture is the principal economic activity.

Myanmar is highly undeveloped. It has a record of defaulting on its payments on public foreign debts. The annual inflation rate has been moving upward and has reached extremely high levels. Unemployment has remained low but there are some questions as to the reliability of the information, which has been provided by the government on this subject.

■ SUMMARY OF FOREIGN INVESTMENT POLICY

The government is anxious to obtain foreign investment and, pursuant to that goal, has enacted the Foreign Investment Law of 1988. The Office of Foreign Investment Commission along with the Ministry of Trade have the primary responsibilities for promoting and controlling foreign investment.

There is a specific interest on the part of the government to increase the level of private investment generally in the country. Among the targets of such economic development are the promotion of exports, heavy investment in the exploitation of natural resources, increasing the levels of technology, and creating more opportunities for employment.

Most economic areas are open to foreign investment. Among those areas closed to foreign investors, or open only with specific government permission, are banking, insurance, radio and television broadcasting, telecommunications, and industries involved with security and defense.

All foreign investments must be submitted for approval to the Foreign Investment Commission and companies engaged in foreign trade must be registered with the Ministry of Trade.

A variety of tax and other incentives have been made available to include tax holidays, exemption from profit taxes, accelerated depreciation, research and development allowances, and customs exemptions.

■ FORMATION AND TYPES OF PERMITTED BUSINESS ORGANIZATIONS

Foreign investors may create a limited company (i.e., a corporation), a partnership, or a sole proprietorship. In addition, foreign investors may establish branch offices of a corporation or partnership that is domiciled in another country.

Joint ventures may be formed with domestic investors, however, the amount of equity provided by the foreign investor must be at least 35 percent of the total business capital.

There is no requirement for domestic management or equity in any business that is wholly formed with foreign investment.

Corporations must be on file with the Registrar of Companies.

MYANMAR

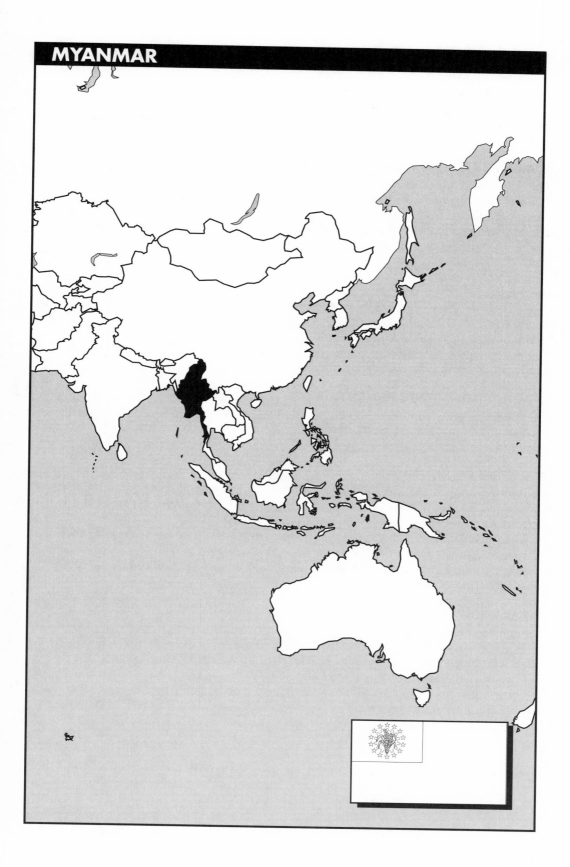

■ ENVIRONMENTAL PROTECTION

There is a high level of government concern regarding environmental protection. Potential foreign investors are advised to contact the Ministry of Trade or the Foreign Investment Commission for complete information about this subject.

■ RIGHTS AND OBLIGATIONS OF FOREIGN INVESTORS

There are government guarantees against nationalization and expropriation.

Foreign investments and profits generated from such investments may be remitted abroad or repatriated after payment of all taxes and other required payments. Repatriation is permitted in cases of liquidation subsequent to required tax payments.

Local financing is available to foreign investors through the Myanmar Economic Bank.

■ LABOR

There is an abundant and highly motivated labor force. A list of available workers will be supplied to any foreign establishment by the local government labor office. Qualified workers are selected from that list.

Foreign nationals may only be employed in cases where specially needed skills are not locally available. Work permits must be obtained by all foreign employees.

■ ACCOUNTING REQUIREMENTS

Companies must maintain complete accounting records for tax and other purposes. Accounting records must be maintained in accordance with internationally accepted standards.

■ CURRENCY CONTROLS

Matters relating to foreign exchange controls are the responsibility of the Exchange Control Board. The nation's currency, the Kyat, is not negotiable abroad, and it is not permitted to move the currency into or from the country.

Foreign businesses or individuals are not permitted to open or maintain foreign currency bank accounts.

Foreign employees may repatriate or remit abroad any portion of income received, after deduction of taxes that are due.

■ TAXATION

Foreign businesses and individuals are subject to the tax laws.

The major tax levied is that in income. There are numerous tax deductions, allowances, and incentives to include tax holidays for up to three years.

The tax year runs from April 1 to March 31.

There are many other taxes that are levied on both business and individual taxpayers to include those on documents, profits, customs, land, real property, and on the use of state-owned activities.

■ LEGAL SYSTEM

The legal system in Myanmar is under review. At present, military courts are a predominant force in the judicial system. The highest court is the Supreme Court, which sits at Yangdon.

■ CUSTOMS AND DUTIES

Customs duties are charged on virtually all imports, and export taxes are assessed on some commodities. Exemptions from customs duties and other relevant taxes may be granted by the government in the case of raw materials for three years following the establishment of a business, and for the importation of machinery and equipment during construction of necessary plants.

■ PROTECTION OF INTELLECTUAL PROPERTY

Potential foreign investors are advised to contact the Ministry of Trade or the Foreign Investment Commission regarding the position of the government about the protection of copyrights, patents, trademarks, and technology transfer.

■ IMMIGRATION AND RESIDENCE

There are two types of visas available for visits to the country. The first is an ordinary visa, which is valid for 14 days, and the second is the Multiple Journey Entry Visa.

Potential foreign investors are advised to contact the Ministry of Trade or the Foreign Investment Commission for complete information regarding visa, work permit, and residence permit requirements.

■ FOREIGN INVESTMENT ASSISTANCE DIRECTORY

Sources that can provide more information about foreign investment in Myanmar include:

Ministry of Trade
228-240 Strand Road
Yangon, Myanmar
Telephone: (0) (1) 87034
Telex: 21338
Fax: (0) (1) 89578

Foreign Investment Commission
228-240 Strand Road
Yangon, Myanmar
Telephone: (0) (1) 07034

Myanmar Economic Bank
P.O. Box 35
564 Merchant Street
Yangon, Myanmar
Telephone: (0) (1) 81819 / (0) (1) 85257
Cable: BANKINDUST

Persons interested in obtaining further information about foreign investment in Myanmar are advised to contact the closest Myanmar embassy or consular office.

Myanmar maintains diplomatic relations with Australia, Bangladesh, People's Republic of China, Czechoslovakia, Egypt, France, Germany, India, Indonesia, Israel, Italy, Japan, Republic of Korea, Laos, Malaysia, Nepal, Pakistan, Philippines, Russia, Singapore, Sri Lanka, Thailand, United Kingdom, United States, and Vietnam.

NAMIBIA, REPUBLIC OF

■ POLITICAL ENVIRONMENT

It is perhaps too early to judge the stability of the government of this relatively new independent state. At the present time it does not appear that there are any threats to the country from either internal or external forces.

There is a major dependence on the Republic of South Africa as a trading partner. Unemployment is high and inflation is above average.

■ SUMMARY OF FOREIGN INVESTMENT POLICY

The government is interested in obtaining foreign investment. It has, to this end, established The Investment Centre, under the authority of the Ministry of Trade and Industry, to promote foreign investment and to provide assistance to potential foreign investors. The principal statute relevant to this effort is the Foreign Investments Act of 1990.

All potential investment activities must be proposed to the government and, if approved, are granted a Certificate of Status Investment. Approval is determined based on the targets that Namibia has identified as essential to its national growth.

Among the points that will be considered in the evaluation of an application for a certificate will be the extent that the investment will assist the country's overall development; the extent to which the nation's resources will be utilized; the potential for increased employment and training; the creation of increased foreign exchange; the advancement of opportunities for disadvantaged individuals, including women; the development of rural areas; and the impact of the proposed activity on the environment.

■ FORMATION AND TYPES OF PERMITTED BUSINESS ORGANIZATIONS

There is no requirement for Namibian participation in a management or ownership capacity in any foreign investment activity. However, in cases where natural resources are being used, the government is entitled to, and may obtain, an interest in such exploitation.

Public and private companies must be on file with the Registrar of Companies and with other relevant government agencies to include the Receiver of Revenue.

Firms that are incorporated outside the country and open branch offices are classified as external companies and must also file with the Registrar of Companies.

■ ENVIRONMENTAL PROTECTION

There is a strong interest in the protection of the environment. Potential foreign investors are advised to contact The Investment Centre for current and complete information concerning laws and regulations regarding the protection of the environment.

■ RIGHTS AND OBLIGATIONS OF FOREIGN INVESTORS

Foreign investors will be afforded equal rights with domestic ones with respect to investment opportunities.

Foreign investors are entitled to purchase convertible foreign currency for use without restriction when remitting abroad or repatriating investments or profits generated

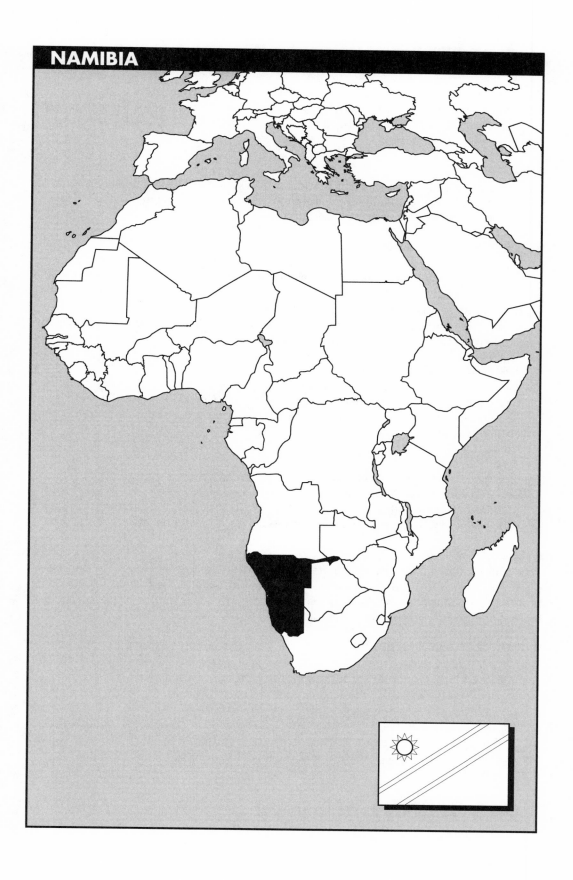

from such investments, subject only to payment of all due taxes.

Any disputes that may arise between a foreign investor and the government regarding compensation or the validity or continued validity of the certificate must be settled by the process of arbitration.

■ LABOR

There are existing laws concerning minimum working conditions and other employment factors. Generally, Namibian workers must be hired by foreign companies unless it can be shown that they do not possess required skill levels.

■ ACCOUNTING REQUIREMENTS

All businesses, including those formed as external companies, as well as public or private corporations, must maintain accurate and complete financial records to include profit and loss statements, balance sheets, cash flow statements, and a directors' report. In addition, there must be an annual report filed by a licensed auditor.

Partnerships and sole proprietors (sole traders) must provide complete accounting information to the Receiver of Revenue on an annual basis.

■ CURRENCY CONTROLS

The Central Bank of Namibia is the fiscal agent of the government.

Potential foreign investors are advised to contact the Central Bank or the Ministry of Trade and Industry for full and up-to-date information on the status of currency controls in the country.

■ TAXATION

The Receiver of Revenue is the government's tax authority.

Foreign businesses and individuals must file tax returns.

Potential foreign investors are strongly advised to seek full and current information as to the tax policy of the government to include possible tax incentives.

■ LEGAL SYSTEM

The court system is on three levels, the Lower Courts that hear petty offenses and civil cases; the High Courts that are courts of general jurisdiction and also possess some power of appellate review; and the Supreme Court, which is the highest appellate body. The Supreme Court sits in Windhoek.

■ CUSTOMS AND DUTIES

Namibia has been recognized as a beneficiary country under the Generalized System of Preferences (GSP). Under this program, many of the country's exports will be accepted in other nations on a sharply reduced or customs exempt basis.

The country is also a member of the Southern African Customs Union, which has eliminated customs duties on trade between member nations and established a common external tariff on all goods and services imported from nations outside the Union. The member states share all customs and excise duties earned from such levies applied to imported goods.

■ PROTECTION OF INTELLECTUAL PROPERTY

Namibia subscribes to the internationally accepted standards of protection accorded to copyrights, patents, trademarks, and technology transfer.

■ IMMIGRATION AND RESIDENCE

Foreign nationals may apply for permanent residence and for work permits if they are employed in Namibia. Potential foreign investors are advised to seek information on current laws and regulations regarding residence and work permits from The Investment Centre.

■ FOREIGN INVESTMENT ASSISTANCE DIRECTORY

Several sources are available to provide further information about foreign investment in Namibia. These sources include:

The Investment Centre
Ministry of Trade and Industry
Private Bag 13340
Windhoek, Namibia
Telephone: (264) 289911
Fax: (264) 220148

Namibia National Chamber of Commerce and Industry
P.O. Box 9355
Windhoek, Namibia
Telephone: (264) 228809
Fax: (264) 228009

Persons interested in obtaining further information about foreign investment in Namibia are also advised to contact the closest Namibian embassy or consular office.

Namibia maintains diplomatic relations with Algeria, Angola, Bangladesh, Botswana, Brazil, Canada, People's Republic of China, Cuba, Denmark, Egypt, Finland, France, Germany, Ghana, India, Iran, Italy, Japan, Kenya, Democratic People's Republic of Korea, Republic of Korea, Malawi, Nigeria, Norway, Portugal, Russia, Spain, Sweden, United Kingdom, United States, Zambia, and Zimbabwe.

NEPAL, KINGDOM OF

■ POLITICAL ENVIRONMENT

The country has experienced severe internal unrest over the past several years. Threats to territory on the Indian-Nepal border are a continuing problem.

Economically, Nepal is extremely underdeveloped. It has a very high external public debt and debt service.

■ SUMMARY OF FOREIGN INVESTMENT POLICY

Nepal recognizes its need for foreign investment. The Foreign Investment and Technology Act of 1981, as amended, is the controlling law. The Foreign Investment Promotion Division of the Ministry of Industry is the government agency charged with the responsibility to develop foreign investment.

Any foreign investment must be approved by the government and must be in the form of a joint venture with either the government or a domestic entity.

Foreign investors are not permitted to participate in any part of the defense industry.

Except where approved by the government, no business may be located within eight kilometers of the nation's borders.

Numerous incentives designed to attract foreign investors are being offered by the government to include tax holidays, exemptions, and reductions. Export promotion zones have been established.

A specific interest exists in attracting foreign investment that will provide modern technology and contribute to an increase in exports.

■ FORMATION AND TYPES OF PERMITTED BUSINESS ORGANIZATIONS

Foreign investments generally take the form of joint ventures between foreign corporations and a domestic business entity or between foreign corporations and the government. Joint ventures are usually formed as separate public companies.

■ ENVIRONMENTAL PROTECTION

Potential foreign investors are advised to contact the Foreign Investment Promotion Division of the Ministry of Industry for current and detailed information on laws and regulations relevant to environmental protection.

■ RIGHTS AND OBLIGATIONS OF FOREIGN INVESTORS

Income generated as a result of foreign investment may be repatriated. However, such repatriation may need to be on the basis of installments as determined by the government.

There is a prohibition against nationalization. However, the law provides that nationalization may occur if required in the national interest and defense. In such a case, just compensation will be provided.

■ LABOR

Local labor must be given hiring preference except in cases where necessary executive, professional, technical, or scientific skills are not locally available. Approval must be

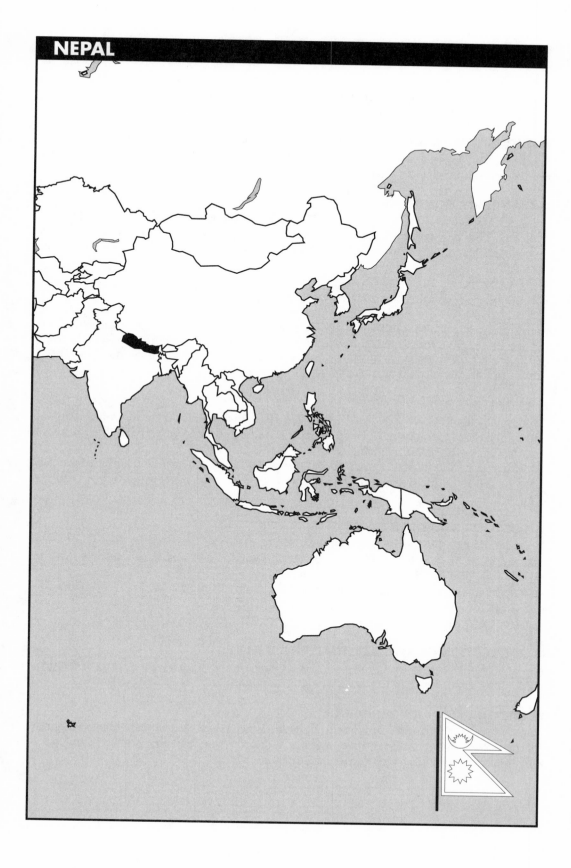

obtained from the Department of Labor to hire foreign nationals. If such approval is obtained, foreign employees may work in Nepal for a period of seven years and, where necessary, that period may be extended for an additional five years.

■ ACCOUNTING REQUIREMENTS

All foreign businesses must maintain appropriate books and records that are essential for tax and other relevant purposes.

■ CURRENCY CONTROLS

Foreign nationals may repatriate up to 75 percent of their incomes in foreign currency.

Convertible currencies may be exchanged for the purpose of purchasing necessary raw materials, goods, and required services.

■ TAXATION

Foreign businesses must file tax returns.

Corporate taxes are paid annually. Tax deductions are available for firms operating in underdeveloped areas of the country. Companies engaged in energy production and mining are eligible for extended tax holidays. Companies that export at least 25 percent of their total production, or that expand manufacturing capacity or make substantial reinvestment, are eligible for significant tax advantages.

■ LEGAL SYSTEM

The legal system is composed of District Courts, which hear and decide most criminal and civil cases. Decisions may be appealed to the Appellate Courts and to the Supreme Court, which sits in Kathmandu.

Disputes arising between any foreign investor and the government under the provisions of the Foreign Investment and Technology Act must be determined by arbitration.

■ CUSTOMS AND DUTIES

No customs or other duties are charged on raw materials received in the export zone that are to be used in the production of goods there, nor on any goods received in the export zone that are destined solely for export.

Any business manufacturing a product that is new in the nation is exempt from the excise tax for a period of three years.

Customs duties on exportable industrial products are limited to 1 percent.

■ PROTECTION OF INTELLECTUAL PROPERTY

Nepal subscribes to the generally accepted international standards relating to the protection of copyrights, patents, trademarks, tradenames, and technology transfer.

■ IMMIGRATION AND RESIDENCE

Visas, work permits, and residence permits are issued on a case-by-case basis. Potential foreign investors are advised to contact the Foreign Investment Promotion Division for current and detailed information on this subject.

■ FOREIGN INVESTMENT ASSISTANCE DIRECTORY

Sources that will be able to provide further information about investing in Nepal include:

Foreign Investment Promotion Division
Ministry of Industry
Kathmandu, Nepal
Telephone: 2-16692
2-15026
2-15030

Federation of Nepalese Chambers of Commerce and Industry
P.O. Box 269
Kathmandu, Nepal
Telephone: 2-12096
Telex: 2574

Nepal Chamber of Commerce
P.O. Box 198
Kathmandu, Nepal
Telephone: 2-21318
Telex: 2349
Fax: 226567

Persons interested in obtaining further information about foreign investment in Nepal are also advised to contact the country's closest embassy or consular office.

Nepal maintains diplomatic relations with Australia, Bangladesh, People's Republic of China, Egypt, France, Germany, India, Israel, Italy, Japan, Democratic People's Republic of Korea, Republic of Korea, Myanmar, Pakistan, Russia, Thailand, United Kingdom, and United States.

NETHERLANDS, KINGDOM OF THE

■ POLITICAL ENVIRONMENT

The government of the Netherlands is democratically elected and stable.

The economy is diversified and sound. Inflation is low and unemployment is considered moderate.

Netherlands has been a member of the European Community (EC) since the organization's inception.

Privatization of some traditional public services have occurred as part of a general government program. A broad tax reduction plan has been designed by the government to promote continued economic growth.

■ SUMMARY OF FOREIGN INVESTMENT POLICY

The government has an interest in the acquisition of foreign investment. The principal government office involved in that process is the Netherlands Foreign Investment Agency, which is active in promotion of the country to potential foreign investors.

Numerous incentives have been made available for foreign investors to include guaranteed, low-interest government loans, cash grants, and export guarantees. The use of tax incentives has largely been eliminated because of the general reduction in taxes that has occurred. In most cases, incentives are now offered to foreign investors for the purpose of attracting them to areas of the country that need economic stimulation, or which have been hardest hit by, for example, unemployment.

Government grants, however, are given to both domestic and foreign enterprises to encourage medical technology, biotechnology, the development and use of advanced materials, and information technology, as well as for the development and use of technology related to environmental protection.

Foreign investments must neither be approved by, nor registered with, any agency of the government.

There are only a few economic areas where foreign investment is either limited or prohibited. Foreign investment is not permitted in the country's airlines, and it is restricted to no more than a one-third ownership of companies engaged in ocean shipping.

No restrictions exist as to the amount or percentage of ownership that foreign investors may hold in any other domestic company.

■ FORMATION AND TYPES OF PERMITTED BUSINESS ORGANIZATIONS

Foreign investors may create public corporations, private companies, general or limited partnerships, or operate as sole proprietors. Additionally, foreign investors may form joint ventures with Netherlands investors.

Subsidiaries or branch offices of foreign corporations may be established.

Corporations, including subsidiaries of foreign corporations, are considered to be legal entities and to have juridical person status, which is acquired upon the filing of the required documents, to include articles of association, with the Chamber of Commerce and with the Commercial Trade Register.

There is no requirement for domestic participation in the management of an enterprise that is wholly or partially owned by foreign investors.

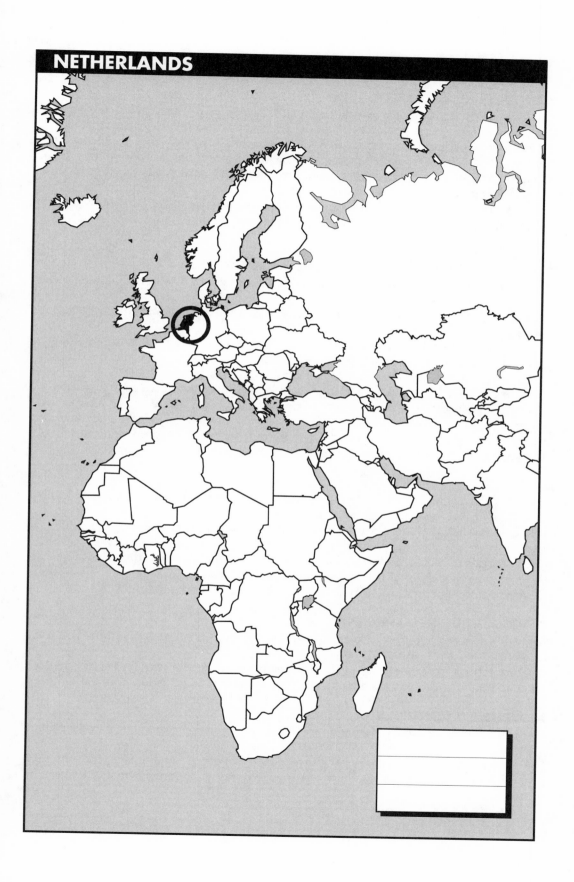

■ ENVIRONMENTAL PROTECTION

There is a very high interest on the part of the government in the protection of the environment. As noted, government grants are provided to investors relevant to the development of equipment or processes that will reduce environmental problems. The Ministry of Housing, Physical Planning and the Environment has a major policy role in this area. Additionally, local government authorities require high standards to be met by all facilities with regard to environmental protection. The government has introduced a broad plan to be carried out over the next several years, i.e., the National Environment Policy, that is designed to provide and maintain environmental protection.

■ RIGHTS AND OBLIGATIONS OF FOREIGN INVESTORS

There are no government restrictions with regard to foreign investors obtaining local financing.

Foreign and domestic investors are guaranteed equal rights and acquire the same obligations under the law.

Foreign investments and all income derived from such investments may be freely remitted abroad or repatriated. In the event of investment liquidation, the foreign investor's share of such an investment may be remitted or repatriated.

Domestic companies may be acquired by or merged with a foreign company subject to the provisions of the nation's Takeover and Mergers Code. Trade unions affected by any merger or acquisition must be advised of such possible action. Acquisitions or mergers that may result in an enterprise with total sales to exceed one billion dollars (U.S.) must be approved by the European Commission.

■ LABOR

The labor force is highly motivated. It is skilled, educated and experienced at all levels to include professional, managerial, and technical ones.

A complete body of laws exists with regard to employment and working conditions. The labor force is highly unionized to include the staff and upper management levels.

Enterprises must obtain permission, in the form of a license issued by the Ministry of Social Affairs and Employment, to maintain more than 20 foreign nationals as employees. All foreign employees must obtain work and residence permits.

■ ACCOUNTING REQUIREMENTS

All businesses are required to keep proper accounting, statistical, and similar records for tax and other purposes.

Corporations, both public and private, must be audited on a yearly basis by a registered accountant who will prepare a report for the Commercial Trade Registry.

■ CURRENCY CONTROLS

The central bank is De Netherlands Bank. It is responsible for matters concerning foreign exchange.

There are very few foreign exchange restrictions. There are no limits on the amount of capital a foreign investor may move into the country to operate or finance an enterprise.

■ TAXATION

Both foreign companies and individuals are subject to the Netherlands tax laws.

The major taxes are those assessed on both corporate and personal income. There are a variety of other taxes to include a Value added tax (VAT) along with those assessed on the transfer of real property, a lottery tax, road taxes, customs duties, and registration and license fees.

Companies may use their fiscal year for tax year purposes.

The Ministry of Finance is the government's tax authority.

In general, partnerships are not considered to be taxable entities. A joint venture that has been incorporated is a taxable entity. Joint ventures established as a partnership, including between two or more corporations, are considered to be a partnership, and the income of the partners is taxable.

Among the deductions and allowances permitted to be taken by corporate taxpayers are those included for business expenses; depreciation; costs of salaries and wages; insurance premiums; contributions to charity; and losses.

Individuals are taxed on income and on net wealth and must use the calendar year as the tax year. Tax deductions and allowances include expenses incurred, travel costs, charitable deductions, and insurance costs, among others.

The Netherlands has entered into numerous bilateral treaties with other nations on the subject of double taxation.

■ LEGAL SYSTEM

The court system essentially includes the local courts thath are empowered to decide petty criminal and civil cases; district courts that hear more serious criminal and civil cases and that hear appeals from the local courts; and the court of appeal, which renders decisions based on cases referred to it from the lower courts. Appeals from the court of appeal are taken to the Supreme Court, which sits at The Hague.

■ CUSTOMS AND DUTIES

The Netherlands is committed to free trade. The nation is a member of the EC, and is a signatory to the General Agreement on Tariffs and Trade (GATT). As an EC member, trade with other member states is duty free. Agreements forged by the European Community Commission (ECC) with other trade groups provide guaranteed preferential access to numerous countries.

Import licenses are required for only a limited number of products. Export licenses are, in the main, required only for goods that are considered by the government to be of strategic importance.

■ PROTECTION OF INTELLECTUAL PROPERTY

The Netherlands is a member of the World Intellectual Property Organization, and is a signatory to the Paris Convention of Patents, the European Patent Convention, the Patent Cooperation Treaty, the Benelux Trademarks Act, the Madrid Agreement, the Berne Convention for the Protection of Literary and Artistic Works, the Universal Copyright Convention, and the Uniform Benelux Design Act

In addition, the country has domestic laws to provide protection of intellectual property.

■ IMMIGRATION AND RESIDENCE

In general, visas are required to enter the country, except for individuals who are citizens of other EC nations.

Potential foreign investors are advised to contact the Netherlands Foreign Investment Agency for complete and current information on requirements for visas, work permits, and residence permits.

■ FOREIGN INVESTMENT ASSISTANCE DIRECTORY

Sources that can provide further information about foreign investment in the Netherlands include:

Netherlands Foreign Investment Agency
Ministry of Development Cooperation
P.O. Box 20061
Bezuidenhoutseweg 67
2500 EB
The Hague, Netherlands
Telephone: (31) (70) 3486486
Telex: 31326

Ministry of Housing, Physical Planning and the Environment
Van Alkemadelaan 85
2597 AC
The Hague, Netherlands
Telephone: (31) (70) 3264201
Telex: 34429

Ministry of Social Affairs and Employment
P.O. Box 90801
Anna Van Hannoverstraat 4
2509 LV
The Hague, Netherlands
Telephone: (31) (70) 3334444
Telex: 331250
Fax: (31) (70) 3334023

De Netherlands Bank NV
P.O. Box 98
Westeinde 1
1000 AB
Amsterdam, Netherlands
Telephone: (31) (20) 5249111
Telex: 11355

Persons interested in obtaining additional information about foreign investment in the Netherlands are advised to contact the country's closest embassy or consular office.

The Netherlands maintains diplomatic relations with Algeria, Argentina, Australia, Austria, Belgium, Brazil, Bulgaria, Canada, Cape Verde, Chile, People's Republic of China, Colombia, Costa Rica, Cuba, Czechoslovakia, Denmark, Egypt, El Salvador,

Finland, France, Germany, Greece, Holy See, Honduras, Hungary, India, Indonesia, Iran, Iraq, Ireland, Israel, Italy, Japan, Kenya, Republic of Korea, Kuwait, Lebanon, Luxembourg, Malaysia, Mexico, Morocco, New Zealand, Nicaragua, Nigeria, Norway, Oman, Pakistan, Peru, Philippines, Poland, Portugal, Romania, Russia, Saudi Arabia, South Africa, Spain, Sudan, Suriname, Sweden, Switzerland, Tanzania, Thailand, Tunisia, Turkey, United Kingdom, United States, Uruguay, Venezuela, Yemen, and Zaire.

NETHERLANDS ANTILLES

■ POLITICAL ENVIRONMENT

Government, on this island group, has a history of fragmentation. Internal stability has not been achieved since independence was granted by the Netherlands in 1954.

Tourism and offshore finance are the dominant economic activities.

Inflation is low. However, unemployment has been rising on a consistent basis.

■ SUMMARY OF FOREIGN INVESTMENT POLICY

There is a definite interest on the part of the government in promoting and acquiring foreign investment. The Department of Trade, Industry and Employment is the key agency for such promotion. In addition, the Foreign Investment Agency Curacao functions in that capacity for the island government factor.

Among the government's priority development interests are to continue to develop the already successful tourism area and to increase offshore finance activities. In addition, the government wants to generate increased trade levels. The Curacao Free Zone has been developed to help achieve this goal.

There is a strong interest in obtaining foreign investment projects that will provide increased employment.

Foreign investment incentives include the development of the Curacao Free Zone and an industrial estate, plus favorable tax and other considerations. Companies engaged in manufacturing for export are entitled to long-term tax holidays that can range up to ten years, exemptions from customs charges on necessary manufacturing related imports, and substantially reduced corporate profit tax rates.

Companies engaged in manufacturing, but not generally for export, are entitled to similar incentives to include tax and other concessions.

In order to achieve eligibility for foreign investor incentives, companies must be established as limited liability companies in the country.

Incentives also are made available to limited liability companies engaged in the tourism and oil industries as well as those engaged in the development of land.

Companies formed in the country and established as offshore firms are entitled to special tax concessions.

Limited liability companies that are established in the Curacao Free Zone are entitled to special tax rates on profits as well as favorable customs considerations.

All foreign investment must be approved by the government. Foreign ownership of any domestic business is limited to 49 percent. There are no limits on the amount of foreign ownership of offshore business activities.

Most economic areas are open to foreign investment. Areas closed to investment, foreign or domestic, are those that usually are carried on by agencies of the government.

■ FORMATION AND TYPES OF PERMITTED BUSINESS ORGANIZATIONS

Foreign investors may participate in the economy through the formation of limited liability companies, general and limited partnerships, and joint ventures with domestic partners. Branch offices and subsidiaries of foreign corporations may be established.

In practical terms, however, most incentives available to foreign investors require

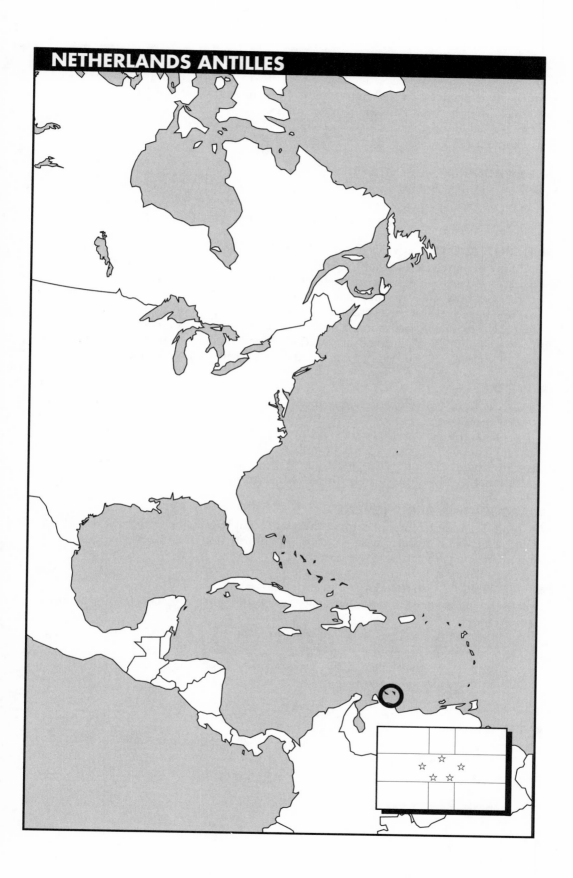

that the investment be formed in the country as a limited liability company. Subsidiaries are eligible for foreign investment incentives.

Limited liability companies enjoy juridical person status and must be registered with the Chamber of Commerce. Branch offices and subsidiaries must also be registered.

■ ENVIRONMENTAL PROTECTION

There is a strong interest in protecting the environment. Potential foreign investors, particularly those planning to be engaged in manufacturing, are advised to contact the Department of Trade, Industry and Employment regarding this subject.

■ RIGHTS AND OBLIGATIONS OF FOREIGN INVESTORS

Land may be purchased without restriction by foreign companies and individuals.

Foreign investors engaged in onshore activities may obtain financing from local sources. Offshore investors may obtain financing from foreign sources subsequent to obtaining approval from the central bank.

Except for offshore activities, foreign investments and income derived from such investments may be repatriated or remitted abroad without restriction. In the case of offshore investments, such repatriation must be approved by the central bank.

■ LABOR

There is a highly developed existing body of laws with regard to employment and working conditions.

In general, foreign employers should provide hiring preferences to local labor. Foreign employers must possess work permits that will only be granted where local workers cannot be located with necessary skills. In most cases, management and professional level positions can be filled by foreign personnel.

■ ACCOUNTING REQUIREMENTS

All limited liability companies must maintain complete financial records for tax and other purposes on a yearly basis. Accounting information must be prepared in accord with internationally accepted standards.

■ CURRENCY CONTROLS

Foreign businesses and foreign nationals are permitted to maintain bank accounts in any currency.

The Bank of the Netherlands Antilles is the central bank and is responsible for operational management of the country's foreign exchange policies.

Any transactions involving foreign loans must be approved by the central bank.

Foreign monetary obligations may be settled without prior approval of the central bank.

■ TAXATION

Foreign companies and individuals are subject to the country's tax laws.

The major taxes are those on corporate profits and individual income. There are minor taxes to include those on international transfers, documents, customs, property, mining rights, and royalties.

In general, the tax year runs concurrently with the calendar year, i.e., January 1 through December 31. Corporations may elect another tax year.

Deductions and allowances in addition to tax incentives available to corporations include depreciation, investment allowances, and business expenses.

Partnerships and joint ventures are not considered to be taxable entities. The partners in such business formations are taxed either as individuals or as corporations.

Individual taxpayers must also claim deductions for business and certain personal expenses.

Netherlands Antilles has entered in several bilateral treaties on the subject of double taxation.

Companies established as offshore entities are taxed on profits but the tax rates are significantly less than those for onshore items.

■ LEGAL SYSTEM

The Courts of First Instance function as the trial courts. Appeals are taken to the Joint High Court of Justice of the Netherlands Antilles and Aruba, which sits at Willemstadt.

■ CUSTOMS AND DUTIES

The country, because of its status as an independent nation within the Kingdom of the Netherlands, is an associate member of the EC and has observer status in CARICOM.

The government is interested in expanding its levels of both importing and exporting. Goods and materials received in the Curacao Free Zone are exempt from import charges. Exports from the zone to another zone or country are free of export charges. Firms established in the free zone must limit their activities to exporting and cannot supply any goods or materials to the domestic market.

In addition to the Curacao Free Zone, St. Maarten operates as a free port.

■ PROTECTION OF INTELLECTUAL PROPERTY

Netherlands Antilles is not a member of the World Intellectual Property Organization. However, Netherlands is a member, and patents and other forms of intellectual property that are registered in the Netherlands are protected in the Netherlands Antilles.

■ IMMIGRATION AND RESIDENCE

Visas may be required to visit the country. Potential foreign investors are advised to contact the Department of Trade, Industry and Employment or the Foreign Investment Agency Curacao for complete information regarding visa and work permit requirements.

■ FOREIGN INVESTMENT ASSISTANCE DIRECTORY

Sources that can provide additional information about foreign investment in Netherlands Antilles include:

Department of Trade, Industry and Employment
De Rouvilleweg 7
Willemstad
Curacao, Netherlands Antilles
Telephone: (599) 626400
Fax: (599) 627590

Bank of the Netherlands Antilles
Breedesraat 1
Willemstad
Curacao, Netherlands Antilles
Telephone: (599) 613600
Fax: (599) 615004

Curacao Chamber of Commerce and Industry
P.O. Box 10
Willemstad
Curacao, Netherlands Antilles
Telephone: (599) 613918

Foreign Investment Agency Curacao
ITC Building, Piscadera Bay
Curacao, Netherlands Antilles
Telephone: (599) 636603
Telex: 1456
Fax: (599) 636481

New Zealand, Dominion of

■ POLITICAL ENVIRONMENT

The government is democratically elected and stable.

This nation has suffered from a prolonged period of minimal economic expansion. Exports are principally derived from agricultural activities. There is very little heavy industry.

The country's low rate of economic growth has led to an increasing level of unemployment; rising inflation; and a balance of payments deficit.

Government efforts to boost the economy have included a program to move away from the high degree of business regulation that has marked its previous policy and to move forward with at least a limited privatization program.

■ SUMMARY OF FOREIGN INVESTMENT POLICY

There are numerous laws that have been enacted with regard to foreign investment. However, the Overseas Investment Regulation of 1985, as amended, and the Overseas Investment Act of 1973, represent the principal material on the subject. The Overseas Investment Commission is the government agency charged with developing and coordinating the country's foreign investment activities.

There is a particular government desire for foreign investment in areas that will generate increased exports, develop advanced technology, and, in an overall sense, improve the national economy. In addition, there is a specific government interest in the acquisition of foreign investment with regard to tourism and the forestry industry.

Many areas of the economy that were formerly closed to foreign investment are no longer so restricted. In effect, government approval (through the Overseas Investment Commission) is no longer required except where a foreign investment would involve the uses of certain rural land, commercial fishing, and the broadcasting industry, to include both radio and television.

Overseas Investment Commission approval is also required whenever a foreign investment will result in a position equal to at least 25 percent of the shares of a company; any acquisition investment involving NZ$10 million or more; or where the consideration involved in any investment exceeds NZ$10 million. In such cases, information required by the Overseas Investment Commission will include the number of personnel to be employed; full details on the proposed investment; background data on the investors; and financing arrangements.

There are special provisions in place with regard to the creation of a bank or other financial institutions. Application procedures for such institutions are set out by the Reserve Bank of New Zealand Act of 1989.

Mergers and acquisitions are subject to review and may be set aside by the Commerce Commission.

Certain minimal requirements have been established with reference to foreign investments and these include a minimum of NZ$500,000 to NZ$750,000 and a proven record of business experience.

Incentives are available on an industry-specific basis to attract investors to designated regions of the country, and, in some cases, tariff protection is used. Effectively, there are no available tax incentives. A wide variety of incentives are available in the

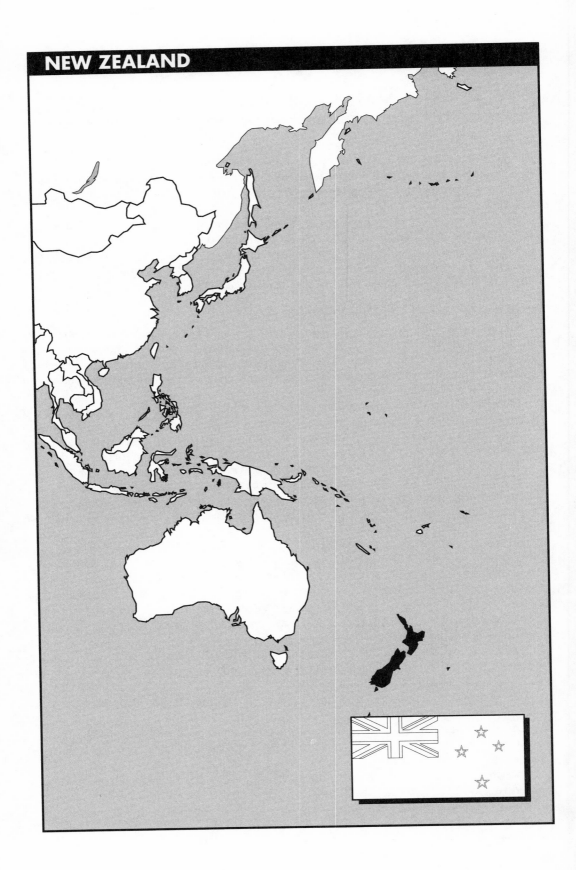

form of government advisory services; technical information; and, for firms engaged in exporting, certain grants and loans, promotional support, and other activities. Enterprises engaged in the tourism industry and the operation of research and development firms are also eligible for financial assistance that can take the form of government loans.

■ FORMATION AND TYPES OF PERMITTED BUSINESS ORGANIZATIONS

Foreign investors may participate in the economy through the creation of a public or private company (i.e., a corporation); a general (ordinary) or limited (special) partnership; or a sole proprietorship.

Joint ventures may be created between foreign and domestic investors.

Subsidiaries, termed overseas companies, of foreign corporations may be established.

All corporations, including foreign subsidiaries, must be registered with the Registrar of Companies. Corporations have a juridical person status.

Foreign subsidiaries must be approved by the Overseas Investment Commission prior to commencing business activities.

In most cases, the number of partners in a partnership is limited to 25. There are exceptions set out for professional partnerships, i.e., those created for the practice of law, medicine, and other professions. Similarly, private corporations are limited to 25 shareholders.

■ ENVIRONMENTAL PROTECTION

The government, through the Ministry of the Environment, maintains a high level of interest in protecting the environment. Local and regional environmental authorities are also active with regard to environmental protection. The principal law with reference to environmental protection is the Resource Management Act of 1991.

Potential foreign investors are advised to contact the Ministry of the Environment for complete information on the provisions of the Resource Management Act and relevant rules and regulations pertaining to this subject.

■ RIGHTS AND OBLIGATIONS OF FOREIGN INVESTORS

There are no restrictions on the repatriation or remittance abroad of foreign investments or income derived from such investments.

Local financing sources are available to foreign investors.

There are guarantees against nationalization and expropriation. Any taking based on reasons of public necessity must be promptly and justly compensated.

■ LABOR

There is a highly developed and comprehensive body of laws with regard to the subjects of employment and working conditions.

The labor force is well educated. The unions represent a major power in the economy.

All foreign nationals, except those from Australia and, under certain conditions, those from other Commonwealth areas, must obtain work permits that are valid for a period of six months and may be renewed.

■ ACCOUNTING REQUIREMENTS

Public corporations are required to maintain accurate and complete financial records, to appoint independent auditors, and to be audited on a yearly basis. Subsidiaries of overseas corporations and New Zealand companies that are owned to the extent of 25 percent or more by foreign investors must also be audited on a yearly basis.

The annual audits of an overseas company must be filed with the Registrar of Companies. Public companies and those that are 25 percent or more owned by foreign investors must file audited statements with the Registrar of Companies together with annual tax returns.

■ CURRENCY CONTROLS

The Reserve Bank of New Zealand is the nation's central bank, which is responsible for management of the country's foreign exchange policy.

No restrictions are in place with regard to the movement of capital. Currency exchanges can be executed only through a bank or other authorized exchange dealer.

■ TAXATION

The principal tax levied is that on both business and personal income. A variety of other taxes are imposed to include those on goods and services; estate and gift taxes (on individual taxpayers); real property taxes; customs duties; excise taxes; stamp taxes with regard to the sale or other transfer of commercial real property; and certain other registration and license fees.

The accounting year runs from April 1 to March 31. Companies may elect to use their fiscal year as the tax year.

Partnerships and joint ventures are not considered as taxable entities. Income earned by such business forms is taxed to the partners of such organizations. Partnerships and joint ventures formed as partnerships are, however, required to file tax returns.

There are numerous deductions to include legitimate business expenses; depreciation on physical assets; interest on loans; depletion allowances with regard to firms engaged in petroleum, mining, and forestry exploration and exploitation; employee enumeration and fringe benefits costs; royalties; insurance premiums, and other costs incurred.

Individual taxpayers are entitled to deduct certain personal allowances in the form of tax rebates, which include but are not limited to, those for dependents and charitable deductions.

New Zealand is a signatory to numerous treaties with other nations on the subject of double taxation.

■ LEGAL SYSTEM

The court structure is comprised of four essential levels. The District Court is organized into divisions that are empowered to hear and decide criminal and civil matters to include family law issues. Trials or more serious criminal and civil cases are heard by the High Court, which also acts in an appellate capacity with regard to decisions referred to it from the District Courts. Decisions of the High Courts may be referred to the Court of Appeal, which sits at Wellington. Final appeals from decisions of the Court of Appeal may be taken to the Judicial Committee of the Privy Council in London, United Kingdom.

■ CUSTOMS AND DUTIES

New Zealand is interested in the expansion of its export trade. There are no trade barriers between Australia and New Zealand. In general, a policy of increased free trade is being pursued by the government, with most import duties being reduced or eliminated. The country is a signatory to the General Agreement on Tariffs and Trade (GATT). Despite these factors, some tariff protection measures may be employed to protect domestic industries. A generalized system of preferences is employed by the government as a means of generating increased trade with less developed nations.

■ PROTECTION OF INTELLECTUAL PROPERTY

New Zealand is a member of the World Intellectual Property Organization and is a signatory to the Berne Convention and the Universal Copyright Convention. In addition, the government has enacted laws designed to protect interests in copyrights, patents, and trademarks.

■ IMMIGRATION AND RESIDENCE

Depending on visitor nationality, visas may be required to enter the country. Persons seeking permanent residence are required to meet certain standards, and in the case of those individuals wishing to open businesses in the country, are required to demonstrate adequate financial standing.

Foreign business executives and investors who wish to visit the country for the purpose of exploring possible investment opportunities or to monitor the progress of such investments may, for reasonable cause, be extended for an additional three months.

Potential foreign investors are advised to contact the Overseas Investment Commission or the New Zealand Immigration Service for complete and current information on visas, work permits, and residence permits.

■ FOREIGN INVESTMENT ASSISTANCE DIRECTORY

Sources that can provide further information about foreign investment in New Zealand include:

Overseas Investment Commission
P.O. Box 2498
Wellington, New Zealand
Telephone: (64) (4) 4722029
Fax: (64) (4) 4723262

Ministry of Commerce
P.O. Box 1473
32 Bowen Street
Wellington, New Zealand
Telephone: (64) (4) 4720030
Fax: (64) (4) 4734638

Ministry of the Environment
P.O. Box 10362
Wellington, New Zealand
Telephone: (64) (4) 4734090
Fax: (64) (4) 4710195

Immigration Service
Business Immigration Section
P.O. Box 4130
120 The Terrace
Wellington, New Zealand
Telephone: (64) (4) 4739100
Fax: (64) (4) 4712118

Reserve Bank of New Zealand
P.O. Box 2498
2 The Terrace
Wellington, New Zealand
Telephone: (64) (4) 4722029
Telex: NZ3368
Fax: (64) (4) 4738554

Persons interested in obtaining additional information about foreign investment in New Zealand are advised to contact the closest New Zealand embassy or consular office.

New Zealand maintains diplomatic relations with Australia, Belgium, Canada, Chile, People's Republic of China, Czechoslovakia, Fiji, France, Germany, Holy See, India, Indonesia, Iran, Israel, Italy, Japan, Republic of Korea, Malaysia, Mexico, Netherlands, Papua New Guinea, Philippines, Poland, Russia, Singapore, Sweden, Switzerland, Thailand, Turkey, United Kingdom, United States, and Western Samoa.

NIGER, REPUBLIC OF

■ POLITICAL ENVIRONMENT

The nation is a troubled one. Politically, its history has been marked by internal struggles between the army and civilian officials, corruption, and numerous takeovers. There is no real semblance of either democratic processes or of stable government.

Agriculture dominates the economy, providing employment for a major percentage of the work force and generating a large share of the nation's exports.

Inflation is low. The external public debt is high. Austerity measures that are needed to generate foreign investment, have proven difficult to sustain in the face of popular resistance. Governmental stability over the long term must be seen as doubtful in the absence of economic success coupled with popular public support for such measures.

■ SUMMARY OF FOREIGN INVESTMENT POLICY

The primary law regarding foreign investment is the Investment Code. The Investment Commission, which functions under the Ministry of the Economy, Finance and Planning, is the government agency responsible for promotion and development of foreign investment.

Areas of the economy that the government has identified as those to which the foreign investment law will be applied are agriculture, to include commercial fishing and food processing for export; manufacturing; energy production; mining and hydrocarbon exploration and exploitation; residential construction; and the maintenance of industrial equipment.

The government is particularly interested in acquiring foreign investment with reference to new economic activities and those that modernize or expand existing facilities.

Under the law, certain special benefits may be provided to firms engaged in hotel construction and motion picture production.

Foreign investment proposals are classified into three groups, i.e., small, medium, and large size. Small investments are those of not less than 25 million FCFA and not more that 100 million FCFA. Medium size investments are those of not less than 100 million FCFA and not more than 500 million FCFA. Large size investments are those of 500 million FCFA or more.

Foreign investment is considered to include capital contributions; in-kind contributions of expertise; loans extended to domestic entities; and other equity capital provided in exchange for shares of existing Niger companies.

All foreign investment proposals must include guarantees that the investor will use local materials, products, and services to the maximum extent possible; that local workers will be given hiring preference and will be trained with the purpose of replacing any foreign nationals; and will maintain high standards of quality in all products and services offered.

Incentives offered to foreign investors are classified into regimes, i.e., identified as Regime A (Promotional), Regime B (Priority), and Regime C (Conventional).

Regime A incentives are offered to foreign investors for a period of ten years. Included among the incentives is a complete exemption necessary for carrying out the investment and which cannot be obtained locally; complete exemption from the busi-

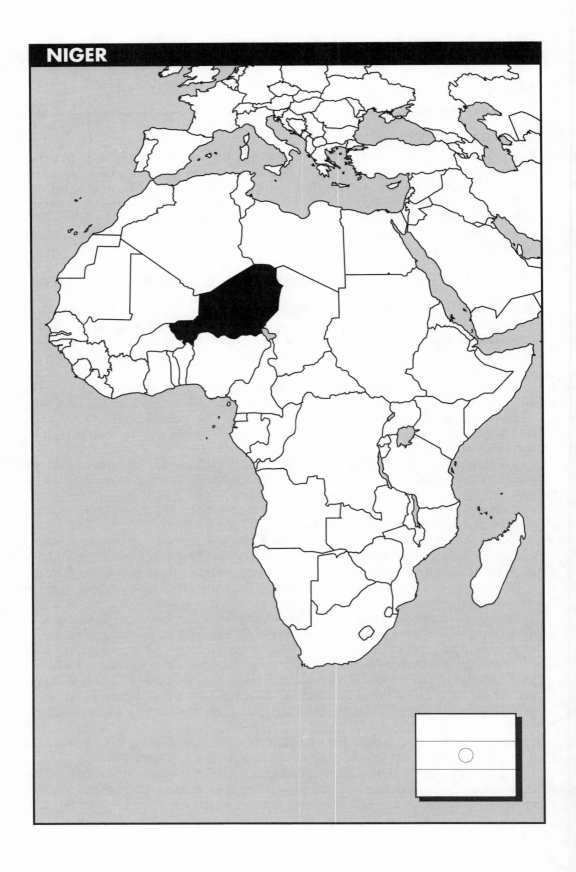

ness tax for the initial four years of the investment; complete exemption from real property and related taxes for the first six years of the investment; and complete exemption from the industrial and commercial profits tax and the fiscal rate tax for the first six years of the investment and a reduction in such taxes in the seventh to tenth year of the investment.

Regime B incentives are granted to new enterprises based on investment amount and employment opportunities that are being provided by such enterprises, and to companies that are engaged in expansion or modernization of existing firms. Small firms are those employing at least five local workers and representing an investment of at least 50 million FCFA. Medium size firms are those providing employment for at least ten local workers and representing an investment of at least 250 million FCFA. Large firms are those providing employment for at least 150 Niger workers and represent an investment level of at least one billion FCFA.

Regime B incentives are offered for ten years to a small firm; 12 years to a medium size firm; and 15 years to a large firm. Incentives include all offered under Regime A, plus exemption for the time periods shown on export taxes and duties.

Regime C incentives are offered for a period of 15 years to firms that represent an investment of two billion FCFA and provide employment for at least 400 Niger workers.

In addition to the incentives provided under Regimes A and B, large firms are entitled to 50 percent rebates on customs duties and taxes on fuel oil, diesel oil, and other energy sources used in buildings.

No subsequent legislation may be used to reduce the incentives provided under the law. However, if a subsequent law should increase the available incentives, enterprises will be permitted to enjoy such incentives.

All foreign investment agreements, or covenants, made between the investor and the government shall set out the purpose of the investment; the arbitration procedure to be followed in case of disagreement between the parties; the incentives that will apply; and conditions for amendment.

In some cases, particularly when an enterprise agrees to locate in an underdeveloped area, the periods of time during which the incentives will be provided may be extended.

Companies and individuals engaged in motion picture production are entitled to exemption from customs duties and taxes, and the value added tax (VAT) relevant to the importation of required motion picture equipment, and on all necessary construction and related materials and equipment when the latter are not locally available.

Artists and others investing in art projects in the country are eligible for exemption from the business tax; the tax on industrial and commercial profits; and other taxes including the value added tax (VAT) for a period of five years.

Similarly, companies or individuals investing at least 500 million FCFA in the construction of hotels will be exempt from customs duties and taxes.

■ FORMATION AND TYPES OF PERMITTED BUSINESS ORGANIZATIONS

Foreign investors may form domestic enterprises in the form of corporations, partnerships, or sole proprietorships. Subsidiaries of foreign corporations may also be established.

There is no requirement for domestic equity participation in any enterprise that is wholly or partially owned by foreign investors.

■ ENVIRONMENTAL PROTECTION

The government has exhibited a continuing interest in the environment and has created a government department, the Ministry of Water Resources and the Environment, to develop policy and programs relevant to this subject area. Potential foreign investors are advised to contact the Investment Commission for complete information about this subject.

■ RIGHTS AND OBLIGATIONS OF FOREIGN INVESTORS

Foreign investors are guaranteed equality with domestic ones.

The government guarantees that nationalization or expropriation will not occur. If, however, public necessity requires any taking of property, just and fair compensation will be provided.

In the event of a dispute between the government and the foreign investor regarding the validity, interpretation, or application of the provisions of the covenant between them, or relevant to any indemnity that may need to be determined, arbitration will be the method of conflict resolution, to include final recourse to the International Center for the Settlement of Investment Disputes.

Foreign investments and income derived from such investments may be repatriated or remitted. However, potential foreign investors are advised that such a transfer may be delayed because of a shortage of foreign exchange. In like manner, a foreign investor may remit or repatriate the proper share of an investment in the event of liquidation.

■ LABOR

Foreign enterprises must give hiring priority to Niger workers. Work permits must be possessed by foreign nationals employed in the country. Foreign personnel may only be hired when it is shown that required skills or training are not locally available.

■ ACCOUNTING REQUIREMENTS

All foreign investments must maintain accurate and complete accounting and financial records in accord with internationally accepted standards.

■ CURRENCY CONTROLS

The Banque Centrale des Etats de l'Afrique de l'Ouest (the Bank of the West African States) fulfills the role of the nation's central bank and, in cooperation with the Ministry of the Economy, Finance and Planning, is responsible for the country's foreign exchange policy and programs.

Foreign businesses and individuals are not permitted to maintain bank accounts in any foreign currencies.

Local financing sources may be available to foreign investors.

Exchange controls are enforced. There is no free flow of currency into or from the country.

■ TAXATION

The major tax is that levied on business income. There are many other taxes levied to include that on personal income; the value added tax (VAT); customs duties and taxes; the fiscal rate tax; real property construction tax; the tax on industrial and commercial benefits; and various registration and license fees.

Deductions and allowances are permitted to include those for legitimate expenses and depreciation of physical assets.

■ LEGAL SYSTEM

The court system includes the Courts of First Instance, which hear minor cases; the Criminal and Assize Courts, which hear more serious matters; and the Court of Appeal. Final appeals are taken to the Supreme Court, which sits at Niamey.

■ CUSTOMS AND DUTIES

Most of the necessities of a modern society are imported. There is a strong government interest in developing a higher level of international trade, particularly exports.

■ PROTECTION OF INTELLECTUAL PROPERTY

Niger is a member of the World Intellectual Property Organization and thus supports internationally accepted standards for the protection of copyrights, tradenames, and patents.

■ IMMIGRATION AND RESIDENCE

Visas are required to enter the country. Potential foreign investors are advised to contact the Investment Commission for complete information about visa, work permit, and residence permit requirements.

■ FOREIGN INVESTMENT ASSISTANCE DIRECTORY

Sources that can provide further information about foreign investment in Niger include:

Investment Commission
Ministry of the Economy, Finance and Planning
P.O. Box 235
Niamey, Niger
Telephone: (0) 723467
Telex: 5214

Chamber of Commerce and Industry of Niger
P.O. Box 209
Niamey, Niger
Telephone: (0) 732210
Telex: 5242

Persons interested in obtaining additional information about foreign investment in Niger are advised to contact the closest Nigerian embassy or consular office.

Nigeria maintains diplomatic relations with Algeria, Belgium, Benin, People's Republic of China, Egypt, France, Germany, Iran, Libya, Mauritania, Morocco, Nigeria, Pakistan, Russia, Saudi Arabia, Tunisia, and United States.

NIGERIA, FEDERAL REPUBLIC OF

■ POLITICAL ENVIRONMENT

The nation has suffered through a series of government changes, widespread and violent unrest, rule by military officers, and a sagging economy.

Nigeria relied on petroleum as its principal export and was a victim of the soft worldwide petroleum market. The country is burdened with a very high external debt.

■ SUMMARY OF FOREIGN INVESTMENT POLICY

Nigeria has a continuing interest in the acquisition of foreign investment. As part of its overall Structural Adjustment Programme to improve the status of the nation's economy, the government has amended the Nigerian Enterprises Promotion Decree, which was originally issued in 1972.

A government agency, the Industrial Development Coordinating Committee, composed of the heads of the Finance, Internal Affairs, Industry and Technology, Agriculture, Labor and Productivity, and Commerce and Tourism ministries, has been created to administer the promotion decree and to provide assistance to potential foreign investors.

The government is determined to increase its industrial sector activities and thus to generate more exports, improve the overall technological skills of the work force, and reduce the currently high level of unemployment. A need is also seen to develop rural areas of the country through the dispersal of new industrial activities.

Among the incentives that Nigeria has developed to attract foreign investment are the promotion of export free zones, a more liberal foreign exchange program, and various fiscal and financial programs.

Various areas of the economy that were formerly operated by the government are being privatized.

In addition to specific steps taken to improve the economy through infusion of foreign investment and assistance to the domestic private sector, Nigeria has established a Debt Conversion Programme, the principal goal of which is to gradually reduce the country's external debt.

A number of business activities have now been opened to complete foreign ownership. While full ownership of what are called Scheduled Enterprises is generally reserved for Nigerians, foreign investment is permitted in such activities if the investment is not less than 20 million Naira (the unit of Nigerian currency) and prior approval of such foreign participation is obtained from the government. Scheduled enterprises include an extensive list of manufacturing fields as well as mass communications activities.

■ FORMATION AND TYPES OF PERMITTED BUSINESS ORGANIZATIONS

Corporations may be formed by foreign investors and may own all or part of a business activity. Joint ventures are also permitted with domestic business. Private limited liability companies may also be formed. Both public companies (i.e., corporations) and private limited ones are accorded juridical status.

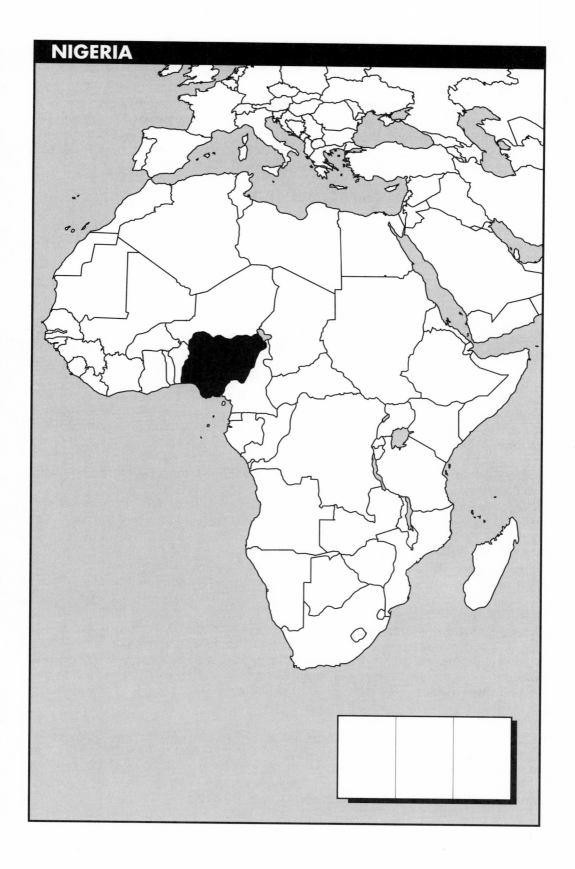

NIGERIA

■ ENVIRONMENTAL PROTECTION

The government requires that any planned industrial activity must provide an environmental impact statement. All activities that may create environmental damage will be continuously monitored. Potential investors should contact the Industrial Development Coordinating Committee for more detailed information about environmental protection regulations.

■ RIGHTS AND OBLIGATIONS OF FOREIGN INVESTORS

Foreign investors must file tax returns with the Nigerian government.

There are no requirements for domestic participation in enterprises that are fully financed by foreign investment.

Foreign investors may remit abroad or repatriate income generated as a result of investment in Nigeria.

All foreign investment must be submitted for prior approval to the Industrial Development Coordinating Committee.

Nigeria has several bilateral agreements regarding foreign investment guarantees. Potential foreign investors are advised to determine the status or existence of such agreements with their national governments.

■ LABOR

Foreign businesses must obtain permits to employ nationals of other countries. Except in situations where the Nigerian work force does not possess specific technical, scientific, or management skills required for the operations of an activity, Nigerian employees must be given hiring preference.

An expatriate quota exists that requires capitalization of five million Naira to hire two foreign nationals, and ten million Naira to entitle the foreign investor to hire four foreign nationals.

Requests for hiring of other than Nigerian employees or to expand on the number of positions permitted under the quota system will be considered on a case-by-case basis.

■ ACCOUNTING REQUIREMENTS

All business enterprises must maintain an accurate system of books and records in accordance with internationally accepted accounting and auditing standards.

■ CURRENCY CONTROLS

The government has established a new trade and exchange rate regimen that is designed to permit quicker and easier access to funds for foreign investors.

Foreign businesses, except those involved in exporting of petroleum and petroleum products, are permitted to maintain bank accounts in foreign currency, subject to the requirements established by the Central Bank of Nigeria.

■ TAXATION

Taxes are payable annually in conformance with the Companies Income Tax Act, as amended. One of the effects of the amended law was to eliminate double taxation on income from investments.

The principal tax levied in Nigeria is the corporate tax although there are a variety of minor taxes. The current corporate tax rate is 40 percent.

The government has created a number of incentives for investors. Among the incentives are tax holidays for companies (both corporations and private limited liability firms) that engage in new fields of activity. The holiday is for a period of five years (seven years if the company is located in an area that is designated by the government as economically disadvantaged) and is not renewable.

Other tax incentives are available to firms that develop local raw materials, provide labor intensive processes, are engaged in export-oriented activities, or provide in-plant training.

Extensive tax reductions are also available for product research and development.

■ LEGAL SYSTEM

There are both federal and state court systems. The appeals court in each state is the High Court. In the federal system, criminal and civil cases are heard by the Federal High Court. Appeals are taken to the Federal Court of Appeal. The nation's highest court is the Nigerian Supreme Court, which sits in Lagos.

■ CUSTOMS AND DUTIES

Customs duties are levied on an ad valorem basis. Excise duties are also payable on goods imported or produced in Nigeria.

Special customs duties may be levied when any goods are dumped in the country, if such an anti-dumping provision will not conflict with the General Agreement on Tariffs and Trade (GATT) to which Nigeria subscribes.

Exporters may claim repayments of customs duties paid on materials that have been used in the production of goods for export from Nigeria pursuant to an established customs drawback provision.

No license is required to export manufactured products, and exports are exempted from the excise tax.

An Export Development Fund has been created by the government as an incentive to promote exports by covering a portion of expenses entailed by businesses engaged in exporting. Exports valued at a minimum of 50,000 Naira are required annually to create eligibility for this fund.

■ PROTECTION OF INTELLECTUAL PROPERTY

Nigeria recognizes the internationally accepted protection standards accorded to copyrights, patents, trademarks, and technological transfer.

■ IMMIGRATION AND RESIDENCE

Visas, work permits, and residence permits are required in Nigeria. These documents are issued after case-by-case consideration. Potential foreign investors are advised to contact the Industrial Development Coordinating Committee for detailed information relevant to visa, residence, and work permit requirements.

■ FOREIGN INVESTMENT ASSISTANCE DIRECTORY

The following sources may be contacted to obtain more detailed information concerning foreign investment in Nigeria:

Industrial Development Coordinating Committee
Ministry of Industry and Technology
Garki, Abuja
Nigeria
Federal Capital Territory

Investment Information and Promotion Centre
Federal Ministry of Industry and Technology
Garki, Abuja
Nigeria
Federal Capital Territory

Nigerian Association of Chambers of Commerce, Industries and Agriculture
Commerce House
Idowu Taylor Street
Victoria Island
Lagos, Nigeria
Telephone: (234) (1) 964737
Telex: 21368

Persons interested in obtaining further information about investing in Nigeria also are advised to contact the closest Nigerian embassy or consular office.

Nigeria maintains diplomatic relations with Algeria, Angola, Argentina, Australia, Austria, Belgium, Benin, Brazil, Bulgaria, Burkina Faso, Cameroon, Canada, Central African Republic, Chad, Chile, People's Republic of China, Columbia, Cote d'Ivoire, Cuba, Czechoslovakia, Denmark, Egypt, Equatorial Guinea, Ethiopia, Finland, France, Gabon, Germany, Ghana, Greece, Guinea, Holy See, Hungary, India, Indonesia, Iran, Iraq, Ireland, Italy, Democratic People's Republic of Korea, Republic of Korea, Lebanon, Liberia, Libya, Malaysia, Mauritania, Morocco, Netherlands, Niger, Pakistan, Philippines, Poland, Portugal, Romania, Russia, Saudi Arabia, Senegal, Sierra Leone, Somalia, Spain, Sudan, Sweden, Switzerland, Syria, Tanzania, Thailand, Togo, Trinidad and Tobago, Turkey, United Kingdom, United States, Venezuela, Zaire, Zambia, and Zimbabwe.

■ POLITICAL ENVIRONMENT

The government is stable.

The infrastructure is highly developed. Inflation and unemployment are both low.

There has been a high dependence on petroleum, a situation that placed the country in a vulnerable economic position during periods of soft oil market prices. The government has embarked on a program to diversify the nation's exports and to expand the industrial base.

■ SUMMARY OF FOREIGN INVESTMENT POLICY

It is the policy of the government to welcome foreign investment although there are no incentive programs that have been created to promote the country to foreign investors. The Ministry of Industry is the principal agency involved with foreign investment.

■ FORMATION AND TYPES OF PERMITTED BUSINESS ORGANIZATIONS

Foreign investors may participate in the Norwegian economy through the creation of a limited company; as a partnership; as a limited liability partnership; as a sleeping partnership; or as a sole proprietorship.

A limited company is the equivalent of a corporation. There are requirements for the promoters to be bona fide Norwegian residents. A limited company enjoys the status of a juridical person.

A limited liability partnership generally involves a limited company as the general partner. In a sleeping partnership, one partner (who has usually funded all or most of the enterprise) is silent and is not liable, under the terms of the partnership agreement, for any debts of the organization.

Foreign investors may form branches, open offices, or create subsidiaries.

■ ENVIRONMENTAL PROTECTION

There is a strong interest in environmental protection. Potential foreign investors are advised to contact the Ministry of the Environment for information as to relevant laws on environmental protection.

■ RIGHTS AND OBLIGATIONS OF FOREIGN INVESTORS

Foreign businesses and individuals incur a tax liability.

There is a guarantee against nationalization or expropriation.

There is no requirement to register a foreign investment with the government. However, enterprises must be registered with the government for purposes of employment, taxation, and other relevant government controls.

There are no restrictions on the repatriation of investments or income generated as a result of such investments. However, the government must be notified of such transfers.

■ LABOR

There is an extensive body of laws with regard to labor, working conditions, and employment rules. There are no requirements with regard to hiring preferences being accorded to Norwegians.

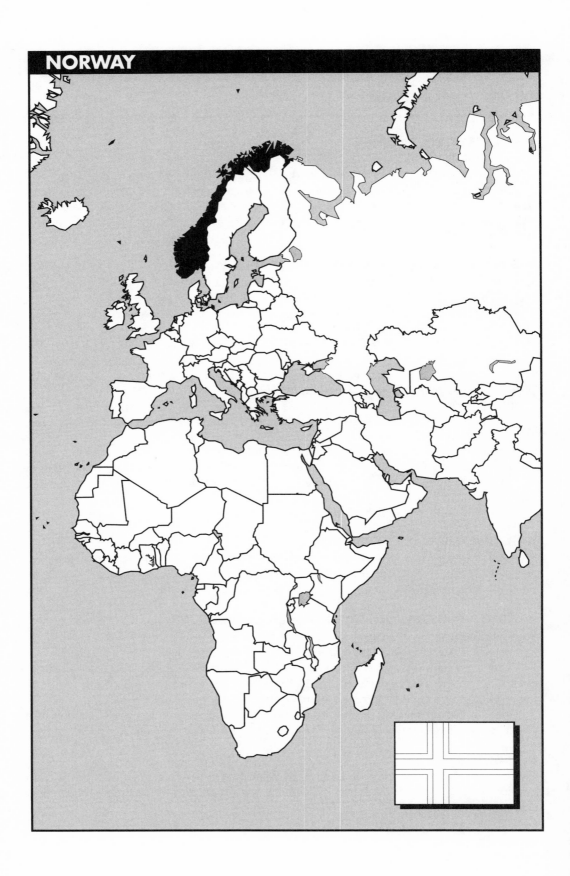

NORWAY

The labor force, at all levels, is well trained and highly motivated. Foreign nationals are required to obtain work permits.

■ ACCOUNTING REQUIREMENTS

All limited companies and partnerships must undergo annual audits by a registered or chartered accountant or auditor.

■ CURRENCY CONTROLS

The Norges Bank is the nation's central banking institution.

All transfers of currency must be reported to the bank and must be made through either the central bank or another bank that is legally permitted to arrange foreign transfers.

Foreign investors may hold and maintain foreign currency accounts subsequent to reporting such accounts to the central bank.

There is a limit of NOK 25,000 in currency or the equivalent in any foreign currency that may be moved into or from the country in cash by any enterprise or individual. Any amount in excess of NOK 25,000 must be reported to customs upon entry or departure.

■ TAXATION

Businesses may use a 12- or 18-month accounting period for tax purposes. Corporations are treated as taxable entities. Firms incorporated in Norway are liable for taxation on worldwide income. There are a variety of deductions and allowances to include depreciation on assets.

Corporate taxes are paid in four installments during the tax year. Tax returns must be filed on or before February 28.

Norway has concluded bilateral treaties on the subject of double taxation with numerous countries.

Individuals who are Norway residents are taxable on their income on a worldwide basis. Individual taxpayers are eligible for a variety of deductions. Foreign nationals employed in Norway are eligible for special tax considerations.

There are numerous minor taxes to include those levied on petroleum, sales of businesses, a value added tax (VAT), and taxes on investments and real estate.

■ LEGAL SYSTEM

The lowest level in the Norwegian court system are the District Courts. The High Courts hear and decide major civil and criminal cases and also perform an appellate function. Appeals from the High Courts are taken to the Supreme Court, which sits in Oslo.

■ CUSTOMS AND DUTIES

No duties are charged on imported items from EC nations or from other Nordic countries. Norway is a member of the General Agreement on Tariffs and Trade (GATT) and of the Organization for Economic Cooperation and Development (OECD).

There are several foreign trade zones into which goods and raw materials are received duty free.

■ PROTECTION OF INTELLECTUAL PROPERTY

Norway is a member of the World Intellectual Property Organization and thus subscribes to internationally accepted standards of copyright, trademark, and patent protection. Norway also has domestic laws relevant to the protection of intellectual property.

■ IMMIGRATION AND RESIDENCE

Visas may or may not be required for entry based on the individual's country of domicile. Visas are valid for three-month periods. Work permits are required for all foreign nationals.

Potential foreign investors are advised to contact the Ministry of Industry or the Ministry of Justice and Police regarding current requirements for visas, working permits, and residence permits.

■ FOREIGN INVESTMENT ASSISTANCE DIRECTORY

Several sources can provide further information about foreign investment in Norway and they include:

Ministry of Industry
Pløensgt 8
P.O. Box 8014
Department 0030
Oslo 1, Norway
Telephone: (47) (2) 34-90-90
Telex: 21428
Fax: (47) (2) 34-95-25

Ministry of the Environment
Myntgt 2
P.O. Box 8013
Department 0030
Oslo 1, Norway
Telephone: (47) (2) 34-90-90
Telex: 21480
Fax: (47) (2) 34-95-60

Norges Bank (Bank of Norway)
Bankplassen 2
P.O. Box 1179
Sentrum 0107
Oslo 1, Norway
Telephone: (47) (2) 31-60-00
Telex: 71369
Fax: (47) (2) 41-31-05

Persons interested in obtaining further information about investing in Norway also are advised to contact the closest Norwegian embassy or consular office.

Norway maintains diplomatic relations with Argentina, Austria, Belgium, Brazil, Bulgaria, Canada, Chile, People's Republic of China, Colombia, Czechoslovakia, Denmark, Egypt, Finland, France, Germany, Greece, Hungary, Iceland, India, Indonesia, Iran, Israel, Italy, Japan, Democratic People's Republic of Korea, Republic of Korea, Mexico, Netherlands, Panama, Poland, Portugal, Romania, Russia, Spain, Sweden, Switzerland, Thailand, United Kingdom, United States, and Venezuela.

Oman, The Sultanate of

■ POLITICAL ENVIRONMENT

The nation enjoys excellent economic health and the government, which has the support of the people, is stable. The national standard of living is very high.

Oman's principal source of income is its production and export of petroleum, which provides approximately 80 percent of all government revenue. Inflation is virtually nonexistent. There is a minimal level of unemployment.

The nation is not a member of OPEC. However, it maintains a membership in the Independent Petroleum Exporting Countries (IPEC), which works closely with OPEC member states in matters relevant to oil pricing and production.

Despite the healthy economic climate that exists in Oman, the government is seeking ways to diversify the nation's sources of revenue, particularly into the area of agriculture and manufacturing. A Development Plan covering the period from 1991 to 1994 has been designed with its features being to expand the activities of the private sector in the economy, to improve and maintain the national infrastructure, and to seek foreign investment.

■ SUMMARY OF FOREIGN INVESTMENT POLICY

The country's basic statute on foreign investment is the Foreign Business and Investment Law, which was enacted in 1973. Other important legislation relevant to foreign investment are the Commercial Agencies Act Law of 1977, and Royal Decree 32/84, which sets out the guidelines for commercial dispute settlements.

There are a number of government agencies that may become involved with the approval of foreign investment proposals. However, the key government office is the Committee on the Investment of Foreign Capital that is comprised of members representing the Chamber of Commerce, the Development Council, the Ministry of Commerce and Industry, the Ministry of Petroleum and Minerals, the Ministry of Agriculture and Fisheries, and the Directorate General of Finance.

All foreign investment proposals must be submitted for approval to this group. The minimum foreign investment that may be considered, under the law, is 150,000 Oman Rial although that amount may be reduced to 30,000 by the Committee.

The key points relevant to approval of a foreign investment proposal, in addition to the size of the investment, include the value of the investment to the nation's overall economic development, the level of modern technology that will be introduced, and the opportunities for employment that are presented.

There are limits on foreign investment with regard to participation in various types of economic activity. In general, the Omani share in the ownership of any firm may not be less than 51 percent. Foreign investment is not permitted in banks, nor in any mass media (press and other information) activities.

Commercial firms that are wholly or partially owned by foreign interests are not permitted to own land.

The areas in which the government has a particular interest for the application of foreign investment include agriculture, light manufacturing, food processing, mining, and tourism.

All companies operating in the country are required to secure the services of a local

OMAN

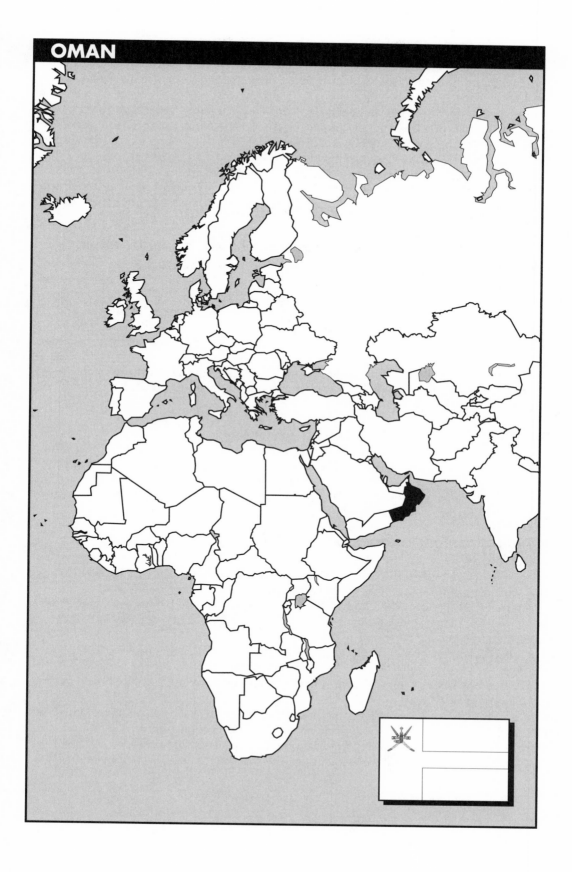

agent on an exclusive basis with regard to the promotion, sale, and distribution of any products.

Numerous incentives are available for eligible companies to include low-interest financing that is provided by the Oman Development Bank, government assistance with the establishment of industrial facilities at any of the several newly developed industrial estates that now exist in the country, long-term (five-year) tax holidays that may be renewed, interest-free loans that may be obtained from the Ministry of Commerce and Industry, the possible imposition of, and benefit from, protective tariffs, and the payment, by the government, of Omani workers while they are being trained by the foreign investor.

■ FORMATION AND TYPES OF PERMITTED BUSINESS ORGANIZATIONS

Foreign investors may participate in the Omani economy through the creation of joint stock companies (publicly held companies) or through joint ventures. Subsidiaries of foreign corporations may be established in the country.

All companies must be members of the Chamber of Commerce and Industry, and all corporations must be on file with the Commercial Registry.

Foreign companies doing business in Oman must be represented by a domestic Omani company.

Most foreign firms operate as joint venture partners with the government, domestic Omani businesses, or individuals. Joint ventures do not need to file with the Commercial Registry.

■ ENVIRONMENTAL PROTECTION

The government has a continuing interest in the subject of environmental protection. Any industrial company, whether foreign or domestic, must obtain necessary approvals for its operations from the Ministry of Environment and Water Resources. Potential foreign investors are advised to contact that agency for complete information on current environmental laws and regulations.

■ RIGHTS AND OBLIGATIONS OF FOREIGN INVESTORS

Local sources of financing are available to foreign firms. The commercial capital sources are, however, limited. Most financing for foreign investments is provided by the Ministry of Commerce and Industry and the Oman Development Bank.

Commercial disputes are handled by the Authority for the Settlement of Commercial Disputes. Oman is not a member of the International Center for the Settlement of Investment Disputes.

Government permission is required before a foreign investment may be made in a domestic company.

Foreign businesses can seek government permission to obtain leaseholds on land for periods of up to 49 years.

Based on the government's history and attitudes, there seems to be no potential for nationalization or expropriation. If such cases should occur based on a legitimate national or public necessity, fair compensation would probably be provided.

Foreign investments and investment income may be remitted abroad or repatriated freely subject to the payment of required taxes.

■ LABOR

The principal statute relevant to labor is the Omani Labor Law of 1973. It is a comprehensive statute that covers virtually all aspects of employment and working conditions. The government agency responsible for ensuring the operation of the law is the Ministry of Labor and Social Affairs.

Foreign employees may not be hired without the approval of the Ministry of Social Affairs and Labor. Government approvals will not normally be provided where qualified Omani workers are available. In practice, however, expatriate hiring is permitted because of a shortage of Omani personnel.

A government program will provide funding for the payment of Omani personnel by foreign companies that will enable such workers to eventually fill positions at all levels.

All foreign nationals employed in Oman must obtain both work and residence permits.

■ ACCOUNTING REQUIREMENTS

All companies established in Oman must maintain accurate and complete accounting and other records for tax and statistical purposes. Joint stock companies must be audited on a yearly basis and audits may be required of any other form of business organization.

■ CURRENCY CONTROLS

The Central Bank of Oman is the nation's central bank and is responsible for management of the country's monetary policies to include financial exchange matters.

All commercial banks in Oman must maintain no more than 40 percent of their capital, to include reserves, in foreign exchange.

There are no restrictions on the movement of capital into or from Oman.

■ TAXATION

Foreign businesses and individuals are subject to Oman's tax laws.

Potential foreign investors should be aware that the Omani tax requirements are changed frequently and often with little or no notice to taxpayers.

There is no personal income tax assessed. The only tax imposed is that on trade or business profits that exceed 20,000 rials. Companies wholly owned by Omanis are exempt from taxation.

The tax year runs from January 1 to December 31. Companies may request that the Director of Income Tax permit filing based on a different fiscal period.

Deductions include reasonable depreciation on assets, legitimate business expenses, and losses incurred. As noted previously, tax incentives include long-term tax holidays and certain other deductions.

Other taxes include a municipal tax levied by Muscat, a payroll tax, and a number of registration assessments.

■ LEGAL SYSTEM

The Omani judicial system is, in addition to a variety of specialized courts, e.g., landlord-tenant and labor, a two-tier system that includes local courts that have authority to hear criminal, civil, and family matters. Appeals from these local courts are taken to the Court of Appeal, which sits at Muscat.

■ CUSTOMS AND DUTIES

Oman is a nation that is heavily dependent on imports. Import licenses are not required. Most food imports are exempt from customs duties. The usual customs charge is 5 percent of import value.

The country employs protective tariffs in some areas that run from 15 to 20 percent of value.

Oman is a member of the Gulf Cooperation Council (GCC) and many goods traded between member states of that group are duty free.

■ PROTECTION OF INTELLECTUAL PROPERTY

Oman is not a member of the World Intellectual Property Organization. The country has, however, enacted a Law of Trademarks and Commercial Data, which became effective in 1987. There are no laws regarding the protection of copyrights or patents.

■ IMMIGRATION AND RESIDENCE

Visas are required to enter Oman. It is possible to arrange the issuance of visas for business purposes. In all cases, the assistance of an Omani sponsor is necessary. Potential foreign investors are strongly advised to contact the Oman Chamber of Commerce for complete and current information on the requirements and procedures relevant to visas, work permits, and residence permits.

■ FOREIGN INVESTMENT ASSISTANCE DIRECTORY

Sources that can provide further information about foreign investment in Oman include:

Committee on the Investment of Foreign Capital
Ministry of Commerce and Industry
P.O. Box 550
Muscat, Oman
Telephone: (968) 799500
Telex: 3665 WIZARA ON
Fax: (968) 794238

Ministry of Environment and Water Resources
P.O. Box 323
Muscat, Oman
Telephone: (968) 696444
Telex: 54404 A/B MININVOY ON
Fax: (968) 602320

Ministry of Finance and Economy
P.O. Box 506
Muscat, Oman
Telephone: (968) 738201
Telex: 5333 MALIYA ON

Ministry of Social Affairs and Labor
P.O. Box 560
Muscat, Oman
Telephone: (968) 602444
Telex: 5002 MOSAL ON

Central Bank of Oman
P.O. Box 4161
Ruwi, Oman
Telephone: (968) 702222
Telex: 3070 MARKAZI ON
Fax: (968) 707913

Oman Development Bank
P.O. Box 309
Muscat, Oman
Telephone: (968) 738021
Telex: 5179 OBEDE ON

Oman Chamber of Commerce and Industry
P.O. Box 4400
Ruwi, Oman
Telephone: (968) 707674
Telex: 33889 AL-GURFA MB

Persons interested in obtaining additional information about foreign investment in Oman are advised to contact the closest Omani embassy or consular office.

Oman maintains diplomatic relations with Algeria, Austria, Bangladesh, People's Republic of China, Egypt, France, Germany, India, Iran, Iraq, Italy, Japan, Jordan, Republic of Korea, Kuwait, Malaysia, Morocco, Netherlands, Pakistan, Qatar, Russia, Saudi Arabia, Somalia, Sri Lanka, Sudan, Sweden, Syria, Thailand, Tunisia, Turkey, United Arab Emirates, United Kingdom, United States, and Yemen.

■ POLITICAL ENVIRONMENT

Given the recent history of political repression, unrest among ethnic minorities, reported official corruption, and a deteriorating national economy, the government cannot be classified as stable.

Inflation is rising although unemployment, based on government estimates, is low. There are ongoing efforts at privatization.

■ SUMMARY OF FOREIGN INVESTMENT POLICY

There is a desire for foreign investment. The government has established the Investment Promotion Bureau as the coordinating agency for foreign investment development. The principal law on the subject is the Foreign Private Investment Act of 1976.

The government is particularly interested in the use of foreign investment because of the addition of capital to the economy, the increased levels of technology that may be gained, and the marketing and management skills that are developed.

Among the government's goals to be achieved through the help of foreign investment are the improvement of the national infrastructure, increased export manufacturing, generation of electric power, opportunities for employment, and development of rural areas of the country.

Most economic activities are open to foreign investment. Government approval for foreign investment is required in some areas, notably in those involving munitions production, radioactive substances, and power generation.

Incentives offered to potential foreign investors include the availability of industrial estates, tax incentives to include exemption from the sales tax, tax holidays of up to three years for operations in built-up areas and for up to eight years in underdeveloped areas, and import concessions in the form of customs duty exemptions.

Additional incentives in the form of customs duty exemptions and four-year tax holidays are available to firms engaged in what are termed as "key industries," i.e., electronics, fibre optics, solar energy, biotechnology, and fertilizer development. Certain other concessions are available, to include those of a tax and non-tax nature, for firms engaged in the tourism industry.

Export processing zones have been established and firms established inside such zones are eligible for special incentives to include tax holidays to the year 2000 and subsequent annual taxes at 25 percent of regular tax rates.

■ FORMATION AND TYPES OF PERMITTED BUSINESS ORGANIZATIONS

Foreign investors are urged to establish either private or public corporations. Subsidiaries of foreign domiciled corporations may be established. All companies must be on file with the Registrar of Companies.

Partnerships and sole proprietorships may also be formed by foreign investors, including partnerships with domestic investors.

■ ENVIRONMENTAL PROTECTION

There is a continuing interest in the subject of environmental protection. Potential foreign investors are advised to contact the Investment Promotion Bureau for complete

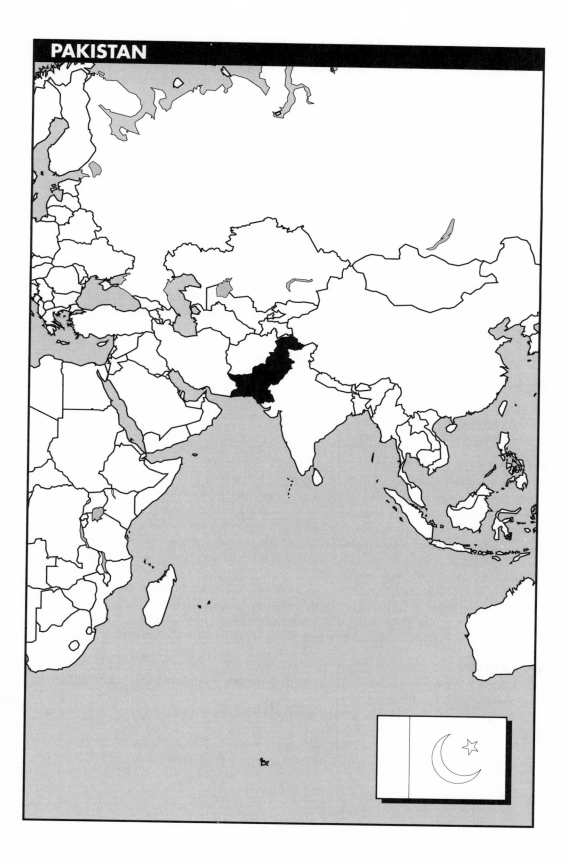

and current information on laws and regulations pertaining to protection of the environment.

■ RIGHTS AND OBLIGATIONS OF FOREIGN INVESTORS

No prior approval or permission is necessary in order to repatriate or remit abroad capital investments or income derived from such investment.

Local financing is available from the Industrial Development Bank of Pakistan, the National Development Finance Corporation, the Regional Development Finance Corporation, and other institutions.

Foreign investors are guaranteed equality with domestic ones.

■ LABOR

The labor force is motivated and skilled. There is a developed body of laws on the subjects of employment and working conditions.

While the employment of Pakistani labor is favored, nothing currently precludes a foreign employer from hiring foreign nationals in managerial and technical positions. Work permits are no longer required.

Any company engaged in manufacturing and that employs more than ten workers must register their names with the Provincial Chief Inspector of Industries.

■ ACCOUNTING REQUIREMENTS

All companies must maintain accurate financial records for tax and other purposes. Public companies must submit audited statements to the Registrar of Companies on a yearly basis.

■ CURRENCY CONTROLS

Foreign exchange controls have been eliminated. There are no limits on the amount of capital that may be moved into or from the country.

Foreign businesses and individuals may open and maintain foreign currency accounts and may use such accounts as collateral for loans that are obtained locally.

Any foreign nationals employed in Pakistan may remit abroad or repatriate up to 50 percent of their wages or salaries and may, in addition, remit all savings held in Pakistan, upon leaving the country.

There are no limits on loans that may be obtained by companies that export at least 50 percent of their production. No permission is required from any government agency, including the State Bank of Pakistan (the central bank), to obtain financing.

There are no restrictions on the payments of royalties or technical fees.

■ TAXATION

In addition to filing with the Registrar of Companies, businesses must be on file with the Income Tax Department.

The principal tax is that levied on company and individual income. There are numerous minor taxes including those on sales.

The tax year runs with the calendar year, i.e., from January 1 to December 31 although other 12-month periods may be used by companies with the approval of the tax authorities.

In addition to tax incentives, there are a variety of deductions and allowances available to include depreciation, business expenses, and losses.

■ LEGAL SYSTEM

The court system includes local courts that hear petty criminal matters and High Courts, which exercise trial level jurisdiction and which are located around the country. Appeals from the High Courts are taken to the Supreme Court, which sits at Islamabad.

■ CUSTOMS AND DUTIES

A variety of goods and materials may now be imported under different forms of concessions. All equipment that will be used for the construction of private electric power plants may be imported free of any customs charges.

An import license is required to import raw materials and equipment used in manufacturing. Machinery that cannot be acquired locally may be imported free of customs duties where used by companies established in underdeveloped areas of the country, and the cost of the import license fee is substantially reduced.

Companies established in the approved industrial estates are eligible for a 50 to 100 percent exemption from customs charges depending on the location of the industrial estate.

In general, the duties on imported raw materials have been reduced and a system of duty drawbacks has been introduced.

Customs exemptions are available on materials and equipment used in pharmaceutical and fertilizer production, on required mining equipment, dairy farming equipment, cement manufacturing, engineering equipment, and specific other capital goods and machinery not produced locally.

Under a special program designed to encourage the tourism industry, goods and materials relevant to that field of activity may be imported free of customs and related charges.

Companies operating in the export processing zones are exempt from the payment of import and export charges.

■ PROTECTION OF INTELLECTUAL PROPERTY

Pakistan is a member of the World Intellectual Property Organization and, in addition, has enacted domestic statutes providing protection for copyrights, trademarks, tradenames, patents, and technology transfer.

■ IMMIGRATION AND RESIDENCE

Visas are normally required to enter the country. Potential foreign investors are advised to contact the Investment Promotion Bureau for complete information regarding the issuance of visas and residence permits.

■ FOREIGN INVESTMENT ASSISTANCE DIRECTORY

Sources that can provide further information about foreign investment in Pakistan include:

Investment Promotion Bureau
Kandawala Building
M.A. Jinnah Road
Karachi, Pakistan
Telephone: (92) (21) 714289
Telex: 3137 SUPLS PK
Fax: (92) (21) 713572

Ministry of Industries
Block-A, Pak Secretariat
Islamabad, Pakistan
Telephone: (92) (51) 820235
Telex: MIND PK 5774
Fax: (92) (51) 825130

Federation of Pakistan Chambers of Commerce & Industry
Federation House, Clifton
Karachi, Pakistan
Telephone: (92) (21) 532179
Telex: 25370 FPCC&J
Fax: (92) (21) 570277

Persons interested in further information about foreign investment in Pakistan are advised to contact the closest Pakistani embassy or consular office.

Pakistan maintains diplomatic relations with Afghanistan, Algeria, Argentina, Australia, Austria, Bangladesh, Belgium, Bulgaria, Canada, Chile, Cuba, Czechoslovakia, Denmark, Egypt, France, Germany, Greece, Holy See, Hungary, India, Indonesia, Iran, Iraq, Italy, Japan, Jordan, Kenya, Democratic People's Republic of Korea, Republic of Korea, Kuwait, Lebanon, Libya, Malaysia, Mauritius, Morocco, Myanmar, Nepal, Netherlands, New Zealand, Nigeria, Norway, Oman, Philippines, Poland, Portugal, Qatar, Romania, Russia, Saudi Arabia, Singapore, Somalia, Spain, Sri Lanka, Sudan, Sweden, Switzerland, Syria, Thailand, Tunisia, Turkey, United Arab Emirates, United Kingdom, United States, and Yemen.

PANAMA, REPUBLIC OF

■ POLITICAL ENVIRONMENT

The nation has suffered from a variety of political and economic ills. Riots, strikes, and general internal unrest have been common. The political situation remains unstable following the removal from power of General Manuel Noriega by U.S. forces in 1989.

Economically, the Panamanian situation is marked by high unemployment and a large public debt, much of that being generated as a result of the withdrawal of American support during the Noriega years.

■ SUMMARY OF FOREIGN INVESTMENT POLICY

The Panama Trade Development Institute has been designated as the principal agency to secure foreign investment and to assist potential foreign investors. It is specifically desired that foreign investment be obtained that will increase the nation's industrial base, provide more employment opportunities, and generate more exports.

A number of steps have been taken to promote foreign investment to include the creation of export processing zones and the enactment of a tax reform program containing numerous tax incentives.

■ FORMATION AND TYPES OF PERMITTED BUSINESS ORGANIZATIONS

Foreign investors may form corporations, unlimited partnerships, limited partnerships (where one or more partners is fully liable), limited liability companies, or sole proprietorships. Foreign investors may also acquire Panamanian companies and form joint ventures with domestic firms.

There is no requirement for Panamanian participation in any business that is financed wholly or partially by foreign capital.

Corporations enjoy juridical person status once they are on file with the Mercantile Register.

■ ENVIRONMENTAL PROTECTION

There are numerous laws dealing with environmental protection to include the prohibition on chemical products that are banned elsewhere. Potential foreign investors are advised to contact the Trade Development Institute for complete information on the laws and regulations that relate to environmental protection.

■ RIGHTS AND OBLIGATIONS OF FOREIGN INVESTORS

In order to establish eligibility for any incentives offered by the government to foreign investors, an application must be filed relevant to business activities with the Ministry of Commerce and Industry.

Foreign companies and individuals must file tax returns with the government.

Invested capital, and profits and income generated by such investments, may be freely repatriated or remitted abroad subject to payment of Panamanian taxes.

■ LABOR

Foreign companies must employ Panamanian nationals except where it can be shown that no available Panamanian workers possess specially required skills. Approval for

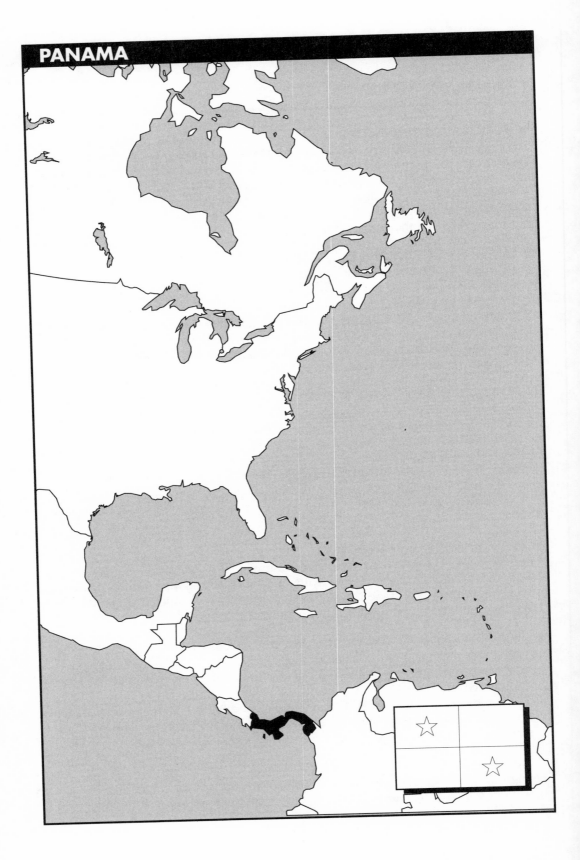

PANAMA

the employment of foreign personnel in such cases must be obtained from the Ministry of Labor and Social Welfare. A program of training of local workers to replace foreign personnel within a certain time period may be required.

■ ACCOUNTING REQUIREMENTS

All companies operating in Panama must maintain complete and accurate records in accordance with internationally accepted accounting standards. Financial records must be examined annually by a licensed auditor.

■ CURRENCY CONTROLS

There are no exchange control regulations in Panama.

Bank accounts may be maintained in any foreign or Panamanian bank in any currency.

■ TAXATION

Foreign businesses and individuals are required to file tax returns. The major tax is that assessed on income. There are many minor taxes to include those on real estate, sales, and documents.

Corporations are required to pay taxes on income generated within Panama.

There are numerous tax incentives designed for foreign investors depending on the business activities in which they are engaged, e.g., agribusiness and exporting. Exemptions include donations to agribusiness research and on the cost of raw materials, equipment, and parts that will be used in the manufacturing of goods for export.

Special exemptions are available to firms that locate in specific areas of the country as well as to companies that choose to operate within the free zones.

■ LEGAL SYSTEM

The system of courts includes those at the municipal level, which hear minor criminal and civil cases, and at the circuit court (trial) level. Appeals are taken to the Superior (or High) courts. The highest appellate level is the Supreme Court of Justice, which sits in Panama City.

■ CUSTOMS AND DUTIES

Companies that operate in the free zones are completely exempt from the payment of customs and export charges as are those firms that produce goods exclusively for export.

Panama has adopted a new policy that does not anticipate any increase in protective tariffs beyond those now in effect. Further, it expects to reduce tariffs on a continuing basis.

■ PROTECTION OF INTELLECTUAL PROPERTY

Panama has a domestic body of law covering copyrights, patents, tradenames, and trademarks, and is a member of the World Intellectual Property Organization.

■ IMMIGRATION AND RESIDENCE

Multiple entry visas, valid for one year, are available to current and potential foreign investors. The visas are renewable. Employees of any foreign enterprise at any level including executive, professional, scientific, or technical are required to obtain a work permit, which is generally valid for a limited time to be determined on a case-by-case basis.

■ FOREIGN INVESTMENT ASSISTANCE DIRECTORY

Several sources are available to provide further information about foreign investment in Panama. They include:

Panama Trade Development Institute
Banco Exterior Building
P.O. Box 6-1897
El Dorado, Panama
Telephone: (507) 25-7244
Telex: 3499 Invest PG
Fax: (507) 25-2193

Chamber of Commerce, Industry and Agriculture of Panama
Avda Samuel Lewis
Panama City, Panama
Telephone: (507) 64-8498
Telex: 2434

Persons interested in obtaining further information about foreign investment in Panama also are advised to contact the closest Panamanian embassy or consular office.

Panama maintains diplomatic relations with Argentina, Bolivia, Brazil, Chile, Taiwan (Republic of China), Colombia, Costa Rica, Cuba, Dominican Republic, Ecuador, Egypt, El Salvador, France, Germany, Guatemala, Haiti, Holy See, Honduras, India, Israel, Italy, Jamaica, Japan, Republic of Korea, Libya, Mexico, Nicaragua, Peru, Russia, Spain, Switzerland, United Kingdom, United States, Uruguay, and Venezuela.

PAPUA NEW GUINEA, INDEPENDENT STATE OF

■ POLITICAL ENVIRONMENT

The nation has experienced recent widespread terrorism and rioting that has been linked to several factors, including demands for higher wages and attempts by rival political groups to seize local areas. There has been at least one attempted coup d'etat.

The situation in the country must be described as currently unstable.

Economically, there are low rates of annual inflation and unemployment. The country is very underdeveloped and the infrastructure requires modernization.

■ SUMMARY OF FOREIGN INVESTMENT POLICY

The government has created an Investment Promotion Authority that has been charged with the responsibility of developing foreign investment. Additionally, a new law, the Investment Promotion Act, was enacted in 1992.

Foreign investors must obtain a certificate of authority from the Investment Promotion Authority to participate in the country's economy.

Pursuant to the Investment Promotion Act, foreign investments may not be nationalized or expropriated except by operation of law and for fair value compensation.

The nation is a signatory to the Multilateral Investment Guarantee Agency Agreement and to the Investment Disputes Convention Act, which provides for the settlement of disputes between states and nationals of other states.

All major areas of economic activity are open to foreign investors.

The government has developed numerous incentives for foreign investors. Included among such incentives are certain tax advantages and import considerations, and subsidies for feasibility studies conducted by foreign investors.

■ FORMATION AND TYPES OF PERMITTED BUSINESS ORGANIZATIONS

Foreign investors may participate in the economy either through the formation of a domestic corporation or through the use of a subsidiary. In either case the enterprise must receive approval and receive a certificate that will be on file with the Register of Certificates maintained by the Investment Promotion Authority.

Foreign investors may enter into joint ventures with domestic enterprises.

■ ENVIRONMENTAL PROTECTION

Foreign investors are advised to contact the Investment Promotion Authority for complete and current information regarding laws and regulations pertaining to environmental protection.

■ RIGHTS AND OBLIGATIONS OF FOREIGN INVESTORS

Foreign investors are generally guaranteed equal treatment with domestic ones relevant to taxation, customs duties, rates, rents, and any other relevant charges relating to investment.

Investments and income derived from such investments may be remitted abroad or repatriated at the prevailing exchange rate.

PAPUA NEW GUINEA

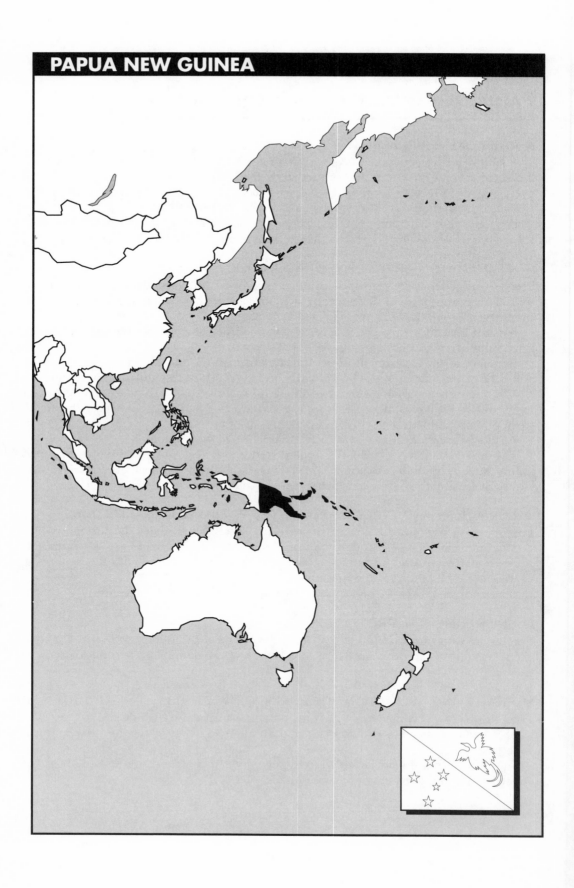

■ LABOR

Foreign companies are expected to provide hiring preferences to the local labor force.

There are laws regarding employment and required working conditions to include holidays, vacations, wages, and related factors.

Enterprises may be granted wage subsidies for up to five years of minimum wages for each local national employed on a full-time basis.

■ ACCOUNTING REQUIREMENTS

All enterprises must maintain complete financial records for tax and other purposes. Financial records must be maintained in accordance with internationally accepted accounting and auditing standards.

■ CURRENCY CONTROLS

The Bank of Papua New Guinea is the nation's central bank, and it is responsible for all matters relevant to exchange control.

Foreign investors may open and maintain foreign currency accounts, subject to the permission of the Bank of Papua New Guinea, for the purpose of meeting necessary financial obligations.

■ TAXATION

There is a corporate income tax that is levied on both foreign and domestic companies.

Among the specific tax incentives that are provided to foreign investors are a five year tax holiday, which may be granted to the establishment of a firm in a new industry; depreciation on industrial plants, warehouses, and storage facilities in an amount of 100 percent of cost; deductions of up to 75 percent of costs incurred in promoting export markets overseas; and tax allowances for various periods when establishing business activities in least developed areas of the country.

■ LEGAL SYSTEM

There are a variety of Local Courts that deal with minor civil and criminal matters or with specialized issues such as compensation. Village Courts function at the local level in the same manner as magistrates' courts.

The District Courts function at the trial level and hear and decide more serious criminal and civil cases. Appeals are taken to the National Courts and then to the Supreme Court, which sits in Boroko.

■ CUSTOMS AND DUTIES

The nation has reduced many of its import duties.

Duties on any machinery, equipment, tools, and other goods required in the manufacturing, agricultural, fisheries, and tourism areas have been virtually eliminated as part of the government's incentives to foreign investors.

■ PROTECTION OF INTELLECTUAL PROPERTY

Foreign investors are advised to contact the Investment Promotion Authority for information regarding the country's position relevant to patents, copyrights, trademarks, tradenames, and technology transfer.

■ IMMIGRATION AND RESIDENCE

Visas are generally required to enter the country. Foreign investors are advised to contact the Investment Promotion Authority or the nation's nearest embassy or consulate regarding information concerning visas, work permits, and residence permits.

■ FOREIGN INVESTMENT ASSISTANCE DIRECTORY

Sources that can provide further information about foreign investment in Papua New Guinea include:

Investment Promotion Authority
P.O. Box 5053
Boroko, Papua New Guinea
Telephone: (675) 258777
Telex: 93128

Tourism Development Corporation
P.O. Box 7144
Boroko, Papua New Guinea
Telephone: (675) 272521
Fax: (675) 259119

Bank of Papua New Guinea
Douglas Street
P.O. Box 121
Port Moresby, Papua New Guinea
Telephone: (675) 212999
Telex: 22128
Fax: (675) 211617

Persons interested in obtaining further information about investing in Papua New Guinea also are advised to contact the country's closest embassy or consular office.

Papua New Guinea maintains diplomatic relations with Australia, People's Republic of China, France, Germany, Holy See, Indonesia, Japan, Republic of Korea, Malaysia, New Zealand, Philippines, Russia, United Kingdom, and United States.

PARAGUAY, REPUBLIC OF

■ POLITICAL ENVIRONMENT

The government of Paraguay is relatively stable since the overthrow of former president Stroessner in 1989.

Goals of the new, reformist government include the creation of a more vibrant and liberal economy. Immediate objectives include the reduction of the large public foreign debt, privatization, and the acquisition of foreign investment.

Currently, both the inflation and unemployment rates are high and increasing.

■ SUMMARY OF FOREIGN INVESTMENT POLICY

The government, largely through the Ministry of Industry and Commerce and under the provisions of Decree Law 19 of 1989, is seeking to promote foreign investment in the country. The Investment Council Office of that ministry is charged with specific responsibilities in this area.

Foreign investment may take place in most economic areas. However, the government is particularly interested in the use of foreign investment to develop and use raw materials and to provide greater employment opportunities.

Incentives provided to foreign investors as part of the general government program include tax exemptions and long-term tax holidays for firms that are established in the nation or that expand, modernize, or otherwise improve existing economic activities. Firms engaged in oil and natural gas exploration, and in agriculture, ranching and forest industries, are exempt from the income tax provisions.

Companies established in Northern Chaco, a largely undeveloped area of Paraguay, are eligible for special incentives.

Foreign investors may acquire unlimited equity in existing domestic businesses.

Additional incentives include the establishment of free trade zones or special zones such as Ciudad del Este into which goods and materials may be imported without payment of customs duties.

Except for those businesses engaged in foreign exchange, where the majority of the investment must be domestic, there are no other requirements relating to domestic management or equity participation in any domestic business activity.

■ FORMATION AND TYPES OF PERMITTED BUSINESS ORGANIZATIONS

Foreign investors may participate in the economy through the creation of corporations, limited liability companies, general or limited partnerships, or sole proprietorships. Branch offices of foreign businesses may also be established. Joint ventures may be undertaken with either foreign or domestic partners.

Corporations and limited liability companies enjoy juridical person status.

Corporations, limited liability companies, and branches of foreign corporations must be on file with the Public Trade Registry.

■ ENVIRONMENTAL PROTECTION

There is a high level of government interest in the protection of the environment. Potential foreign investors are advised to contact the Investment Council Office for complete information on this subject.

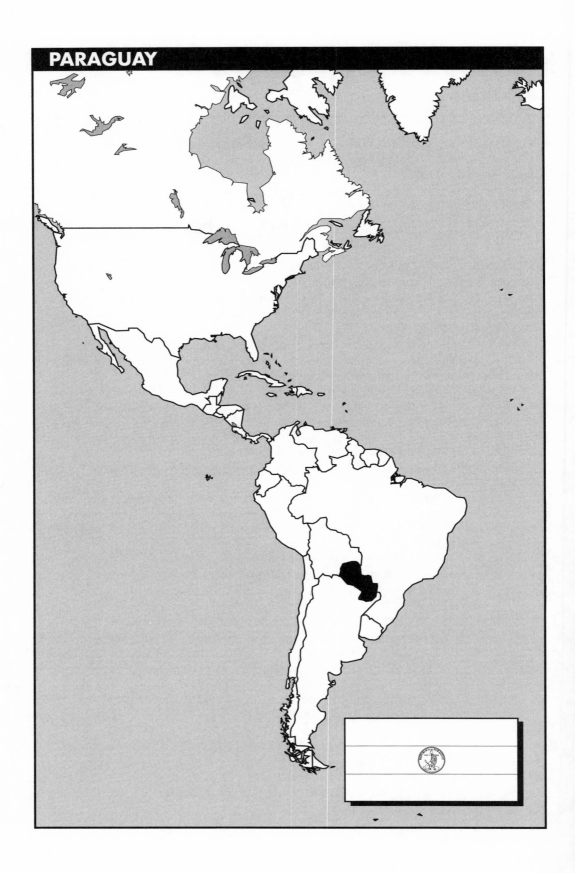

PARAGUAY

■ RIGHTS AND OBLIGATIONS OF FOREIGN INVESTORS

Foreign investments may be easily repatriated or remitted abroad, along with profits derived from such investments. Taxes must be paid before such repatriation occurs.

Foreign and domestic investors are guaranteed equality of treatment.

Both local and foreign financing may be obtained.

■ LABOR

Paraguay has a developed body of laws covering the subject of employment and working conditions.

There is a large supply of Paraguayan labor. Foreign firms must hire local personnel unless required special skills are not available.

Foreign nationals must obtain work permits and temporary residence permits.

■ ACCOUNTING REQUIREMENTS

All corporations and limited companies must maintain complete accounting and associated records for tax and other purposes. Audited financial statements must be prepared on a yearly basis and provided to the Ministry of Finance.

■ CURRENCY CONTROLS

The Bank of Paraguay is the central bank, and it is responsible for management of the foreign exchange policy.

No foreign exchange controls are presently in force. Foreign companies and individuals may open and maintain bank accounts in any currency.

■ TAXATION

There are numerous taxes assessed in Paraguay. The most important, as a revenue measure, is the income tax that is levied on both businesses and individuals.

The tax year runs with the calendar year, i.e., from January 1 to December 31. However, companies may, with permission of the appropriate tax office located within the Ministry of Finance, apply for a different 12-month tax period.

In addition to the tax holidays and exemptions offered as incentives, there are deductions and allowances that include depreciation, business expenses, uninsured losses, and bad debts.

Under the tax laws, partnerships are considered to be taxable entities.

Individual taxpayers may also claim certain deductions and allowances.

Taxes in addition to that on income include those assessed on services, documents, consumption, sales, and real estate, among others.

■ LEGAL SYSTEM

The court system includes local or magistrates' courts that hear lesser offenses, and the Courts of First Instance that are the general trial level courts and decide more serious cases of both a criminal and civil nature. Appeals are taken to the Court of Appeal, which sits at Asuncion.

■ CUSTOMS AND DUTIES

Paraguay is interested in expanding its foreign trade. It has joined in the MERCOSUR trading bloc with Argentina, Brazil, and Uruguay to create a South Atlantic common market.

Export incentives are available in the form of export and related charges on manufactured and other products that are received in Paraguay, finished there with local labor, materials, and other resources, and reexported.

Raw materials and required tools and equipment used in manufacturing for export are eligible for reduced customs charges.

■ PROTECTION OF INTELLECTUAL PROPERTY

Paraguay is a member of the World Intellectual Property Organization and of other international organizations seeking to provide intellectual property protection. In addition, the country has enacted domestic laws with regard to the protection of copyrights, patents, and trademarks.

■ IMMIGRATION AND RESIDENCE

In most cases, visas are not required to visit Paraguay. However, potential foreign investors are advised to contact the Investment Council Office for complete and current information regarding requirements for work permits and residence permits.

■ FOREIGN INVESTMENT ASSISTANCE DIRECTORY

Sources that can provide further information about foreign investment in Paraguay include:

Investment Council Office
Ministry of Industry and Commerce
Avda Espana 323
Ascunción, Paraguay
Telephone: (595) (21) 204693
Telex: 259
Fax: (595) (21) 210570

Central Bank of Paraguay
Avda Pablo VI
Ascunción, Paraguay
Telephone: (595) (21) 608019 / (595) (21) 608020
Telex: 134
Fax: (595) (21) 608150

Chamber of Commerce of Paraguay
Estrella 540
Ascunción, Paraguay
Telephone: (595) (21) 47312

Persons interested in obtaining additional information about foreign investment in Paraguay also are advised to contact the closest Paraguayan embassy or consular office.

Paraguay maintains diplomatic relations with Argentina, Belgium, Bolivia, Brazil, Chile, Republic of China (Taiwan), Colombia, Costa Rica, Ecuador, El Salvador, France, Germany, Holy See, Israel, Italy, Japan, Republic of Korea, Mexico, Panama, Peru, South Africa, Spain, Switzerland, United Kingdom, United States, Uruguay, and Venezuela.

■ POLITICAL ENVIRONMENT

In recent years the country has been severely troubled by rampant inflation coupled with internal political dissent, which has often taken on violent forms. The workers, despite the presence of a powerful labor faction, have traditionally been poorly paid and thus hit by inflation. General strikes have been a consequence.

A particularly difficult problem is that of export earnings. Coffee was the major Peruvian export, and it has been the victim of a depressed worldwide market. Meanwhile, the country's other major export is coca, from which cocaine is derived. Some experts believe, in view of the fact that at least a portion of the profits earned from the sale of cocaine become, indirectly, a part of Peru's foreign earnings, that curtailment of drug trafficking negatively impacts Peru's already fragile economy.

Meanwhile, internal political difficulties have included a full scale terrorism campaign in the nation's rural sections, much of that being attributed to the Sendero Luminoso (Shining Path), a left wing guerrilla group.

■ SUMMARY OF FOREIGN INVESTMENT POLICY

The position of Peru's new government is that foreign investment is an essential part of the nation's economic recovery. Peru has established a government agency, the National Commission on Foreign Investment and Technology (CONITE), to promote foreign investment. Several laws have been enacted as part of the government's liberalization program. However, the key legislation relevant to the infusion of foreign capital has been the Foreign Investment Promotion Law.

Among the various steps taken by the government to promote foreign investment in that country are the creation of free zones, changes in the nation's basic laws that now permit foreign participation in all sectors of the economy including the provision of public services, insurance, agriculture, and the petroleum industry.

Tax reform has been accomplished with an intent to simplify the taxation system while broadening the tax base.

Additionally, Peru has embarked on a privatization program and has engaged in discussions with various nations, as well as the World Bank, regarding the payment of its foreign debt.

Foreign investors are guaranteed equality of treatment with domestic ones.

All foreign investments are considered as immediately authorized and registered with the government.

■ FORMATION AND TYPES OF PERMITTED BUSINESS ORGANIZATIONS

Under Peruvian law, foreign investors may form or participate in corporations, limited liability companies, general and limited partnerships, limited partnerships that issue shares, and joint ventures. In addition, foreign firms may establish branch offices.

Corporations and limited liability companies enjoy a juridical person status upon formation.

■ ENVIRONMENTAL PROTECTION

There is a strong interest in the protection of the environment. Potential foreign inves-

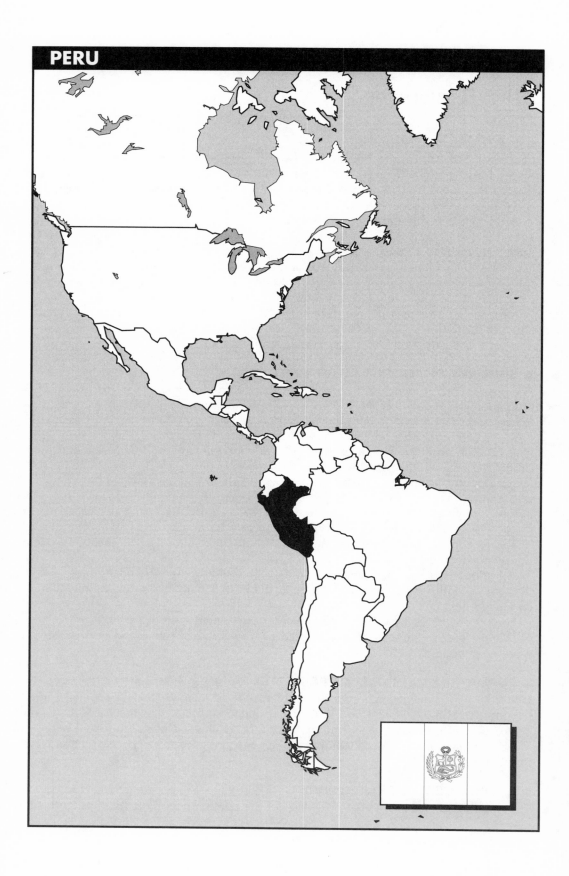

PERU

tors are advised to make inquiries of the National Commission on Foreign Investment and Technology regarding specific environmental regulations as they impact industrial activities.

■ RIGHTS AND OBLIGATIONS OF FOREIGN INVESTORS

The law provides that foreign investors are free to remit abroad or repatriate all profits and other income, including royalties, without limit and without government approval, and subject only to payment of such Peruvian taxes as may be due.

Foreign businesses, as investors, may own and hold land.

The government will guarantee what it terms as "juridical stability" to foreign investments, to include the right of repatriation, if such foreign investments are maintained for at least two years and meet certain minimum investment levels. The guarantees so provided are valid for a period of ten years.

Foreign investors, both business entities and individuals, must file tax returns with the government.

■ LABOR

The government has changed the labor laws with the view toward creating less of a burden on business activities. Among the changes were those that tended to restrict more narrowly the right of the employees to profit sharing and the rights of workers to membership on corporate boards.

The number of foreign workers that may be employed in a business enterprise in Peru is limited to not more than 20 percent of the total work force, and the salary of such foreign employees cannot equal more than 30 percent of the total salaries paid by the company in Peru.

■ ACCOUNTING REQUIREMENTS

All business entities must maintain appropriate books and records in accordance with internationally accepted accounting standards.

Firms operating in the export processing or tourist free zones are exempt from all customs and taxes.

■ CURRENCY CONTROLS

At the present time, no exchange controls are imposed by Peru.

Both residents and non-residents may maintain savings and checking accounts in foreign currencies.

Foreign investors may exchange hard currency into Peruvian currency when desired, using the facilities of the domestic banking system.

■ TAXATION

The most important Peruvian taxes are the income and the value added tax (VAT).

Business entities and individuals who are considered as domiciled are subject to the Peruvian income tax. Non-resident companies, individuals, and branches of foreign businesses are only taxed on income gained in the country.

Royalties are subject to a withholding tax of 28 percent. There are a variety of minor taxes.

The VAT is assessed at 16 percent of the value of all goods and services provided by businesses and individuals.

■ LEGAL SYSTEM

There is a system of provincial or Courts of First Instance located throughout the country that hear criminal and civil cases. Appeals are taken to a system of superior courts and then to the Supreme Court. The Supreme Court sits in Lima.

■ CUSTOMS AND DUTIES

Imports are taxed at rates of 15 and 25 percent of value. Most imports are taxed at the latter percentage.

The government has enacted legislation that will create free zones, special trade treatment zones, special development, and tourist free zones. Free zones are reserved for the production of goods that will be exported. Business enterprises operating in these zones, as they are created, will enjoy special tax, customs, and labor provisions.

■ PROTECTION OF INTELLECTUAL PROPERTY

Peru is a member of the World Intellectual Property Organization and has ratified the Geneva Convention on copyrights. The nation has enacted domestic laws relevant to the protection of patents, copyrights, trademarks, tradenames, and technology transfer.

■ IMMIGRATION AND RESIDENCE

Peru has created a program for entry into the country of "qualified immigrants," i.e., foreign investors and their families. The status of "qualified immigrant" is governed by numerous regulations that are within the control of the Ad Hoc Commission that administers the Migration-Investment Program under the general supervision of the Ministry of Foreign Relations.

■ FOREIGN INVESTMENT ASSISTANCE DIRECTORY

The following sources may be contacted to obtain more detailed information concerning foreign investment in Peru:

National Commission on Foreign Investment and Technology (CONITE)
Ministry of Industry, Commerce, Tourism, and Integration
Calle 1 Oeste
Corpac, San Isidro
Lima, Peru
Telephone: (51) (14) 407120
Telex: 21094

Confederation of Chambers of Commerce of Peru
Avda Gregorio Escobedo 398
Lima, Peru
Telephone: (51) (14) 633434

Persons interested in obtaining further information about investing in Peru also are advised to contact the closest Peruvian embassy or consular office.

Peru maintains diplomatic relations with Algeria, Angola, Argentina, Austria, Belgium, Bolivia, Brazil, Bulgaria, Canada, Chile, People's Republic of China, Colombia, Costa Rica, Cuba, Czechoslovakia, Dominican Republic, Ecuador, Egypt, El Salvador, Finland, France, Germany, Guatemala, Haiti, Holy See, Honduras, Hungary, India, Israel, Italy, Japan, Democratic People's Republic of Korea, Republic of Korea, Mexico, Morocco, Netherlands, New Zealand, Nicaragua, Panama, Paraguay, Philippines, Poland, Portugal, Romania, Russia, Saudi Arabia, Spain, Sweden, Switzerland, United Kingdom, United States, Uruguay, and Venezuela.

PHILIPPINES, REPUBLIC OF

■ POLITICAL ENVIRONMENT

The recent history of internal unrest is widely known. The nation is suffering from severe economic distress that is largely, though not totally, the result of its inability to resolve its internal political difficulties.

There are moderately high rates of both unemployment and inflation. The country has a large external public debt and a high debt service.

■ SUMMARY OF FOREIGN INVESTMENT POLICY

The government has recognized the need for a liberalized policy on foreign investment and to that end has taken a number of steps designed to obtain such investment. A new law, the Foreign Investments Act, was passed in 1991, and the National Economic and Development Authority, responsible to the Department of Trade and Industry, was established.

There are a number of specific areas in which foreign investment is to be particularly encouraged, and they include those that increase employment opportunities, expand the export base, improve the level of technology, and raise the nation's standard of living.

Foreign investors may own 100 percent of any enterprise that is not on the negative list, i.e., the list of activities in which foreign participation is either prohibited or limited to no more than 40 percent ownership.

Firms that generally direct their business activities to Filipinos are encouraged to involve them more into the management and overall participation of the enterprise.

The government has created various incentives designed for foreign investors. Eligibility of these incentives requires that the foreign investor register with the government.

Foreign investment is not desired in the areas of small and mid-sized firms, i.e., such enterprises possessing paid-in capital of less than $500,000 (U.S.), and no foreign investment may be made in such companies.

■ FORMATION AND TYPES OF PERMITTED BUSINESS ORGANIZATIONS

Foreign investors may carry on business in the Philippines as a foreign corporation, through a branch or representative office of a foreign corporation, as a partnership, as a sole proprietor, or as a joint venture with a Filipino enterprise. Foreign investors may also form a Filipino corporation, however, such a corporation must have at least 60 percent Filipino ownership.

■ ENVIRONMENTAL PROTECTION

The law requires that all companies must comply with the existing rules and regulations concerning environmental protection.

■ RIGHTS AND OBLIGATIONS OF FOREIGN INVESTORS

Foreign investors may repatriate or remit profits and other income derived from investment after payment of all due taxes and if registered with the Central Bank.

There are guarantees against nationalization or expropriation of property.

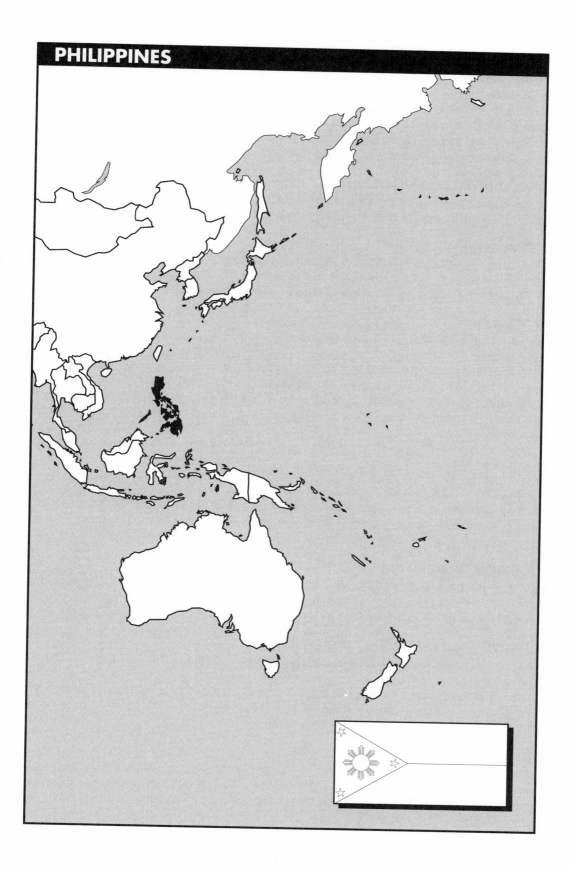

■ LABOR

There is a complete body of laws relevant to required working conditions, wages, salaries, and other employment factors.

Filipino nationals must be given hiring preference except in cases where available local labor does not possess the required technical skill level.

■ ACCOUNTING REQUIREMENTS

All businesses must maintain accurate financial records.

Companies must file annual statements that are certified by a licensed accountant.

■ CURRENCY CONTROLS

The Central Bank is responsible for all matters relevant to foreign exchange.

Potential foreign investors are advised to contact the Central Bank for information on current rules and regulations pertaining to currency controls.

■ TAXATION

The major taxes are those on income, which are levied against both corporations and individuals.

There are various deductions, allowances, and exemptions for which companies may be eligible, to include depreciation and tax holidays.

There are numerous minor taxes to include a value added tax (VAT), and taxes imposed on franchises, documentary (stamp) taxes, and taxes on real estate and mining operations.

Companies operating in less developed areas of the country are eligible for a variety of special incentives.

■ LEGAL SYSTEM

The court system includes municipal courts, regional courts that function at the trial court level, and the Court of Appeals. The highest level court is the Supreme Court, which sits in Manila.

■ CUSTOMS AND DUTIES

Raw materials, equipment, tools, and other items used in the production of goods for export are exempt from customs and duties.

Companies operating in the free zones are eligible for additional customs incentives.

■ PROTECTION OF INTELLECTUAL PROPERTY

There are domestic statutes concerning copyrights, trademarks, tradenames, and patents.

The Philippines are a member of the World Intellectual Property Organization and subscribe to the internationally accepted standards of protection accorded to patents, copyrights, trademarks, and technology transfer.

■ IMMIGRATION AND RESIDENCE

Potential foreign investors may apply for multiple entry visas that are valid for one year. Foreign employees who possess managerial, scientific, or technical skills may be issued work permits that are valid for five years and may be renewable.

Complete information relevant to current rules on visas, work permits, and residence permits may be obtained from the National Economic and Development Authority.

■ FOREIGN INVESTMENT ASSISTANCE DIRECTORY

Several sources exist that can provide additional information about foreign investment in the Philippines. They include:

Department of Trade and Industry
385 Sen. Gil J. Puyat Avenue
1200 Makatu, Metro Manila, Philippines
Telephone: (63) (2) 868-403 / (63) (2) 867-895 / (63) (2) 875-602
Telex: 45555 BOI/PM
122661 BOI PH
Fax: (63) (2) 632-851166

Philippine Chamber of Commerce
ODC International Plaza Building
219 Salcedo Street
Makati, Metro Manila 2801
Telephone: (63) (2) 8176981
Telex: 62042

Persons interested in obtaining further information about investing in the Philippines also are advised to contact the country's closest embassy or consular office.

The Philippines maintain diplomatic relations with Argentina, Australia, Austria, Bangladesh, Belgium, Brazil, Brunei, Bulgaria, Canada, Chile, People's Republic of China, Colombia, Cuba, Czechoslovakia, Denmark, Egypt, Finland, France, Germany, Holy See, India, Indonesia, Iran, Iraq, Israel, Italy, Japan, Republic of Korea, Libya, Malaysia, Malta, Mexico, Myanmar, Netherlands, New Zealand, Nigeria, Norway, Pakistan, Panama, Papua New Guinea, Peru, Romania, Russia, Saudi Arabia, Singapore, Spain, Sri Lanka, Sweden, Switzerland, Thailand, United Kingdom, United States, and Vietnam.

POLAND, REPUBLIC OF

■ POLITICAL ENVIRONMENT
The nation is now a multi-political party state with an official position of having a free market economy. During the current period of transition from a centrally planned economy, the country is experiencing some difficulties particularly in relation to its growing external public debt.

Inflation is extremely high but the rate of unemployment is quite low. It is anticipated that in the short run there will be some popular dissatisfaction with economic progress and its impact on living standards. There is an ongoing program of privatization.

■ SUMMARY OF FOREIGN INVESTMENT POLICY
Poland is interested in generating foreign investment. It has enacted a Law on Companies with Foreign Participation and has charged the Ministry of Privatization with the primary responsibility of promoting foreign investment.

No permission to establish foreign investment is required except in cases where foreign interests intend to enter the banking or telecommunications industries.

Government concessions must be applied for and received in order to engage in any mining activities as well as the production of liquor, weapons, and related materials, insurance, air transportation, motion picture and record production, postal services, pharmacies, and pharmaceutical and related production. There is a specific government interest in foreign investment that will improve the infrastructure.

Permits also are required in cases where foreign investment interest intends to take over property in Poland that is owned by a state enterprise.

There is no requirement for Polish participation in a foreign enterprise.

Foreign investment capital may take the form of Polish currency or in non-monetary form, i.e., equipment and other assets.

There is a guarantee against expropriation up to the amount of enterprise participation. The guarantee is based on the principle of reciprocity.

■ FORMATION AND TYPES OF PERMITTED BUSINESS ORGANIZATIONS
Foreign investors may form either limited liability companies or joint stock companies with domestic partners, or establish wholly owned foreign firms. Such investors may also purchase partial or total control of limited liability or joint stock companies that already exist in Poland.

Branches and representative offices of foreign firms may also be established.

The minimum capital requirement, either in currency or in-kind contribution (i.e., equipment), is 40 million zlotys ($3,000 U.S.) for a limited liability company and one billion zlotys ($80,000 U.S.) for a joint stock company.

Limited liability and joint stock companies, upon filing appropriate documents with the Ministry of Privatization, enjoy juridical person status.

■ ENVIRONMENTAL PROTECTION
Potential foreign investors are advised to contact either the Ministry of Privatization or the Ministry of Environmental Protection, Natural Resources and Forestry for full and

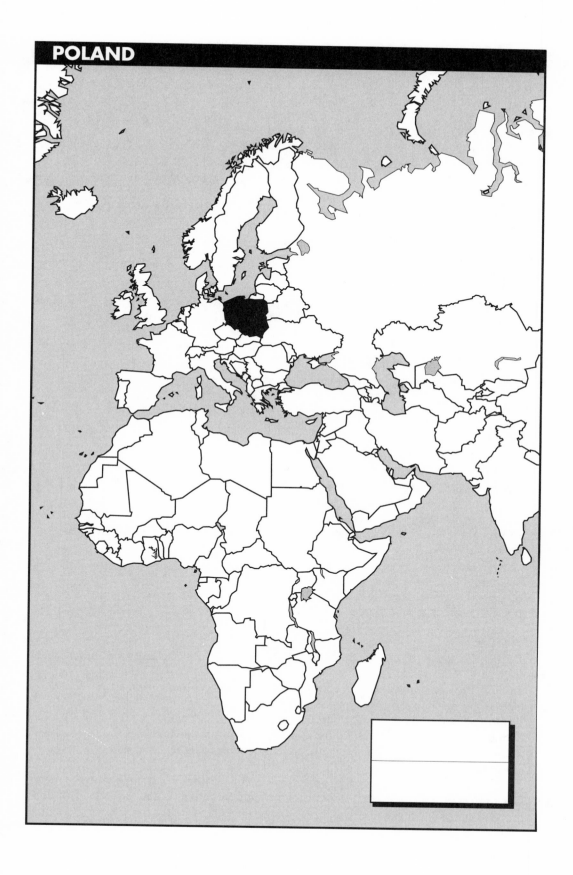

current information on Poland's laws and regulations concerning environmental protection.

■ RIGHTS AND OBLIGATIONS OF FOREIGN INVESTORS

All foreign investment activities must be registered in the Commercial Court and must obtain a code number from the Central Statistical Office.

Capital investment, net profits after taxes derived from such investment, and receipts after enterprise dissolution may be freely repatriated.

There is no limit on the percentage of salary of foreign employees that may be repatriated.

Land may be purchased or leased by foreign businesses or individuals. A permit to purchase or lease land must be obtained from the Ministry of Internal Affairs.

■ LABOR

There is a highly productive and highly unionized labor force and a major body of laws regarding requirements for working conditions, wages, and relevant considerations.

Foreign businesses must register with the Polish Social Security Fund.

■ ACCOUNTING REQUIREMENTS

All foreign investors must maintain a system of books and records for inspection by the Minister of Ownership Changes and for tax purposes. Accounting and financial records must be maintained in accord with internationally accepted standards.

■ CURRENCY CONTROLS

The National Bank of Poland is responsible for exchange control.

Currency movements into and from the country require a foreign exchange permit.

Foreign investors have the right to obtain foreign currency from the National Bank in order to meet obligations or to remit or repatriate investment capital and income.

Foreign employees may purchase foreign currency in exchange for Polish currency. Such purchases require proper employer certification of the amount of which the employees are compensated.

A foreign exchange permit is not required by foreign employees to remit abroad or repatriate any percentages of their wages or salaries.

Foreign companies may open bank accounts with a foreign currency only with the permission of the National Bank.

■ TAXATION

All businesses must register with the Treasury Office and make appropriate tax payments.

Foreign firms are subject to a corporate income tax and other minor taxes.

Individuals are liable for personal income tax.

A value added tax (VAT) on goods and services is also levied.

Poland has entered into bilateral treaties relevant to double taxation.

There are numerous exemptions and deductions available relevant to both business and individual taxation.

The Minister of Finance, based on an evaluation of certain factors such as investment size, type of economic activity, impact on employment and exports, and the introduction of new technology, may exempt a business from the corporate income tax.

Employers of foreign employees must withhold income for purposes of personal income tax payment.

■ LEGAL SYSTEM

The court system includes the General Courts that comprise the trial court level and that hear and decide both civil and criminal cases. Appeals are taken to the Supreme Court, which sits in Warsaw.

■ CUSTOMS AND DUTIES

Poland is a member of the General Agreement on Tariffs and Trade (GATT) and, pursuant to its desires to increase exports, has adopted a liberal international trade policy.

■ PROTECTION OF INTELLECTUAL PROPERTY

Poland is a member of the World Intellectual Property Organization and subscribes to the internationally accepted standards of protection to be accorded copyrights, patents, tradenames, trademarks, and technology transfer.

■ IMMIGRATION AND RESIDENCE

Visas are generally required to enter Poland. Potential foreign investors are advised to contact the Ministry of Privatization for full and current information concerning visas, work permits, and resident permits.

■ FOREIGN INVESTMENT ASSISTANCE DIRECTORY

There are several sources that can provide further information about investing in Poland and they include:

Ministry of Privatization
ul. Krucza 36
00-525 Warsaw, Poland
Telephone: (48) (22) 628-0281
Fax: (48) (22) 625-1114

Ministry of Industry and Trade
ul. Wspólna 4
00-921 Warsaw, Poland
Telephone: (48) (22) 210-351
Fax: (48) (22) 212-550

Ministry of Environmental Protection, Natural Resources and Forestry
ul. Wawelska 52/54
00-922 Warsaw, Poland
Telephone: (48) (22) 250-001 / (48) (22) 254-001
Fax: (48) (22) 253-335 / (48) (22) 253-972

National Bank of Poland
ul. Swietokrzyska 11/12
00-950 Warsaw, Poland
Telephone: (48) (22) 200-321
Fax: (48) (22) 269-955

Polish Chamber of Commerce
Promotion Center
ul. Trebacka 4
00-074 Warsaw, Poland
Telephone: (48) (22) 260-221 / (48) (22) 267-376
Fax: (48) (22) 274-673 / (48) (22) 6355-137

Persons interested in obtaining further information about foreign investment in Poland are also advised to contact the closest Polish embassy or consular office.

Poland maintains diplomatic relations with Afghanistan, Albania, Algeria, Argentina, Australia, Austria, Bangladesh, Belgium, Brazil, Bulgaria, Canada, Chile, People's Republic of China, Colombia, Costa Rica, Cuba, Czechoslovakia, Ecuador, Egypt, Finland, France, Germany, Greece, Holy See, Hungary, Indonesia, Iran, Iraq, Ireland, Israel, Italy, Democratic People's Republic of Korea, Republic of Korea, Laos, Libya, Malaysia, Mexico, Mongolia, Morocco, Netherlands, Nigeria, Norway, Pakistan, Peru, Philippines, Portugal, Romania, Russia, Spain, Sweden, Switzerland, Thailand, Tunisia, Turkey, United Kingdom, United States, Uruguay, Venezuela, Vietnam, Yemen, and Zaire.

PORTUGAL, REPUBLIC OF

■ POLITICAL ENVIRONMENT

Portugal is a representative democracy. It has a stable government and faces no external threats to its sovereignty. The nation is a member of the European Community (EC).

There have been ongoing efforts to privatize the economy with notable success. There has been some internal unrest, partially created by a high rate of inflation, and there are dissident political factions, some of which are engaged in domestic terrorism.

■ SUMMARY OF FOREIGN INVESTMENT POLICY

There is a major interest in acquiring foreign investment. The principal statute relevant to this effort is the Decree Law on Foreign Investment of 1977, as amended. The primary government agency involved in the promotion and regulation of foreign investment is the Portuguese Foreign Trade Institute.

The government has created a wide variety of foreign investment incentives to include tax exemptions and cash grants. Eligibility for incentives under this program is dependent on both the amount of foreign investment and the areas of foreign participation.

Several free zones have been established throughout the nation that provide special trade and tax incentives to foreign investors.

At present, Portugal's principal interest in foreign investment is its value in improving the economy's general level of productivity. The areas of the economy that have been targeted specifically for improvement and where the incentives for foreign investment are the most significant are communications technology and data processing; biotechnology; agribusiness; tourism; the automotive industry; specific areas within the chemical industry; and the production of hospital and medical surgical equipment.

■ FORMATION AND TYPES OF PERMITTED BUSINESS ORGANIZATIONS

Foreign investors may participate in the Portuguese economy through several types of business organizations to include the formation of a sociedade anónima - S.A. (the equivalent of a corporation); the quota company (sociedade por quotas - Lda.); limited partnerships; unlimited partnerships; and sole proprietorships.

In most cases, the corporate form, or sociedade anónima - S.A., is used by larger companies. Both the corporation and the quota company acquire juridical person status.

Foreign investors may also either wholly or partially acquire existing firms that are Portuguese owned, as well as form joint venture agreements with Portuguese-owned business organizations.

All potential foreign investment activities must be submitted to the Foreign Trade Institute for approval.

■ ENVIRONMENTAL PROTECTION

Air and water pollution are major issues of concern in Portugal. Potential foreign investors are strongly advised to seek guidance on environmental protection requirements from the Foreign Trade Institute.

PORTUGAL

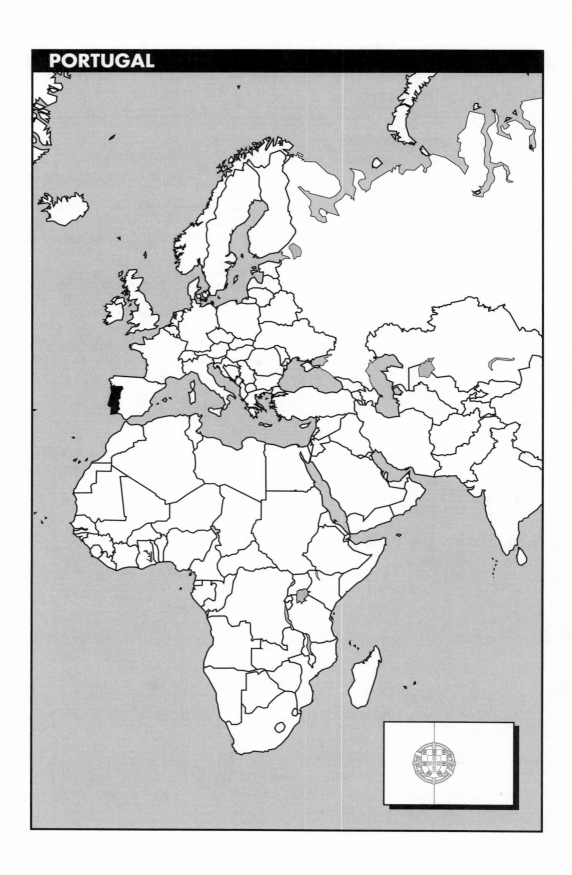

■ RIGHTS AND OBLIGATIONS OF FOREIGN INVESTORS

Foreign and domestic investors are accorded the same rights with respect to participation in the Portuguese economy.

There is no history of nationalization programs having been undertaken by the Portuguese government. Foreign investment is guaranteed protection from nationalization or expropriation.

Foreign businesses and individuals employed by such businesses must pay taxes to Portugal.

Profits and other income gained through foreign investment may be repatriated abroad after payment of all taxes, subsequent to approval from the Bank of Portugal.

■ LABOR

Portugal has a large and well qualified labor force. The Portuguese labor unions are powerful and exert a major political influence.

Working conditions, fringe benefits, salaries, and wages are matters generally established by law.

In most cases, foreign employees may only be hired where no Portuguese workers are available. Such foreign workers must have proper residence permits. Permission may be granted by the Ministry of Labor to employ non-Portuguese workers when special technical knowledge, possessed only by available foreign individuals, is required.

■ ACCOUNTING REQUIREMENTS

Portugal has introduced an Official Accounting Plan that must be used by all businesses operating in the country with regard to the maintenance of proper books and records.

Most companies with limited liability must be annually examined by independent auditors pursuant to standards that have been adopted by the Portuguese Institute of Statutory Auditors.

■ CURRENCY CONTROLS

There is an increased level of liberalization relevant to the movement of capital in and out of Portugal. The process will continue to become more simplified because of the membership of Portugal in the EC with regard to capital flows across Europe's borders, and because of the policy based on easing capital flow restrictions generally. Approval for the movement of capital must be obtained from the Bank of Portugal, which is the government agency responsible for currency and exchange controls.

■ TAXATION

The corporate income tax is based on the calendar year. There are no estimated tax provisions.

Corporate taxes, in addition to that levied on income, include those on capital gains, royalties, and income produced by investments. Minor taxes include a value added tax (VAT), stamp, and real estate taxes.

Individuals working in Portugal must pay a tax on personal income on a worldwide basis if they are considered as residents. Individuals who qualify as non-residents must pay taxes only on the income earned in Portugal. Personal income tax calculations are based on the calendar year. Returns are generally due to be filed by March 1.

There are numerous tax deductions and exemptions that may be claimed by both corporations and individuals.

All businesses operating in the free zones may be eligible for tax advantages resulting from those locations.

■ LEGAL SYSTEM

The Courts of First Instance, located around the country, serve a trial function. The Courts of Second Instance have an appellate function. The highest court of appeal is the Supreme Court, which decides cases coming to it from the Courts of Second Instance. The Constitutional Court decides on the legality of the nation's basic laws when they come into issue. Both the Constitutional Court and the Supreme Court sit in Lisbon.

■ CUSTOMS AND DUTIES

Foreign investors operating within any of the free zones are exempt from customs duties.

As an EC member, Portugal will continue to move forward, in terms of trade with other EC members, to eliminate all customs and related charges.

■ PROTECTION OF INTELLECTUAL PROPERTY

Portugal is a member of the World Intellectual Property Organization. However, problems have been encountered with regard to inadequate enforcement of relevant provisions of treaties to which Portugal is a party and that deal with copyrights, trademarks, and patents.

■ IMMIGRATION AND RESIDENCE

Generally, there are no visas required to enter Portugal. However, individuals intending to establish residence must obtain a residence visa that is valid for ninety (90) days. Individuals who visit Portugal for business purposes without the intention of becoming residents may obtain a visa that is valid for sixty (60) days and is renewable.

Work permits must be obtained to be employed in Portugal.

■ FOREIGN INVESTMENT ASSISTANCE DIRECTORY

Sources that can provide additional information about foreign investment in Portugal include:

Portugese Foreign Trade Institute
Avenue 5 de Outubro 101
Lisbon, Portugal
Telephone: (351) (1) 7930103
Telex: 16498
Fax: (351) (1) 7935028

The Portuguese Foreign Trade Institute (ICEP) maintains offices in Alger, Algeria; Luanda, Angola; Vienna, Austria; Brussels, Belgium; Sao Paulo, Brazil; Montreal and Toronto, Canada; Praia, Cape Verde; Prague, Czechoslovakia; Copenhagen, Denmark; Cairo, Egypt; Helsinki, Finland; Paris, France; Dusseldorf, Stuttgart, and Berlin, Germany; Budapest, Hungary; Baghdad, Iraq; Dublin, Ireland; Milan and Rome, Italy; Tokyo, Japan; Macao; Rabat, Morocco; Maputo, Mozambique; Den Haag, Denmark;

Oslo, Norway; Islamabad, Pakistan; Warsaw, Poland; Johannesburg, South Africa; Moscow, Russia; Seoul, South Korea; Madrid, Barcelona, Vigo, and Seville, Spain; Stockholm, Sweden; Geneva, Switzerland; London, United Kingdom; New York and Washington, D.C., United States; and Caracas, Venezuela.

Ministry of Trade and Tourism
Avenue de República 79
Lisbon, Portugal
Telephone: (351) (1) 730412
Telex: 13455

Ministry of the Environment
Ave Don Carlos I
Lisbon, Portugal

Bank of Portugal
Rua do Comercio 148
Lisbon, Portugal
Telephone: (351) (1) 3462931
Telex: 16554
Fax: (351) (1) 3467341

Persons interested in obtaining further information about investing in Portugal are also advised to contact the closest Portuguese embassy or consular office.

Portugal maintains diplomatic relations with Algeria, Angola, Argentina, Australia, Austria, Belgium, Bolivia, Brazil, Bulgaria, Canada, Cape Verde, Chile, People's Republic of China, Colombia, Costa Rica, Cuba, Czechoslovakia, Denmark, Egypt, Finland, France, Germany, Greece, Guatemala, Guinea-Bissau, Holy See, Hungary, India, Iran, Iraq, Ireland, Israel, Italy, Japan, Democratic People's Republic of Korea, Republic of Korea, Libya, Luxembourg, Mexico, Morocco, Mozambique, Netherlands, Nigeria, Norway, Pakistan, Panama, Peru, Poland, Romania, Russia, Sao Tome and Principe, South Africa, Spain, Sweden, Switzerland, Thailand, Turkey, United Kingdom, United States, Uruguay, Venezuela, and Zaire.

QATAR, STATE OF

■ POLITICAL ENVIRONMENT

The government is politically stable. Economically, the nation is richly endowed with hydrocarbon reserves. The annual inflation rate is extremely low and there is no measurable rate of unemployment. There is a long-term interest in diversifying the economic base to reduce dependence on hydrocarbons as the principal export.

■ SUMMARY OF FOREIGN INVESTMENT POLICY

The government, through both the Ministry of Economy and Trade and the Industrial Development Technical Center, is interested in acquiring foreign investment, particularly in the area of light industry and in the continuing development of the country's infrastructure.

There are restrictions on foreign ownership. As a result, investment cannot generally take the form of equity participation.

There are no specific restrictions regarding areas in which foreign investment may or may not be accepted.

Any foreign business or investment must be registered with the Controller of Companies of Qatar.

In those cases where foreign investors are permitted to establish businesses, there are incentives offered by the government to include the availability of industrial estates, preferred public utility rates, preferred interest loans, and exemptions from customs duties, as well as tax holidays.

In virtually all cases where foreign equity participation is permitted, there must be at least a 51 percent domestic interest.

■ FORMATION AND TYPES OF PERMITTED BUSINESS ORGANIZATIONS

Foreign investors may legally participate in the economy as corporations, limited liability companies, partnerships, or in joint ventures.

It must be stressed, however, that any foreign business or investment requires government approval and that virtually any company will involve either government or domestic enterprise participation and control.

■ ENVIRONMENTAL PROTECTION

Potential foreign investors are advised to contact the Ministry of Economy and Trade or the Industrial Development Technical Center for complete and current information regarding the government's position on environmental protection.

■ RIGHTS AND OBLIGATIONS OF FOREIGN INVESTORS

Investments and any income derived from such investments may be freely repatriated or remitted abroad. Financing may be obtained from local banks.

■ LABOR

There is a shortage of labor in the country. As a result of high wages at all employment

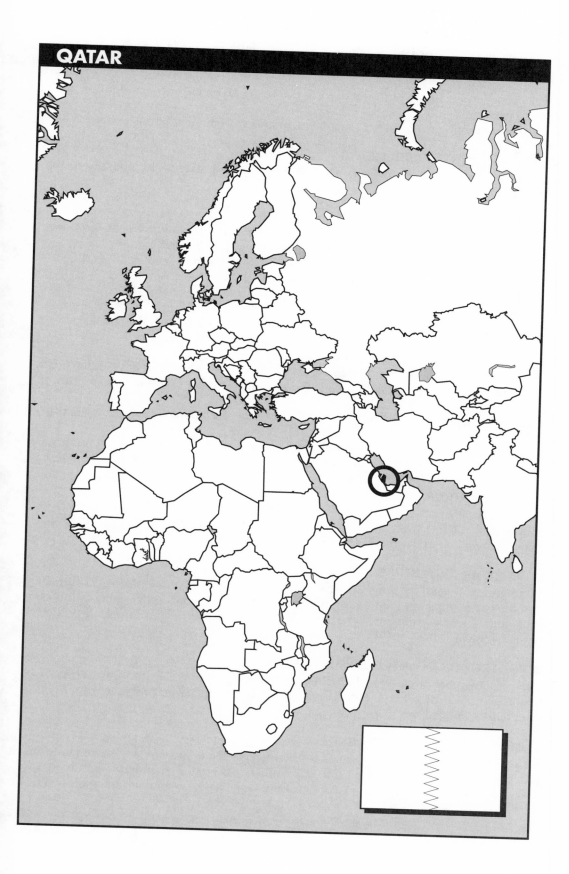

levels, a major percentage of the labor force is foreign. Work permits are required of all foreign personnel.

A large body of laws regarding employment and working conditions exists.

■ ACCOUNTING REQUIREMENTS

All businesses established in Qatar must submit audited statements annually to the Office of the Director of Income Tax.

■ CURRENCY CONTROLS

The government office, which acts in the capacity of a central bank, is the Qatar Monetary Agency, and it is responsible for foreign exchange and related matters.

There are no restrictions on currency amounts moved into the country.

The currency is freely convertible.

■ TAXATION

The principal tax is the corporate income tax. There is no individual income tax.

The corporate tax is assessed on all income generated in the country.

There are a variety of minor taxes on services.

The taxable period is the calendar year although businesses that have other fiscal 12-month periods may use such a period if approved by the Office of the Director of Income Tax.

There are deductions for business expenses and depreciation of physical assets used in business.

Tax incentives, to include long-term tax holidays and other special considerations, may be provided by the government where it is deemed to be in the national interest.

■ LEGAL SYSTEM

The court system includes Lower Criminal Courts that hear and decide petty cases and Commercial, Civil, Labor, and Higher Criminal Courts that function at the trial level. Appeals are taken to the Court of Appeal, which sits in Doha.

■ CUSTOMS AND DUTIES

There are no general customs exemptions created as incentives to foreign investment. In some cases, depending on the significance of the project to the government, imports of materials and equipment to be used in such a project will be imported without customs duties.

■ PROTECTION OF INTELLECTUAL PROPERTY

Qatar is a member of the World Intellectual Property Organization and thus subscribes to the accepted international standards of protection to be accorded to copyrights, trademarks, and patents.

■ IMMIGRATION AND RESIDENCE

Visas are normally required to enter the country. Often a sponsor will be required in order to obtain a visa, a work permit, or a residence permit. Potential foreign investors are advised to contact the Ministry of Economy and Trade, the Industrial Development

Technical Center, or the Ministry of the Interior regarding current laws and regulations pertaining to this subject.

■ FOREIGN INVESTMENT ASSISTANCE DIRECTORY

Sources that can provide further information about foreign investment in Qatar include:

Ministry of Economy and Trade
P.O. Box 1968
Doha, Qatar
Telephone: (974) 434888
Telex: 4488

Ministry of the Interior
P.O. Box 3883
Doha, Qatar
Telephone: (974) 330000
Telex: 4238
Fax: (974) 324430

Industrial Development Technical Center
P.O. Box 2599
Doha, Qatar
Telephone: (974) 832121
Telex: 4323

Qatar Chamber of Commerce
P.O. Box 402
Doha, Qatar
Telephone: (974) 425131
Telex: 4078
Fax: (974) 324338

Persons interested in obtaining further information about foreign investment in Qatar are advised to contact the country's closest embassy or consular office.

Qatar maintains diplomatic relations with Algeria, Bangladesh, People's Republic of China, Egypt, France, Germany, India, Iran, Iraq, Japan, Jordan, Republic of Korea, Kuwait, Lebanon, Mauritania, Morocco, Oman, Pakistan, Russia, Saudi Arabia, Somalia, Sudan, Syria, Tunisia, Turkey, United Kingdom, United States, and Yemen.

ROMANIA

■ POLITICAL ENVIRONMENT

Romania is another of the eastern European countries that has moved from a centrally planned economy to one based on free market principles.

The transition has not been an easy one. Inflation has been extremely high. Unemployment has begun to rise as a result of the government's aggressive program of privatization, which has resulted in the closure of state-owned enterprises. Romania's public external debt is negligible.

The government appears to have achieved stability and is democratically elected. Its continued stability is, however, clearly linked to a level of economic success that must be both visible and of direct benefit to the general public.

Government actions to improve the economy have thus far included the development of a program to generate a higher level of foreign investment; currency devaluation; and the introduction of a floating exchange rate.

■ SUMMARY OF FOREIGN INVESTMENT POLICY

The two principal laws relevant to foreign investment in Romania are the Commercial Company Law of 1990 and the Foreign Investment Law of 1991. The Romanian Development Agency is the primary government office with respect to the promotion and development of foreign investment.

Areas of the economy that the government considers as being of priority interest in terms of foreign investment are services, to include banking, insurance, and consulting activities; consumer goods; tourism; transportation, to include automobile manufacturing; energy, to include both exploration and exploitation of energy sources; and manufacturing of telecommunications equipment.

The government's general policy on foreign investment is that foreign and domestic investors should be given equal access to investment opportunities; that there should be minimal governmental interference in investment activities; and that investors should have access to all markets and economic sectors.

Most economic activities are open to foreign investors. Among the principal areas not open to foreign investment are the manufacturing of ammunition, explosives, and pharmaceuticals.

All foreign investments must be registered with the Romanian Development Agency. The registration process begins with the filing of an application with the agency that sets out complete information about the investor and the investment as proposed. Upon acceptance of the proposal by the agency, a registration certificate is provided that entitles the investor to available incentives.

Tax incentives for firms engaged in the agricultural, industrial, and construction areas include a five-year profits tax holiday. Three-year tax holidays are available for firms engaged in communications, energy exploitation and exploration, communications and transportation activities. Firms active in tourism, banking, insurance, and other service areas are entitled to a two-year tax holiday. Subsequent tax reductions are available when a firm provides substantial employment opportunities; is active in the elimination of environmental problems; engages in research and development; or makes other uses of enterprise profits.

ROMANIA

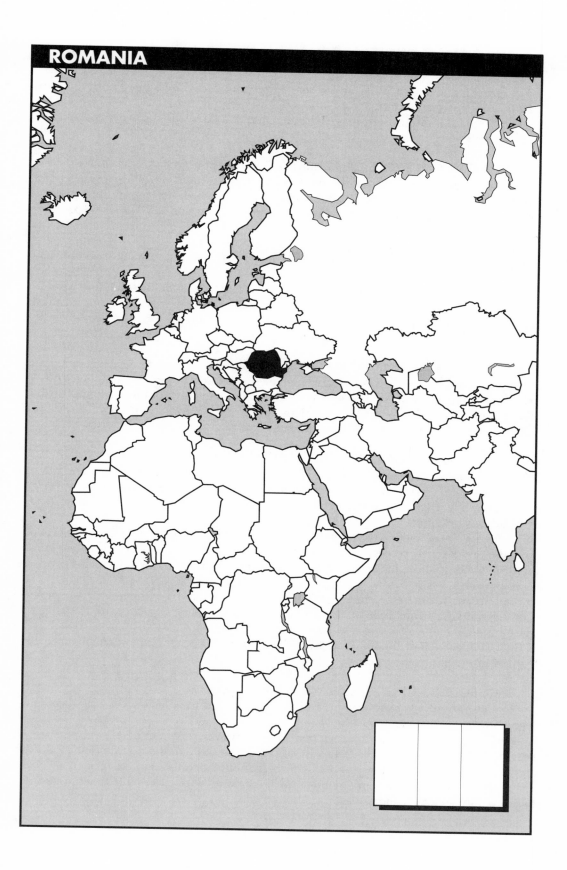

Equipment, machinery, tools, and other capital goods used by a foreign investor are exempt from customs duties.

There is no limit on the percentage of ownership of a domestic company that may be held by foreign investors.

■ FORMATION AND TYPES OF PERMITTED BUSINESS ORGANIZATIONS

Foreign investors may participate in the Romanian economy through the creation of a corporation either in the form of a joint stock or limited liability company; a general partnership; a limited partnership; a limited partnership by shares; or as a sole proprietorship.

Branch offices of foreign enterprises may be established.

There are no specific provisions for a joint venture. However, such organizations are formed as partnerships.

Foreign corporations represented by branch offices, and as joint stock and limited companies and partnerships, are considered to be legal entities and acquire juridical person status on the date that formation papers are filed with the Commerce Register.

The number of shareholders in a limited liability company cannot exceed 50.

■ ENVIRONMENTAL PROTECTION

The government has exhibited an increasing level of interest in the environment. Potential foreign investors are advised to contact the Romanian Development Agency or the Ministry of the Environment for complete and current information about laws and regulations pertaining to environmental protection.

■ RIGHTS AND OBLIGATIONS OF FOREIGN INVESTORS

There are guarantees against the nationalization, confiscation, expropriation, and other government takings of private property without proper legal process and as a result of public necessity. In the event of such an action, property owners are entitled to fair and prompt consideration.

All foreign investments and profits derived from such investments may be remitted abroad or repatriated subject to the payment of taxes that may be due. In the event of investment liquidation, the foreign investor may repatriate, or remit abroad, the proper share of such investment.

Profits may be reinvested in the same enterprise or in another Romanian enterprise.

Foreign investors are to be treated equally with domestic ones with respect to incentives that may be provided by the government.

Real property may be acquired by either natural or legal Romanian persons, to include Romanian companies that are controlled wholly or partially by foreign investors.

Local financing sources are available to foreign investors.

Foreign individuals cannot own land but are entitled to enter into leasing arrangements for real property.

Foreign nationals may import personal effects without payment of customs charges. Foreign individuals who have been employed in the country may, at the end of such employment, repatriate their personal effects without customs charges.

Romania has entered into many bilateral agreements with other nations with regard to mutual investment guarantees.

■ LABOR

The Romanian labor force is industrious and highly skilled.

There is a complete and extensive body of laws with regard to both employment and working conditions.

Foreign nationals may be employed only in managerial, scientific, or other positions where a special level or skill is required that is not locally available.

■ ACCOUNTING REQUIREMENTS

All business enterprises must maintain accurate and complete accounting records. Joint stock companies and limited liability companies with 15 or more shareholders must appoint auditors. Accounting activities must be in accord with internationally accepted standards.

■ CURRENCY CONTROLS

The Banca Nationala (the National Bank of Romania) is the nation's central bank. The bank is responsible for the management of the country's foreign exchange and related activities.

Foreign enterprises may maintain bank accounts in foreign currencies.

There are stringent foreign exchange controls that include restrictions on the movement of foreign exchange and Romanian currency both into and from the country.

Enterprises that are wholly or partially owned by foreign investors must open and maintain a domestic currency account in a Romanian bank and must employ that account to carry out business activities.

■ TAXATION

The principal tax is levied on corporate profits. Other taxes are assessed on personal income and on sales of most goods and services.

There are numerous deductions that may be taken from gross income to determine taxable profit that include but are not limited to legitimate business expenses; research and development costs, losses, and charitable contributions.

Romania has entered into many bilateral treaties with other nations on the subject of double taxation.

Potential foreign investors should be aware that the nation's tax laws are undergoing certain revisions. The Romanian Development Agency should be consulted for current and complete tax law information.

■ LEGAL SYSTEM

The court system essentially includes local courts that hear petty civil and criminal cases and county courts that are empowered to try more serious matters and that have appellate authority with regard to decisions of the local courts. Final appeals from the county courts are referred to the Supreme Court, which sits at Bucharest.

■ CUSTOMS AND DUTIES

Romania is a signatory to the General Agreement on Tariffs and Trade (GATT).

Import and export licenses are required.

Several free ports are being developed as part of the country's interest in expanding its level of foreign trade. In addition, Romania has instituted a customs draw back program with respect to imported goods that are subsequently exported.

Equipment, to include office equipment and supplies, to be used by a foreign investment, may be imported exempt from customs charges.

■ PROTECTION OF INTELLECTUAL PROPERTY

Romania is a member of the World Intellectual Property Organization, and is a signatory to the Paris Convention for the Protection of Industrial Property and the Madrid Convention for the International Register of Trademarks. In addition, domestic laws have been passed to provide protection for patents and trademarks.

■ IMMIGRATION AND RESIDENCE

Visas are required to enter the country. Potential foreign investors are advised to contact the Romanian Development Agency for current and complete information on the requirements for visas, work permits, and residence permits.

■ FOREIGN INVESTMENT ASSISTANCE DIRECTORY

Sources that can provide further information about foreign investment in Romania include:

Romanian Development Agency
7 Boulevard Magheru
Bucharest, Romania
Telephone: (40) (0) 156686 / (40) (0) 154698
Telex: 11027
Fax: (40) (0) 120371

Ministry of the Environment
12 Boulevard Libertatii
Bucharest, Romania
Telephone: (40) (0) 316104
Telex: 11457
Fax: (40) (0) 316486

National Bank of Romania
25 Lipscani Street
Bucharest, Romania
Telephone: (40) (0) 155528
Telex: 11136 BN BUCR
Fax: (40) (0) 145910

Persons interested in obtaining additional information about foreign investment in Romania are advised to contact the closest Romanian embassy or consular office.

Romania maintains diplomatic relations with Albania, Algeria, Argentina, Austria, Bangladesh, Belgium, Brazil, Bulgaria, Canada, Chile, People's Republic of China, Colombia, Congo, Costa Rica, Cuba, Czechoslovakia, Denmark, Ecuador, Egypt, Finland, France, Germany, Ghana, Greece, Guinea, Holy See, Hungary, India, Indonesia, Iran, Iraq, Israel, Italy, Japan, Jordan, Democratic People's Republic of Korea, Republic of Korea, Lebanon, Liberia, Libya, Malaysia, Mauritania, Mongolia, Morocco, Netherlands, Nigeria, Pakistan, Peru, Philippines, Poland, Russia, Spain, Sudan, Sweden, Switzerland, Syria, Thailand, Tunisia, Turkey, United Kingdom, United States, Uruguay, Venezuela, Vietnam, Yemen, and Zaire.

RUSSIA

■ POLITICAL ENVIRONMENT

The nation is engaged in working through the myriad problems that have been presented as a result of fundamental changes in government and economic philosophies.

It appears that governmental stability has been achieved. However, in the long term, stability will surely hinge on economic considerations.

Presently, Russia, as a nation, and its people are facing national and individual challenges that are created by democracy and the adoption of a free market economic system—both concepts with which neither the government nor the people have any experience.

If it can be understood, during the pressure of events, that democracy is not an economic panacea and that the benefits, despite their multiplicity, of the free market system, are long term, then both democracy and the free market will survive.

Meanwhile, the Russian government, still encumbered by an in-depth bureaucracy that continues to generate conflicting rules and regulations, is attempting to increase the level of foreign investment, is continuing an ongoing program of privatization, has become a member of the International Monetary Fund (IMF), and is seeking to play a more active part in world economic affairs.

■ SUMMARY OF FOREIGN INVESTMENT POLICY

The principal Russian law on the subject of foreign investment is the Legal Foundations for Foreign Investments Act of 1990.

All foreign investments must be approved or accredited by the government office involved, e.g., the Ministry of Foreign Economic Relations, the State Bank of the Russian Federation, and others, as may be appropriate.

Foreign investors may hold 100 percent ownership in an enterprise established in Russia; investment may take the form of property, securities, or shares, and may include partial ownership with Russian investors.

The government is interested in receiving proposals, in most cases, from major international companies that can provide modern technology, increase the nation's overall economic development, and help to develop export trade.

Foreign investment is restricted with reference to those economic activities involving national defense, internal security, telecommunications, air and surface transportation, and the financial sector.

Information that must be provided to the appropriate accrediting office includes the period of time that the investment will be carried out, the number of foreign nationals that will be employed, any conditions under which the investment will function, and the purpose of the investment.

Incentives may include tax holidays and other tax and non-tax benefits for enterprises that are at least 30 percent owned by foreign investors and that are established in certain geographic areas of the country.

■ FORMATION AND TYPES OF PERMITTED BUSINESS ORGANIZATIONS

Foreign investors may participate in the Russian economy through the operation of wholly owned subsidiaries of foreign corporations, through joint ventures, i.e., joint enterprises, with one or more Russian partners, or as joint stock companies.

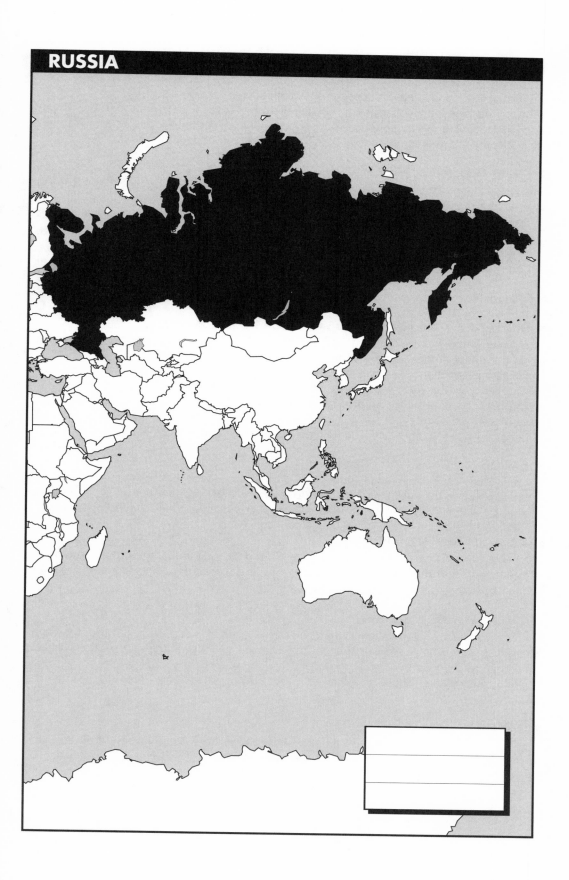

RUSSIA

Foreign firms may also open representatives offices.

Joint enterprises are considered to be legal entities upon registration with the Ministry of Finance. However, potential foreign investors are cautioned that Russian law on the subject of limited legal liability is still in the process of development.

■ ENVIRONMENTAL PROTECTION

The issue of environmental protection has only recently taken on a relatively high degree of priority in Russia. There is a central government office, the Ministry of Ecology and Use of Natural Resources, that is charged with the development and monitoring of a national policy on this subject. Local officials are also becoming more involved in environmental efforts.

Potential foreign investors are advised to contact the Ministry of Ecology and Use of Natural Resources, as well as any appropriate local authorities, with regard to laws and regulations pertaining to environmental protection.

■ RIGHTS AND OBLIGATIONS OF FOREIGN INVESTORS

The government has guaranteed that foreign and domestic investors will be granted equal treatment and legal protection.

Foreign investments and income generated from such investments may be repatriated or remitted abroad, or reinvested in Russia.

Concessions may be granted to foreign enterprises for the development of natural resources in the country.

Foreign investors may seek financing from Russian and foreign banks.

■ LABOR

There is a large labor force with uneven educational and skill levels. An extensive body of laws exists on the subjects of working conditions and employment.

Foreign nationals employed in Russia must obtain both work and residence permits.

■ ACCOUNTING REQUIREMENTS

All enterprises, including joint enterprises and foreign subsidiaries, must maintain complete and accurate accounting and other financial records. All enterprises are subject to auditing by the government.

■ CURRENCY CONTROLS

The State Bank of the Russian Federation is the country's central bank and has been given responsibility for establishing control relevant to the exchange rate of the Russian currency unit, the ruble.

Foreign investors should be aware that the ruble is not yet considered to be convertible.

■ TAXATION

The major tax assessed is that on enterprise income. There are a variety of other taxes to include import and export taxes, a consumption tax, a turnover tax, a sales tax, a documents (stamp) tax, and numerous registration and license fees.

The tax year is the same as the calendar year, i.e., from January 1 to December 31, for all taxpayers.

Tax deductions include, but are not limited to, those for depreciation of physical assets; research and development; employee income and benefits, and interest payments on bank loans.

Joint enterprises, foreign subsidiary corporations, domestic corporations, and representative offices of foreign companies are considered to be taxable entities.

Individual taxpayers may claim several dependents as a deduction.

Russia is a signatory to bilateral treaties with numerous nations on the subject of double taxation.

■ LEGAL SYSTEM

The Russian court system includes local (magistrates' level) courts; and district (regional) courts that function at the trial court level regarding civil and criminal matters. Appeals may be taken to the Supreme Court of the Russian Federation, which sits at Moscow.

■ CUSTOMS AND DUTIES

The government is interested in increasing its levels of foreign trade and has moved toward acquiring full participation through the General Agreement on Tariffs and Trade (GATT). Export and import licenses are required for significant numbers and types of goods.

Goods may be imported without payment of customs fees if they are reexported within one year from date of importation.

■ PROTECTION OF INTELLECTUAL PROPERTY

Russia is a member of the World Intellectual Property Organization. The government has enacted some legislation that is designed to protect interests in copyrights, patents, trademarks, and other forms of intellectual property. Potential foreign investors should contact the Ministry of External Economic Relations pertaining to the complete and current status of the entire body of laws on intellectual property, which are presently undergoing review.

■ IMMIGRATION AND RESIDENCE

Visas are required to enter the country. Special visas are available for business purposes. Potential foreign investors should contact the Ministry of External Economic Relations for complete and current information about visas, work permits, and residence permits.

■ FOREIGN INVESTMENT ASSISTANCE DIRECTORY

Sources that can provide further information about foreign investment in Russia include:

Ministry of External Economic Relations
Smolenskaya-Sennaya Square, 32-34
121200 Moscow, Russia
Telephone: (7) (095) 2201350

Ministry of Ecology and Use of Natural Resources
Vadkovsky, 18-20
101474 Moscow, Russia
Telephone: (7) (095) 2893065

State Bank of the Russian Federation
Zhitnaya, 4
Moscow, Russia
Telephone: (7) (095) 2373065

Chamber of Commerce and Industry of the Russian Federation
Ilyinka, 6
103864 Moscow, Russia
Telephone: (7) (095) 9234323
Fax: (7) (095) 2302455

Persons interested in obtaining additional information about foreign investment in Russia are advised to contact the closest Russian embassy or consular office.

Russia maintains diplomatic relations with Afghanistan, Albania, Algeria, Angola, Argentina, Armenia, Australia, Austria, Bahrain, Bangladesh, Belgium, Benin, Bolivia, Brazil, Bulgaria, Burkina Faso, Burundi, Cambodia, Cameroon, Canada, Cape Verde, Central African Republic, Chad, Chile, People's Republic of China, Colombia, Congo, Costa Rica, Côte d'Ivoire, Cuba, Cyprus, Czechoslovakia, Denmark, Ecuador, Egypt, Equatorial Guinea, Estonia, Ethiopia, Finland, France, Gabon, Germany, Ghana, Greece, Guinea, Guinea-Bissau, Guyana, Holy See, Hungary, Iceland, India, Indonesia, Iran, Iraq, Ireland, Israel, Italy, Jamaica, Japan, Jordan, Kenya, Democratic People's Republic of Korea, Republic of Korea, Kuwait, Laos, Latvia, Lebanon, Libya, Lithuania, Luxembourg, Madagascar, Malaysia, Mali, Malta, Mauritania, Mexico, Mongolia, Morocco, Mozambique, Myanmar, Namibia, Nepal, Netherlands, New Zealand, Nicaragua, Niger, Nigeria, Norway, Oman, Pakistan, Peru, Philippines, Poland, Portugal, Qatar, Romania, Rwanda, Saudi Arabia, Senegal, Sierra Leone, Singapore, Somalia, South Africa, Spain, Sri Lanka, Sudan, Sweden, Switzerland, Syria, Tanzania, Thailand, Togo, Tunisia, Turkey, Uganda, United Arab Emirates, United Kingdom, United States, Uruguay, Venezuela, Vietnam, Yemen, Zaire, Zambia, and Zimbabwe.

Saint Christopher and Nevis, Federation of

■ POLITICAL ENVIRONMENT

The government is relatively stable. Its economy is largely dependent on sugar exports and tourism. There is a strong interest in diversification of the economy to provide some insulation against the inherent weaknesses of agriculture.

Inflation and unemployment rates are both low.

■ SUMMARY OF FOREIGN INVESTMENT POLICY

In order to diversify its present industrial and export base, the government is interested in obtaining increased levels of foreign investment. It has established the Investment Promotion Agency that is charged with the responsibility of promoting foreign investment. The Ministry of Trade, Industry and Development is also involved in that effort.

The government is particularly interested in acquiring foreign investment in the agricultural section, in tourism, and in accelerating the development of the country's industrial sector, with special attention being focused on light industry. Three industrial estates are in existence.

Numerous types of incentives are being offered to foreign investors including several developed industrial estates, tax holidays and rebates, and customs exemptions.

Foreign investors are required to submit proposals to the Investment Promotion Agency. Preliminary discussions with the government ministry directly concerned with the prospective investment should be undertaken, i.e., the Ministry of Trade, Industry and Development, or the Ministry of Agriculture, Lands, Housing and Development, and generally, in all cases, the Ministry of Finance.

All factories must be registered and inspected by the Ministry of Agriculture, Lands, Housing and Development.

■ FORMATION AND TYPES OF PERMITTED BUSINESS ORGANIZATIONS

Foreign investors may form corporations, partnerships, or sole proprietorships as well as operating through subsidiaries. All companies must be registered under the provision of the country's Company Act.

Corporations enjoy juridical person status.

Joint ventures may be formed with domestic enterprises.

■ ENVIRONMENTAL PROTECTION

Potential foreign investors are advised to contact the Investment Promotion Agency for complete and current information about laws and regulations pertaining to environmental protection.

■ RIGHTS AND OBLIGATIONS OF FOREIGN INVESTORS

Foreign investors purchasing land must obtain an Aliens Land Holding License from the Ministry of Agriculture.

Raw materials may be imported after obtaining a license from the Ministry of Trade, Industry and Development.

Local financing is available to foreign investors.

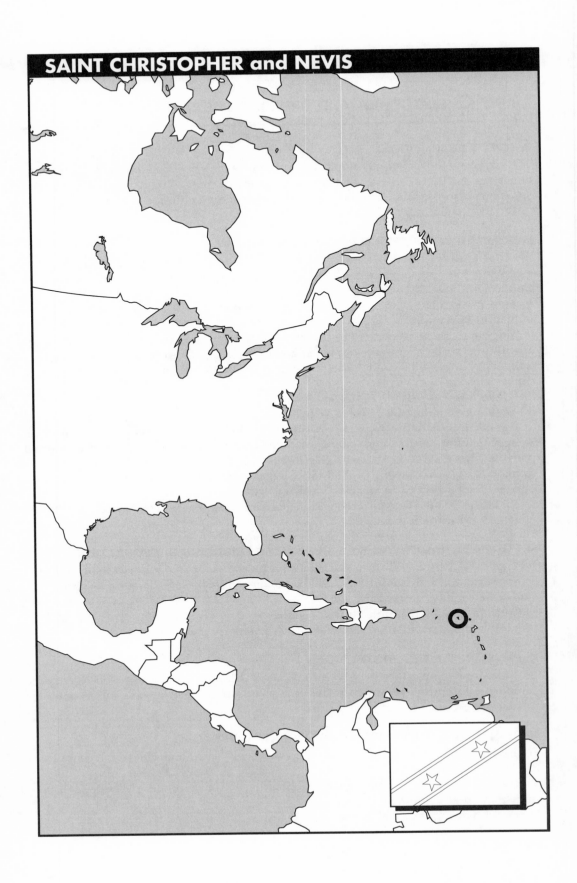

There is an investment protection guarantee agreement between the government and the United States.

Capital investments and all profits, dividends, and royalties derived from the investment may be repatriated or remitted abroad after payment of taxes. Such repatriation or remittance is accomplished through procedures established by the Ministry of Finance.

■ LABOR

There is an existing body of laws regarding employment and working conditions. The labor force is motivated and is generally unionized.

There is a hiring preference for local labor. Foreign nationals must obtain work permits.

■ ACCOUNTING REQUIREMENTS

All companies must maintain accurate financial records in accord with internationally accepted accounting and auditing standards.

■ CURRENCY CONTROLS

The Eastern Caribbean Central Bank is charged with the responsibility of currency issue and exchange control.

Foreign currency taken into the country must be sold to an approved local bank. Investors may open and maintain bank accounts in local currency.

Foreign assets must be registered with the St. Kitts National Bank.

■ TAXATION

The country has entered in numerous treaties relevant to double taxation. Such agreements include those with the United States, New Zealand, Norway, Sweden, Switzerland, Jamaica, Barbados, Trinidad and Tobago, and Guyana.

There is no tax on personal income.

Among the tax incentives available to foreign investors are a total tax holiday relevant to corporate income tax for up to 15 years and additional tax exemptions of 75 percent on corporate earnings derived from exports.

Firms engaged in the tourism industry are eligible for special tax incentives.

There is no tax imposed on capital gains.

In general, taxes imposed on corporate income have been reduced over the past several years. There are a variety of minor taxes including those on services and motor vehicles.

■ LEGAL SYSTEM

There are Magistrates' Courts that handle minor civil and criminal matters, and High Courts that function at the trial level. Appeals are taken to the Court of Appeals and to the Supreme Court, both of which sit in St. Lucia.

■ CUSTOMS AND DUTIES

Raw materials and equipment that are to be used in manufacturing or other businesses are exempt from customs duties.

The country is a member of the Caribbean Common Market (CARICOM) and is a signatory to the Lome Convention.

An export processing zone is under development.

■ PROTECTION OF INTELLECTUAL PROPERTY

Foreign investors are advised to contact the Investment Promotion Agency relevant to current information about the protection of copyrights, tradenames, trademarks, patents, and technology transfer.

■ IMMIGRATION AND RESIDENCE

Visas are required depending on the visitor's country of origin. Visas have a valid duration of six months and may be renewed.

Work permits are required for all foreign employees. Permits are valid for one year and may be renewed.

Potential foreign investors are advised to contact the Investment Promotion Agency for complete and current information regarding visas, work permits and residence permits.

■ FOREIGN INVESTMENT ASSISTANCE DIRECTORY

Sources that can provide additional information about foreign investment in St. Christopher and Nevis include:

Investment Promotion Agency
P.O. Box 600
Bay Road, St. Christopher
Telephone: (809) 465-4106
Telex: 6852 IPA KC

Ministry of Trade, Industry and Development
P.O. Box 186
Government House
Church Street
Basseterre, St. Christopher
Telephone: (809) 465-2302

Ministry of Finance
Government House
Church Street
Basseterre, St. Christopher
Telephone: (809) 465-2612

Ministry of Agriculture, Lands, Housing and Development
Government House
Church Street
Basseterre, St. Christopher
Telephone: (809) 465-2521

Eastern Caribbean Central Bank
P.O. Box 89
Basseterre, St. Christopher
Telephone: (809) 465-2536
Telex: 6828
Fax: 465-1051

St. Kitts-Nevis National Bank Ltd.
P.O. Box 343
Church Street
Basseterre, St. Christopher
Telephone: (809) 465-2205
Telex: 6826

St. Kitts-Nevis Chamber of Commerce and Industry
P.O. Box 232
South Square Street
Basseterre, St. Christopher
Telephone: (809) 465-2980
Telex: 6822
Fax: (809) 465-4490

Persons interested in obtaining further information about investing in St. Christopher and Nevis also are advised to contact the country's closest embassy or consular office.

St. Christopher and Nevis maintain diplomatic relations with Antigua and Barbuda, Argentina, Austria, Barbados, Canada, Chile, Republic of China (Taiwan), Denmark, El Salvador, France, Germany, Guatemala, Guyana, India, Israel, Jamaica, Japan, People's Democratic Republic of Korea, Republic of Korea, Malaysia, Mexico, Netherlands, Nicaragua, Norway, Peru, Seychelles, Singapore, Spain, United Kingdom, United States, Uruguay, and Venezuela.

SAINT LUCIA

■ POLITICAL ENVIRONMENT

The government appears to be stable. There are some economic strains, notably in the form of increasing unemployment. Inflation is low to moderate.

Agriculture and tourism dominate the nation's economy. There is a strong government desire to achieve economic diversification. This goal would be achieved, pursuant to the government's plan, by increasing the country's manufacturing base.

■ SUMMARY OF FOREIGN INVESTMENT POLICY

There is a major interest in acquiring foreign investment. The government has created the St. Lucia National Development Corporation as the principal agency charged with the responsibility of developing investment from foreign sources. This agency acts to create a relationship between potential foreign investors and the Ministry of Trade and Industry.

All foreign companies operating in St. Lucia must obtain a trade license every year.

The government has devised numerous incentives that are available to foreign investors. Included among such incentives are the creation of free trade zones; completely functioning industrial estates at various locations; and long-term (i.e., periods ranging up to 15 years) tax holidays. In addition, foreign investors may import raw materials, spare parts, tools, and machinery for use in production on a customs-exempt basis.

Subsequent to the expiration of the long-term tax holiday, the government will grant tax relief in the form of a deduction or allowance from the profits tax.

Applications for tax incentives must be filed by foreign investors with the Ministry of Trade and Industry. A trade license is a prerequisite to filing for any tax incentives offered by the government.

■ FORMATION AND TYPES OF PERMITTED BUSINESS ORGANIZATIONS

Foreign investors may participate in the national economy through the formation of public or closed corporations, general or limited partnerships, or sole proprietorships.

Subsidiaries of foreign corporations may be established. Foreign investors may form joint ventures with domestic partners and, in fact, such joint ventures are encouraged by the government.

Corporations acquire juridical person status.

There are no requirements for domestic managerial participation in a foreign enterprise. Businesses may be wholly funded by foreign capital.

■ ENVIRONMENTAL PROTECTION

There is a very high level of interest on the part of the government regarding protection of the environment. Potential foreign investors are advised to contact the National Development Corporation for complete and current information on laws and regulations intended to provide environmental protection.

■ RIGHTS AND OBLIGATIONS OF FOREIGN INVESTORS

Foreign investors are guaranteed equal rights with domestic ones.

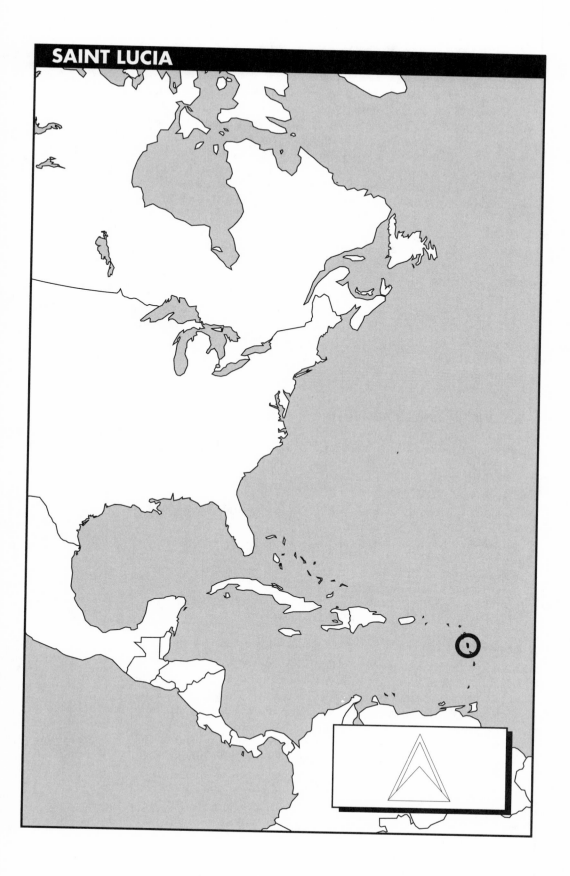

Financing may be obtained by foreign investors either directly from local sources or through an application filed with the National Development Corporation.

Foreign investments and income from such investments may be remitted abroad or repatriated at any time subject only to the payment of outstanding taxes.

Investment guarantees are available to United States investors granted under the provisions of the Overseas Private Investment Corporation (OPIC).

Licenses may be obtained by foreign investors for the purpose of acquiring, through leasing and other means, real property and mortgages on such property.

■ LABOR

The labor force of St. Lucia is considered to be highly motivated, intelligent, and generally skilled. A comprehensive body of laws exists with regard to employment and working conditions.

Foreign enterprises must, except in cases where special skills are not locally available, hire from the available labor force. Work permits must be obtained for foreign workers. When foreign nationals are employed, it is usually required that a local worker be hired for the purpose of being trained, in as short a time period as possible, to fill the position.

The Ministry of Health, Housing and Labor is the agency responsible for issuing work permits, which are valid for a period of 12 months.

■ ACCOUNTING REQUIREMENTS

All companies must maintain complete and accurate financial and other records. Accounting records must be maintained in accord with internationally accepted standards. Public companies must be audited on a yearly basis.

■ CURRENCY CONTROLS

The Eastern Caribbean Central Bank operates as the central bank for St. Lucia. The bank is located in St. Christopher.

Purchases of foreign currency are controlled. Permission must be obtained from the Ministry of Finance.

Foreign investors desiring to maintain accounts in United States currency must request permission from the Ministry of Finance.

Businesses operating in the free trade zones are generally granted permission to open and maintain foreign currency accounts.

■ TAXATION

Both foreign businesses and individuals are subject to the tax law of St. Lucia.

The major tax is levied on businesses and individual income. There are other taxes to include those on property, customs, foreign exchange, and documents.

A variety of allowances and deductions are available to include those relevant to business expenses and depreciation of plant and equipment. Tax incentives made available by the government include provisions for long-term tax holidays and significant tax reductions designed to encourage foreign investment. Export tax concessions are also available.

St. Lucia is a party to treaties with numerous nations on the subject of double taxation.

■ LEGAL SYSTEM

The judicial system includes Magistrates' Courts, which hear petty criminal cases, and High Courts that hear more serious criminal and civil matters. Appeals are taken to the Court of Appeal. Both the High Court and the Court of Appeal are part of the Eastern Caribbean Supreme Court, which functions as a regional court to serve the needs of Grenada, St. Lucia, the British Virgin Islands, St. Christopher and Nevis, St. Vincent, and the Grenadines.

Appeals from the Eastern Caribbean Supreme Court's appellate jurisdiction are taken to the Judicial Committee of the Privy Council in the United Kingdom.

■ CUSTOMS AND DUTIES

St. Lucia is a member of the Caribbean Common Market (CARICOM), which is a group of Caribbean countries that are intending to create an essentially duty free trade bloc. In addition, St. Lucia is a signatory to the Lome Convention, which provides certain advantages when engaged in trade with members of the European Community (EC).

The nation also participates in the Generalized System of Preferences in terms of trade with the United States and through CARIBAN with Canada.

Licenses are required to import certain products.

There are minimal customs requirements encountered with regard to the importation of raw materials or finished products that are received in the free trade zones.

■ PROTECTION OF INTELLECTUAL PROPERTY

Potential foreign investors are urged to contact the National Development Corporation for current information regarding the nation's position relevant to the protection of interests in copyrights, trademarks, and patents.

■ IMMIGRATION AND RESIDENCE

Visas are not usually required to enter the country. Individuals residing in St. Lucia for more than six months and desiring to attain temporary residence status may file an application with the Office of the Prime Minister. Individuals who have resided in St. Lucia for seven years may file for permanent residence.

Potential foreign investors are advised to contact the National Development Corporation for more complete and current information on visas, work permits, and residence permits.

■ FOREIGN INVESTMENT ASSISTANCE DIRECTORY

Sources that can provide further information about foreign investment in St. Lucia include:

National Development Corporation
P.O. Box 495
27 Brazil Street
Castries, St. Lucia, West Indies
Telephone: (809) 452-3614 / (809) 452-3615
Telex: 341-6387 NDC SLU LC

Ministry of Finance, Statistics, Development and Negotiations
Old Government Buildings
Laborie Street
Castries, St. Lucia, West Indies
Telephone: (809) 452-5315
Telex: 6223
Fax: (809) 453-1648

Ministry of Health, Housing and Labor
Chausee Road
Castries, St. Lucia, West Indies
Telephone: (809) 452-2827

Ministry of Trade, Industry and Tourism
NIS Building
John Compton Highway
Castries, St. Lucia, West Indies
Telephone: (809) 452-2429

Eastern Caribbean Central Bank
P.O. Box 89
Basseterre, St. Christopher
Telephone: (809) 465-2537
Telex: 6828
Fax: (809) 465-1051

St. Lucia Chamber of Commerce, Industry and Agriculture
P.O. Box 482
Monplaisir Building
Brazil Street
Castries, St. Lucia, West Indies
Telephone: (809) 452-3165
Fax: (809) 452-6907

Persons interested in obtaining additional information about foreign investment in St. Lucia are advised to contact the country's closest embassy or consular office.

St. Lucia maintains diplomatic relations with Republic of China (Taiwan), France, United Kingdom, and Venezuela.

SAINT VINCENT AND THE GRENADINES

■ POLITICAL ENVIRONMENT

This country has a stable and democratically elected government.

Agriculture, to include commercial fishing, is the nation's principal economic activity. Bananas are the major crop. Tourism is a burgeoning industry.

The government has acted to expand and modernize the country's infrastructure to support a growth-oriented economy.

Inflation is moderate. Unemployment, however, is quite high.

■ SUMMARY OF FOREIGN INVESTMENT POLICY

The government is seeking to acquire additional foreign investment. The principal government agency that has been designated to promote foreign investment is The Development Corporation. The St. Vincent and the Grenadines Chamber of Commerce and Industry is also active in promoting the nation with reference to foreign investors.

Foreign investment is particularly desired in the tourism, large-scale agriculture, and commercial fishing industries.

There are no economic areas that appear to be considered closed to foreign investors.

No restrictions are imposed on the percentage of any companies that may be held by foreign investors.

Incentives that are made available by the government to foreign investors include special tax considerations, low-cost financing, and (for major investments in agriculture), government financial assistance relevant to planting and crop propagation, as well as customs exemptions for necessary equipment and materials.

Modern industrial facilities have been developed at several locations to meet the needs of smaller industrial companies.

■ FORMATION AND TYPES OF PERMITTED BUSINESS ORGANIZATIONS

Foreign investors may participate in the national economy through the creation of public or private corporations, general or limited partnerships, or as sole proprietorships. Subsidiaries and branch offices of foreign corporations may be established. Joint ventures may be created between foreign and domestic investors.

Corporations acquire a juridical person status.

There are no requirements with regard to either local participation in company management or in an ownership capacity with regard to foreign investments.

■ ENVIRONMENTAL PROTECTION

The government maintains a continuing interest in all matters relevant to the environment. A cabinet level position, the Ministry of Health and Environment has the responsibility of recommending laws and regulations pertaining to the protection of the environment.

Potential foreign investors are advised to contact either The Development Corporation or the Ministry of Health and Environment with regard to current or proposed laws and regulations relevant to this subject.

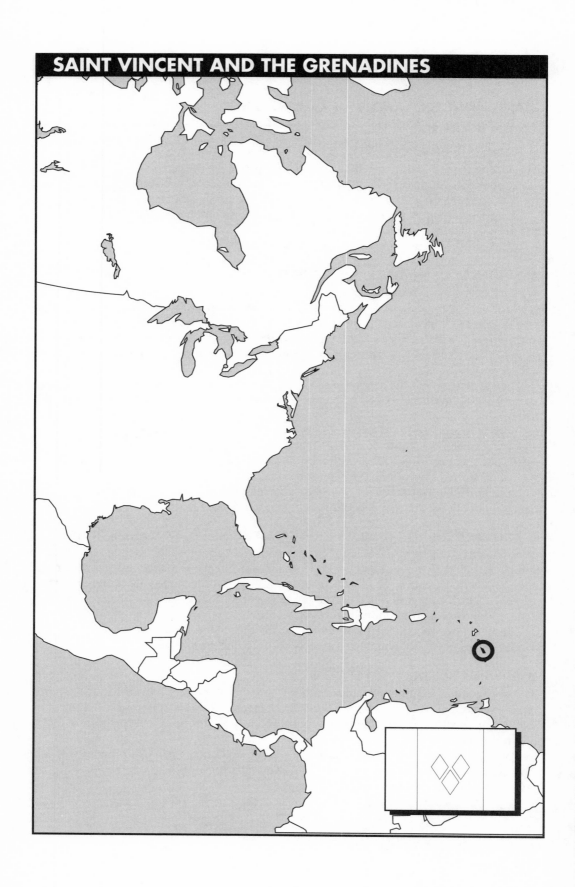

■ RIGHTS AND OBLIGATIONS OF FOREIGN INVESTORS

Foreign investors are guaranteed equal protection of the law and equal rights to business opportunities.

Foreign investments and income derived from such investments may be freely repatriated or remitted abroad.

Local sources of financing are available to foreign investors.

Foreign property interests are guaranteed to be protected against any nationalization or expropriation. Any required taking of private property by the government for any purpose must be under color of law and must give rise to fair compensation.

■ LABOR

There is a comprehensive body of laws in existence with regard to employment and working conditions.

The labor force is well educated and motivated.

Foreign nationals employed in St. Vincent and the Grenadines must possess work permits.

■ ACCOUNTING REQUIREMENTS

All companies operating in the country must maintain an accurate and complete accounting and financial system. Public companies must be audited yearly by a chartered accountant.

■ CURRENCY CONTROLS

The Eastern Caribbean Central Bank, with its main office located at Saint Christopher, functions as the country's central bank.

Foreign businesses and individuals may open and maintain bank accounts in foreign currencies.

Foreign employees may remit or repatriate their income subject to payment of required taxes.

■ TAXATION

The major tax assessed is on business income. There are a variety of taxes including customs charges, property taxes, and license and registration fees. A departure tax is imposed on individuals remaining in the country for a period of more than 24 hours.

■ LEGAL SYSTEM

The court system includes three levels. The Magistrates' Court is empowered to decide petty offenses. The High Court, which sits at Saint Lucia, is the trial court and hears more serious criminal issues and civil matters, as well as hearing appeals from the Magistrates' Courts. Final appeals are taken to the Court of Appeal of the Eastern Caribbean Supreme Court, which also sits at Saint Lucia.

■ CUSTOMS AND DUTIES

There is a strong government interest in developing an increased level of foreign trade, particularly in terms of manufacturing for export.

The country is a member of CARICOM, a group of nations formed into a regional common market arrangement. It also enjoys certain trading benefits through the Lome

Convention relevant to exports to the EC, and under both the U.S. and Canadian trade arrangements through the CARIBAN and Caribbean Basin initiatives, respectively.

■ PROTECTION OF INTELLECTUAL PROPERTY

The country is not a member of the World Intellectual Property Organization although the protection afforded to copyrights, patents, trademarks, and technology transfer under various laws enacted in the United Kingdom may be applicable.

■ IMMIGRATION AND RESIDENCE

Visas are required to visit the country, depending on the visitor's citizenship.

Potential foreign investors are advised to contact The Development Corporation, or the St. Vincent and the Grenadines Chamber of Commerce and Industry for complete information pertaining to the requirements for visas, work permits, and residence permits.

■ FOREIGN INVESTMENT ASSISTANCE DIRECTORY

Sources that can provide further information about foreign investment in Saint Vincent and the Grenadines include:

The Development Corporation
P.O. Box 841
Kingstown, St. Vincent
Telephone: (809) 457-1358
Fax: (809) 457-2838

St. Vincent and the Grenadines Chamber of Commerce and Industry
P.O. Box 134
Kingstown, St. Vincent
Telephone: (809) 457-1464
Fax: (809) 457-2944

Ministry of Health and Environment
Government Offices
Kingstown, St. Vincent
Telephone: (809) 457-6111

Persons interested in obtaining additional information about foreign investment in Saint Vincent and the Grenadines are advised to contact the country's closest embassy or consular office.

St. Vincent and the Grenadines maintains diplomatic relations with the Republic of China (Taiwan), United Kingdom, and Venezuela.

SAUDI ARABIA, KINGDOM OF

■ POLITICAL ENVIRONMENT

The government is very stable. Saudi Arabia has a very high standard of living and a strong economy based almost exclusively on the export of petroleum, natural gas, and related products.

Inflation and unemployment rates are extremely low.

The principal government interest in terms of long-range economic development lies in the recognized need to expand the nation's industrial base and to reduce Saudi Arabia's heavy dependence on petroleum and related activities.

■ SUMMARY OF FOREIGN INVESTMENT POLICY

A key element of the government's Fifth Five Year Development Plan (January 1990-December 1994) is the acquisition of foreign investment. The principal law applied to this area is the Foreign Capital Investment Law that, among other salient points, created the Foreign Capital Investment Committee, which is directly responsible to the Ministry of Industry and Electricity.

All foreign investments and industrial firms must obtain licenses from the Ministry of Industry and Electricity. License applications are made through the Foreign Capital Investment Committee.

The main interests of the government regarding foreign investments include the promotion of non-petroleum oil revenues, substitution of locally manufactured products for imports, and economic development throughout the entire nation.

There are no restrictions on the use of foreign investment regarding industrial activities. While there are no restrictions on 100 percent ownership, it is the desire of the government to promote joint ventures between foreign and domestic interests.

Numerous incentives are available to foreign investors principally in the form of tax considerations and credit. Exemptions from the income and company taxes are only available to enterprises where invested Saudi capital is equal to at least 25 percent of the total investment and is not reduced at any time during the life of the investment.

Foreign investments are limited to projects that are part of the National Development Plan. Such projects are considered to be valuable to the national interest and generally include those relating to industrial development, agricultural production, health services, service sector development, and infrastructure development.

The government's tax incentives are primarily long-term tax holidays and customs exemptions. Loans are available to eligible projects, i.e., those involved in activities within the National Development Plan. These loans are provided by the government, principally through the Saudi Development Fund. All loans are provided with no interest charges and can, depending on the activity, range from 50 to 80 percent of project cost.

Additionally, the government has established two industrial cities, Yanbu and Jubail. Enterprises formed in either of these locations are eligible for other government incentives including public utilities, plant sites, and worker training. The government, depending on the size of the enterprise, may agree to act as a joint venture partner with regard to activities in these two areas.

Special foreign investment rules are in effect with regard to investors from any of the

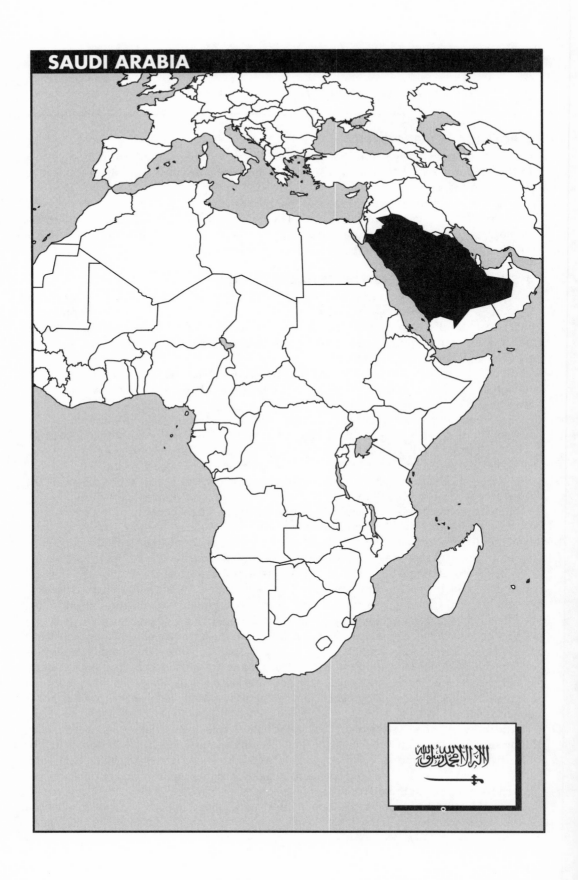

SAUDI ARABIA

other member states of the Cooperation Council of the Arab Gulf States (GCC). There are particular customs advantages available between GCC members.

■ FORMATION AND TYPES OF PERMITTED BUSINESS ORGANIZATIONS

According to law, foreign investors may create corporations, general and limited partnerships, partnerships limited by shares, and derivatives of such business organizations, i.e., variable capital companies and cooperative companies, which are partnership and corporate forms, respectively.

Foreign investors may also establish joint ventures with the government or domestic private investors.

Most foreign investors create a limited liability company, which is a hybrid organization with some characteristics of a corporation (in terms of limited liability) and some of a partnership. Partners must number no less than two and no more than 50.

There are limitations on the operations of limited liability companies to the extent that they may not be used to carry on financial or insurance activities.

Foreign investors may also establish branches in Saudi Arabia if the need for total foreign control of the branch can be shown to exist. Foreign companies with less than 25 to 50 percent Saudi participation are not eligible for tax incentives.

In general, because of the stated interest of the government, joint ventures seem to be the preferred method of foreign investment in Saudi Arabia.

■ ENVIRONMENTAL PROTECTION

Potential foreign investors are advised to contact the Ministry of Industry and Electricity or the Foreign Capital Investment Committee relevant to current laws and regulations pertaining to environmental protection.

■ RIGHTS AND OBLIGATIONS OF FOREIGN INVESTORS

Foreign investors are guaranteed equality of treatment and opportunity with domestic ones. However, there is a preference granted to local companies with regard to obtaining government contracts.

Low-cost financing is available to foreign investors from government sources.

Foreign investments and all income, including profits and interest, may be remitted abroad or repatriated after payment of all due taxes.

Real property may not be held by foreign companies.

■ LABOR

There is a complete body of laws regarding employment and working conditions. Work permits must be possessed by foreign nationals employed in the country. Any employment that will require staying in the country for more than three months requires the issuance of a residence permit. Both permits are issued by the Ministry of Labor and Social Affairs.

Foreign nationals may be hired without government approval until and unless the percentage of Saudi workers becomes less than 75 percent of the work force or where total wages or salaries paid to Saudi employees becomes less than 51 percent of overall employee compensation.

It is expected that foreign employers will train Saudi workers to fill positions held by foreign nationals.

■ ACCOUNTING REQUIREMENTS

All companies are required to maintain accurate financial records according to accepted international standards. Joint stock companies and limited liability companies are required to have financial statements prepared by an independent auditor on a yearly basis.

■ CURRENCY CONTROLS

The functions of a central bank are carried out by the Saudi Arabian Monetary Agency. There are no exchange controls in effect.

Foreign companies and individuals may open and maintain bank accounts in any currency.

■ TAXATION

There is no personal income tax assessed on employees. A tax is levied on the incomes of self-employed individuals.

Limited liability companies are considered to be taxpaying entities. Partnerships are not. Partnership income is considered to be that of the partners.

Joint ventures are considered as partnerships for tax paying purposes.

Depreciation, losses, and other business expenses are deductible.

Companies active in the petroleum and hydrocarbon industries are subject to a different tax rate than firms engaged in other activities.

Tax returns must be filed within three months of the end of the taxpaying entity's accounting or fiscal year, unless the calendar year is selected by the taxpayer.

As previously noted, tax holidays may be granted that can range from a period of five to 10 years.

■ LEGAL SYSTEM

The Saudi court system includes summary courts, which essentially hear and decide minor cases; general courts, which are responsible for deciding more serious criminal matters; and the Court of Cassation, which hears major civil cases and some criminal cases.

Final appeals are taken to the Supreme Court of Justice, which sits in Riyadh.

■ CUSTOMS AND DUTIES

The customs duties charged range from 12 to 30 percent. There is some protection of local industry. There are no free trade zones.

Foreign nationals may not act as importers.

Special customs provisions are in effect among the members of the Arab League. In addition, Saudi Arabia has entered into bilateral trade agreements with other Arab countries that involve special trade provisions.

■ PROTECTION OF INTELLECTUAL PROPERTY

Saudi Arabia is a member of the World Intellectual Property Organization. In addition, there are domestic laws to cover the protection of trademarks, copyrights, and patents.

■ IMMIGRATION AND RESIDENCE

Visas are required to enter Saudi Arabia. Potential foreign investors are advised to contact the Foreign Capital Investment Committee or the Ministry of Industry and Electricity for complete and current information on the requirements for visas, work permits, and residence permits.

■ FOREIGN INVESTMENT ASSISTANCE DIRECTORY

Sources that can provide additional information about foreign investment in Saudi Arabia include:

Foreign Capital Investment Committee
P.O. Box 5729
Omar bin Al-Khatab Road
Riyadh, Saudi Arabia 11127
Telephone: (966) (1) 4775302

Ministry of Industry and Electricity
P.O. Box 5729
Omar bin Al-Khatab Road
Riyadh, Saudi Arabia 11127
Telephone: (966) (1) 4772722
Telex: 401154 INDEL SJ

Saudi Arabian Monetary Agency
P.O. Box 2992
Riyadh, Saudi Arabia 11461
Telephone: (966) (1) 4636000
Telex: 400350 SAMA SJ

Saudi Industrial Development Fund
P.O. Box 4143
Riyadh, Saudi Arabia 11491
Telephone: (966) (1) 4774002
Telex: 401065 SAMA SJ

Council of Saudi Arabian Chambers of Commerce
P.O. Box 16683
Riyadh Chamber of Commerce and Industry Building
Riyadh, Saudi Arabia 11474
Telephone: (966) (1) 4053200
Telex: 405808
Fax: (966) (1) 402747

Persons interested in obtaining further information about foreign investment in Saudi Arabia are advised to contact the nation's closest embassy or consular office.

Saudi Arabia maintains diplomatic relations with Afghanistan, Algeria, Argentina, Australia, Austria, Bahrain, Bangladesh, Belgium, Brazil, Burkina Faso, Burundi, Cameroon, Canada, Chad, People's Republic of China, Denmark, Djibouti, Egypt, Ethiopia, Finland, France, Gabon, Gambia, Germany, Ghana, Greece, Guinea, India, Indonesia, Iran, Ireland, Italy, Japan, Jordan, Kenya, Republic of Korea, Kuwait, Lebanon, Libya, Malaysia, Mali, Mauritania, Mexico, Morocco, Nepal, Netherlands, New Zealand, Niger, Nigeria, Norway, Oman, Pakistan, Philippines, Portugal, Qatar, Russia, Rwanda, Senegal, Sierra Leone, Singapore, Somalia, Spain, Sri Lanka, Sudan, Sweden, Switzerland, Syria, Tanzania, Thailand, Tunisia, Turkey, Uganda, United Arab Emirates, United Kingdom, United States, Uruguay, Venezuela, and Yemen.

SENEGAL, REPUBLIC OF

■ POLITICAL ENVIRONMENT

The last several years have been troubled ones for this country. Internal political strife has been exacerbated by student and general rioting, while economic difficulties, at least partially created by the nation's essentially single-crop agricultural economy, have concurrently required austerity measures that further alienated the people from the government. Externally, military confrontations between Senegal and Mauritania have occurred over disputed border territory.

There is a high external public debt with an accompanying debt service that cuts deeply into Senegal's fragile foreign earnings base. Inflation and unemployment rates are significantly high. Some foreign debt has been rescheduled by creditors in order to avoid default.

■ SUMMARY OF FOREIGN INVESTMENT POLICY

The government has an active interest in the development of foreign investment and, to this end, has enacted an Investment Code that contains numerous incentives.

Priority foreign investment areas include expansion of the tourist industry, modernization of agriculture, development of the industrial base, and research activities. A major interest applicable to all areas is that of providing increased employment opportunities.

There are restrictions on foreign investment in certain areas of the economy to include those that provide essential services.

Among the incentives provided to attract foreign investment are wide-ranging tax and customs exemptions, the development of tax-free industrial zones, and the creation of industrial estates.

Foreign investments must be registered with the government. The principal agency involved with foreign investment is the Investment Committee, which is responsible to the President.

A special program of incentives is available to small and medium-sized companies in which the majority control is held by domestic interests.

There is a strong government desire to promote joint ventures between foreign and domestic investors. Joint ventures in which domestic interests have provided at least 60 percent of the invested capital are entitled to additional special incentives to include long-term tax holidays and general exemption from other taxes including those assessed on documents.

Companies established within the industrial tax free zones are eligible for exemption from taxes on income, various registration assessments, and the transactions tax. Such companies must meet certain minimal levels of capital investment and must provide employment for a stipulated number of local workers in addition to receiving government approval.

■ FORMATION AND TYPES OF PERMITTED BUSINESS ORGANIZATIONS

Foreign investors may create corporations, limited liability companies, general, limited, and silent partnerships, and sole proprietorships. Branch offices of foreign companies may also be established. Foreign investors may enter into joint ventures with domestic partners.

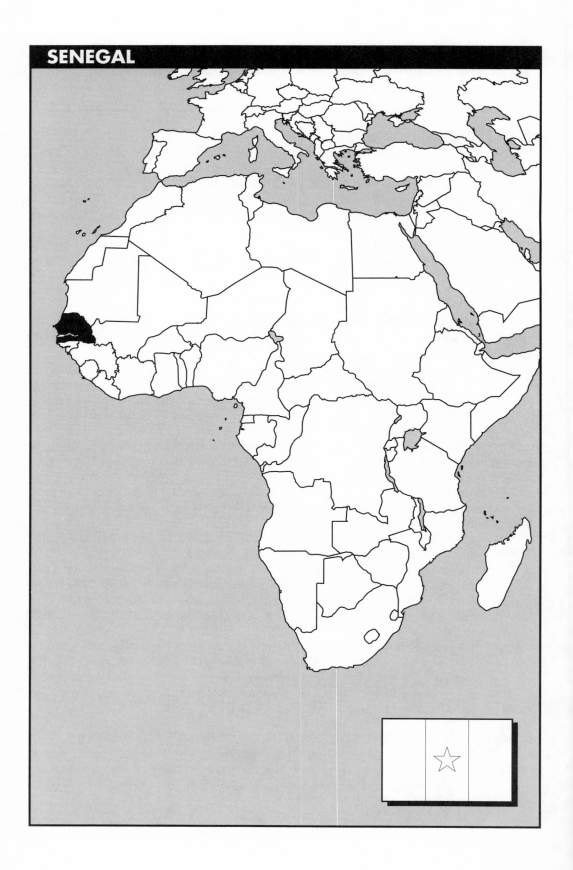

SENEGAL

Corporations and limited liability companies acquire juridical person status.

There is no requirement for domestic equity or managerial participation in a firm financed by foreign investment.

Partnerships, joint ventures, and branch offices of foreign corporations are not considered to be legal entities.

■ ENVIRONMENTAL PROTECTION

The government has a strong interest in environmental protection. Potential foreign investors are advised to contact the Ministry of Tourism and Environmental Protection for complete information about this subject.

■ RIGHTS AND OBLIGATIONS OF FOREIGN INVESTORS

Investments and income derived from such investments may be repatriated or remitted abroad.

Land may be purchased by foreign businesses or individuals without restriction.

Foreign businesses and individuals are guaranteed equality of treatment with domestic investors to include the right to compete for government contracts.

Local financing may be obtained.

In the event that changes in the investment laws should occur that are unfavorable to foreign investor interests, the investor may elect to be covered under the present law.

■ LABOR

Senegal has a highly developed body of laws covering the areas of employment and working conditions.

Local labor must be accorded hiring preference by foreign employers. Foreign nationals may be hired if necessary skills are not locally available. All foreign employees must obtain work and residence permits.

■ ACCOUNTING REQUIREMENTS

All corporations and limited liability companies must maintain accurate and completed financial information for tax and other purposes. Independently audited financial statements must be filed annually with shareholders.

■ CURRENCY CONTROLS

The Central Bank of West Africa is the central bank not only for Senegal but for all member states that comprise the Monetary Union of West Africa. Foreign exchange controls are operationally managed by the bank.

All foreign currency transactions, including the repatriation or remittance abroad of investments and investment income, must be approved in advance by the central bank. Approval authority has, in general, been delegated by the central bank to the commercial banks established in Senegal.

■ TAXATION

Foreign businesses and individuals are subject to the Senegal tax laws.

The major taxes are those imposed on corporate and personal income. Other taxes include those assessed on services, licenses, documents, and income derived from personal property.

The tax year normally runs concurrently with the calendar year, i.e., January 1 to December 31. However, companies may use their adopted fiscal year for tax filing, upon approval of the Office of Tax, Ministry of the Economy, Finance and Planning.

Deductions include depreciation of plant and equipment, business expenses, royalties, salaries, and operating losses. Allowances include those for reinvested profits.

Senegal is a party to several bilateral treaties on the subject of double taxation.

■ LEGAL SYSTEM

The court system includes local (or district) courts and the high courts. The latter function as trial courts and hear major criminal and civil cases. Appeals are taken to the Court of Appeal and then to the Supreme Court, which sits at Dakar.

■ CUSTOMS AND DUTIES

Senegal is a member of several trading groups including the Franc Zone which is comprised of several nations in West Africa. Imports from the EC and from the Franc Zone are exempt from customs duties.

Goods and materials received and used for manufacturing by businesses established in the industrial estates are exempt from customs duties. Similarly, goods and materials received and reexported are exempt from customs charges.

■ PROTECTION OF INTELLECTUAL PROPERTY

Senegal is a member of the World Intellectual Property Organization and several other international organizations created to provide intellectual property protection including the Union of Paris and the Berne Convention. In addition, Senegal has enacted domestic laws for the protection of copyrights, patents, trademarks, and technology transfer.

■ IMMIGRATION AND RESIDENCE

Visas are normally required to enter the country. Potential foreign investors are advised to contact the Investment Committee or any Senegalese embassy or consular office for information on visa, work permit, and residence permit requirements.

■ FOREIGN INVESTMENT ASSISTANCE DIRECTORY

Sources that can provide additional information about foreign investment in Senegal include:

Investment Committee
Office of the President
P.O. Box 168
Avenue Roume
Dakar, Senegal
Telephone: (221) 231088
Telex: 258

Ministry of the Economy, Finance and Planning
P.O. Box 462
Rue Charles Laisné
Dakar, Senegal
Telephone: (221) 226550
Telex: 61203

Ministry of Tourism and Environmental Protection
P.O. Box 4049
Avenue André Peytavin
Dakar, Senegal
Telephone: (221) 225376

Central Bank of West Africa
P.O. Box 3108
Avenue Abdoulaye Fadiga
Dakar, Senegal
Telephone: (221) 231615
Telex: 21815
Fax: (221) 239345

Persons interested in obtaining further information about foreign investment in Senegal are advised to contact the closest Senegalese embassy or consular office.

Senegal maintains diplomatic relations with Algeria, Argentina, Austria, Bangladesh, Belgium, Brazil, Bulgaria, Cameroon, Canada, Cape Verde, People's Republic of China, Congo, Côte d'Ivoire, Czechoslovakia, Egypt, Ethiopia, France, Gabon, Gambia, Germany, Guinea, Guinea-Bissau, Haiti, Holy See, India, Indonesia, Iraq, Italy, Japan, Democratic People's Republic of Korea, Republic of Korea, Kuwait, Lebanon, Mali, Mauritania, Mexico, Morocco, Netherlands, Nigeria, Pakistan, Philippines, Poland, Romania, Russia, Saudi Arabia, Somalia, Spain, Switzerland, Syria, Thailand, Tunisia, Turkey, United Kingdom, United States, Zaire, and Zimbabwe.

SEYCHELLES, REPUBLIC OF

■ POLITICAL ENVIRONMENT

The nation has witnessed numerous attempts at armed rebellion and takeover, some of them successfully staged, since achieving independence from the United Kingdom in 1976.

Currently, and since late 1991, there has been a semblance of governmental stability.

Economically, the nation is dependent on tourism and agriculture (principally coconut production) as the major sources of foreign exchange. However, tourism will continue to be a major source of foreign exchange only as long as the environment is considered to be reasonably secure from armed violence or the real and imminent threat of it.

Seychelles has a large public external debt and a high debt service. Inflation and unemployment levels are low.

The government introduced a Development Plan for the period of 1990 through 1994 that set out the need, among other points, for an increased level of foreign investment.

■ SUMMARY OF FOREIGN INVESTMENT POLICY

As part of its commitment to acquire an increased level of foreign investment, the government has established the Seychelles Investment Development Corporation (SIDEC). Although this agency was created as an autonomous entity, it remains closely identified, both in terms of policy development and management, with the Department of Industry.

There is no specific investment law or code in existence at this time. However, a number of other laws are directly applicable to include the Companies Act of 1972, the Business Tax Act of 1987, and the Seychelles Licensing Act of 1987.

The government is dedicated to a national economic program that will increase the country's economic base; develop a light industry manufacturing sector that will produce high-quality items; correct the presently large trade imbalance; and generate employment opportunities.

All potential foreign investments must be approved by the government with the starting point of such an approval being the Investment Development Corporation.

All approved foreign investments must be registered with the government through the offices of the Investment Development Corporation and must be licensed pursuant to the requirements of the Seychelles Licensing Act of 1987.

Generally, well considered foreign investment proposals are welcomed by the government if they can be shown to provide a long-term benefit to the country.

Foreign investment proposals are classified into four categories: tourism; industrial development; those projects with a capital cost of more than 100,000 Seychelle rupees; and any other project involving foreign participation.

In particular, projects involving foreign participation must include a feasibility study and financial considerations. The impact of the project on the country's balance of payments, government revenue, employment opportunities, and the environment are among the key factors to be considered relevant to government approval.

The proposal is reviewed by a Project Appraisal Committee, which includes key

SEYCHELLES

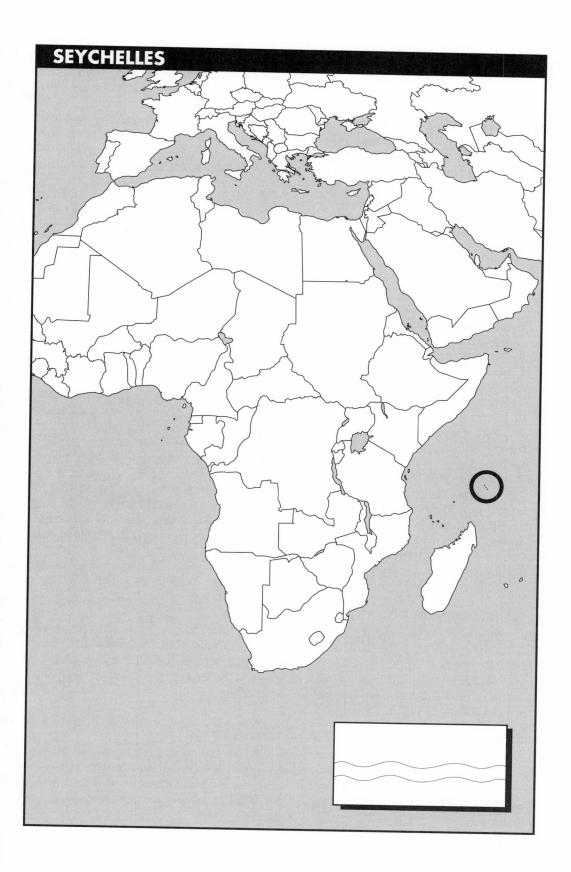

members of the government and representatives of the Ministry of Finance and the Ministry of Manpower.

Incentives that are available to foreign investors are largely in the form of customs exemptions that permit the importation of goods and equipment necessary for carrying on the approved investment activity.

The geographic location of a foreign investment is subject, in large measure, to government approval. Manufacturing activities must be established in areas classified for industrial use.

Foreign investment may comprise cash, equipment, land, buildings, or technology. If the investment is other than in cash, the value is determined by the Ministry of National Development and the Ministry of Finance.

■ FORMATION AND TYPES OF PERMITTED BUSINESS ORGANIZATIONS

Foreign investments may be established in Seychelles in the form of publicly held or privately held corporations, general or limited partnerships, or sole proprietorships.

Subsidiaries or branch offices of foreign corporations may be established. Joint ventures may be created between foreign investors and state-owned businesses, private businesses controlled by Seychelles interests, and with the government.

In most cases where the government is a partner in a joint venture, the government holds a 51 percent interest.

There are no requirements with regard to either management or equity participation of firms wholly financed by foreign investors. However, there is an unstated preference for some kind of equity participation involving domestic interests. In addition, there may be situations in which the government will seek a majority interest in any enterprise created to exploit natural resources, or in any industrial activity where the investment will be greater than one million rupees.

Corporations are considered to be domestic investors if registered in the country, if a minimum of 51 percent of its shares are owned by resident Seychelles interests, and if the corporate headquarters are located in the country. Partnerships are considered to be domestic ones under the application of the same general rules and if at least half of the partners are resident Seychelles nationals.

Corporations, both subsidiaries of foreign companies and those established in the country, are considered to have a juridical person status.

■ ENVIRONMENTAL PROTECTION

The government has an interest in the area of environmental protection although no ministry level office has, to date, been charged with that specific responsibility. Some environmental protection regulations are under the control of the Ministry of Health.

Potential foreign investors are advised to contact the Investment Development Corporation for current and complete information on regulations and laws in effect relevant to environmental protection.

■ RIGHTS AND OBLIGATIONS OF FOREIGN INVESTORS

There is a history of nationalization in the Seychelles, the most prominent case involving a major oil company in 1985. The government now claims that expropriation or nationalization will not occur without full legal process and with fair compensation.

Seychelles is a member of the International Bank for Reconstruction and Development and the International Center for the Settlement of Investment Disputes.

Foreign investors are, according to the government, to be accorded full and equal rights with domestic investors.

Foreign investments and all income derived from such investments may be fully repatriated or remitted abroad, subject to all required taxes.

Local financing from any source, government or private, is not generally available to foreign investors. This rule, however, does not apply to raising share capital, which may be borrowed based on the percentage of shares owned by resident Seychelles investors.

■ LABOR

There is an existing and extensive body of laws regarding employment and working conditions, the key statute being the Employment Act.

There is a general requirement that while foreign managers and technical personnel may be hired when a firm is initially established, Seychelles workers must be employed as trainees to fill such positions. Foreign workers may be hired only where it can be shown that required training and experience are not locally available. Seychelles workers are hired through the offices of the Ministry of Employment and Social Services, the Manpower Division of the Office of the President, and the Department of Industry.

■ ACCOUNTING REQUIREMENTS

All companies established in the Seychelles must maintain complete and accurate financial and other records for tax and other government reporting purposes. Accounting information must be maintained in accordance with internationally accepted standards.

■ CURRENCY CONTROLS

The Central Bank of Seychelles is the country's central bank and, among other related responsibilities, manages the nation's foreign exchange system.

Foreign exchange activities are closely monitored by the bank and other government agencies, particularly the Ministry of Finance. Outward remittances of both domestic and foreign currencies require advance notification and permission.

Foreign investors must provide necessary capital without any reliance on raising funds locally.

■ TAXATION

The major Seychelles tax is that on business income based on the provisions of the Business Tax Act of 1987, which sets out the basic and excess profits tax structure. The law provides that business taxes are to be estimated and paid on a monthly basis. Tax adjustments are made in the year subsequent to payment. New businesses must pay monthly taxes based on investor-supplied information.

There is no personal income tax beyond that which is collected under the Social Security statute.

There are other taxes levied to include those on royalties and interest income; a tax on locally produced goods and locally provided trades and services, and customs duties.

Tax exemptions are rarely provided by the government as incentives. However, customs exemptions are provided relevant to the importation of raw materials and equipment necessary for business operations, and depreciation allowances are permitted on the basis of 40 percent in the first year and 20 percent for three subsequent years on plant and equipment.

■ LEGAL SYSTEM

The judicial system essentially functions at three levels. Magistrates' Courts operate at the local level and hear civil and criminal matters. Appeals from this level are taken to the Supreme Court that also has a trial function relevant to more serious criminal and civil cases. Appeals from the Supreme Court are taken to the Court of Appeal, which sits at Victoria.

■ CUSTOMS AND DUTIES

The nation imports far more than it exports. Most imports are heavily taxed. Trade quotas are also in place. Importers must be licensed. An import substitution policy has been adopted by the government and is enforced by the Seychelles Marketing Board.

■ PROTECTION OF INTELLECTUAL PROPERTY

Seychelles is not a member of the World Intellectual Property Organization. However, the country has enacted statutes to effectively protect copyrights, patents, technology transfer, and trademarks. All technology transfer agreements must receive government approval before incentives may be offered.

■ IMMIGRATION AND RESIDENCE

Information on visa, work permit, and residence permit requirements should be obtained from the Industrial Development Corporation by any potential foreign investor.

■ FOREIGN INVESTMENT ASSISTANCE DIRECTORY

Sources that can provide additional information about foreign investment in Seychelles include:

Seychelles Industrial Development Corporation
P.O. Box 537
Victoria, Seychelles
Telephone: (0) (0) 24911
Telex: 2415
Fax: (0) (0) 25121

Ministry of Finance
P.O. Box 313
State House
Victoria, Seychelles
Telephone: (0) (0) 25252
Telex: 2363
Fax: (0) (0) 25265

Office of the President
State House
Victoria, Seychelles
Telephone: (0) (0) 24391

Ministry of Administration and Manpower
P.O. Box 50
National House
Victoria, Seychelles
Telephone: (0) (0) 24041
Telex: 2333
Fax: (0) (0) 24936

Central Bank of Seychelles
P.O. Box 791
Independence Avenue
Victoria, Seychelles
Telephone: (0) (0) 25200
Telex: 2301
Fax: (0) (0) 24958

Chamber of Commerce and Industry
P.O. Box 443
Premier Building
Victoria, Seychelles
Telephone: (0) (0) 23812

Seychelles Marketing Board
P.O. Box 516
Oceangate House
Victoria, Seychelles
Telephone: (0) (0) 76618

Persons interested in obtaining further information about foreign investment in Seychelles are advised to contact the country's closest embassy or consular office.

Seychelles maintains diplomatic relations with People's Republic of China, Cuba, Germany, India, Netherlands, Russia, United Kingdom, and United States.

Sierra Leone, Republic of

■ POLITICAL ENVIRONMENT

This nation has an unfortunate history of politically motivated violence; coups; attempted coups; and high-level government corruption. These political problems have been exacerbated by economic ones that, to at least some extent, have been beyond the power of the government to control.

Despite a change from one party to a multi-party system, the political conditions in Sierra Leone are still very unstable.

Sierra Leone is principally an agricultural country. The growing of coffee and cocoa, among other crops, provides employment for most of the nation's workers, generates about one-third of the country's national income, and, according to the government, sustains some 75 percent of the population. Foreign earnings are also obtained from mining exports (notably rutile), bauxite, and diamonds. These exports are responsible for most of Sierra Leone's foreign exchange.

The nation imports almost all of its fuel and, as a result, was hard hit by the increased cost of oil during the 1980s. The oil price increase led to major inflation levels from which the country has not yet recovered. Unemployment is extremely high, and there is a substantial public debt. The government has, in the past few years, been in arrears on the debt.

In order to become eligible for further multilateral assistance, the government has agreed with the International Monetary Fund (IMF) to the development of a structural adjustment program. Despite a slow start in meeting the requirements of that program, the government has taken steps to help restore the national economy to include a reduction in public spending, the promotion of foreign trade, limited privatization, and a commitment to developing foreign investment.

■ SUMMARY OF FOREIGN INVESTMENT POLICY

The major law on this subject is the Development of Industries Act of 1983. Under the provisions of the law, a new government agency, the Industrial Development Department, which is part of the Ministry of Trade and Industry, was created. The responsibilities of the Industrial Development Department include overall promotion for the acquisition of foreign investment and providing assistance and guidance to potential and actual foreign investors.

Among the priority areas of the economy where the government desires foreign investment are agriculture (to include raw materials processing); commercial fishing; mining (to include exploration and development); and manufacturing.

The law provides that various incentives and guarantees will be available to foreign investors who are engaged in export-oriented and resource-based industries; building material industries; export-oriented industries partially based on imported materials and services; and import substitution industries that can generate or save foreign exchange and produce a domestic added value in excess of 30 percent of the value of the finished product.

All foreign investment proposals must be submitted to the Ministry of Trade and Industry for approval. Any proposed foreign investment that exceeds $40,000 (U.S.) must contain a complete feasibility study that reflects the general criteria for approval

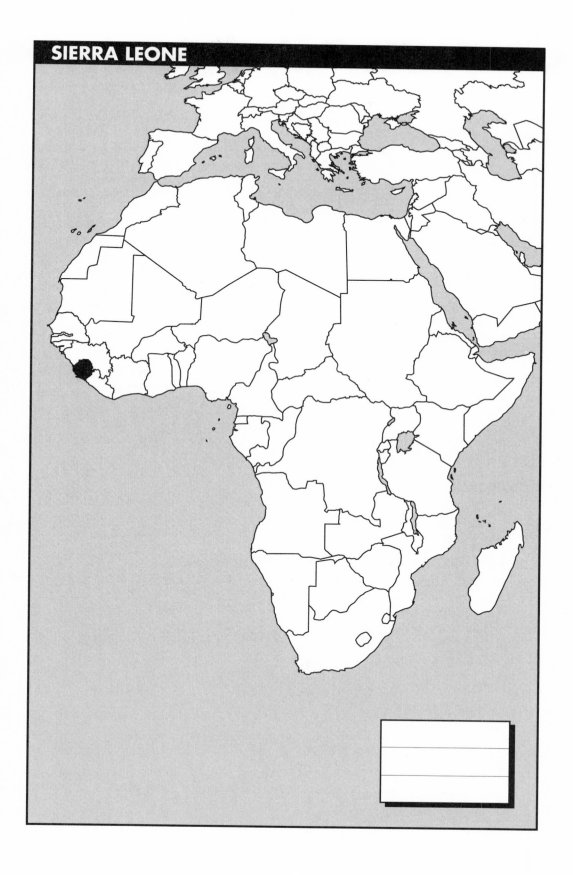

used by the government's Project Approval Committee, the agency charged with the responsibility of reviewing all submitted proposals.

The criteria used includes the current and future markets that will be served by the project; a requirement for the use of modern technology; the location of the project; costs; raw materials used and their availability; management capabilities; financial return; overall value to the national economy; value added considerations; foreign exchange benefits; and opportunities for employment of the country's labor force.

The Ministry of Trade and Industry will provide guidance and assistance to foreign investors to ensure the implementation of the project once it is approved.

Among the incentives and guarantees that are provided to approved foreign investors are long-term tax holidays of up to five years; capital and investment allowance on taxes; relief from the income tax surcharge for a period not to exceed five years; and full or partial customs duties exemptions.

In addition, special incentives in the form of government guidance and assistance, low-interest loans, and buildings and land access are available to foreign investors who locate outside of the Freetown area.

Companies that manufacture or process goods primarily for export are entitled to exemptions from the export tariff.

■ FORMATION AND TYPES OF PERMITTED BUSINESS ORGANIZATIONS

Foreign investors may participate in the country's economy through the creation of corporations, partnerships, or sole proprietorships. Subsidiaries of foreign corporations may be established. Joint ventures may be formed with domestic investors.

There is no requirement for domestic participation in the management or in the ownership of an enterprise that is funded with foreign capital.

■ ENVIRONMENTAL PROTECTION

Potential foreign investors are advised to contact the Industrial Development Department to determine the status of any environmental protection laws or regulations that could impact facilities of any kind that are or will be established in Sierra Leone.

■ RIGHTS AND OBLIGATIONS OF FOREIGN INVESTORS

The government has guaranteed that approved industrial enterprises are fully protected against nationalization except when required by public need. In any such case, fair and adequate compensation is to be quickly provided. There have been no recent cases of nationalization in Sierra Leone.

Local financing is available to foreign investors to include that provided by the National Development Bank on a low-interest basis.

Foreign investments and income derived from such investments may be remitted abroad or repatriated subject to the payment of taxes. In the event of investment liquidation, foreign investors may repatriate or remit abroad their proper share in such investment.

Potential foreign investors should recognize that, as a practical matter, remittances on foreign investments may be delayed because of the country's shortage of foreign exchange.

■ LABOR

There is a complete body of existing laws covering the subjects of employment and working conditions.

The labor force in Sierra Leone is large and is primarily composed of unskilled workers. The literacy rate is low.

Foreign employers are urged to provide training to local employees, to include management level training. Training of local personnel is tax deductible.

Except in those cases where required skills or experience are not locally available, foreign employers must provide preferential hiring to indigenous workers. Foreign workers must possess work permits.

■ ACCOUNTING REQUIREMENTS

All companies established in Sierra Leone must maintain complete and accurate financial and other records as required by the government.

Accounting records must be maintained in accord with internationally recognized standards.

■ CURRENCY CONTROLS

The Bank of Sierra Leone is the country's central bank and is responsible for management of the nation's foreign exchange program and related activities.

Bank accounts may be maintained in a foreign currency, designated in U.S. dollars. Such accounts must be generated based on the sale of goods and services and may be used for any legitimate private or commercial purpose.

The current exchange rate is a floating one, based on supply and demand principles.

Foreign exchange can be purchased at the prevailing rate from any of the banks or foreign exchange bureaus that have been established in the country.

■ TAXATION

The principal tax imposed is on corporate income pursuant to the Income Tax Act. Partnerships are not considered to be taxable entities. Partnership income is taxed to the partners as individual taxpayers.

A 25 percent initial capital allowance is granted on equipment and machinery, followed by an annual 10 percent allowance during the tax holiday period. A 16 percent investment allowance is also provided.

While income tax and surtax holidays are provided, neither can exceed 150 percent of the amount of the capital invested.

Additional allowances including that provided for training of local personnel, other legitimate business expenses, losses incurred, and research and development costs are permitted.

■ LEGAL SYSTEM

The principal courts are at the Magistrates', High Court, Court of Appeal, and Supreme Court levels.

Magistrates' Courts have a limited jurisdiction with regard to petty criminal matters. The High Court exercises unlimited trial court jurisdiction in more serious criminal cases and civil issues, as well as acting in an appellate role with regard to decisions of the Magistrates' Courts. Decisions of the High Court may be referred to the Court of Appeal. Final appeals are taken to the Supreme Court, which sits at Freetown.

■ CUSTOMS AND DUTIES

The government is interested in expanded foreign trade and has a particular desire to increase the country's level of exports.

Foreign investors will be provided preferential treatment with regard to import license applications procedures.

Complete or partial import duty exemptions will be granted with regard to capital equipment, raw materials, and other goods required by an approved foreign investor to operate in the country, provided that such equipment is not a replacement of labor intensive techniques, if such raw materials are not locally available, and if any intermediate goods will not reduce domestic added value.

Export tariff exemptions may be available to approved companies that are manufacturing essentially for export.

Companies engaged in export production may be eligible to participate in the Export Credit Guarantee Scheme that is provided by the Bank of Sierra Leone. Under this program, any preshipment financing required to purchase, produce, process, and pack items for export and provided by credit institutions to exporters is guaranteed by the central bank's Export Credit Guarantee Institution.

■ PROTECTION OF INTELLECTUAL PROPERTY

Sierra Leone is not a member of the World Intellectual Property Organization. Potential foreign investors are advised to contact the Industrial Development Department for current information on the status of existing or contemplated laws that provide protection for copyrights, patents, trademarks, and technology transfer.

■ IMMIGRATION AND RESIDENCE

Visas are required to enter the country. Potential foreign investors are advised to contact the Industrial Development Department for complete and current information on the requirements for visas, work permits, and residence permits.

■ FOREIGN INVESTMENT ASSISTANCE DIRECTORY

Sources that can provide additional information about foreign investment in Sierra Leone include:

Industrial Development Department
Ministry of Trade and Industry
Ministry Buildings
George Street
Freetown, Sierra Leone
Telephone: (0) (0) 25211
Telex: 3218

Bank of Sierra Leone
P.O. Box 30
Siaka Stevens Street
Freetown, Sierra Leone
Telephone: (0) (0) 26501
Telex: 3232

Sierra Leone Chamber of Commerce
P.O. Box 502
Lanina Sankoh Street
Freetown, Sierra Leone
Telephone: (0) (0) 26305

Persons interested in obtaining further information about foreign investment in Sierra Leone are advised to contact the country's closest embassy or consular office.

Sierra Leone maintains diplomatic relations with People's Republic of China, Côte d'Ivoire, Egypt, France, Gambia, Germany, Guinea, Italy, Republic of Korea, Lebanon, Liberia, Nigeria, United Kingdom, and United States.

SINGAPORE, REPUBLIC OF

■ POLITICAL ENVIRONMENT

The government is stable and there are no external threats to the nation. Inflation and unemployment rates are both very low. There is an ongoing program of privatization of former public sector industries.

■ SUMMARY OF FOREIGN INVESTMENT POLICY

The government has a traditional policy of welcoming foreign investment. The Economic Development Board is charged with the responsibility of promoting foreign investment in Singapore.

The priority interests of the government in terms of foreign investment include the development and maintenance of modern industrial and related technology.

Numerous incentives have been made available by the government through the Economic Development Board for foreign investors. Some of the incentives are those that include pioneer company status, tax holidays, expanded tax allowances, low-cost local financing, and financial grants for research and development. Small-scale industry is eligible for technical assistance if there is a minimum of 30 percent local ownership of a manufacturing enterprise or a labor force of at least 50 individuals in the service sector.

The country has entered into bilateral investment guarantee agreements with a number of countries.

A number of industrial estates and research facilities have been created. Singapore is a duty free port.

Offshore banking activities are encouraged.

No requirement exists to register foreign investments with the government or to obtain approval for any foreign investment.

There is no requirement for domestic participation in a company that is formed by foreign investors, nor is there any requirement for domestic participation in the management of a firm that is wholly funded by foreign investment. The exception is in the case of domestic banks where foreign interests may not exceed 40 percent.

Some industries, notably those dealing with the production of weapons and ammunition, public utilities, telecommunications, and newspaper publishing, are restricted in terms of foreign investment.

■ FORMATION AND TYPES OF PERMITTED BUSINESS ORGANIZATIONS

Foreign investors may establish corporations, form partnerships, or operate as sole proprietors. In addition, foreign investors may establish a branch or a subsidiary of a corporation domiciled in another country, and may create a joint venture with a domestic enterprise.

Companies may be limited (by shares or by guarantee), and they may be either public or private. Companies must be registered with the Registrar of Companies.

Partnerships may be general or limited. Joint ventures may be formed between corporations, partnerships, individuals, or any combination of them.

Corporations enjoy the status of a juridical person.

Partnerships and sole proprietorships must be registered with the government.

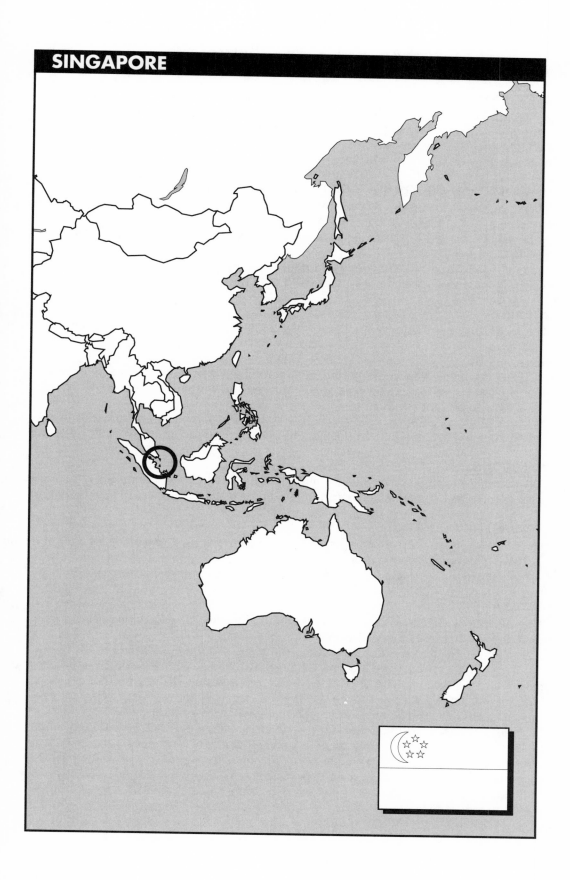

■ ENVIRONMENTAL PROTECTION

There is an ongoing interest in environmental protection. All new industrial projects are required to meet strict government standards that are rigorously enforced. Potential foreign investors are advised to contact the Economic Development Board for complete information on this subject.

■ RIGHTS AND OBLIGATIONS OF FOREIGN INVESTORS

There are no restrictions on the percentages of ownership of companies held by foreign investors.

Investments and all profits derived from such investments may be repatriated or remitted abroad.

Local financing may be obtained by foreign investors.

Foreign investment need not be registered with the government.

■ LABOR

The labor force is productive and well trained. There is a history of good labor-management relations. A body of law exists relevant to employment and working conditions.

There are restrictions on the employment of foreign labor. In the service sector of the economy, no more than 20 percent of all employees may be foreign nationals, and no more than 50 percent in other industries including construction.

In all other areas, there is a levy imposed on every foreign national employed. Foreign personnel are required to obtain either a work permit or an employment pass.

■ ACCOUNTING REQUIREMENTS

All companies must be professionally audited on a yearly basis. Accounting and other records must be maintained in conformity with internationally accepted standards.

■ CURRENCY CONTROLS

The Monetary Authority of Singapore is the government's principal financial office.

There are no exchange controls.

No restrictions exist on the maintenance of foreign currency banking accounts.

■ TAXATION

The major tax levied is on business and individual income. There are numerous minor taxes to include those on documents and property transfers.

The tax year is the calendar year, and returns must be filed before March 31.

There are a variety of deductions for business taxpayers to include those for expenses and depreciation. Tax incentives for foreign investors include exemptions from withholding taxes levied on royalties, losses incurred from various investment and business activities, and allowances for the creation of a new investment.

Additional tax incentives are also provided to companies that are established as offshore headquarters for corporations operating outside of Singapore.

Double tax exemptions may be made available to firms established in the country that manufacture for export and for expenses they incur in such activities as overseas marketing, advertising, the creation of overseas trade offices, and involvement in trade missions and trade fairs.

Individual taxpayers are entitled to various deductions and allowances.

There is no capital gains tax.

Singapore is a party to numerous bilateral treaties on the subject of double taxation.

■ LEGAL SYSTEM

The lowest functioning court levels are the Magistrates' Courts, District Courts, Juvenile Courts, and Small Claims Courts. The trial court level for major criminal and civil matters is found with the High Court, which also has an appellate function. Appeals from the High Court are taken to the Court of Criminal Appeal or, in civil cases, to the Court of Appeal.

Final appeals are taken to the Privy Council in the United Kingdom.

■ CUSTOMS AND DUTIES

Singapore is a member of the Association of Southeast Asian Nations (ASEAN), a trading bloc, as well as being a participant in the Generalized System of Preferences, as developed through GATT with the EC and other major trading nations.

The government endorses a policy of free trade. Several free trade zones have been established.

Import duties are levied on very few items, generally to include vehicles, clothing, some foods, liquor, petroleum products, and tobacco.

Materials and equipment imported for use in business may be received without import duty.

■ PROTECTION OF INTELLECTUAL PROPERTY

Singapore is a member of the World Intellectual Property Organization. In addition, it has domestic statutes on the protection of copyrights and trademarks. Patents are covered by registration under the United Kingdom Patents Act.

■ IMMIGRATION AND RESIDENCE

Visas may be required to enter the country, depending on the citizenship of the foreign national. All foreign nationals employed in the country must obtain either a work permit or employment passes.

Potential foreign investors are advised to contact the Economic Development Board for current information on the issuance of visas, employment passes, work permits, and residence requirements.

■ FOREIGN INVESTMENT ASSISTANCE DIRECTORY

Sources that can provide further information about foreign investment in Singapore include:

Economic Development Board
250 North Bridge Road #24-00
Raffles City Tower
Singapore 0617
Telephone: (65) 3362288
Telex: RS 26233 SINEDB
Cable: INDUSPROMO
Fax: (65) 3396077

The Economic Development Board maintains offices in Boston, Chicago, Dallas, Los Angeles, New York, San Francisco, and Washington, D.C., USA; Frankfort, Germany; London, United Kingdom; Milan, Italy; Paris, France; Stockholm, Sweden; Hong Kong, Osaka, and Tokyo, Japan; Beijing, People's Republic of China; and Jakarta, Indonesia.

Trade Development Board
1 Maritime Square #10-40 (Lobby D)
World Trade Centre
Telok Blangah Road
Singapore 0409
Telephone: (65) 2719388
Telex: RS 28617 TRADEV
RS 28170 TRADEV
Cable: SINTRADEV
Fax: (65) 2782518

The Trade Development Board maintains offices in Beijing and Shanghai, People's Republic of China; Bombay and New Delhi, India; Budapest, Hungary; Dubai, United Arab Emirates; Dusseldorf and Frankfort, Germany; Suva, Fiji; Geneva, Switzerland; Hong Kong; Jakarta, Indonesia; Jeddah, Saudi Arabia; London, United Kingdom; Los Angeles, New York, and Washington, D.C., United States; Osaka and Tokyo, Japan; Rotterdam, The Netherlands; Seoul, Republic of Korea; Stockholm, Sweden; Sydney, Australia; and Vancouver, Canada.

Singapore International Chamber of Commerce
50 Raffles Place #03-02
Shell Tower
Singapore 0104
Telephone: (65) 2241255
Telex: RS 25235 INTCHAM
Fax: (65) 2242785

Persons interested in obtaining further information about foreign investment in Singapore also are advised to contact the country's closest embassy or consular office.

Singapore maintains diplomatic relations with Argentina, Australia, Bangladesh, Belgium, Brazil, Brunei, Bulgaria, Canada, Chile, People's Republic of China, Denmark, Egypt, Finland, Germany, Holy See, India, Indonesia, Israel, Italy, Japan, People's Democratic Republic of Korea, Republic of Korea, Malaysia, Myanmar, Netherlands, New Zealand, Norway, Pakistan, Panama, Philippines, Poland, Romania, Russia, Saudi Arabia, Sri Lanka, Sweden, Switzerland, Thailand, Turkey, United Kingdom, and United States.

SOLOMON ISLANDS

■ POLITICAL ENVIRONMENT

The government is stable. There are no external threats, and internal political disagreements have been generally resolved through democratic processes.

The country is underdeveloped with most of its economic activities being agriculturally related. Inflation is somewhat high and there is a moderate rate of unemployment. There is a major privatization program in progress.

■ SUMMARY OF FOREIGN INVESTMENT POLICY

The government desires foreign investment particularly in the areas of natural resource exploitation, agriculture, and tourism. The Ministry of Commerce and Primary Industries is the principal government agency responsible for the promotion and development of foreign investment. Foreign investments in any area of the economy are initially examined by the Foreign Investment Advisory Committee, which acts in a clearing house and liaison role.

Most sectors of the economy are open to foreign participation. However, foreign investors may find it difficult to receive approval from the government for any investment project or business in which domestic interests do not maintain majority control.

There are some incentives designed for foreign investors, most being in the areas of tax considerations and local financing.

■ FORMATION AND TYPES OF PERMITTED BUSINESS ORGANIZATIONS

Foreign investors may form and operate corporations, partnerships, and sole proprietorships. Corporate forms include private and public companies where liability is limited by shares. Corporations must be registered with the Registrar of Companies.

Corporations domiciled in another country must be registered with the Registrar of Companies and with the Foreign Investment Advisory Committee.

Foreign investors may form joint ventures with the government or with domestic enterprises.

■ ENVIRONMENTAL PROTECTION

The government has a continuing interest in protecting the environment. Potential foreign investors are advised to contact the Ministry of Commerce and Primary Industries or the Foreign Investment Advisory Committee regarding the laws and regulations.

■ RIGHTS AND OBLIGATIONS OF FOREIGN INVESTORS

Foreign investments and all income derived from such investments may be freely remitted abroad or repatriated subject to the knowledge and approval of the Central Bank of Solomon Islands.

Financing is generally available to foreign investors either from commercial banks or from government sources to include the Development Bank of Solomon Islands.

■ LABOR

There is a considerable body of existing laws regarding employment and working conditions to include wages, fringe benefits, and other relevant factors.

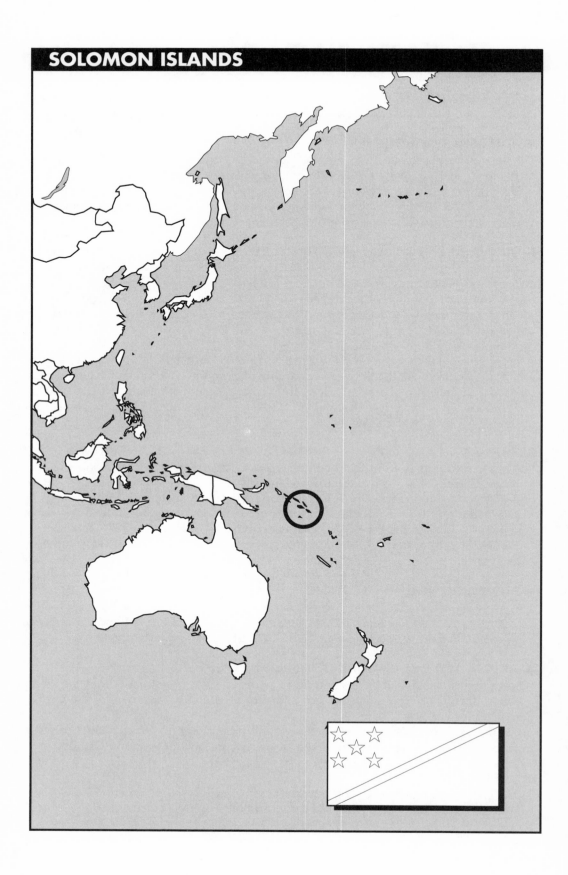

SOLOMON ISLANDS

Hiring preference must generally be accorded to local personnel unless unavailable special skills are required. Foreign employers may be required to train local personnel to eventually fill such positions. Foreign employees are required to obtain work permits.

■ ACCOUNTING REQUIREMENTS

All companies must maintain accurate and complete accounting and other records for tax and other purposes. Companies must be audited annually. Accounting and auditing procedures are expected to be in accord with those adopted in the United Kingdom.

■ CURRENCY CONTROLS

The Central Bank of Solomon Islands has responsibility for exchange controls.

Movement of capital from the country for any purpose is closely monitored although it is permitted for required business purposes.

■ TAXATION

Foreign businesses and individuals are subject to the tax laws, which are administered by the Inland Revenue Division of the Ministry of Finance.

There are treaties in effect with several nations on the subject of double taxation.

The tax year is the calendar year although another 12-month period may be used for reporting purposes. Various deductions including depreciation of physical assets, research and development costs, and business expenses are permitted.

Depending on the national need, special incentives, to include long-term tax holidays, may be granted to foreign investors.

Individual taxpayers must file annual tax returns. There are a variety of allowances for which individuals may be eligible.

There are numerous minor and local taxes.

■ LEGAL SYSTEM

The court system includes Magistrates' Courts, which hear petty criminal and civil cases. Major cases are heard by the High Courts, which are trial courts of record. Appeals are taken to the Court of Appeal.

■ CUSTOMS AND DUTIES

There are no export licensing requirements.

In those cases where it is deemed to be in the national interest, protective tariffs may be employed.

All companies, both foreign and domestic, may be granted exemptions from import duties, particularly relevant to materials and equipment necessary for establishing and operating an enterprise.

■ PROTECTION OF INTELLECTUAL PROPERTY

Potential foreign investors are advised to contact the Ministry of Commerce and Primary Industries or the Foreign Investment Advisory Committee regarding the government's position on the protection of copyrights, patents, trademarks, and technology transfer.

■ IMMIGRATION AND RESIDENCE

Visas are normally required for entry. Potential foreign investors are advised to contact the Foreign Investment Advisory Committee regarding complete information on visas, work permits, and residence permits.

■ FOREIGN INVESTMENT ASSISTANCE DIRECTORY

Sources that can provide further information about foreign investment in the Solomon Islands include:

Foreign Investment Advisory Committee
P.O. Box 26
Honiara, Solomon Islands
Telephone: (0) 23700
Telex: 66337

Ministry of Commerce and Primary Industries
P.O. Box G26
Honiara, Solomon Islands
Telephone: (0) 21140
Telex: 66311

Central Bank of Solomon Islands
P.O. Box 634
Honiara, Solomon Islands
Telephone: (0) 21791
Telex: 66320
Fax: (0) 23513

Persons interested in obtaining further information about investing in Solomon Islands are also advised to contact the country's closest embassy or consular office.

Solomon Islands maintains diplomatic relations with Australia, Republic of China (Taiwan), Japan, New Zealand, United Kingdom, and United States.

SOUTH AFRICA, REPUBLIC OF

■ POLITICAL ENVIRONMENT

As a result of recent elections, this nation is governed by a black majority for the first time in history. Despite the country's natural resources and a highly developed infrastructure, significant economic and political problems must be solved. Inflation is rising and unemployment remains high.

While the newly empowered black leadership has promised protection to the white minority and to white-owned property, there are serious questions about the ability of the government to maintain internal stability. There can be no guarantees that what has occurred in other African countries, such as governmental mismanagement and corruption, coupled with the emergence of old tribal rivalries that lead to violence, will not be witnessed in South Africa. The implications with regard to current and potential foreign investment are clear if such a scenario develops.

■ SUMMARY OF FOREIGN INVESTMENT POLICY

There are a number of laws that are related directly or indirectly to foreign investment. The principal government agency charged with promoting and acquiring foreign investment is the Department of Trade and Industry, which is located within the Ministry of Finance, Trade and Industry.

The government's economic planning includes almost complete privatization accompanied by the decentralization of industry throughout the nation, particularly in those areas where unemployment is high.

No restrictions exist that limit the ownership of foreign investors in companies doing business in South Africa, except in the banking area where limited equity participation is required. Equally, there are no areas of the South African economy where foreign investment is prohibited.

Proposals for foreign investments must be submitted to the Department of Trade and Industry and must include complete information on the size of the business to be established, the amount of capital involved, environmental considerations, and labor opportunities to be provided, along with other information that the government may desire. No projects should be commenced without government approval.

Incentives provided by the government principally include financial loans from the Industrial Corporation of South Africa, particularly to firms willing to establish in previously underdeveloped areas.

In the main, government incentives are equally available to both foreign and domestic investors, to include tariff schedules that will benefit and protect domestic industry.

Export incentives are provided to include exemptions from export charges.

■ FORMATION AND TYPES OF PERMITTED BUSINESS ORGANIZATIONS

Foreign investors may participate in the South African economy through the creation of public companies, private companies, close corporations, general partnerships, limited partnerships, and sole proprietorships.

Subsidiaries and branch offices of foreign corporations may be established. Joint ventures between foreign investors and either domestic private investors or the South African government may be formed.

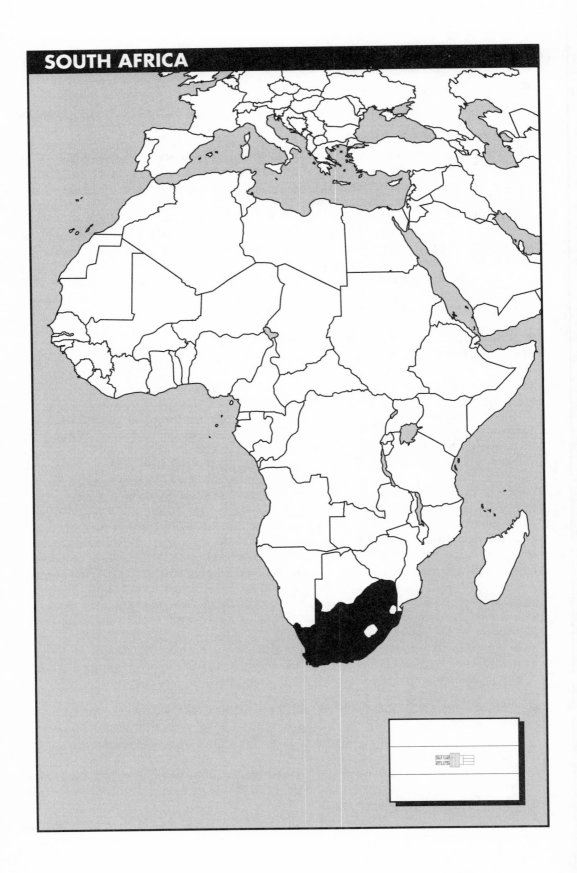

Essentially, the difference between a close corporation and a private company involves the fact that private companies are limited to 50 members, while close corporations are limited to ten members. Additionally, there are fewer requirements to meet in the formation of the close corporation.

South African law also permits the creation of a business trust whereby a trustee operates an enterprise for the benefit of beneficiaries. The liability of the trust is limited to the extent of trust assets.

Partnerships cannot involve more than 20 members.

Corporations, i.e., public companies, private companies, and close corporations, are legal entities and attain juridical person status.

Subsidiaries of foreign corporations are considered to possess the same legal rights and obligations as held by corporations formed in South Africa.

■ ENVIRONMENTAL PROTECTION

There is a great deal of interest on the part of the government in the protection of the environment. Several major laws have been enacted to ensure protection of the air, surface, and underground water (including the ocean), as well as controlling the handling and disposal of hazardous materials.

A cabinet level office, the Ministry of Home Affairs and Environment Affairs, is actively involved in this issue and coordinates the environmental efforts of the local government authorities. Potential foreign investors are advised to contact the Ministry of Home Affairs and Environment Affairs to ascertain the status of current and proposed laws with regard to this subject.

■ RIGHTS AND OBLIGATIONS OF FOREIGN INVESTORS

Foreign investors may obtain local financing from commercial banks and from several government agencies including the Industrial Development Corporation, the Development Bank of Southern Africa, and others. In some cases, depending on the level of equity held by a foreign investor in a domestic company, the South African Exchange Control office must provide approval of financing.

Domestic enterprises may be acquired by foreign investors.

Foreign nationals employed in the country may remit abroad or repatriate a predetermined amount of their income, and may move all savings abroad upon permanently leaving South Africa.

Foreign investments and income derived from such investments may be freely remitted or repatriated.

■ LABOR

There is an extensive body of laws covering the subjects of employment and working conditions.

The South African labor force that is skilled, trained, and available for management, professional, or technical positions is almost exclusively white and in short supply. Black labor, which is mostly unskilled, is available.

Foreign workers may be employed in South Africa in cases where it can be shown that required experience or skills are not locally available. All foreign nationals working in the country must possess work permits and, depending on the anticipated length of stay, residence permits.

There are no requirements that businesses maintain a stated payroll percentage paid to South African workers or that a specific number of South African employees be hired.

■ ACCOUNTING REQUIREMENTS

All companies operating in South Africa are required to maintain accurate books and records for tax, statistical, and other purposes. Public and private companies must be audited on a yearly basis by a qualified independent auditor. Close corporations require the firm's internal accountant or similar executive to examine the books on a yearly basis. Subsidiaries and branch offices of foreign corporations are required to file annual audits with the Registrar of Companies.

■ CURRENCY CONTROLS

The South African Reserve Bank is the nation's central bank and manages the foreign exchange system. There is a dual currency system, one for financial and investment purposes, and another that is used in trade and for income.

Foreign currency may be moved into the country only with the permission of the central bank.

■ TAXATION

Both foreign companies and individuals are subject to the South African tax laws. The principal tax is that levied on business and individual income. Other taxes include those assessed on sales, natural resources, property, and income, among others.

Partnerships and joint ventures are not considered to be taxable entities. Partnership and joint venture income is taxable to the partners.

The tax year for companies is that which the enterprise uses as its fiscal year. Individual taxpayers use a tax year that runs from March 1 to the final day of February.

There are a variety of deductions and allowances to include business expenses, depreciation of plant, equipment, and other assets, research costs, insurance premiums, income to employees, and charitable deductions.

Individual taxpayers are also allowed certain deductions and allowances to include business expenses, medical, and insurance costs. Gift and inheritance taxes are also levied.

South Africa has entered into numerous bilateral treaties with other nations on the subject of double taxation.

■ LEGAL SYSTEM

There are several local courts that are empowered to hear and decide petty criminal, small claims, juvenile cases, and family law issues, and certain specialized areas to include labor and tax matters.

The Supreme Court of South Africa is the trial court for major civil and criminal cases. Appeals are taken to the Appellate Division of the Supreme Court, which sits at Bloemfontein.

■ CUSTOMS AND DUTIES

South Africa is a signatory to the General Agreement on Tariffs and Trade (GATT) and is a member of the Southern African Customs Union.

The government is interested in the expansion of the nation's export trade and provides numerous incentives in the form of government assistance, allowances, and export insurance programs.

South Africa can and has employed protective tariffs to protect its industries from foreign competition.

Import and export licenses are not generally required.

■ PROTECTION OF INTELLECTUAL PROPERTY

South Africa is a member of the World Intellectual Property Organization and is a signatory to the Paris Union Convention for the Protection of Industrial Property, and the Berne Convention.

In addition, the government has enacted domestic laws providing protection of copyrights, patents, trademarks, and designs.

■ IMMIGRATION AND RESIDENCE

In most cases, visas are required to enter the country. Potential foreign investors are advised to contact the Department of Immigration, Ministry of Justice for complete and current information about visas, work permit, and residence permit requirements.

■ FOREIGN INVESTMENT ASSISTANCE DIRECTORY

Sources that can provide additional information about foreign investment in South Africa include:

Department of Trade and Industry
Ministry of Finance, Trade and Industry
P.O. Box X84
240 Vermeulen Street
Pretoria, South Africa
Telephone: (27) (12) 260261
Telex: 320153

Ministry of Home Affairs and Environment Affairs
P.O. Box X152
Post Office Building
Pretoria, South Africa
Telephone: (27) (12) 2931911
Telex: 350013

Department of Immigration
Ministry of Justice
P.O. Box X276
Presidia Building
Pretoria, South Africa
Telephone: (27) (12) 3238581
Fax: (27) (12) 211708

South African Reserve Bank
P.O. Box 427
Pretoria, South Africa
Telephone: (27) (12) 261611
Telex: 320455
Fax: (27) (12) 3133197

Persons interested in obtaining further information about foreign investment in South Africa are advised to contact the closest South African embassy or consular office.

South Africa maintains diplomatic relations with Australia, Austria, Belgium, Brazil, Canada, Chile, Republic of China (Taiwan), Denmark, Finland, France, Germany, Greece, Holy See, Israel, Italy, Japan, Malawi, Netherlands, Paraguay, Poland, Portugal, Spain, Sweden, Switzerland, United Kingdom, United States, and Uruguay.

Spain, Kingdom of

■ POLITICAL ENVIRONMENT

Spain is relatively new to democratic government, having been under the dictatorship of Francisco Franco from the end of the Spanish Civil War in 1939 until Franco's death in 1975. There were some periods of intense domestic trial during the 1980s, some of it involving dissent within the military, some as a result of government corruption, and some caused by Basque separatists. Despite these problems, the government (which is democratically elected), appears to have achieved stability.

There are problems with a somewhat aging national infrastructure.

Spain is a member of the European Community (EC).

The annual inflation level has been rising. Unemployment is very high. Spain's large public external debt is a serious economic problem.

■ SUMMARY OF FOREIGN INVESTMENT POLICY

The government is interested in acquiring increased levels of foreign investment. The General Directorate for External Investment, which is part of the Ministry of Industry, Trade and Tourism, together with the Spanish Institute for Foreign Trade (ICEX), are the major government agencies involved with the development and promotion of foreign investment. The underlying legal framework for foreign investment in Spain is comprised of the Royal Decree of 1986 regarding the Regulation of Foreign Investment.

Priority uses of foreign investment are those that will help to create employment opportunities and will help to further the overall development of the nation.

In most economic areas, there are few, if any, restrictions on foreign investment. Services that are traditionally provided by the government are not open to investors, either foreign or domestic. Other activities that are closed to foreign investment are those dealing with national security and defense, telecommunications, broadcasting, and air transportation.

Foreign ownership of up to 50 percent of any domestic company does not require any notification to the government. Any percentage of ownership above that amount requires prior central bank approval. Upon approval, all foreign investments must be filed with the Foreign Investment Register.

A variety of incentives are provided to foreign investors to include central government grants to train employees and for technical assistance programs in agriculture, energy development, electronics, mining activities, environmental improvement, and other areas.

Regions of the nation (in most cases, those which are underdeveloped) offer various incentives in the form of tax benefits and low-interest loans.

Central government tax incentives are available to both foreign and domestic investors and are related to the promotion of new industries and technologies. Generally, these incentives are in the form of reductions from the corporate profits or income tax.

Some incentives are industry specific to include tax reductions and bank credit for companies engaging in oil and gas exploration, book publishing, and exporting.

Firms engaged in exporting are entitled to a special tax credit. Enterprises formed as holding companies in Spain, but not doing business in the country beyond holding shares in other firms, are eligible for major corporate profits tax reductions.

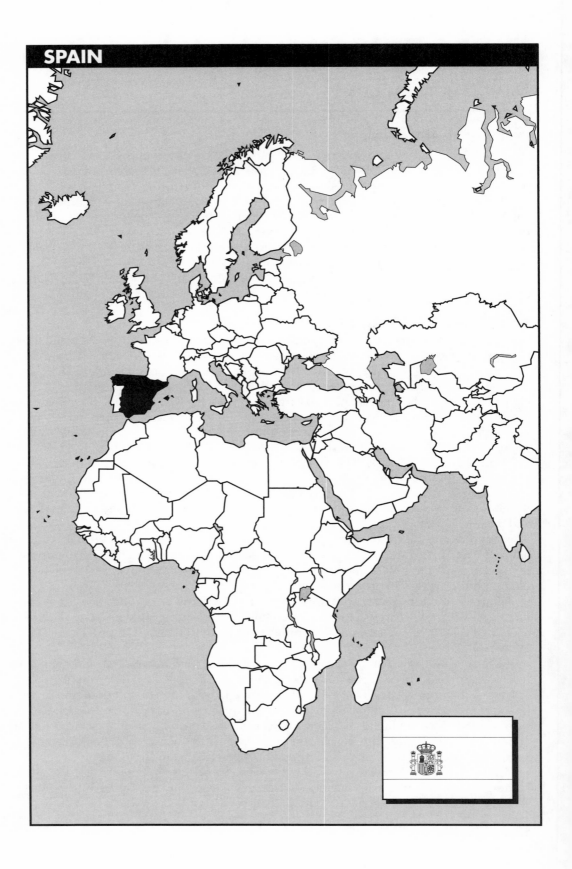

■ FORMATION AND TYPES OF PERMITTED BUSINESS ORGANIZATIONS

Foreign investors may form public and limited corporations; general and limited partnerships; and sole proprietorships.

Joint ventures with domestic investors may be created and they may be formed, depending on their ultimate purpose, either as a separate legal entity or merely as a temporary business agreement to carry out a specific project.

Subsidiaries and branches of foreign corporations may be established.

Companies are considered to be legal entities upon filing of appropriate documents with the Mercantile Register. Branches are not considered to be legal entities.

There is no requirement for local participation in the management of any firm that is wholly or partially owned by foreign investors.

■ ENVIRONMENTAL PROTECTION

The Ministry of Agriculture has the overall responsibility for environmental protection. Potential foreign investors are advised to contact that ministry or the General Directorate for External Investment with regard to laws and regulations pertaining to this subject.

■ RIGHTS AND OBLIGATIONS OF FOREIGN INVESTORS

Local financing sources are available to foreign investors.

Foreign investments and all income derived from such investments may be remitted abroad or repatriated.

Any government taking of property must be through proper legal means and must involve prompt and fair compensation.

■ LABOR

There is an existing and extensive body of laws with regard to both employment and working conditions. Labor unions are a major force in the economy.

All foreign nationals employed in Spain must obtain work and residence permits.

There are no general requirements with respect to the number of local workers who must be hired or any percentage as to the total number of such workers that must be employed.

■ ACCOUNTING REQUIREMENTS

All businesses operating in Spain must maintain full and accurate accounting records in accordance with internationally accepted standards. Companies, depending on size and activities, are required to appoint independent auditors and to be audited on a yearly basis.

■ CURRENCY CONTROLS

The Banco de Espana (the Bank of Spain) is the nation's central bank. The General Directorate of Foreign Transactions, under the Ministry of Economy and Finance, is responsible for policy development and management of the nation's foreign exchange program.

Foreign nationals employed in Spain are permitted to repatriate or remit abroad as much as 50 percent of their total income.

Spain's foreign exchange controls are now generally within the umbrella of EC requirements.

■ TAXATION

The principal taxes levied are on corporate and personal income and a value added tax (VAT). The central government, the community, and the local governments also possess the power to tax.

Other assessments include the excise tax, the transfer tax, a stamp tax, and customs duties. In addition to the personal income tax, individuals are also liable for net worth and inheritance taxes.

Local taxes are imposed on real property, motor vehicles, and various business and construction activities.

The tax year is the calendar year, i.e., January 1 to December 31. Business firms can elect to use their fiscal year for tax filing purposes.

Partnerships and joint ventures are required to file tax returns in the same manner as corporations and are generally considered to be taxable entities.

Various deductions are allowed including, but not limited to, legitimate business expenses, depreciation of physical assets, certain charitable donations, insurance premiums, and amortization of intangible assets.

Companies engaged in hydrocarbons exploitation and exploration are taxed under the special provisions of the Hydrocarbons Law.

Individual taxpayers are generally allowed a variety of tax credits with reference to, for example, dependent children, and certain percentages of expenses such as insurance premiums, medical expenses, and certain charitable donations.

Spain is a signatory to numerous bilateral treaties with other nations on the subject of double taxation.

■ LEGAL SYSTEM

There are a number of inferior courts, i.e., Magistrates' level which hear petty criminal and other special matters to include, for example, juvenile matters. The Provincial Courts hear more serious cases and act as appellate courts with regard to decisions of the lower courts. The Superior Courts hear certain types of civil and criminal cases and function in an appellate role with regard to decisions of the provincial courts. The National Court hears major criminal cases.

Appeals may be taken to the Supreme Court, which sits at Madrid.

■ CUSTOMS AND DUTIES

Spain is a signatory to the General Agreement on Tariffs and Trade (GATT) and is a member of the European Community. The government, as evidenced by EC membership, is committed to a free trade policy.

A number of free trade zones have been established throughout the country where materials and goods that are destined for reexport may be received without the imposition of customs charges.

■ PROTECTION OF INTELLECTUAL PROPERTY

Spain is a member of the World Intellectual Property Organization. In addition, the government has enacted laws for the protection of copyrights, patents, and trademarks.

■ IMMIGRATION AND RESIDENCE

Potential foreign investors are advised to contact the General Directorate for External

Investment for complete and current requirements pertaining to visas, work permits, and residence permits.

■ FOREIGN INVESTMENT ASSISTANCE DIRECTORY

Sources that can provide further information about foreign investment in Spain include:

Spanish Institute for Foreign Trade (ICEX)
Paseo de la Castellana, 14-16
28012 Madrid, Spain
Telephone: (34) (1) 4311240
Telex: 44838
Fax: (34) (1) 4316128

General Directorate for External Investment
Ministry of Industry, Trade and Tourism
State Department of Trade
Paseo de la Castellana, 162
28046 Madrid, Spain
Telephone: (34) (1) 5837400
Telex: 42112
Fax: (34) (1) 4581766

Banco de Espana (Bank of Spain)
Alcalá 50
28014 Madrid, Spain
Telephone: (34) (1) 4469055
Telex: 49461
Fax: (34) (1) 5216356

Persons interested in obtaining additional information about foreign investment in Spain are advised to contact the closest Spanish embassy or consular office.

Spain maintains diplomatic relations with Algeria, Angola, Argentina, Australia, Austria, Belgium, Bolivia, Brazil, Bulgaria, Cameroon, Canada, Chile, People's Republic of China, Colombia, Costa Rica, Côte d'Ivoire, Cuba, Czechoslovakia, Denmark, Dominican Republic, Ecuador, Egypt, El Salvador, Equatorial Guinea, Finland, France, Gabon, Germany, Greece, Guatemala, Haiti, Holy See, Honduras, Hungary, India, Indonesia, Iran, Iraq, Ireland, Israel, Italy, Japan, Jordan, Republic of Korea, Kuwait, Lebanon, Libya, Luxembourg, Malaysia, Mauritania, Mexico, Monaco, Morocco, Netherlands, New Zealand, Nicaragua, Nigeria, Norway, Pakistan, Panama, Paraguay, Peru, Philippines, Poland, Qatar, Romania, Russia, Saudi Arabia, South Africa, Sweden, Switzerland, Syria, Thailand, Tunisia, Turkey, United Arab Emirates, United Kingdom, United States, Uruguay, Venezuela, and Zaire.

SRI LANKA, DEMOCRATIC SOCIALIST REPUBLIC OF

■ POLITICAL ENVIRONMENT

Over the years, the country has experienced severe internal difficulties, essentially as the result of ethnic problems involving the Tamils, a minority group with religious ties to the Hindu religion. The Hindu connection with India has, on several occasions, created serious confrontations between Sri Lanka and that country.

The continuous problem of internal terrorism and the potential for a military confrontation with India over the Tamil issue have greatly strained the nation's fragile economic base. There is a high rate of unemployment. The annual rate of inflation is also high. There is an ongoing privatization program.

■ SUMMARY OF FOREIGN INVESTMENT POLICY

The government is actively seeking foreign investment and to that end has created the Greater Colombo Economic Commission, which has been given the responsibility of attracting foreign investment.

Principal goals of the government's program to obtain foreign investment are to increase the nation's industrial base, generate more foreign earnings, and provide employment opportunities.

The government permits foreign investment in all areas of the economy with the exception of small retail and personal services businesses.

There are numerous regulated industries to include banking, transportation, and defense-oriented activities in which foreign investors may be able to participate. Applications by foreign investors to participate in such areas will be determined by the government on a case-by-case basis. Application must be made through the Greater Colombo Economic Commission.

Minimum investments of $250,000 (U.S.) are required.

Manufacturing enterprises funded by foreign investment must produce 90 percent of production for export.

Overall, the government desires foreign investment in export-oriented activities; agribusiness; tourism; and in projects that will improve the country's infrastructure.

A number of incentives are offered to foreign investors to include long-term tax holidays, duty free imports if goods and materials are necessary for operations, and various concessions, many of which are related to the specific activities, e.g., tourism, agribusiness, export manufacturing, etc., in which a firm is engaged.

Companies that invest over $50 million (U.S.) and that create businesses that are not presently operating in the country are categorized as flagship or pioneer firms and are entitled to additional incentives.

Export processing zones have been established. Foreign firms operating in those zones are entitled to additional tax, customs, and other incentives.

■ FORMATION AND TYPES OF PERMITTED BUSINESS ORGANIZATIONS

Foreign investors may create corporations or partnerships as well as operating as sole proprietorships. Joint ventures may also be formed with domestic enterprises.

Branch offices or subsidiaries of firms incorporated outside the country may not be established without the permission of the government.

SRI LANKA

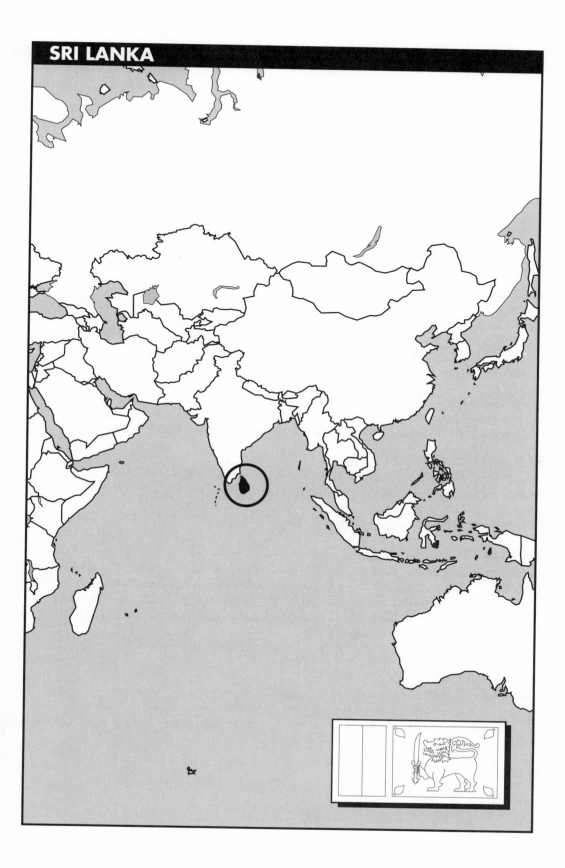

■ ENVIRONMENTAL PROTECTION

The government is interested in protecting the environment. Potential foreign investors are advised to contact the Greater Colombo Economic Commission regarding current laws and regulations pertaining to environmental protection.

■ RIGHTS AND OBLIGATIONS OF FOREIGN INVESTORS

In the majority of cases, foreign investors will have the right to obtain financing from local banks.

Foreign investors will generally have the right to open and maintain foreign currency accounts.

Investments and profits generated as a result of such investments may be repatriated.

■ LABOR

The labor force is well trained. There is an existing body of laws regarding employment and working conditions.

There is a requirement that local labor be accorded hiring preference except where personnel do not possess required technical skills.

Foreign nationals must obtain work permits.

■ ACCOUNTING REQUIREMENTS

All businesses must maintain complete records for tax and other purposes. Accounting and auditing procedures must meet internationally accepted standards.

■ CURRENCY CONTROLS

The Central Bank of Sri Lanka is responsible for the nation's monetary policy and affairs, including exchange control matters. In recent years, the country has removed virtually all exchange controls.

Foreign employees may repatriate earnings.

■ TAXATION

Foreign businesses and individuals are subject to taxation. Among the various tax incentives created for foreign investors are total tax exemptions from corporate income taxes for up to 15 years, and a reduced rate imposed on the turnover tax. Other tax advantages are also available for companies depending on their areas of activity, e.g., tourism and agribusiness, among others.

Individual taxpayers are eligible for a variety of deductions and allowances.

■ LEGAL SYSTEM

The Magistrates' Courts and Primary Courts hear and decide petty criminal and civil cases. The District Courts and the High Courts are trial level courts. Appeals from these courts are taken to the Court of Appeal as a matter of right. Final appeals may be taken to the Supreme Court, which sits in Colombo.

■ CUSTOMS AND DUTIES

The government has acted to reduce customs duties on a significant array of items.

Machinery, equipment, raw materials, and other goods and items necessary for operations may generally be imported without payment of duties.

■ PROTECTION OF INTELLECTUAL PROPERTY

Sri Lanka is a member of the World Intellectual Property Organization and thus subscribes to internationally accepted standards for the protection of copyrights, patents, and trademarks.

■ IMMIGRATION AND RESIDENCE

Visas are generally required to enter the country. Potential foreign investors are advised to contact the Greater Colombo Economic Commission for complete information regarding visas, work permits, and residence permits.

■ FOREIGN INVESTMENT ASSISTANCE DIRECTORY

Sources that will be able to provide further information about foreign investment in Sri Lanka include:

Greater Colombo Economic Commission
P.O. Box 1768
14 Sir Baron Jayatilleke Mawatha
Colombo 1, Sri Lanka
Telephone: (94) 448880 / (94) 422447 / (94) 434403 / (94) 435027
Telex: 21332 ECONCOM CE
Fax: (94) 447995

Ministry of Trade and Commerce
21 Rakshana Mandlraya
Vauxhall Street
Colombo 2, Sri Lanka
Telephone: (94) 35601
Telex: 21245

Central Bank of Sri Lanka
34-36 Janadhipathi Mawatha
P.O. Box 590
Colombo 1, Sri Lanka
Telephone: (94) 421191
Telex: 21176
Fax: (94) 540353

Federal of Chambers of Commerce and Industry
People's Bank Building
220 Deans Road
Colombo 1, Sri Lanka
Telephone: (94) 699530

Persons interested in obtaining further information about foreign investment in Sri Lanka also are advised to contact the country's closest embassy or consular office.

Sri Lanka maintains diplomatic relations with Australia, Bangladesh, Canada, People's Republic of China, Cuba, Czechoslovakia, Egypt, Finland, France, Germany, Holy See, India, Indonesia, Iraq, Italy, Japan, Republic of Korea, Libya, Malaysia, Maldives, Myanmar, Netherlands, Norway, Pakistan, Philippines, Poland, Russia, Sweden, Switzerland, Thailand, United Kingdom, and United States.

SUDAN, REPUBLIC OF

■ POLITICAL ENVIRONMENT

The nation is currently governed by a revolutionary command council that has been in power following a military coup d'etat in June 1989.

At the present time, the country's legislative and executive powers are both held by the National Salvation Revolutionary Command Council. The constitution has been suspended.

Most of the foreign investment that was present in Sudan before the 1989 (and its predecessor) coup, has been removed from the country. There are concerns about Sudan's stability.

There is a very high foreign debt, and Sudan has a history of being in arrears on debt payments. In addition, there is continuing military-civilian conflict in some parts of the nation.

■ SUMMARY OF FOREIGN INVESTMENT POLICY

Despite the country's current political instability, there remains a continuing desire for foreign investment.

In 1990, the National Salvation Revolutionary Command Council created The Encouragement of Investment Act that is administered by the Investment Public Corporation, a government organization which reports directly to the Ministerial Council that is composed of the prime minister, the minister of justice, the attorney general, the governor of the Bank of Sudan, and the president of the corporation.

The government is specifically interested in obtaining foreign investment in agricultural, industrial, mining, and tourism areas, as well as in the improvement of basic services and the overall infrastructure.

Sudan is a party to the Convention for the Settlement of Disputes Between States and Nationals of Other States, and several similar regional agreements with Arab nations.

■ FORMATION AND TYPES OF PERMITTED BUSINESS ORGANIZATIONS

The investment law is silent on the formation and type of business organization that a foreign investor may use in the country.

■ ENVIRONMENTAL PROTECTION

Potential foreign investors are advised to contact the Sudanese government for details regarding details on any laws applicable to the protection of the environment.

■ RIGHTS AND OBLIGATIONS OF FOREIGN INVESTORS

According to the law, there will be no discrimination as between a foreign or domestic investor, or between a public, private, cooperative, or mixed sector investment project.

Foreign investors and the employees of such investors are guaranteed freedom of movement, transport, and residence.

There are guarantees against nationalization, confiscation, expropriation, sequestration, custody, or freezing of property or funds without a judicial order and fair compensation.

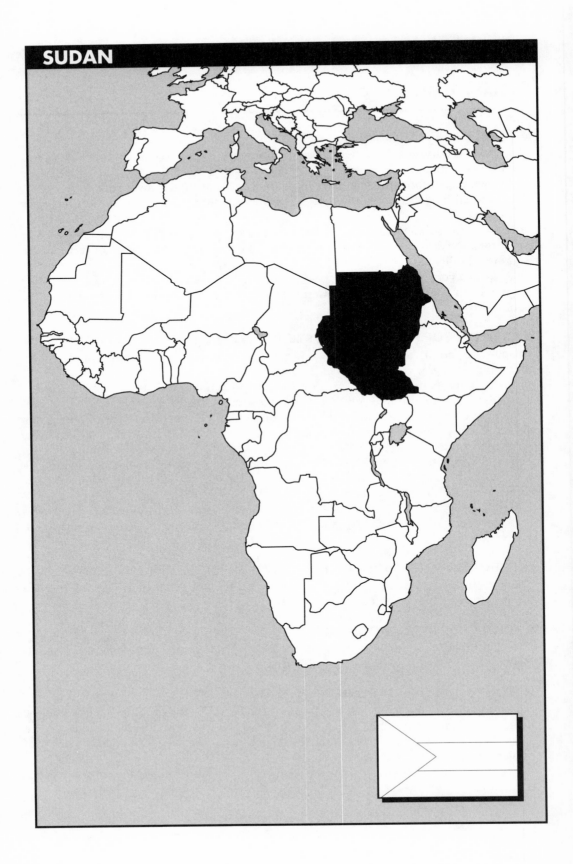

SUDAN

Foreign investors are guaranteed the right to repatriate investments in cases where the project is not implemented, or is liquidated either partially or totally.

There is a requirement that no project funded by foreign capital may begin without a technical and economic feasibility study being submitted and approved by the government.

■ LABOR

Approved projects that are funded by foreign investment are permitted to employ foreign nationals who possess expertise not available within the Sudanese labor force.

■ ACCOUNTING REQUIREMENTS

All foreign investors are required to maintain complete accounting records, which must be submitted annually to the Investment Public Corporation. Accounting records must be accredited by a chartered auditor.

The records must also show all assets that are exempt from customs duties and all materials that were imported for use in the project that have been exempted from such duties.

■ CURRENCY CONTROLS

Foreign investors are advised to contact the Investment Public Corporation for details as to the government's regulations on currency and exchange controls. Foreign nationals, employed by foreign investors, may repatriate their savings.

■ TAXATION

Taxes must be paid by all foreign investors whether formed as legal entities or individuals.

Details on current taxation programs should be obtained from the Investment Public Corporation.

Tax deductions and exemptions are available to include depreciation on plant and equipment.

■ LEGAL SYSTEM

The current system of courts is operated by the military forces. Islamic law is used in those courts.

■ CUSTOMS AND DUTIES

Foreign investors may enjoy total or partial exemption from customs duties pertaining to equipment and materials required for their project activities.

■ PROTECTION OF INTELLECTUAL PROPERTY

Sudan is a member of the World Intellectual Property Organization and thus subscribes to internationally agreed-upon standards concerning the protection of copyrights, trademarks, and patents.

■ IMMIGRATION AND RESIDENCE

Foreign nationals, including both potential investors and employees of foreign investors, must obtain visas to enter the country. Detailed information on visas, work permits, and residency permits should be obtained from the Investment Public Corporation.

■ FOREIGN INVESTMENT ASSISTANCE DIRECTORY

The principal source that can provide further information about foreign investment in Sudan is:

The Investment Public Corporation
21 Al Amarat
P.O. Box 701
Khartoum, Sudan
Telephone: (00) 42425
Telex: 24078

Persons interested in obtaining further information about investing in Sudan are also advised to contact the closest Sudanese embassy or consular office.

Sudan maintains diplomatic relations with Algeria, Central African Republic, Chad, People's Republic of China, Czechoslovakia, Denmark, Egypt, Ethiopia, France, Germany, Greece, Holy See, Hungary, India, Iraq, Italy, Japan, Jordan, Kenya, Democratic People's Republic of Korea, Republic of Korea, Kuwait, Lebanon, Libya, Morocco, Netherlands, Niger, Nigeria, Oman, Pakistan, Poland, Qatar, Romania, Russia, Saudi Arabia, Somalia, Spain, Switzerland, Syria, Tunisia, Turkey, Uganda, United Arab Emirates, United Kingdom, United States, Yemen, and Zaire.

SWAZILAND, KINGDOM OF

■ POLITICAL ENVIRONMENT

This country has been in an almost continuous state of governmental instability since its founding in 1973. Intrigue, successful and attempted coups, and both real and suspected treason have been commonplace.

There is a high inflation rate, a largely uneducated labor force, and, predictably, a high level of unemployment.

■ SUMMARY OF FOREIGN INVESTMENT POLICY

The government is interested in acquiring foreign investment and offers numerous incentives. Among the incentives are a five-year tax holiday to firms that bring new industry to the country or that produce only for export.

The country is a member of the Multilateral Investment Guarantee Agency Agreement. In addition, both expropriation and nationalization are prohibited by law.

A private company, the Swaziland Industrial Development Company, has been created to work as a joint venture partner with the country and international development institutions, to help develop the nation's private sector. The company provides advisory services to potential foreign investors, provides equity and loan financing, and works with foreign investors to both construct and lease factory buildings.

Industrial estates have been created, and land in those estates is made available by the Ministry of Commerce and Industry to foreign investors at low cost.

All loan applications, except those involving the Swaziland Industrial Development Company, require the approval of the Central Bank.

Any dealings in corporate securities or other documents that indicate ownership require approval by the Central Bank.

■ FORMATION AND TYPES OF PERMITTED BUSINESS ORGANIZATIONS

The most common form of business organization created by foreign investors is the corporation.

Corporations must be registered with the Ministry of Commerce, Industry and Tourism.

■ ENVIRONMENTAL PROTECTION

Foreign investors are advised to contact the Ministry of Commerce, Industry and Tourism for complete information as to relevant laws and regulation concerning environmental protection.

■ RIGHTS AND OBLIGATIONS OF FOREIGN INVESTORS

Foreign investors must file tax returns.

Companies operating in Swaziland are considered as permanent residents.

Profits and other income generated as a result of investment may be freely repatriated subsequent to tax payment.

Foreign investors should be aware that there may be a desire on the part of the government for domestic participation in businesses that are funded partially or wholly by foreign investment.

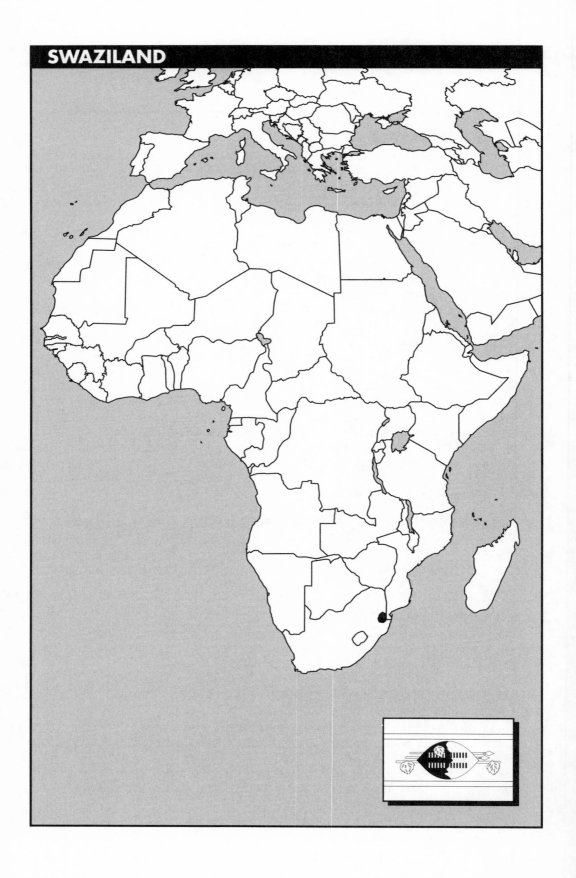

SWAZILAND

■ LABOR

In most cases, local labor must be accorded hiring preference. However, executive, professional, scientific, and technical positions may generally be filled by foreign nationals by showing that the available members of the local work force do not possess the necessary education or training.

■ ACCOUNTING REQUIREMENTS

Companies should maintain accurate and complete records for tax and exchange purposes and in accord with generally recognized accounting and auditing standards.

■ CURRENCY CONTROLS

All foreign exchange control is the responsibility of the Central Bank of Swaziland.

There are no controls on the flow of currency between Lesotho, the Republic of South Africa, and Swaziland, i.e., the Rand Monetary Area.

No company or individual may hold or deal in foreign currency other than an authorized dealer.

Any payments made to countries beyond the Rand Monetary Area must be approved by the Central Bank.

Temporary residents may transfer to countries outside the Rand Monetary Area up to one-third of their local monthly earned income, or up to one-half of such income if they maintain families abroad.

Foreign investment must be approved before any capital may be moved into the country.

■ TAXATION

Swaziland is a party to numerous bilateral treaties on the subject of double taxation.

The major tax is the income tax, which is assessed on both businesses and individuals. The tax year for individuals runs from July 1 to June 30. For companies, the tax year will run concurrently with the organization's fiscal year.

Businesses are permitted a variety of deductions to include those for training expenses of workers, depreciation on plant, machinery, equipment, and other allowances. Companies engaged in certain activities including, for example, mining and agriculture, are entitled to additional deductions.

Individuals are also granted certain exemptions from their taxable income.

There are numerous minor taxes to include those on casino revenue, mineral rights, sugar exports, and unused land, as well as on documents, property transfers, and sales.

■ LEGAL SYSTEM

There is a system of courts on a national basis that include those that hear and decide petty criminal offenses and the Superior Court, which sits as a trial court in major criminal and civil cases. Appeals are taken to the Court of Appeal, which sits at Mbabane.

■ CUSTOMS AND DUTIES

Imports are regulated by the Ministry of Finance, which issues import permits.

Swaziland is a party to the Lome Convention that allows free trade to the EC and enjoys preferred access to most other international markets, including the Southern African Customs Union with Botswana, Lesotho, Namibia, and South Africa.

Customs duties are generally ad valorem. Customs and excise charges are not applied to some types of raw materials and semi-processed goods.

■ PROTECTION OF INTELLECTUAL PROPERTY

Swaziland is a member of the World Intellectual Property Organization and thus subscribes to the internationally accepted standards of protection to be accorded to copyrights, patents, tradenames, trademarks, and technology transfer.

■ IMMIGRATION AND RESIDENCE

Visas, work permits, and residence permits are issued by the Ministry of Home Affairs. Applications are considered on a case-by-case basis. Individuals may attain a temporary residence permit that is valid for six years and may be renewable for additional three-year periods.

Potential investors are advised to contact the Ministry of Home Affairs or the Ministry of Commerce, Industry and Tourism for additional information about visas, work, and residence permits.

■ FOREIGN INVESTMENT ASSISTANCE DIRECTORY

There are several sources of additional information about foreign investment in Swaziland. These sources include:

Ministry of Commerce, Industry and Tourism
P.O. Box 45
Mbabane, Swaziland
Telephone: (268) 43201
Telex: 2232

Swaziland Industrial Development Company
Tin and Walker Streets
P.O. Box 866
Mbabane, Swaziland
Telephone: (268) 43391
Telex: 2052
Fax: (268) 45619

Swaziland Chamber of Commerce and Industry
P.O. Box 72
Mbabane, Swaziland
Telephone: (268) 44408
Telex: 2032
Fax: (268) 44408

Persons interested in obtaining further information about investing in Swaziland also are advised to contact the closest Swaziland embassy or consular office.

Swaziland maintains diplomatic relations with Taiwan (Republic of China), Israel, Mozambique, United Kingdom, and United States.

SWEDEN, KINGDOM OF

■ POLITICAL ENVIRONMENT

The nation has maintained a strict policy of neutrality in military affairs. Sweden, as a result, was never a member of the North Atlantic Treaty Organization.

The country has, however, applied for EC membership. Internal debate over the question of membership was bitter.

There are no threats to the Swedish sovereignty from either external or internal sources. The government is very stable. The Swedish standard of living is one of the highest in the world.

■ SUMMARY OF FOREIGN INVESTMENT POLICY

Sweden desires foreign investment as part of its continuing effort to modernize and expand the manufacturing and service sectors of the economy. The Ministry of Industry and Commerce is charged with the primary responsibility of promoting and regulating foreign investment.

Among the steps that the government has taken to encourage foreign investment are a privatization movement, a policy of deregulation, and a reduction in corporate and other taxes.

Sweden has adopted a policy of regional development which is designed to increase employment and aid the economy of specific geographic sections of the country. Incentives for foreign investment include export promotion assistance, government grants, and tax considerations.

Free trade zones have been created at various locations.

■ FORMATION AND TYPES OF PERMITTED BUSINESS ORGANIZATIONS

There are several types of business organization forms used in Sweden to include the limited liability company, the general or limited partnership, and the sole proprietorship. Branches of foreign businesses and subsidiaries of foreign corporations may also be established.

A limited liability company is the equivalent of the corporate form. Such companies are required to hold annual shareholder meetings. There is no requirement for domestic participation except for the fact that at least half of the members of the board of directors must reside in the country, as must the managing director.

Limited liability companies enjoy juridical person status upon filing with the Registrar's Office.

■ ENVIRONMENTAL PROTECTION

There are strong laws relevant to the protection of the environment, chief among them being the Environmental Protection Acts of 1969 and 1988. Potential foreign investors should contact the Ministry of Industry and Commerce or the Ministry of the Environment for details on the application of these laws.

■ RIGHTS AND OBLIGATIONS OF FOREIGN INVESTORS

Generally, there is equality of treatment under the law between foreign and domestic investors.

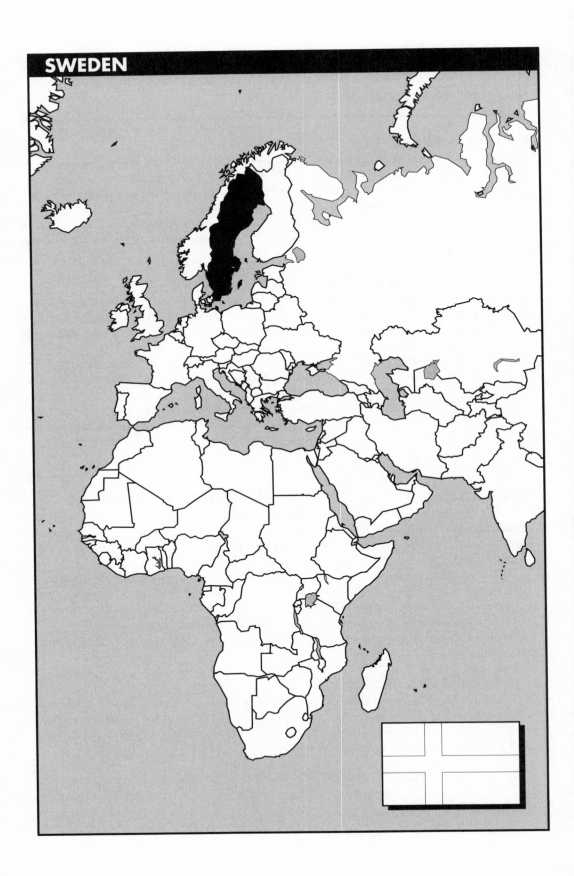

SWEDEN

Foreign companies and individuals must file tax returns with the government.

There are no current restrictions on foreign participation in any Swedish business activity.

Profits and other income derived from foreign investments in Sweden may be remitted abroad or repatriated after payment of required taxes. All such remittances must be conducted through a Swedish exchange bank.

■ LABOR

The Swedish work force is well educated and highly unionized. There is a substantial body of existing law that provides for working conditions, salaries, wages, and fringe benefits.

There is a requirement that nationals of Nordic countries, i.e., Sweden, Norway, Finland, Iceland, and Denmark, be given hiring preference. Work permits must be possessed by individuals from any other country.

■ ACCOUNTING REQUIREMENTS

All limited liability companies must maintain a system of accounting records to include an annual statement and must issue an annual report. These records must be prepared pursuant to internationally accepted standards. Company books must be independently audited on an annual basis.

■ CURRENCY CONTROLS

Swedish controls on the movement of currency into and out of the country are relatively liberal.

Individuals residing in Sweden or limited liability companies formed in Sweden are prohibited from maintaining active bank accounts abroad.

Foreign investors should be aware that virtually all currency movements from Sweden, exclusive of those involving repatriation or remittance abroad of investment income, must be processed through authorized currency dealers.

■ TAXATION

The present policy is dedicated to the concept of tax reduction.

Companies are taxed on all business income. Depreciation is allowed relevant to machinery and equipment, buildings, patents and other intangible assets, and, where applicable, on natural resource depletion.

Sweden is a party to many agreements with other countries relevant to double taxation.

The 12-month tax year for businesses is usually the fiscal year for that business although another 12-month period may be used if approved by the Swedish tax authorities, i.e., the National Tax Board.

There are a variety of minor taxes assessed to include stamp duties, value added taxes (VAT), sales and excise taxes, and taxes on real property and security transactions.

Individuals who are non-residents are taxed only on their income earned in the country. Residents must pay on income earned worldwide.

■ LEGAL SYSTEM

In addition to a system of administrative courts, Sweden has District Courts that hear both petty and major criminal and civil cases. Decisions are referred to the Appellate

Courts. The Supreme Court may agree to hear decisions of the Appellate Courts. The Supreme Court sits in Stockholm.

■ CUSTOMS AND DUTIES

As an applicant for EC membership, Sweden will continue to move forward with plans to reduce and eliminate customs and related charges. Presently, however, customs charges are based on the ad valorem principle.

Sweden is a party to the General Agreement on Tariffs and Trade (GATT) and a member of the European Economic Community and the European Free Trade Association. All customs duties involving trade with other EC members have been eliminated.

■ PROTECTION OF INTELLECTUAL PROPERTY

Sweden is a member of the World Intellectual Property Organization and supports the protection of rights relevant to copyrights, patents, tradenames, trademarks, and technology transfer.

■ IMMIGRATION AND RESIDENCE

Renewable visas may be issued to potential foreign investors. Complete information concerning both visas and residence permits may be obtained from the Ministry of Industry and Commerce.

■ FOREIGN INVESTMENT ASSISTANCE DIRECTORY

The following source may be contacted to obtain more detailed information concerning foreign investment in Sweden:

Ministry of Industry and Commerce
Invest in Sweden Office
Fredsgt. 8 103 33
Stockholm, Sweden
Telephone: (46) (8) 763-10-00
Telex: 14180
Fax: (46) (8) 11-36-16

Persons interested in obtaining further information about investing in Sweden also are advised to contact the closest Swedish embassy or consular office.

Sweden maintains diplomatic relations with Albania, Algeria, Angola, Argentina, Australia, Austria, Bangladesh, Belgium, Bolivia, Botswana, Brazil, Bulgaria, Canada, Chile, People's Republic of China, Colombia, Costa Rica, Cuba, Czechoslovakia, Denmark, Dominican Republic, Ecuador, Egypt, Ethiopia, Finland, France, Germany, Greece, Guatemala, Guinea-Bissau, Hungary, Iceland, India, Indonesia, Iran, Iraq, Ireland, Israel, Italy, Japan, Kenya, People's Democratic Republic of Korea, Republic of Korea, Laos, Lebanon, Libya, Malaysia, Mexico, Morocco, Mozambique, Netherlands, Nicaragua, Nigeria, Norway, Pakistan, Panama, Peru, Philippines, Poland, Portugal, Romania, Russia, Saudi Arabia, Senegal, Somalia, South Africa, Spain, Sri Lanka, Switzerland, Tanzania, Thailand, Tunisia, Turkey, United Kingdom, United States, Uruguay, Venezuela, Vietnam, Zambia, and Zimbabwe.

SWITZERLAND (THE SWISS CONFEDERATION)

■ POLITICAL ENVIRONMENT

Switzerland has a stable and democratically elected government.

The nation, historically, has been a world center for finance and financial services operations. These activities, along with tourism, represent Switzerland's principal sources of revenue.

Both the annual rate of inflation and the unemployment level of the nation are low.

■ SUMMARY OF FOREIGN INVESTMENT POLICY

The Federal Office for Labor and Industry, within the Department of Industry, is the central government's main point of contact for potential foreign investors.

There are no specific federal incentives that have been developed toward foreign investors. Most incentives, including tax incentives, are those provided by the various cantons. In some cases, these locally provided incentives are dedicated to foreign investment interests.

Those few incentives offered by the federal government are usually in the form of tax holidays or grants. In most cases, such federal level incentives are provided to both foreign and domestic investors and are based on a recognized need to generate employment opportunities.

Local or canton incentives can include grants of cash, low-interest loans, tax holidays for periods that can range up to 10 years, and real property provided at low cost by the local government for commercial use. In some cantons, special tax considerations are only for the benefit of foreign investors.

Federal incentives often require that desiring investors incorporate in the country.

Foreign investors may own complete control of companies in Switzerland. There is no requirement for Swiss ownership.

While there are no limits on the percentage of foreign ownership, the majority of the board members of a corporation formed in the country must be resident Swiss nationals.

There is no requirement for registration or approval of a foreign investment by the government except in cases of banks and insurance companies. However, foreign businesses or individuals are required to obtain permission to obtain real property.

Tourism and financial industry enterprises are generally considered to represent special categories of foreign investment. The various cantons, through their economic development offices, may offer long-term, low-interest loans or loan guarantees to tourism enterprises and significant tax incentives to financial industry organizations to include holding companies.

Foreign investors, in general, are not restricted in the areas of the Swiss economy in which they may become engaged. The exceptions are postal services, broadcasting, and rail transportation.

■ FORMATION AND TYPES OF PERMITTED BUSINESS ORGANIZATIONS

Foreign investors may participate in the Swiss economy through the creation of a corporation, a partnership, or a sole proprietorship (i.e., a single owner company).

SWITZERLAND

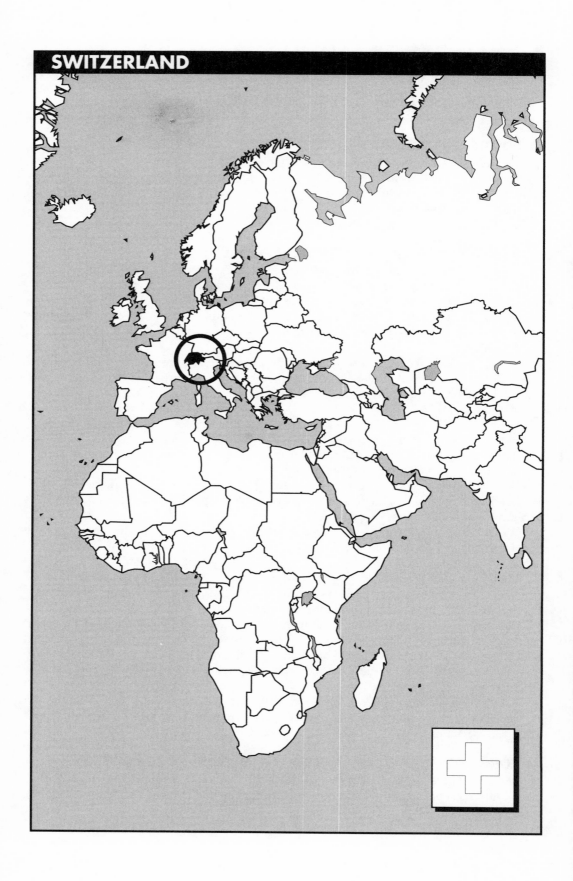

Corporations include joint stock companies, limited liability companies (the latter being primarily designed for the use of small enterprises), and cooperative societies.

Partnerships may be either general or limited in nature.

Subsidiaries or branch offices of foreign corporations may be established. Joint ventures (i.e., ordinary partnerships) may be formed between foreign and Swiss investors or enterprises.

Corporations, including subsidiaries of foreign corporations and cooperative societies, acquire juridical person status upon filing required documents with the Register of Commerce.

■ ENVIRONMENTAL PROTECTION

There is a very high governmental interest at both the federal and cantonal levels with regard to the environment. The Federal Environmental Protection Office is the principal government agency responsible for developing environmental policy.

Cantonal approval is required before development may occur of any facility that may create air, water, or land surface damage or excessive noise levels.

Potential foreign investors are advised to contact the Federal Office for Labor and Industry for complete information on the cantonal agencies that are responsible for environmental protection.

■ RIGHTS AND OBLIGATIONS OF FOREIGN INVESTORS

Foreign enterprises may obtain financing from Swiss banks.

Real property may be purchased by foreign companies or individuals only after acquiring a permit for such purchase from the canton on which the property is located.

Nationalization has never occurred in Switzerland. Any taking by the government for public purposes would require legal process and a payment of fair compensation to the property holder. Switzerland is a party to the Multilateral Investment Guarantee Agency Agreement.

Foreign investments and all income derived from such investments may be remitted abroad or repatriated. Upon liquidation of an investment, the foreign investor's proper share may be remitted abroad or repatriated.

Domestic companies may be merged into or acquired by foreign enterprises without any prior notice to, or approval by, the government.

■ LABOR

The Swiss labor force is highly motivated, extremely skilled, and well educated. There is an extensive body of laws dealing with working conditions and employment.

Foreign nationals may be employed in cases where special qualifications are required and where no Swiss national is available with such a background. All foreign employees must possess work permits of which there are several types that are valid for specific and differing periods of time.

■ ACCOUNTING REQUIREMENTS

All businesses are expected to maintain complete and accurate accounting and other records. Corporations must be audited on a yearly basis unless, in the case of limited companies, the articles of incorporation provide otherwise. Partnerships, except those engaged in banking or other financial activities, are not required to be audited.

Accounting and auditing procedures must be in conformity with internationally accepted standards.

■ CURRENCY CONTROLS

The Swiss National Bank is the nation's central bank and, among other functions, is responsible for the management of the foreign exchange policy.

There are no current restrictions on the movement of investor funds into or from the country.

No requirements exist with regard to the registration of foreign capital, foreign loans, or technology transfer agreements.

Foreign businesses and individuals may open and maintain bank accounts in any foreign currencies.

■ TAXATION

Companies and individuals are subject to the tax laws. Tax incentives, as noted, are generally provided by the individual cantons and take the form of tax holidays or tax reductions. In rare situations, tax incentives are granted at the federal level.

There are a number of taxes levied in Switzerland. The principal tax is on business and individual income. Income taxes are levied at the federal, canton, and municipal (communal) levels on both companies and individuals.

Partnerships are not considered as taxable entities. Income generated by a partnership is considered as income to the individual partners. The same rule is applied to joint ventures.

In general, the tax year is the calendar year, i.e., January 1 to December 31, although there are circumstances where the dates may vary from canton to canton.

Deductions include, among others, depreciation of assets and legitimate business expenses such as insurance premiums, royalties, certain taxes, and contributions to charity.

Individual taxpayers may deduct expenses related to their employment, insurance premiums, charitable contributions, and medical expenses, among others. Personal allowances include those for taxpayer dependents.

There are a number of other taxes assessed to include a wealth tax, and estate and gift taxes on individuals; a turnover (sales) tax; a stamp (or document) tax at the federal and cantonal levels; real property taxes; customs charges; and a variety of minor taxes, license, and registration fees.

Switzerland has entered into numerous bilateral treaties with other nations on the subject of double taxation.

■ LEGAL SYSTEM

The court system includes local (justice of the peace) courts, district and jury courts that hear more serious civil and criminal matters, and appeals courts. The federal system includes the Federal Supreme Court, the ultimate appellate court that sits at Lausanne. The Federal Supreme Court is comprised of several branches that hear bankruptcy, constitutional, civil, and criminal cases.

■ CUSTOMS AND DUTIES

Switzerland is a member of the European Free Trade Association (EFTA) that is comprised of Austria, Finland, Iceland, Liechtenstein, Norway, and Sweden, and which is associated in agreement on most free trade issues with the European Community (EC). Switzerland is a signatory of the General Agreement on Tariffs and Trade (GATT).

The government is basically committed to the principles of free trade although import permits are sometimes required and customs duties are charged on imports from non-EFTA or non-EC countries. Customs charges are based on weight.

Export incentives are provided through the Federal Export Risk Guarantee program that supplies financial risk coverage with regard to certain exports.

Traditionally, Switzerland has protected its agricultural sector with quota restrictions.

■ PROTECTION OF INTELLECTUAL PROPERTY

Switzerland is a member of the World Intellectual Property Organization; the Berne and Universal Copyright Conventions; the Madrid and Nice Agreements on Trademark Registration and Classification; the Paris Convention for the Protection of Industrial Property; the International Patent Classification Agreement; the European Patent Convention; and the Patent Cooperation Treaty.

In addition, Switzerland has enacted domestic laws that are designed to protect interests in copyrights, patents, trademarks, and industrial designs.

■ IMMIGRATION AND RESIDENCE

In most cases, visas are not required to visit the country.

Work permits, however, are required, and are issued in conjunction with residence permits. There are several classes of residence permits granted after five or ten years residence in the country and that are considered permanent permits; temporary permits that must be renewed yearly; short-term permits that are limited to nine or 18 months; and border community permits that are used by workers living in areas outside Switzerland but who work in the country.

Potential foreign investors are advised to contact the Federal Office for Labor and Industry for complete and current information regarding laws and procedures pertaining to visas, work permits, and residence permits.

■ FOREIGN INVESTMENT ASSISTANCE DIRECTORY

Sources that can provide additional information about foreign investment in Switzerland include:

Federal Office for Labor and Industry
Department of Industry
Mattenhofstrasse 5
Berne, Switzerland
Telephone: (41) (31) 612871
Fax: (41) (31) 612768

Swiss National Bank
Bundesplatz
3003 Berne, Switzerland
Telephone: (41) (31) 210211
Fax: (41) (31) 210207

Persons interested in obtaining further information about foreign investment in Switzerland are advised to contact the closest Swiss embassy or consular office.

Switzerland maintains diplomatic relations with Algeria, Argentina, Australia, Austria, Belgium, Brazil, Bulgaria, Cameroon, Canada, Chile, People's Republic of China, Colombia, Costa Rica, Côte d'Ivoire, Cuba, Czechoslovakia, Denmark, Ecuador, Egypt, Finland, France, Germany, Ghana, Greece, Holy See, Hungary, India, Indonesia, Iran, Iraq, Ireland, Israel, Italy, Japan, Jordan, Democratic People's Republic of Korea, Republic of Korea, Lebanon, Libya, Liechtenstein, Luxembourg, Malaysia, Mexico, Monaco, Morocco, Netherlands, Nigeria, Norway, Pakistan, Peru, Philippines, Poland, Portugal, Romania, Russia, Rwanda, Saudi Arabia, Senegal, South Africa, Spain, Sweden, Thailand, Tunisia, Turkey, United Kingdom, United States, Uruguay, Venezuela, Yemen, and Zaire.

SYRIAN ARAB REPUBLIC

■ POLITICAL ENVIRONMENT

The government of Syria has been controlled for the past three decades by the Ba'thist political party, which has an extremely left wing socialist orientation. In recent years, the nation has suffered from a variety of economic problems that the government has not moved quickly or effectively enough to correct. Despite these considerations, the government appears to be both strong and stable.

Syria's government, pursuant to its socialist philosophy, has employed a high degree of central government control of virtually all areas of significant economic activity to include banking, insurance, manufacturing, and large scale agriculture. As part of that control, the government has been deeply involved in the management of foreign and domestic trade, quality and levels of production, distribution of goods, and pricing.

The major Syrian economic sector is agriculture. The petroleum industry has been growing in importance but is still small by comparison with other oil-producing Middle East states.

Syria backed Iran in the Iran-Iraq conflict and, as a result, lost favor with its former Arab allies in the region. These allies had been important sources of aid to Syria, and when that aid ceased, the nation's perennially limited foreign trade assisted by some newly discovered crude oil locations were employed to maintain badly sagging foreign exchange reserves. The net result, however, was an inability to maintain the nation's essential infrastructure. In addition, the government, as the general manager of the economy, was unable to keep factories in operation.

During this entire period, the government has maintained a major military program, largely (if not exclusively) as a result of its real and potential confrontations with Israel.

Inflation, unemployment, and a massive public external debt have been the inevitable results. Inflation was reported at a level of 38 percent in 1988 and 45 percent in 1989. The country has experienced extreme problems in meeting its bilateral debt obligations and those incurred as a result of loans received from such multinational organizations as the World Bank.

In recognition of the problems facing the country, the government, despite its ideology, has pushed through a series of economic reforms designed to revitalize the private sector. These reforms include investment by the private sector in previously closed areas of the economy; encouragement of joint ventures between the private and public sectors that will allow the private sector a management majority position; incentives to exporters that will permit them to retain 75 percent of their foreign exchange profits for import financing; and a liberalization of the nation's views on foreign investment.

■ SUMMARY OF FOREIGN INVESTMENT POLICY

As a part of its reforms relevant to foreign investment, Syria, in 1991, enacted the Investment Law, also known as Law Number 10. A new agency, the Higher Council for Investment, was established to regulate foreign investments.

The law provides incentives to foreign investors that take the form of tax holidays and customs exemptions on required raw materials, equipment, and other imports used in the investor's business operations. There are ongoing discussions with regard

SYRIAN ARAB REPUBLIC

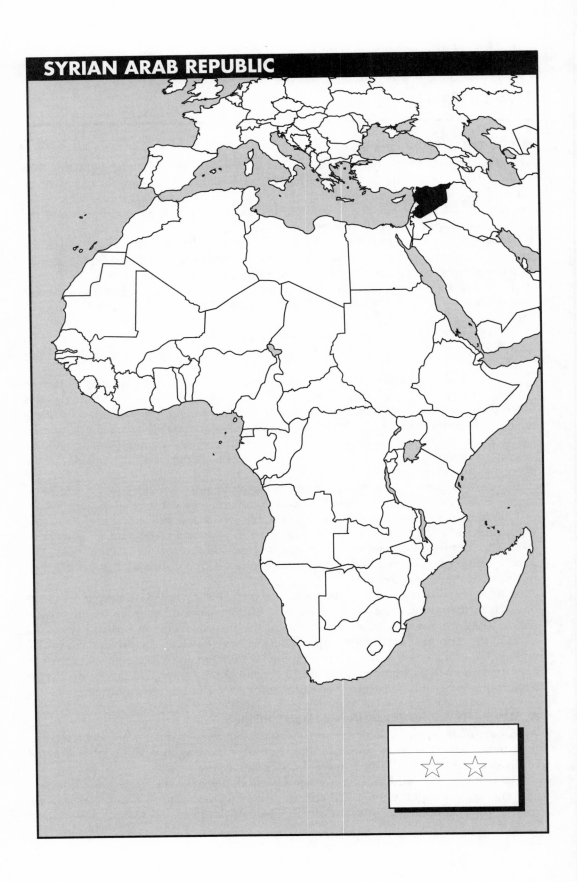

to revitalization of the Free Trade Zones that were originally established at Aleppo, Lattakia, Tartous, Damascus, and Adra and on the Syrian-Jordanian border.

All foreign investment proposals must be submitted for approval to the Higher Council for Investment. Proposals are submitted by this agency to those ministries that may have an interest. The process can be prolonged and complicated.

■ FORMATION AND TYPES OF PERMITTED BUSINESS ORGANIZATIONS

Foreign investors will find that the government of Syria will encourage participation through joint ventures. The foreign joint venture partner will almost without exception be a foreign corporation. The Syrian partner may well be the government. Tourism and agricultural projects are of major foreign investment interest to the Syrian government.

Foreign joint venture partners usually will hold a 75 percent interest with the government maintaining a 25 percent share. In general, the government does not seek a management role in the joint venture's activities.

■ ENVIRONMENTAL PROTECTION

The Syrian government has announced its interest in the need for proper environmental protection measures. A separate office, the Minister of State for Environmental Affairs, has been created.

Potential foreign investors are advised to contact the Higher Council for Investment for complete and current information on current laws and regulations pertaining to this subject area.

■ RIGHTS AND OBLIGATIONS OF FOREIGN INVESTORS

The Investment Law specifically provides for the remittance abroad or repatriation of invested foreign capital and profits created by such investment. The profits that investors seek to transfer abroad must, however, have been the result of investment activities.

There are no guarantees against nationalization. Syria's government remains essentially committed to a socialist economy and central planning. While some private sector companies have been permitted to exist, there is no known government plan to permit the private and public sectors to compete against each other.

No government policy exists with regard to ensuring that foreign investors are accorded equal opportunities with domestic ones.

■ LABOR

The Syrian government has enacted a complete body of laws with regard to the subjects of employment and working conditions.

Based on the country's socialist political ideology, foreign participants in the Syrian economy can expect labor to be favored in any confrontation with management except where the government is involved in an enterprise.

Foreign nationals who are employed in Syria in any capacity must obtain work permits. In general, foreign personnel will only be employed in positions requiring skills and experience that are not locally and immediately available.

The Syrian labor pool is large and contains both skilled and unskilled workers.

■ ACCOUNTING REQUIREMENTS

All economic activities carried on in Syria must maintain complete and current records, including accounting and financial information, for use by the government for tax, statistical, and other purposes.

■ CURRENCY CONTROLS

The Central Bank of Syria is responsible for all matters relevant to operational management of the nation's foreign exchange policy. There are stringent controls on foreign exchange.

The Syrian government uses a two-tier system of exchange rates, the official one and a Neighboring Country rate. The latter is the rate used by the Commercial Bank of Syria when converting currency for cash, personal remittances, and other exchange transactions.

Exchange controls do not permit the movement of Syrian currency out of the country. Transfer of any foreign currency out of the nation is permitted with the approval of the Central Bank of Syria. Official exchange transfers must be approved by the Central Bank and the Ministry of Finance. The ability of the Central Bank to approve transfers may be limited by a foreign exchange shortage that does not permit the transfer.

■ TAXATION

The major taxes in Syria are those levied on income. Anticipated increased foreign investment will result in foreign businesses becoming major taxpayers. While tax holidays and other fiscal incentives are being offered by the government, it would be advisable for potential foreign investors to contact the Higher Council for Investment to determine what current or projected tax laws will pertain to foreign firms.

■ LEGAL SYSTEM

The Syrian court system includes a Supreme Court that is responsible for decisions concerning the application of the nation's constitution and other laws, and to resolve issues of conflicting jurisdiction between the other courts in the system. The Supreme Court also has initial jurisdiction on matters relevant to election of public officers and impeachment.

The court system also includes Personal Status Courts that handle family law matters; Tribunals of Peace that function in the same manner as Magistrates' Courts and decide petty criminal and civil cases; Tribunals of the First Instance, which hear more serious civil and criminal matters; and Courts of Appeal, which have a civil and criminal appellate function on matters brought up from the Tribunals of Peace and from the Tribunals of the First Instance.

Appeals from the Courts of Appeal are taken to the Court of Cassation, which sits at Damascus.

■ CUSTOMS AND DUTIES

There is a strong government interest in generating a greater level of trade and, in particular, of increasing the level of exports.

The government's main interest in reestablishing Free Trade Zones, mentioned previously, represents a key element in its efforts to increase export trade.

Additionally, the government has acted to increase the list of items that the private sector may import, e.g., rice, tea, and sugar. Pick-up trucks, usually prohibited from being imported, may be brought into the country by exporters of agricultural products.

■ PROTECTION OF INTELLECTUAL PROPERTY

Syria is not a member of the World Intellectual Property Organization. Potential foreign investors are advised to contact the Higher Council for Investment to determine the status of any current or projected laws designed to provide protection with regard to copyrights, patents, trademarks, and technology transfer.

■ IMMIGRATION AND RESIDENCE

Visas are generally required to enter Syria. Potential foreign investors are advised to contact the Higher Council for Investment for complete and current information on visa, work permit, and residence permit requirements.

■ FOREIGN INVESTMENT ASSISTANCE DIRECTORY

Sources that can provide further information about foreign investment in Syria include:

Higher Council for Investment
Office of the Prime Minister
Government Offices
Damascus, Syria
Telephone: (0) 113513
Telex: 227981

Central Bank of Syria
29 Ayar Square
Damascus, Syria
Telephone: (0) 224800
Telex: 269007

Persons interested in obtaining additional information about foreign investment in Syria are advised to contact the closest Syrian embassy or consular office.

Syria maintains diplomatic relations with Afghanistan, Algeria, Argentina, Australia, Austria, Belgium, Brazil, Bulgaria, Canada, Chile, People's Republic of China, Cuba, Cyprus, Czechoslovakia, Denmark, Egypt, Ethiopia, Finland, France, Germany, Greece, Holy See, Hungary, India, Indonesia, Iran, Italy, Japan, Jordan, Democratic People's Republic of Korea, Kuwait, Libya, Mauritania, Morocco, Netherlands, Oman, Pakistan, Panama, Poland, Qatar, Romania, Russia, Saudi Arabia, Somalia, Spain, Sudan, Sweden, Switzerland, Tunisia, Turkey, United Arab Emirates, United Kingdom, United States, Venezuela, Vietnam, and Yemen.

TAIWAN, REPUBLIC OF CHINA

■ POLITICAL ENVIRONMENT

The government is internally stable and there is no current external threat to its sovereignty.

A future, and major, consideration is the possibility of closer political ties to be forged between the country and the People's Republic of China. One potential solution that has been advanced to resolve political reunification, and which has apparently received attention both in Taipei and Beijing, has been a scheme whereby Taiwan would become a separate, self-governing unit, similar to the situation that will be effective relevant to mainland China and Hong Kong in 1997.

■ SUMMARY OF FOREIGN INVESTMENT POLICY

The Republic of China has shown a continuing interest in the acquisition of foreign investment and has liberalized many of its national policies toward the accomplishment of that goal.

Major responsibilities for the promotion and regulation of foreign investment are assigned to the Industrial Development and Investment Center, which functions under the general authority of the Ministry of Economic Affairs. An extensive body of law relevant to foreign investment has been enacted with the principal legislation being the Statute for Upgrading Industries, the Statute for Investment by Foreign Nationals, and the Statute for Investment by Overseas Chinese, all as amended.

The government has developed a Six-Year National Development Plan that, in large measure, depends on the infusion of foreign investment for its success. Essential elements of the plan are dedicated to the improvement of the country's transportation and telecommunications systems; housing; development of industries in the fields of optical electronics, computer software, new materials applications, energy conservation, industrial automation, and resource exploitation.

The overall concern of the government is to improve the nation's industrial productivity and to generally raise the quality of life within the country.

Various incentive programs are offered by the government to potential foreign investors. A number of industrial estates, export processing zones, and a science-based industrial park have been developed. There are numerous tax incentives for which foreign businesses, depending on their field of activity, may be eligible.

■ FORMATION AND TYPES OF PERMITTED BUSINESS ORGANIZATIONS

The types of companies that are recognized under the provisions of the nation's Company Law are companies limited by shares, unlimited companies, limited companies, and unlimited companies with limited liability shareholders.

Foreign investors are more likely to create companies limited by shares because of the greater flexibility provided under the law. Limited companies may have no more than 21 shareholders of which at least half must be Chinese. Companies limited by shares and limited companies enjoy juridical person status.

Foreign firms may engage with domestic companies in joint ventures.

In all cases, foreign firms must file for approval, before beginning operations, with the Investment Commission of the Ministry of Economic Affairs.

TAIWAN

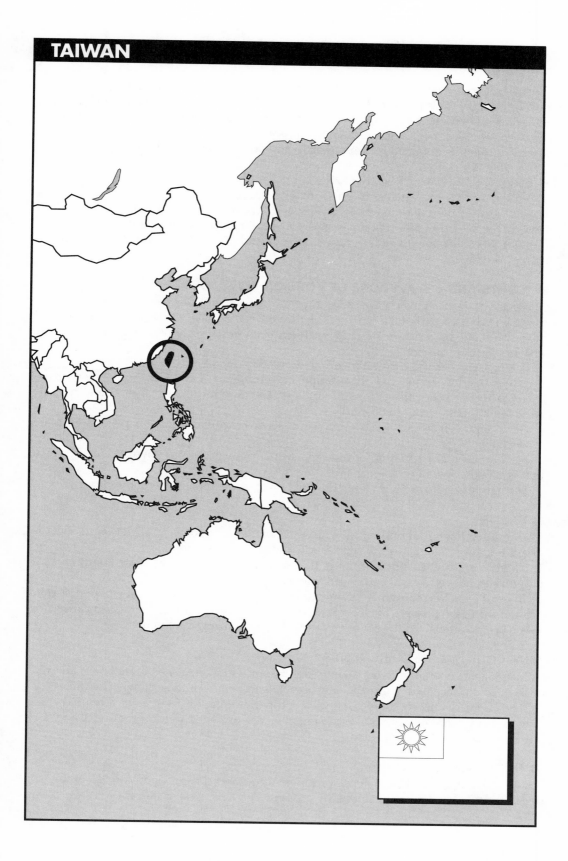

The Negative List for Investment by Overseas Chinese and Foreign Nationals sets out the areas of the economy where foreign investment is not permitted. In addition to the areas shown on the Negative List, certain other areas, to include public utilities, mass communications, finance, and insurance, are considered as restricted. Special approval must be obtained for foreign investors to participate in those areas.

■ ENVIRONMENTAL PROTECTION

There is a continuing interest in environmental protection. Potential foreign investors should consult the Guidelines on Review and Approval of Pollution Prevention and Control for Set-Up of New Factories, and, for specific information, the Industrial Development and Investment Center, regarding laws and regulations pertaining to environmental protection.

■ RIGHTS AND OBLIGATIONS OF FOREIGN INVESTORS

There are no restrictions on the percentage of domestic businesses that may be held by foreign investors except in the case of limited companies where not more than 50 percent of the shares may be held by foreign interests without the approval of the Investment Commission.

Foreign and domestic investors are guaranteed equality of treatment.

While restrictions on the repatriation or remittance abroad of profits have been eased in recent years, there are still limits on the amount of such capital that may be removed annually from the country.

All foreign companies and foreign nationals are required to file tax returns with the government.

No domestic participation is required in the management or ownership of a firm that is wholly owned by foreign investment.

Foreign investors are guaranteed protection from nationalization or expropriation.

■ LABOR

The country has an abundant and highly trained labor force at all levels to include executive, professional, technical, clerical, and production workers.

There is an extensive body of laws that sets out the required working conditions for employees, as well as wage and salary levels, and fringe benefits.

In most cases, except where permitted by the Ministry of Labor, and where domestic workers do not possess the required special knowledge to fill certain technical or executive positions, Chinese workers must be given hiring preference.

■ ACCOUNTING REQUIREMENTS

All companies operating in the country are required to maintain accurate books and records in accordance with internationally accepted accounting and auditing standards.

The rights of shareholders in either a company limited by shares or a limited company must be contained in the documents that are prepared to form the entity and that are submitted to the government.

■ CURRENCY CONTROLS

Despite the liberalization of the government's rules on currency and foreign exchange, the country's laws relevant to the inward and outward flow of currency remain stringent. Potential foreign investors are advised to make specific inquiries as to currency control regulations with the Industrial Center or directly with the Investment Commission.

■ TAXATION

The Ministry of Finance is the government agency charged with the reponsibility of administering tax programs.

Taxes are levied on both businesses and individuals. Income taxes are based on the calendar year but businesses may adopt a fiscal year after approval of such an alternative by the Ministry of Finance.

In addition to income taxes, there are a variety of minor taxes to include those on commodities, real estate, securities, transactions, and local taxes.

Individuals must pay taxes on personal income and, where applicable, business income, as well as estate and gift taxes. Individuals who reside in the country for more than six months in any calendar year are considered residents for tax purposes. Non-resident taxpayers are those who remain in the country for 90 or more days, but less than six months.

Non-residents are generally eligible for a larger number of deductions, exemptions, and tax allowances.

Firms that operate in the export processing zones are exempt from the business tax as well as from the commodity tax and various other minor taxes.

Tax incentives applicable to businesses include various accelerated depreciation schedules and deductions ranging from five to 30 percent depending on the activities in which the business is engaged.

■ LEGAL SYSTEM

There is a system of District Courts that hears civil and criminal cases at the trial level. Appeals from those courts are taken to the High Courts and, where applicable, to the Supreme Court, which is the final appellate level. The Supreme Court sits in Taipei.

■ CUSTOMS AND DUTIES

Businesses that operate in the export processing zones are exempt from the payment of customs charges.

Customs duties are applied to imported goods. Duties have been gradually reduced to the present rate of 3.5 percent of import value.

■ PROTECTION OF INTELLECTUAL PROPERTY

There are domestic laws designed to protect trademarks, patents, and copyrights. However, there has been a past history of intellectual property violations and, apparently, a poor government record of prosecutions under the existing statutes.

■ IMMIGRATION AND RESIDENCE

Foreign nationals who have been approved as investors, executives of foreign businesses in the country, and children and spouses of such individuals, may enter the Republic of China after acquiring a resident visa. The visa is valid for one year.

Visas that permit multiple entry to the country may be issued to other foreign nationals.

■ FOREIGN INVESTMENT ASSISTANCE DIRECTORY

The following offices should be contacted to obtain detailed information concerning foreign investment in Taiwan, Republic of China:

Industrial Development and Investment Center
10th Floor
7 Roosevelt Road
Sec. 1
Taipei, Taiwan, Republic of China
Telephone: (886) (2) 394-7213
Telex: 10634 INVEST
Fax: (886) (2) 392-6835

Investment Commission
8th Floor
7 Roosevelt Road
Sec. 1
Taipei, Taiwan, Republic of China
Telephone: (886) (2) 351-3151
Fax: (886) (2) 396-3970

Ministry of Economic Affairs
15 Foo Chow Street
Taipei, Taiwan, Republic of China
Telephone: (886) (2) 321-2200
Fax: (886) (2) 391-9398
Telex: 19884

Council for Economic Planning and Development
9th Floor
87 Nanking E. Road
Sec. 2
Taipei, Taiwan, Republic of China
Telephone: (886) (2) 551-3522
Fax: (886) (2) 551-9011

Board of Foreign Trade
Ministry of Economic Affairs
1 Hu Kou Street
Taipei, Taiwan, Republic of China
Telephone: (886) (2) 351-0271
Fax: (886) (2) 331-5387

Industrial Development Bureau
Ministry of Economic Affairs
41-2 Hsin Yi Road
Sec. 3
Taipei, Taiwan, Republic of China
Telephone: (03) 754-1255
Fax: (03) 7030160

Persons interested in obtaining further information about investing in Taiwan, Republic of China, are also advised to contact the closest Taiwan, Republic of China, embassy or consular office.

Taiwan, Republic of China, maintains diplomatic relations with Costa Rica, Dominican Republic, El Salvador, Guatemala, Guinea-Bissua, Haiti, Holy See, Honduras, Republic of Korea, Naura, Nicaragua, Panama, Paraguay, Saint Lucia, South Africa, and Swaziland.

TANZANIA, UNITED REPUBLIC OF

■ POLITICAL ENVIRONMENT

The country has experienced severe internal political problems, some due to rivalries between inhabitants of the mainland and the island of Zanzibar, which forms part of the republic. Economic difficulties have been massive with a very high external public debt and accompanying debt service, high inflation, and a high level of unemployment.

The currency has been devalued several times.

A development plan has been put in place to improve the nation's economy.

■ SUMMARY OF FOREIGN INVESTMENT POLICY

The government has created a National Investment Promotion Policy that is designed to generate economic growth, increase employment, eliminate economic dependence on outside sources, and create a generally improved standard of living.

A new law, the National Investment Promotion and Protection Act, and the creation of the Investment Promotion Centre, which is responsible for the development of foreign investment, form essential parts of the government's plan.

Foreign investment is accepted in most areas of the economy, particularly in areas of high technology, agribusiness, tourism, manufacturing, transportation, mining, and petroleum development.

While there are controlled and reserved areas that are generally considered as set aside for public investment or joint public and private investment, to include iron and steel production, chemical production, machine tool production, mass media, banking and insurance services, and other activities, exceptions can be made when the foreign investment is of sufficient magnitude. In addition to the investment size, other considerations would include the impact of such investment on the country's balance of payments, and the potential for improvement of the nation's infrastructure and technical advancement.

Foreign investments must receive approval from the government through the Investment Promotion Centre.

There is no requirement for domestic participation in any foreign investment.

Foreign investment may be in the form of any freely convertible currency. Where the approval of the Bank of Tanzania has been obtained, foreign investment may also be in the form of equipment and technology and the reinvestment of profits.

A variety of incentives for foreign investment has been created by the government to include special tax considerations and the creation of Designated Special Growth Areas. Firms established in such areas are entitled to additional incentives.

■ FORMATION AND TYPES OF PERMITTED BUSINESS ORGANIZATIONS

Foreign investors may participate in the economy either on the basis of wholly owned or partially owned ventures, the latter being in the form of joint ventures with enterprises currently operating in Tanzania.

The extent of any local participation in any project funded by foreign investment shall be determined between the parties involved.

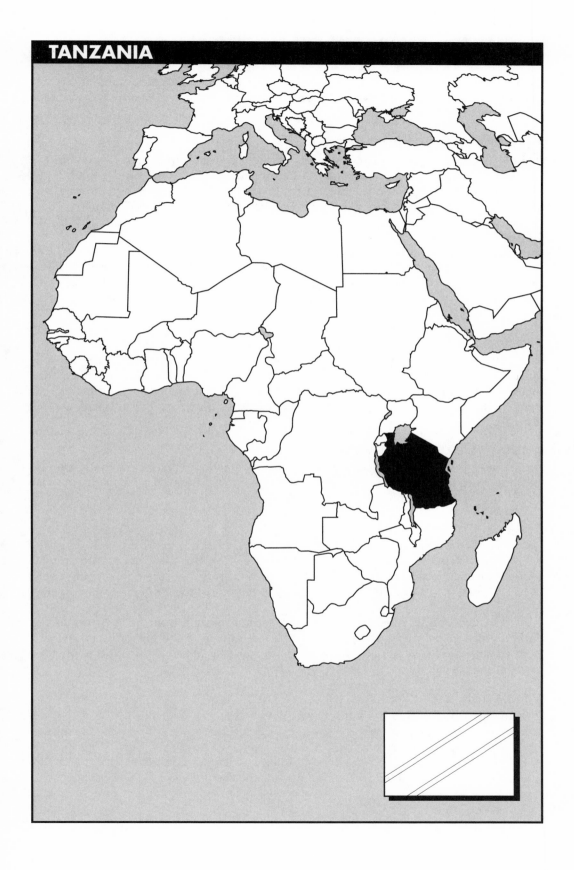

TANZANIA

The government, however, does encourage joint ventures between foreign investors and local cooperatives and parastatal organizations and between foreign investors and local private investors.

■ ENVIRONMENTAL PROTECTION

There is a continuing interest in the protection of the environment. Any major industrial or construction project must meet environmental standards. Potential foreign investors are advised to contact the Investment Promotion Centre for current information relevant to laws and regulations pertaining to the protection of the environment.

■ RIGHTS AND OBLIGATIONS OF FOREIGN INVESTORS

There are guarantees against nationalization and expropriation.

Land cannot be owned by foreign investors. However, long- short-, and medium term leases may be arranged with the government. Leases cannot exceed 99 years.

Foreign and domestic investors are guaranteed equal protection regarding investments in Tanzania.

■ LABOR

Foreign employers must provide hiring preference to local workers. However, foreign nationals may be employed who possess special technical and scientific qualifications. Such personnel are expected to provide technical training to domestic personnel.

Tanzania has a body of existing laws relevant to employment and working conditions.

■ ACCOUNTING REQUIREMENTS

Companies operating in Tanzania are expected to maintain current and complete accounting records for tax and other purposes. Financial records must be maintained in accordance with internationally accepted standards.

■ CURRENCY CONTROLS

The Bank of Tanzania is responsible for all matters concerning exchange control.

Foreign enterprises may, with the permission of the Bank of Tanzania, maintain foreign currency accounts for use in acquiring necessary raw materials, equipment, tools, supplies, and to make other purchases necessary to maintain continued operations.

Foreign investors may remit abroad or repatriate income from investments to include dividends, net profits, and net proceeds subsequent to the sale or liquidation of the investment. Such remittance or repatriation must be in the approved foreign currency, at the prevailing exchange rate, and after payment of all taxes.

■ TAXATION

Foreign enterprises and individuals incur a tax liability.

Individual foreign nationals employed by foreign firms are entitled to tax concessions. Sole proprietors are eligible for a five-year income tax holiday. Withholding taxes may be reduced for both resident and non-resident foreign investors.

Corporations are eligible for a tax holiday for the first five years of operation.

Numerous deductions including depreciation and losses are available. There is a capital gains tax applied to the sale of real property.

Mining and agricultural activities are eligible for tax incentives and deductions relevant to those areas.

Tanzania has concluded bilateral treaties with several countries on the subject of double taxation.

■ LEGAL SYSTEM

The Primary (or Magistrates') Courts hear minor criminal and civil matters. The District Courts have a broader original jurisdiction as well as functioning as the first level of appeal from decisions of the Primary Courts.

The High Courts function at the trial level and hear major criminal and civil cases. Appeals from the High Courts are taken to the Court of Appeal, which sits in Dar es Salaam.

■ CUSTOMS AND DUTIES

Imports of raw materials, machinery, and other supplies and items necessary to the business of a foreign investor and used by that investor for that purpose are exempt from customs duties, sales, and excise taxes.

In some cases, as an alternative to exemption, the government may refund duty and sales taxes, or the sales tax and excise duty.

Tanzania is a member of the Preferential Trade Areas for Eastern and Southern African States, and of the Southern African Development Coordination Conference, and is committed to regional and international trade expansion.

■ PROTECTION OF INTELLECTUAL PROPERTY

Tanzania is a member of the World Intellectual Property Organization and thus subscribes to the internationally accepted standards for the protection of copyrights, patents, tradenames, trademarks, and technology transfer.

■ IMMIGRATION AND RESIDENCE

Visas are normally required to enter Tanzania. Potential foreign investors are advised to contact the Investment Promotion Centre for information concerning current requirements on visas, work permits, and residence permits.

■ FOREIGN INVESTMENT ASSISTANCE DIRECTORY

Sources that can provide further information about foreign investment in Tanzania include:

Investment Promotion Centre
P.O. Box 9242
Dar es Salaam, Tanzania
Telephone: (0) 29411
Telex: 41641

Ministry of Industry and Trade
P.O. Box 9503
Dar es Salaam, Tanzania
Telephone: (0) 27251

Bank of Tanzania
P.O. Box 2939
Dar es Salaam, Tanzania
Telephone: (0) 21291
Telex: 41024

Dar es Salaam Chamber of Commerce
P.O. Box 41
Dar es Salaam, Tanzania
Telephone: (0) 36303
Telex: 41408
Fax: (0) 36303

Persons interested in obtaining further information about investing in Tanzania are advised to contact the country's closest embassy or consular office.

Tanzania maintains diplomatic relations with Albania, Algeria, Angola, Belgium, Brazil, Burundi, Canada, People's Republic of China, Cuba, Czechoslovakia, Denmark, Egypt, Finland, France, Germany, Guinea, Holy See, Hungary, India, Indonesia, Iran, Iraq, Italy, Japan, Kenya, Democratic People's Republic of Korea, Madagascar, Malawi, Mozambique, Netherlands, Nigeria, Norway, Pakistan, Poland, Romania, Russia, Rwanda, Spain, Sudan, Sweden, Switzerland, Syria, United Kingdom, United States, Vietnam, Yemen, Zaire, Zambia, and Zimbabwe.

THAILAND, KINGDOM OF

■ POLITICAL ENVIRONMENT

During the past two decades, numerous governments have been replaced following internal problems. In addition to continuing unrest, there are unresolved issues involving the bordering states of Cambodia and Vietnam.

Thailand has embarked on a limited program of privatization that has been opposed by some powerful factions in the nation. The country is experiencing a high inflation rate and suffers from both a shortage of skilled labor and an insufficient infrastructure to internally develop a major industrial base.

■ SUMMARY OF FOREIGN INVESTMENT POLICY

Thailand recognizes that foreign investment is necessary in order to expand its industrial base and to acquire a greater level of technology. As part of its program to promote foreign investment, the government has established the Office of the Board of Investment, which reports directly to the Office of the Prime Minister. The primary enabling legislation is the Investment Promotion Act.

Thailand has established three categories of businesses, namely, A, B, and C. The general position of the government is that categories A and B, which together encompass most of the categories, are closed to foreign investment. Category C businesses that, generally, are all other activities not covered in Categories A and B, are open to foreign investment but, as a practical matter, no permits are being currently issued to foreign interests to engage in those businesses. The exception to the rule is where the government is convinced that the opening and operation of a category C business cannot be competently accomplished by a company where the majority ownership is Thai.

Foreign businesses may also be permitted to engage in a category B business if there is a specific duration of the investment or if the foreign business is domiciled in a country that has a reciprocal treaty with Thailand.

■ FORMATION AND TYPES OF PERMITTED BUSINESS ORGANIZATIONS

Foreign investors may operate as sole proprietorships, or may form general or limited partnerships, private limited companies, or public limited companies. Both private and public limited companies are equivalent to corporations and enjoy juridical status.

There is no requirement that directors of either form of limited company be Thai.

Foreign businesses may form a joint venture with a domestic business, although the joint venture does not enjoy any specific legal recognition and is treated as a form of partnership.

Foreign firms may also establish branches or representative offices. The latter may carry out certain ministerial functions.

Permits to operate as a foreign investment must be obtained from the government.

■ ENVIRONMENTAL PROTECTION

There is a high degree of interest in protecting the environment. Manufacturing or any other business activity, for example, mining or logging, are particularly subject to government monitoring. Potential foreign investors are advised to contact the Office of

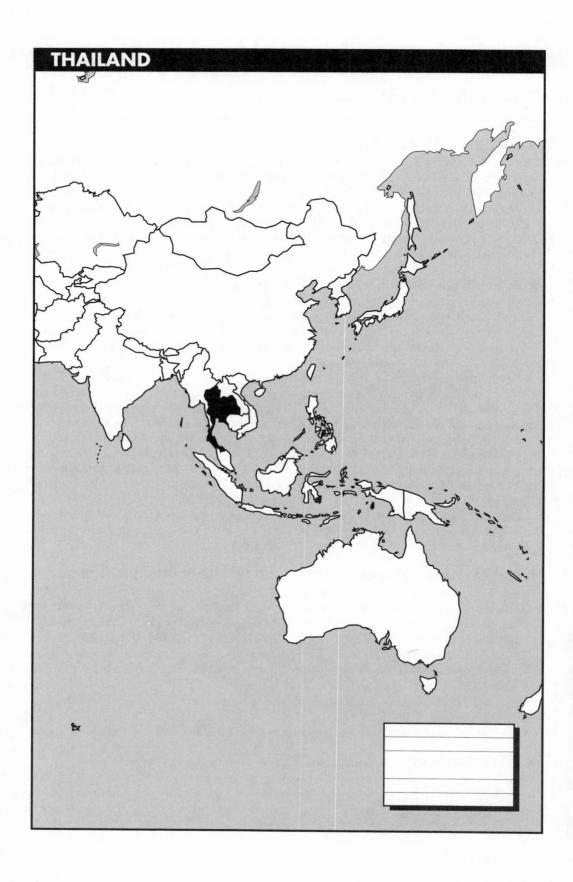

THAILAND

the Board of Investment for detailed information regarding current laws and regulations concerning environmental protection.

■ RIGHTS AND OBLIGATIONS OF FOREIGN INVESTORS

Restrictions as to the percentage of permitted foreign ownership in many kinds of businesses exist in Thailand. This is particularly true relevant to financial activities, transportation, mining, and communications.

There are restrictions, including significant tax considerations, involved with the remittance or repatriation of profits and other income realized from investments in Thailand.

Potential foreign investors should be aware that foreign companies involved in any business transaction with the government may not stand on an equal footing with domestic competitors.

■ LABOR

There are laws regulating working conditions, salaries, wages, and other employment considerations. In general, there is a hiring preference favoring Thai workers.

■ ACCOUNTING REQUIREMENTS

All companies must maintain accurate books and records in accordance with regulations established by the Ministry of Commerce. Copies of income statements, balance sheets and other relevant documents must be filed yearly with the Department of Commercial Registration and with the Revenue Department. Documents filed with the government must be certified by an auditor or auditing firm licensed to practice in Thailand.

■ CURRENCY CONTROLS

All currency moved into or from Thailand must receive approval of the revenue authorities and may be subject to relevant tax laws.

■ TAXATION

Thailand has entered into bilateral treaties on the subject of double taxation with many countries.

There are taxes imposed on income and consumption. All foreign companies and partnerships are subject to the income tax. Individuals are subject to personal taxation.

Corporate income taxes are payable on a semi-annual basis. The tax-paying company may select any year as its fiscal and tax year.

Individuals who are present in the country for more than 180 days in a calendar year are considered as residents of Thailand and are taxed on income obtained on a world-wide basis.

The tax year for individual taxpayers is the calendar year and tax returns are filed by the end of March for the preceding tax year.

There are special taxes relevant to companies engaged in petroleum operations.

In addition to personal and corporate income taxes there are a variety of minor taxes to include the stamp duty, excise tax, property taxes, and a value added tax (VAT).

A number of exclusions, exemptions, and deductions are available for companies and individuals.

■ LEGAL SYSTEM

There is an extensive court system to include the Courts of First Instance (or provincial courts); magistrates' or local courts that hear minor criminal and civil cases; juvenile courts; and special courts that hear labor issues, tax cases, and bankruptcy matters. Appeals are taken to the Court of Appeals. Final appellate authority is exercised by the Supreme Court, which sits in Bangkok.

■ CUSTOMS AND DUTIES

Thailand levies both ad valorem and specific customs duties. There are exceptions to the customs duties that are available under the terms of the Investment Promotion Act and the Petroleum Act. In addition there are generally reduced customs duties charged in the case of trade with members of the Association of Southeast Asian Nations.

The drawback system is also employed whereby the customs duty assessed on goods imported, and within one year exported after assembly or other processing, may be refunded.

A variety of other export incentives has also been developed by the government and more are planned.

■ PROTECTION OF INTELLECTUAL PROPERTY

Thailand is a member of the World Intellectual Property Organization and supports internationally accepted standards for the protection of copyrights, patents, and trade-marks.

■ IMMIGRATION AND RESIDENCE

With few exceptions based on nationality, individuals visiting Thailand must possess a visa. While there are several categories of visas, potential foreign investors should apply for a transit visa that is valid for 30 days and is renewable for an additional seven to ten days.

Employees of foreign businesses may be eligible for a Non-Immigrant Visa, which is valid for a year and is subject to renewal on a year-to-year basis. Applications for such visas are determined on a case-by-case basis.

■ FOREIGN INVESTMENT ASSISTANCE DIRECTORY

The following source may be contacted to obtain more information about foreign investment in Thailand:

Office of the Board of Investment
555 Vipavadee Rangsit Road
Bangkhen, Bangkok 10900
Thailand
Telephone: (66) (2) 270-1400 / (66) (2) 270-1410 / (66) (2) 270-1420
Telex: 72435 BINVEST TH
Cable Address: BINVEST
Fax: (66) (2) 271-0777

The Office of the Board of Investment also maintains offices in Frankfurt, Germany; New York, USA; Sydney, Australia; and Tokyo, Japan.

Thailand maintains diplomatic relations with Argentina, Australia, Bangladesh, Belgium, Brazil, Brunei, Canada, Chile, People's Republic of China, Czechoslovakia, Denmark, Egypt, Finland, France, Germany, Holy See, Hungary, India, Indonesia, Iran, Iraq, Israel, Italy, Japan, People's Democratic Republic of Korea, Republic of Korea, Laos, Malaysia, Myanmar, Nepal, Netherlands, New Zealand, Norway, Pakistan, Philippines, Poland, Portugal, Romania, Russia, Saudi Arabia, Singapore, Spain, Sri Lanka, Sweden, Switzerland, Turkey, United Kingdom, United States, and Vietnam.

Togo, Republic of

■ POLITICAL ENVIRONMENT

The country achieved its independence in 1960. It is governed by one party, which creates the ever present potential for the growth of major and sometimes violent dissent.

Major exports, including coffee, are generated by the agricultural sector. There are low levels of inflation and unemployment.

As a principal means to overcome reliance on agricultural exports and to generally improve the nation's economic difficulties, there is an interest in acquiring foreign investment. A privatization program of former state enterprises has begun.

■ SUMMARY OF FOREIGN INVESTMENT POLICY

The government has enacted an Investment Code to help attract foreign investment. Responsibilities for the promotion of foreign investment and providing assistance to potential foreign investors has been assigned to the EPZ Promotion Board.

Foreign investment in the Export Processing Zone (EPZ) is a major part of the government's program. Companies that will establish operations in the EPZ will be entitled to numerous incentives, assuming that an investment of at least 25 million CFA francs is made.

Small investments may be accepted that will qualify for incentives if there is significant Togolese participation in the enterprise.

Industrial zones have also been established. Companies that function within those zones are eligible for corporate tax reductions and exemptions.

Among the tax incentives for which foreign investors may be eligible are customs exemptions, tax holidays, reduced taxes on the salaries of local employees, refunds on export duties, and tax advantages for operating in rural areas.

Foreign investments that will be established within the EPZ projects will require permits from the EPZ Promotion Board.

All other foreign investment projects will require the completion of successful negotiations with the Ministry of Planning and Mines or the Ministry of Industry and State Enterprises.

■ FORMATION AND TYPES OF PERMITTED BUSINESS ORGANIZATIONS

The new Investment Code provides opportunities for foreign investors to participate in the Togolese economy through a variety of business forms.

It is anticipated that corporations, partnerships, and joint ventures with existing Togolese business enterprises will be the principal types of organizations employed by foreign investors.

■ ENVIRONMENTAL PROTECTION

There is an interest in environmental protection. Potential foreign investors are advised to contact the Ministry of the Environment and Tourism for complete and current information regarding laws and regulations on this subject.

TOGO

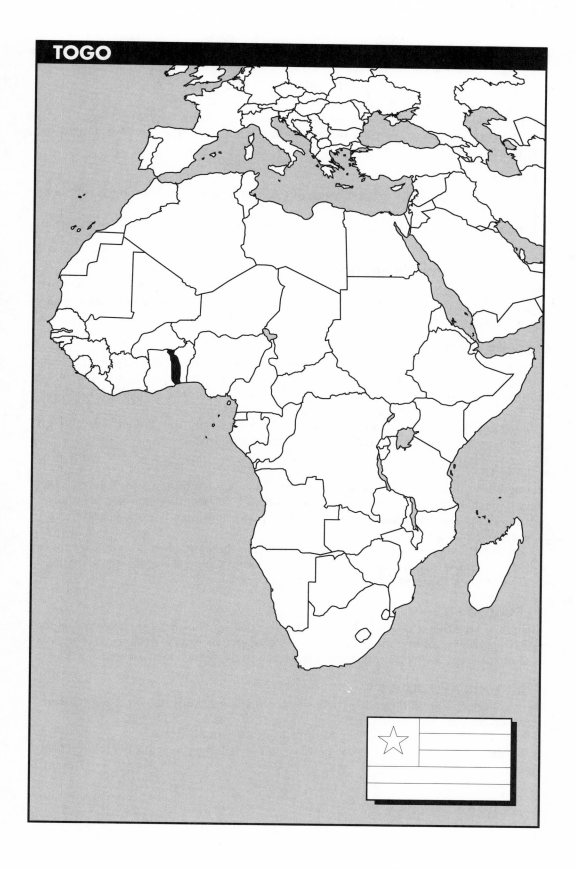

■ RIGHTS AND OBLIGATIONS OF FOREIGN INVESTORS

Foreign businesses and individuals are required to file tax returns.

There is no discrimination between foreign and domestic investors.

Investment capital and profits derived from it may be freely remitted abroad or repatriated.

■ LABOR

There is an existing body of laws regarding employment, i.e., working conditions, salaries and wages.

Companies established in the EPZ are exempt from current regulations on hiring and firing of employees.

■ ACCOUNTING REQUIREMENTS

All business enterprises must maintain complete financial records for tax and other purposes. Such records must be maintained in accordance with internationally accepted standards of accounting and auditing.

■ CURRENCY CONTROLS

There has been an ongoing effort to ease controls on the movement of currency into and from the country. Potential foreign investors are advised to contact the Ministry of Industry and State Enterprises, the EPZ Promotion Board, or the Ministry of Economy and Finance for current information about this subject.

In general, foreign investments are expected to be exempt from any or most foreign exchange controls as the government creates more definitive rules.

■ TAXATION

The new Investment Code provides for a variety of tax exemptions for foreign firms that establish operations either in or outside of the EPZ. Incentives include tax holidays of from three to seven years and exemptions on plant, equipment, services, and fuel for a period of from five to 12 years.

Corporate tax advantages are also enjoyed in the three established industrial zones with two of those, specifically Zones 2 and 3, offering the most significant advantages because of the government's desire to develop those areas.

■ LEGAL SYSTEM

There is a three-tiered system of courts. The first tier, or Tribunaux de premiére, is the trial court level. Appeals are taken to Cours d'Appel, or Courts of Appeal. The final level of appeal is the Cour Suprême, or Supreme Court, which sits in Lome.

■ CUSTOMS AND DUTIES

Through agreement with the EC, Togolese-manufactured products will enter EC member states duty and quota free.

Firms established in the EPZ are exempt from all customs duties.

Tax incentives include a 10-year holiday and a flat 15 percent profits tax for firms operating in the EPZ.

■ PROTECTION OF INTELLECTUAL PROPERTY

Togo is a member of the World Intellectual Property Organization and thus subscribes to internationally accepted standards concerning the protection of copyrights, patents, trademarks, tradenames, and technology transfer.

■ IMMIGRATION AND RESIDENCE

Depending on country of origin, visas may be required for entry. Potential foreign investors are advised to contact the Ministry of Industry and State Enterprises or the EPZ Promotion Board for complete information relevant to visas, work permits, and residence permits.

■ FOREIGN INVESTMENT ASSISTANCE DIRECTORY

Several sources can provide information about foreign investment in Togo. Among those sources are:

EPZ Promotion Board
P.B. 3250
Lome, Togo
Telephone: (228) 21-13-74
Telex: (986) 5012
Fax: (228) 21-52-31

Ministry of Industry and State Enterprises
P.B. 2748
Lome, Togo
Telephone: (228) 21-07-44
Telex: 5396

Ministry of Planning and Mines
ave de la Marina
Lome, Togo
Telephone: (228) 21-27-01
Telex: 5380

Persons interested in obtaining further information about investing in Togo also are advised to contact the closest Togolese embassy or consular office.

Togo maintains diplomatic relations with Belgium, Brazil, People's Republic of China, Egypt, France, Gabon, Germany, Ghana, Israel, Democratic People's Republic of Korea, Libya, Nigeria, Russia, Tunisia, United States, and Zaire.

TRINIDAD AND TOBAGO, REPUBLIC OF

■ POLITICAL ENVIRONMENT

The nation, since its founding in 1962, has been immersed in political difficulties that have to a major extent been the result of its economic policies. Petroleum and related products are the principal exports. As with other major oil producing nations, the soft market of the 1980s forced the country to borrow money thus creating a large public debt. While an improved oil market has reduced the country's cash flow problems, unemployment remains high.

■ SUMMARY OF FOREIGN INVESTMENT POLICY

The government has established the Industrial Development Corporation to promote foreign investment and to provide necessary assistance to potential foreign investors. Specifically, the government is interested in investment that will result in the increased use of raw materials, improvement of technology, introduction of new skills, increased employment, and a higher level of exports.

There is a desire that foreign investments involve significant amounts of capital and that foreign investors participate with domestic investors in joint ventures.

All foreign investment projects must be approved by the Industrial Development Corporation, which issues a license for such activities to be carried out.

A variety of incentives is offered by the government to acquire foreign investment. These incentives include import duty concessions, partial or total corporation tax exemptions, tax allowances, accelerated depreciation, and tax holidays, depending on the business in which engaged.

Export incentives are also available to include financial assistance, export allowances, and major tax deductions to enterprises engaged in export activities.

Free zones have been designated, and companies operating within those zones are eligible for a program of additional incentives.

■ FORMATION AND TYPES OF PERMITTED BUSINESS ORGANIZATIONS

Foreign investors may establish public or private companies that are the equivalent of the corporate form of business organizations. Both public and private companies enjoy juridical status.

Government approval, in the form of a license, must be obtained if a foreign investor intends to form a joint venture with a domestic business or individual; intends to form or acquire shares in an existing private company; or intends to acquire more than a 30 percent interest in an existing public company.

■ ENVIRONMENTAL PROTECTION

Potential foreign investors are urged to contact the Industrial Development Corporation for complete information on the current laws relevant to environmental protection.

■ RIGHTS AND OBLIGATIONS OF FOREIGN INVESTORS

Foreign businesses and individuals must file tax returns with the government.

There are no restrictions on the percentage of foreign ownership in a business entity.

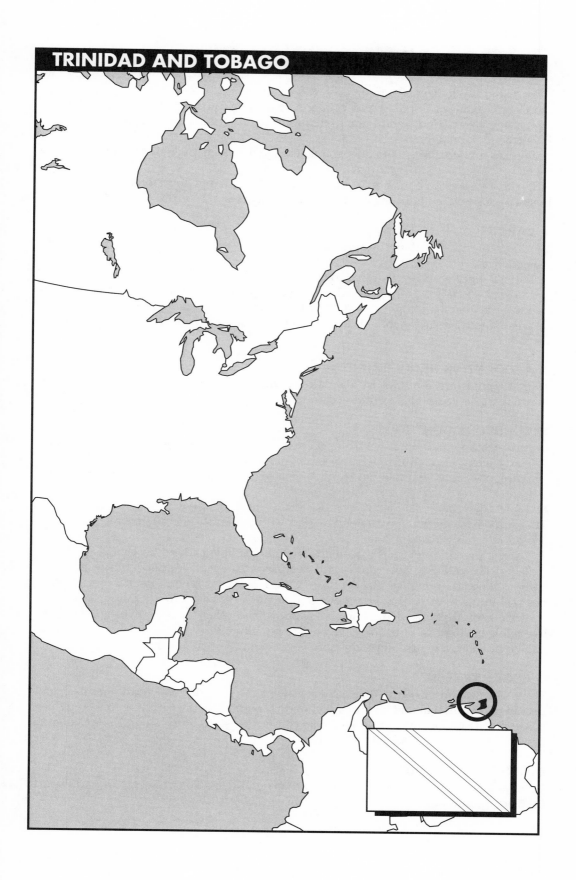

TRINIDAD AND TOBAGO

Foreign investors, once having achieved an approved investment status granted by the Central Bank of Trinidad and Tobago, are eligible to repatriate investment capital over a five-year period, and to repatriate profits and dividend income generated by the investment on an annual basis.

Foreign investors may obtain local financing to the extent of 30 percent of the investment.

Up to five acres of land may be acquired by a foreign investor for purposes of business or trade, without the requirement of a license.

■ LABOR

Working conditions, salaries, wages, and other employment factors are generally established by law.

Foreign employees are required to possess work permits.

In cases where foreign personnel are to be employed because of their special skills and training that are not possessed by Trinidad and Tobago nationals, a program must be created to train such nationals to replace the foreign personnel within an acceptable period.

■ ACCOUNTING REQUIREMENTS

All companies are required to maintain accurate books and records in accord with internationally accepted accounting standards.

■ CURRENCY CONTROLS

Companies and individuals with approved investor status are entitled to maintain foreign currency accounts in local and foreign banks.

Employees may repatriate up to 30 percent of their salaries on an annual basis.

■ TAXATION

The nation has entered into bilateral treaties with a number of countries relevant to the subject of double taxation.

There are numerous taxes assessed to include the value added tax that is applied at a 15 percent rate on most goods and services created or supplied. There are both corporation and individual income taxes. Companies engaged in manufacturing activities within the free zones are exempt from payment of the corporation tax.

Various exemptions, deductions, allowances, and other tax incentives are available to eligible businesses. These include, but are not limited to, allowances on capital plant and equipment, patents, oil production, housing, and research and development.

■ LEGAL SYSTEM

There is a system of courts that includes magistrates' or district courts that hear and decide petty criminal and civil cases; superior courts; and the Court of Appeal, which has appellate review over all subordinate courts. Decisions of the Court of Appeal may be taken to the Privy Council in London.

■ CUSTOMS AND DUTIES

Companies operating in the free zones are generally exempt from import and export licensing requirements.

The country is a signatory to the Caribbean Basin Initiative, the CARIBAN Agreement, and the Lome Convention, which provides preferential trade status with the United States, Canada, and Europe.

There is a 15 percent value added tax (VAT) on imports outside of the free zones.

■ PROTECTION OF INTELLECTUAL PROPERTY

Trinidad and Tobago is a member of the World Intellectual Property Organization and supports internationally accepted standards regarding the protection of copyrights, patents, and trademarks.

■ IMMIGRATION AND RESIDENCE

Visa requirements are determined based on the foreign investor's country of origin. The Immigration Section of the Ministry of Justice and National Security can provide detailed information regarding visa or other requirements necessary to visit the country as a potential investor as well as to supervise ongoing investments.

■ FOREIGN INVESTMENT ASSISTANCE DIRECTORY

There are several sources that can provide detailed information relevant to foreign investment in Trinidad and Tobago. Among them are:

The General Manager
Industrial Development Corporation
P.O. Box 949
Port of Spain, Trinidad
Telephone: (809) 623-7291 / (809) 623-7298
Fax: (809) 625-9124

Central Bank of Trinidad and Tobago
Eric Williams Plaza
P.O. Box 1250
Port of Spain, Trinidad
Telephone: (809) 625-4835
Telex: 22532
Fax: (809) 627-4696

Trinidad and Tobago Chamber of Industry and Commerce
31 Frederick Street, P.O. Box 499
Port of Spain, Trinidad
Telephone: (809) 623-1561
Telex: 22462
Fax: (809) 623-5363

Persons interested in obtaining further information about investing in Trinidad and Tobago also are advised to contact the closest Trinidad and Tobago embassy or consular office.

Trinidad and Tobago maintains diplomatic relations with Argentina, Barbados, Brazil, Canada, People's Republic of China, Colombia, France, Germany, Holy See, India, Jamaica, Japan, Republic of Korea, Netherlands, Nigeria, Peru, United Kingdom, United States, and Venezuela.

TUNISIA, REPUBLIC OF

■ POLITICAL ENVIRONMENT

The government is unstable, principally as a result of internal threats mounted by Islamic fundamentalists.

The economy is largely dependent on agriculture. Poor crop years can, as expected, have widespread negative effects on the overall economy.

Despite such periodic problems, Tunisia has moved forward with economic reforms and has adopted a privatization program.

Annual inflation and unemployment levels are considered low to moderate.

■ SUMMARY OF FOREIGN INVESTMENT POLICY

The government is actively encouraging foreign investment. The Industrial Investment Codes are the principal laws enacted in this area. A government organization, the Agency for Promotion of Industry, has been specifically created to develop foreign investment.

Foreign investment is of particular interest in the areas of manufacturing for export; the creation of increased levels of technology; improvement of the agricultural and fisheries industries; tourism; services; international trading; and hydrocarbon exploration and development.

Incentives are provided, based on areas of investment activity, to include favorable tax rates; financial grants; tax rebates; and government assumption of certain labor-related costs.

Foreign investments, except in the tourism industry, must be approved by the government. No direct foreign investment is approved in the agricultural and fisheries areas. Such investments must be made, instead, through public companies controlled by domestic interests. Foreign equity cannot exceed 50 percent in such a company.

In most cases, there are no limits on the amount or percentage of foreign participation in a business enterprise. If a firm is engaged in manufacturing only partially for export, foreign investment is limited to no more than 49 percent.

■ FORMATION AND TYPES OF PERMITTED BUSINESS ORGANIZATIONS

Most foreign investors operate through branch offices of corporations domiciled abroad.

All foreign companies are required to register with the government. In many cases, and depending on the fields in which a company will engage, registration will be required with several agencies and departments.

■ ENVIRONMENTAL PROTECTION

Potential foreign investors are advised to contact the Agency for Promotion of Industry or the Ministry of the Environment and Land Planning for complete information on this subject.

■ RIGHTS AND OBLIGATIONS OF FOREIGN INVESTORS

Profits and other income derived from foreign investment made in Tunisia may be freely repatriated or remitted abroad subsequent to the payment of all due taxes.

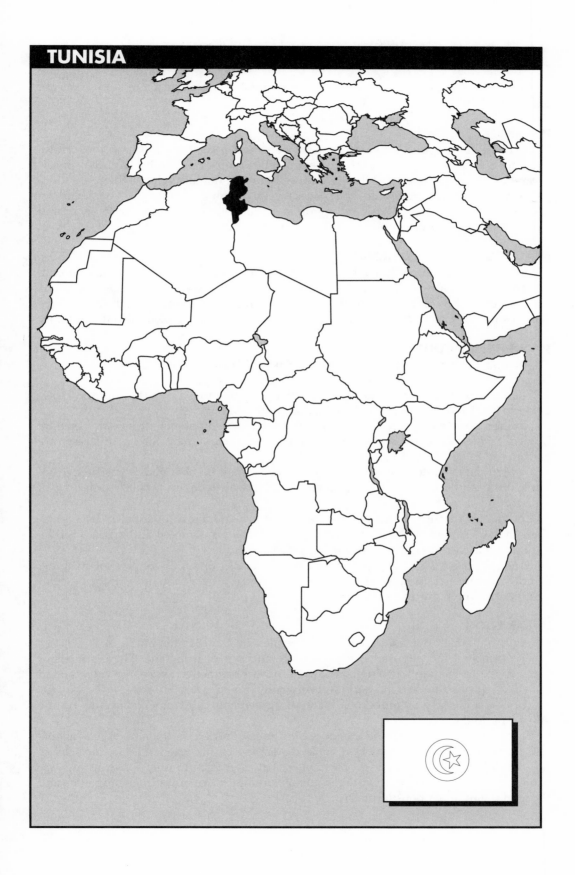

TUNISIA

Land, manufacturing plants, and office space may be rented on a long-term basis not exceeding 40 years.

■ LABOR

There are no requirements to hire Tunisian personnel for supervisory positions. However, general clerical and non-management positions must be filled by Tunisians unless it can be shown that special skills are required that are not locally available.

Foreign personnel are required to possess work permits, valid for one year, from the Ministry of Social Affairs. Residence permits, obtained from the Interior Ministry and valid for one year, are also required. These permits may be renewed.

■ ACCOUNTING REQUIREMENTS

All companies operating in Tunisia are required to prepare and maintain accounting records for tax and other purposes. Depending on the level of financial operations conducted by the company, it may either file its regular statements with the government using internal auditors or may be required to hire independent outside auditors.

■ CURRENCY CONTROLS

The Banque Centrale de Tunisie (Central Bank of Tunisia) is the central bank and has responsibilities for all matters concerning foreign exchange.

There are no limits on foreign currency that may be moved into the country. However, no Tunisian currency may be taken out of the country.

Non-residents are generally exempt from exchange regulations. Companies that are owned to the extent of at least 66 percent of total capital by foreign interests are considered to be non-resident.

Foreign currency to pay for necessary imports may be obtained from the Central Bank upon authorization of the Ministry of National Economy and the Ministry of Finance.

Companies that manufacture only for export are entitled to operate under regulations that are somewhat less stringent, i.e., with fewer government authorizations relevant to the use of foreign currency for payments abroad.

Foreign employees may repatriate or remit abroad up to 50 percent of their net salaries or wages. If the employee's family lives abroad, there is no limit on the percentage that may be remitted or repatriated.

■ TAXATION

Foreign companies and individuals are subject to the Tunisian tax laws.

The principal tax imposed is on corporate and personal income. There are minor taxes levied to include those on consumption and documents. There is a value added tax (VAT) applied to certain goods and services.

Tunisia is a party to numerous bilateral agreements with other countries on the subject of double taxation.

There are a variety of tax deductions, allowances, and exemptions that are available and for which companies may be eligible depending on the areas of economic activity in which they are engaged, e.g., companies that manufacture only for exporting are exempt from the tax on corporate income as are international trading companies and those in the hydrocarbons industry.

■ LEGAL SYSTEM

The judicial system functions at essentially four levels. Local courts hear petty criminal and civil matters. The Courts of First Instance are the trial courts. Appeals are taken to the Court of Appeal, which sits in Tunis, Sousse, and Sfax. The highest court is the Cour de Cassation, which sits at Tunis.

■ CUSTOMS AND DUTIES

Tunisia is a member of the General Agreement on Tariffs and Trade (GATT).

Depending on the activities in which engaged, companies enjoy different exemptions under the relevant import and export regulations, e.g., firms manufacturing only for export may import, free of duty, those materials needed for production.

Export licenses are generally required and most goods, to be exported, must receive approval from the Ministry of National Economy. Export licenses are valid for three months.

Imported goods that are not exempted from customs duties are subject to customs service fees, value added and consumption taxes, and tariffs that generally range to about 25 percent of value.

Firms that manufacture partially for export are entitled to customs refunds on raw materials used in production.

In some cases, foreign employees may be entitled to import personal goods and one car exempt from customs duties.

Companies engaged in the hydrocarbons area enjoy an exemption relevant to customs charges on imports and exports.

■ PROTECTION OF INTELLECTUAL PROPERTY

Tunisia is a member of the World Intellectual Property Organization and has enacted statutes on the protection of rights relevant to copyrights, patents, trademarks, and technology transfer.

■ IMMIGRATION AND RESIDENCE

Visas are normally required to enter the country. Potential foreign investors are advised to contact the Agency for Promotion of Industry for complete information regarding requirements and procedures for the issuance of visas, work permits, and residence permits.

■ FOREIGN INVESTMENT ASSISTANCE DIRECTORY

Sources that can provide additional information relevant to foreign investment in Tunisia include:

Agency for Promotion of Industry
63 Rue du Syrie
1002 Tunis-Belvédère
Tunisia
Telephone: (216) (1) 288091
Telex: 12280
Fax: (216) (1) 782482

Ministry of National Economy
Avenue Kheireddine Pacha
1002 Tunis
Tunisia
Telephone: (216) (1) 780366
Telex: 14341

Chamber of Commerce and Industry
Rue des Entrepreneurs, Tunis
Tunisia
Telephone: (216) (1) 242872
Telex: 14718
Fax: (216) (1) 354714

Persons interested in obtaining further information about foreign investment in Tunisia are advised to contact the closest Tunisian embassy or consular office.

Tunisia maintains diplomatic relations with Algeria, Argentina, Austria, Bahrain, Belgium, Brazil, Bulgaria, Canada, People's Republic of China, Côte d'Ivoire, Cuba, Czechoslovakia, Denmark, Djibouti, Egypt, France, Germany, Greece, Hungary, India, Indonesia, Iran, Iraq, Italy, Japan, Jordan, People's Democratic Republic of Korea, Republic of Korea, Kuwait, Libya, Mauritania, Morocco, Netherlands, Pakistan, Poland, Qatar, Romania, Russia, Saudi Arabia, Senegal, Somalia, Spain, Sweden, Switzerland, Syria, Turkey, United Arab Emirates, United Kingdom, United States, Venezuela, Yemen, and Zaire.

TURKEY, REPUBLIC OF

■ POLITICAL ENVIRONMENT

The nation is a representative democracy of rather recent origin. During the past five years, there have been numerous indications of internal instability to include widespread domestic terrorism and a general strike. Economic problems, largely in the form of high inflation and an unfavorable international balance of payments, have been, and continue to be, of major concern.

■ SUMMARY OF FOREIGN INVESTMENT POLICY

The promotion and regulation of foreign investment activities is the responsibility of the State Planning Organization, which is a part of the Ministry of the Economy and Commerce. The Foreign Investment Directorate has been created within the State Planning Organization to directly assist foreign investors.

The principal statute relevant to foreign investment is the Law Concerning the Encouragement of Foreign Capital, as amended.

Foreign investment is encouraged in any economic area that does not create a monopoly, which is beneficial to the economy, and which is open to the domestic private sector.

The government has embarked on a major program of privatization which has, to date, focused on the textile, petrochemical, telecommunications, iron and steel, and aviation fields.

While the government maintains a general interest in foreign investment, there are special areas where foreign investment is particularly desired, to include agriculture, fish hatcheries, and cut flowers industries; mining and petroleum; tourism; and manufacturing.

Free zones have been established in various locations.

A system of incentives to promote foreign investment has been developed. These incentives include tax exemptions, a reduction or exemptions relevant to customs and export duties, and foreign exchange allocation credits. Eligibility for these incentive programs is largely determined by the amount of foreign capital invested.

Turkey is a party to the Convention for the Settlement of Disputes Between States and Nationals of Other States, and to the Multilateral Investment Guarantee Agency Agreement.

■ FORMATION AND TYPES OF PERMITTED BUSINESS ORGANIZATIONS

Any type of business organization, or any individual, may qualify as a foreign investor. Corporations and limited liability companies may be formed by foreign interests to carry out business activities in Turkey. Branch or liaison offices of existing foreign companies may be created and partnerships may be formed with existing foreign or domestic business organizations in Turkey.

The minimum capital investment that is acceptable to qualify as a foreign investor is $50,000 (U.S.) per juridical person or individual, exclusive of any incentives or shares held by any member(s) of a corporate board of directors.

Businesses funded wholly or partially by foreign investment and already operating in Turkey, and which desire an increased level of capitalization for purposes of expan-

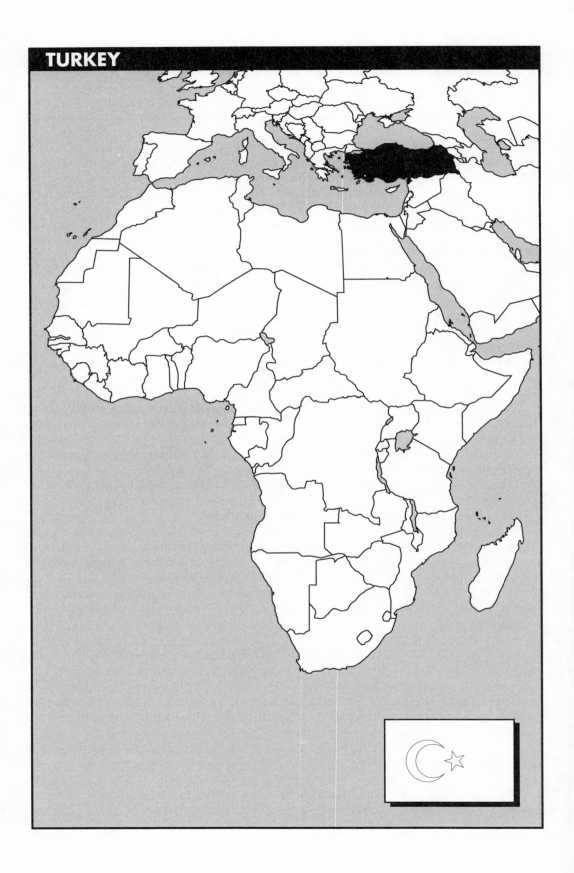

TURKEY

sion, modernization or other necessary purpose, must file a report containing the sources of the acquired capital and the purpose for its use with the Foreign Investment Directorate of the State Planning Organization.

Foreign business entities or individuals may form a joint venture with domestic businesses subsequent to receiving approval for such joint venture from the Foreign Investment Directorate of the State Planning Organization. Documents filed must include balance sheets for the past five years and a copy of the Articles of Association.

■ ENVIRONMENTAL PROTECTION

Potential foreign investors are advised to seek guidance from the Foreign Investment Directorate of the State Planning Organization on environmental protection regulations in Turkey.

■ RIGHTS AND OBLIGATIONS OF FOREIGN INVESTORS

Turkey guarantees equal treatment for domestic and foreign investment capital.

Foreign investors must pay such taxes as are required by law.

There is no requirement for domestic participation in any activity that is wholly or partially financed by foreign investment.

The net amount of income, after the payment of taxes, may be transferred or repatriated following submission to the bank(s) where such capital has been on deposit, of relevant tax declarations, balance sheets, profit and loss statements (as approved by the tax authorities), tax payment verifications, and profit distribution tables. These documents are forwarded by the bank(s) concerned to the Foreign Investment Directorate of the State Planning Organization.

■ LABOR

There is an existing and highly qualified labor force, most of it unionized.

During the establishment of a business activity that is financed by foreign investment, there are no restrictions on the employment of foreign experts, supervisors, technicians, and other skilled personnel. The establishment period is generally considered not to exceed six months.

Working conditions and benefits that must be provided are set forth in Turkey's laws relevant to labor and employment.

■ ACCOUNTING REQUIREMENTS

All business enterprises are required to maintain a system of accounts, to include balance sheets and profit and loss information, in accordance with internationally accepted accounting standards.

Accounting information relevant to the operation of any enterprise financed wholly or partially by foreign investment must be reported annually to the Foreign Investment Directorate of the State Planning Organization.

■ CURRENCY CONTROLS

Potential foreign investors are advised to contact the Foreign Investment Directorate for detailed information on the current laws and regulations relevant to the amount of capital (except for matters involving remittance or repatriation of profits) that may be taken into Turkey or removed from that nation by business organizations and by individuals.

■ TAXATION

Corporate taxes are based on annual income. An extensive system of tax exemptions has been created and may be claimed depending on the fields of activity, e.g., manufacturing for export, in which a business is engaged.

Taxes are based on income gained in a calendar year. A different 12-month period may be used by a business for tax purposes if permission is requested from the Ministry of Finance and Customs.

Individuals who are residents of Turkey are subject to income tax on a worldwide basis. Individuals who are not considered Turkish residents must pay taxes on income derived from their activities in Turkey.

There are a variety of minor taxes including a value added tax (VAT), stamp, banking and insurance transactions, and real estate taxes that may be imposed. Exemptions from such taxes may be claimed by business organizations where applicable.

Turkey is a party to numerous bilateral agreements relevant to the issue of double taxation.

■ LEGAL SYSTEM

There is an extensive system of courts with trial and appellate responsibilities. The Court of Cassation is the judicial organ with appellate review authority of civil and criminal cases heard in the courts below. The highest court is the Constitutional Court which is responsible for deciding on the legality of laws. In exceptional cases it may sit as a court of original jurisdiction.

■ CUSTOMS AND DUTIES

Most machinery and equipment intended to be used by businesses financed by foreign investment are exempt from customs duties.

Imports and exports from the free zones are exempt from taxes and duties.

■ PROTECTION OF INTELLECTUAL PROPERTY

Turkey is a member of the World Intellectual Property Organization and is a party to various international agreements concerning the protection of intellectual property to include patents, trademarks, and copyrights.

■ IMMIGRATION AND RESIDENCE

Visas, which are subject to renewal, may be issued to potential foreign investors. Complete information concerning both visas and residence requirements may be obtained from the Foreign Investment Directorate.

■ FOREIGN INVESTMENT ASSISTANCE DIRECTORY

The following sources may be contacted to obtain more detailed information concerning foreign investment in Turkey:

Foreign Investment Directorate
State Planning Organization
Ministry of the Economy and Commerce
Sanayi ve Ticaret Bakanhgh
Ankara, Turkey
Telephone: (90) (41) 229-2834
Telex: 44598

Union of Chambers of Commerce and Industry of Turkey
149 Ataturk Boulevard
Ankara, Turkey
Telephone: (90) (41) 117-7700
Telex: 42343

Persons interested in obtaining further information about investing in Turkey also are advised to contact the closest Turkish embassy or consular office.

Turkey maintains diplomatic relations with Afghanistan, Albania, Algeria, Argentina, Australia, Austria, Bangladesh, Belgium, Brazil, Bulgaria, Canada, Chile, People's Republic of China, Czechoslovakia, Denmark, Egypt, Finland, France, Germany, Greece, Holy See, Hungary, India, Indonesia, Iran, Iraq, Israel, Italy, Japan, Jordan, Republic of Korea, Kuwait, Lebanon, Libya, Malaysia, Mexico, Morocco, Netherlands, Norway, Pakistan, Poland, Portugal, Romania, Russia, Saudi Arabia, Somalia, Spain, Sweden, Switzerland, Syria, Thailand, Tunisia, Turkish Republic of Northern Cyprus, United Kingdom, United States, and Venezuela.

UGANDA, REPUBLIC OF

■ POLITICAL ENVIRONMENT

This nation has endured a troubled history. It has suffered through numerous violent takeovers of government carried out by a series of dictators, and through a bloody civil war. Charges of government corruption and of human rights violations have been repeatedly made over the passage of many years.

In economic terms, Uganda has also fared poorly. Most of the labor force is engaged in agriculture, the backbone of which is coffee production. The downturn in coffee prices on the international market in the 1980s had a major and negative effect on the already fragile Ugandan economy.

There is a high external public debt and debt service and a troubling annual rate of inflation.

In order to obtain international financial assistance, the Ugandan government has embarked on a limited privatization program and has moved to acquire foreign investment.

■ SUMMARY OF FOREIGN INVESTMENT POLICY

The government is actively seeking foreign investment for a variety of priority reasons to include the creation of an import substitution industrial base; to rebuild the national infrastructure; and to diversify its exports with a view toward achieving less dependence on coffee revenues.

The principal law with regard to foreign investments is the Investment Code of 1991. The Uganda Investment Authority, which reports to the Ministry of Planning and Economic Development, has been designated in the Code as the chief government agency with responsibilities for foreign investment.

Under the provisions of the Code, a foreign investor is defined as a person who is not a citizen of Uganda; a company where the majority of the shares is held by persons who are not citizens of Uganda; and any partnership where the majority of the partners are not citizens of the country.

No foreign investment may be undertaken in the country without first obtaining an investment license issued by the Ministry of Planning and Economic Development. The application for such a license must include complete information on the nature and type of the proposed investment; the incentives that are desired; the amount of capital being invested; anticipated growth; opportunities for local employment; and the qualifications of the investors and managers.

The Uganda Investment Authority will review the application and will determine if the proposed investment will create new earnings and foreign exchange, utilize locally available raw materials, create employment opportunities and will introduce new levels of technology, as well as contribute generally to the economic development of this nation.

If approved, the license issued will be valid for a period of five years. If the investment project cannot for valid reasons be commenced within the five-year period, it may be extended upon application to the Authority.

In most cases, licenses are conditioned upon the foreign investor providing employment to Ugandan citizens; investing a required amount of capital, or in lieu of or in

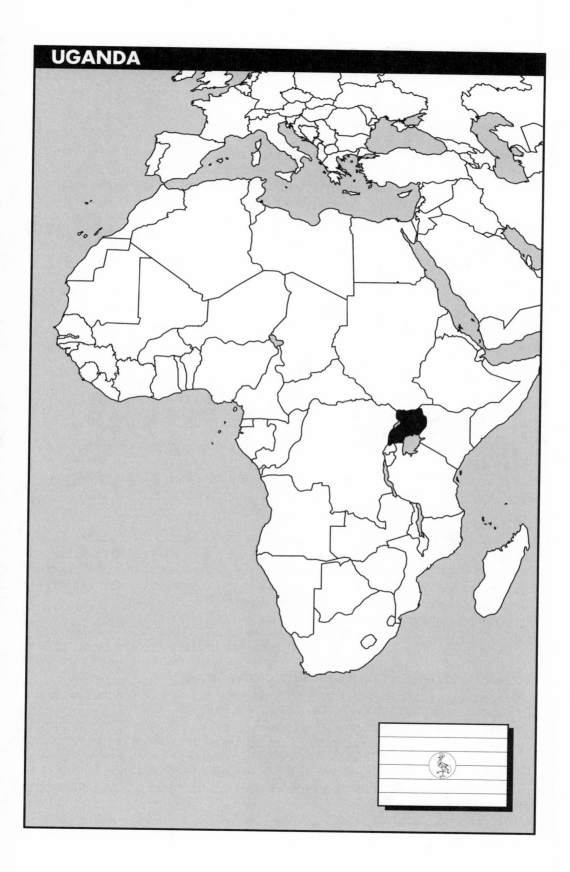

UGANDA

addition to capital, providing plant, equipment, and other capital assets; purchasing to the maximum extent possible, raw materials, goods, and services locally; and doing minimal damage to the environment.

All foreign investments will be registered with the Uganda Investment Authority.

Incentives that are available to foreign investors under the provisions of the Investment Code include customs exemptions on all raw materials, goods, and equipment that are necessary, that are not available in Uganda, and that are not more than five years old; a three-year tax holiday in the case of any investment that is no less than $50,000 (U.S.) and no greater than $300,000 (U.S.); a five-year tax holiday for investments that exceed $300,000 (U.S.); and one additional year of tax exemption in special cases as determined by the Uganda Investment Authority. The tax holidays relate to exemptions from the corporation tax, withholding tax, and the tax on corporate dividends.

In addition, foreign investors and foreign nationals employed by such an investor will be exempt from import charges and the sales tax for a period of 12 months on the importation of one motor vehicle per person and other personal and household effects.

Other incentives include customs drawbacks and the right to obtain local credit.

There are no requirements for Ugandan equity participation or management in companies that are financed by foreign investment.

■ FORMATION AND TYPES OF PERMITTED BUSINESS ORGANIZATIONS

Foreign investors may participate in the economy through the creation of corporations, partnerships, or sole proprietorships.

Subsidiaries of foreign corporations and joint ventures with domestic investors may be established.

Corporations, including subsidiaries of foreign corporations, acquire juridical person status.

■ ENVIRONMENTAL PROTECTION

The government maintains a continuing interest in the protection of the environment. The Ministry of Water, Energy, Minerals and Environment Protection, and the Ministry of Tourism, Wildlife and Antiquities are both involved in aspects of environmental protection. A condition of investment licensing includes the requirement that a foreign investor will not create damage to either the environment or the ecology.

Potential foreign investors are advised to contact the Uganda Investment Authority or the Ministry of Water, Energy, Minerals and Environment Protection for current and complete information on laws and regulations pertaining to this subject.

■ RIGHTS AND OBLIGATIONS OF FOREIGN INVESTORS

Local financing is available from the Bank of Uganda for foreign investors who have been granted investment licenses by the Uganda Investment Authority.

The Investment Code provides that licensed foreign investments or property forming part of such investments may not be taken by the government except as provided by the nation's constitution and must be fairly compensated within a period of not more than 12 months following taking by the government. Such compensation may be freely remitted abroad or repatriated and shall be exempt from any Ugandan foreign exchange controls.

Disputes arising between a foreign investor and the government should be settled through negotiation. If such negotiations are not successful, the parties should submit the issue to arbitration to include the use of the International Center for the Settlement of Investment Disputes.

In the event that arbitration is not successful, the matter may be referred to the High Court. Appeals from the High Court may be taken to the Supreme Court of Uganda.

All agreements relevant to the transfer of foreign technology must be registered with the Uganda Investment Authority.

Properly registered foreign investments, investment income, payments of shareholder dividends, royalties, and fees with respect to technology transfer, payments to employees and others in connection with the investment, and repayment of foreign loan principal and interest may be remitted abroad or repatriated upon application for, and receipt of, a certificate of approval for such remittance or repatriation as granted by the Bank of Uganda. Foreign investors should recognize that delays may occur because of the nation's acute shortage of foreign exchange.

■ LABOR

There is a body of existing laws with regard to working conditions and employment.

All foreign nationals employed in Uganda must possess work and residence permits. Foreign personnel may be employed in cases where it can be shown that required training or special skills are not locally available.

Foreign investors are required to provide employment and training to Ugandan citizens and to replace foreign personnel with such local workers as quickly as possible.

■ ACCOUNTING REQUIREMENTS

All foreign enterprises are required to maintain proper and complete accounting and other business records in accordance with internationally accepted standards.

■ CURRENCY CONTROLS

The Bank of Uganda is the country's central bank. It is responsible for all matters relevant to the nation's foreign exchange policy.

Foreign businesses and individuals are not permitted to open or maintain bank accounts in any foreign currency.

There are stringent controls on the movement of capital into and from the country.

■ TAXATION

Foreign businesses and individuals are subject to the Ugandan tax laws.

The major tax is that imposed on corporate and personal income. There are a variety of other taxes to include those on customs, duties and fee charges, and other assessments.

In addition to tax incentives and exemptions that are available in connection with registered foreign investments, certain deductions and allowances may be taken by corporations and individuals.

The nation's tax laws are currently undergoing revision.

■ LEGAL SYSTEM

There are Magistrates' Courts located throughout the country that are empowered to decide petty criminal and civil cases. The High Court is the trial court and has cognizance over more serious criminal and civil matters, as well as acting in an appellate role with regard to decisions referred to it from the Magistrates' Courts.

Appeals from the High Court are taken to the Supreme Court, which sits at Kampala.

■ CUSTOMS AND DUTIES

The government is interested in the expansion of trade, particularly exports. Registered foreign investors engaged in the manufacturing of goods for export are entitled to a drawback of duties and on sale taxes that are generally payable on imported goods and materials used in such production.

Uganda is a member of the Preferential Trade Areas for Eastern and Southern African States.

■ PROTECTION OF INTELLECTUAL PROPERTY

Uganda is a member of the World Intellectual Property Organization and thus supports internationally recognized measures for the protection of copyrights, patents, trademarks, and technology transfer.

■ IMMIGRATION AND RESIDENCE

Visas are required to enter the country. Potential foreign investors are advised to contact the Uganda Investment Authority for current and complete information regarding requirements for visas, work permits, and residence permits.

■ FOREIGN INVESTMENT ASSISTANCE DIRECTORY

Sources that can provide further information about foreign investment in Uganda include:

Uganda Investment Authority
P.O. Box 7418
Crest House
Nkruman Road
Kampala, Uganda
Telephone: (0) 234105
Fax: (0) 242903

Ministry of Commerce, Industry and Cooperatives
P.O. Box 7103
Kampala, Uganda
Telephone: (0) 759785
Telex: 61183

Ministry of Water, Energy, Minerals and Environment Protection
P.O. Box 7270
Kampala, Uganda
Telephone: (0) 234995
Telex: 61098

Bank of Uganda
P.O. Box 7120
Kampala, Uganda
Telephone: (0) 258441
Telex: 61059
Fax: (0) 242903

Persons interested in obtaining additional information about foreign investment in Uganda are advised to contact the country's closest embassy or consular office.

Uganda maintains diplomatic relations with Algeria, Burundi, People's Republic of China, Cuba, Egypt, France, Germany, Holy See, India, Italy, Kenya, Democratic People's Republic of Korea, Republic of Korea, Nigeria, Russia, Rwanda, Somalia, Sudan, Tanzania, United Kingdom, United States, and Zaire.

UKRAINE, REPUBLIC OF

■ POLITICAL ENVIRONMENT

The government is currently engaged in the difficult task of transforming the economy from a centrally planned one into a free market system.

Ukraine is endowed with significant natural resources that should permit the development of a major industrial base as well as the maintenance of a significant export economy.

■ SUMMARY OF FOREIGN INVESTMENT POLICY

The government of Ukraine is highly interested in obtaining foreign investment as part of its ongoing program to achieve a free market economy.

There are three laws that have been enacted by the government and that bear on the subject of foreign investments and they are the Law on Economic Association, the Law on Investment Activity, and the Law on External Economic Activity.

The government agency principally responsible for the development and regulation of foreign investment is the Ministry of External Economic Relations and Trade. The ministry reports to the Supreme Council (or Parliament), which has overall responsibility for regulating foreign investment activities.

The government's overall desires for the use of foreign investment include achieving a balanced domestic market; stimulating structural changes in the economy; and establishing the country as an integral part of the world economic system.

In terms of specific goals, the government seeks foreign investment in order to improve the national standard of living; increase technological levels and production; create more employment opportunities; improve the agricultural and industrial sectors through the infusion of new techniques, inventions, and applications; and to increase cultural health and education programs.

Under the provisions of the Law on Investment Activity, foreign investments are considered to include capital, movable and immovable properties, intellectual property, technical knowledge, and rights of use to property.

Foreign investments must be registered with the Ministry of External Economic Relations. Any change(s) in the terms of the foreign investment must be filed with the Ministry of External Economic Relations within 14 days of such change(s).

Incentives for foreign investment are principally in the form of tax concessions, government subsidies and loans, and general government assistance and counsel. In addition, the Law on External Economic Activity provides for the creation of special economic zones where foreign enterprises may be established and gain certain tax or tariff advantages.

■ FORMATION AND TYPES OF PERMITTED BUSINESS ORGANIZATIONS

Foreign investors may function within the economy of the country through the creation of what are called economic associations that include joint stock companies, limited responsibility associations, additional responsibility associations, and complete associations.

All economic associations are considered to be legal entities with a juridical person status immediately upon registration with the government. Associations that are

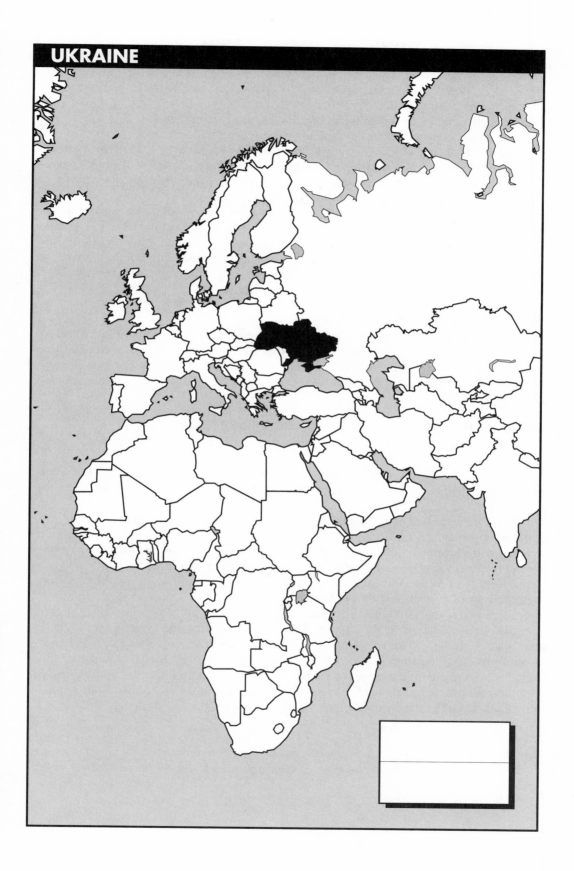

formed to carry out banking activities must become registered with the National Bank of Ukraine, the central bank.

Foreign corporations may establish branch offices or subsidiaries.

A joint stock company is the equivalent of a corporation. Joint stock associations are either open or closed. Open joint stock associations are publicly held. The shares of closed joint stock associations are held only by the founders. Closed joint stock associations may be transformed into open joint stock associations through registration of shares and relevant charges in the association's charter.

Limited responsibility associations are composed of individual participants who are liable for the debts of the enterprise to the limit of their contributions.

A complete association is one where all of the participants are jointly liable for the debts of the enterprise. It is the equivalent of a general partnership. By comparison, in a limited association, the liability of one or more of the participants in the enterprise is limited to the extent of such a participant's contribution.

■ ENVIRONMENTAL PROTECTION

There is a continuing and growing interest on the part of the government in protecting the environment. The agency charged with the primary responsibility of maintaining environmental standards is the Ministry of Environmental Protection. Potential foreign investors are advised to contact that ministry for current regulations and laws on this subject.

■ RIGHTS AND OBLIGATIONS OF FOREIGN INVESTORS

The government has guaranteed equal protection to both foreign and domestic investors.

Selection and extent of foreign investments will not be subject to government interference. However, foreign investments must be registered with, and approved by, the government.

Foreign investments may be transferred from one investor to another without government approval.

Foreign investments and income derived from such investments may be remitted abroad or repatriated subject only to the payment of taxes that may be due.

Property held by foreign investors may be used as collateral with regard to obtaining financing of projects or other debt obligations.

Foreign investment may be reinvested in Ukraine.

Under the provisions of the Law on Investment Activity, the government seeks to guarantee a stable investment environment. If any legislation is enacted that causes losses to foreign investors, compensation will be provided by the government. Similarly, the government guarantees to fairly compensate foreign investors in the event of nationalization or requisition of property or bank deposits. Nationalization or requisition cannot occur in the absence of legislative action.

■ LABOR

The labor force is well trained. Foreign workers may be employed only in cases where required skills are not locally available. Work permits must be obtained by foreign workers.

■ ACCOUNTING REQUIREMENTS

All economic associations must maintain complete accounting, statistical data, and other information for tax and other purposes as may be required for submission to the government. Accounting records must be maintained in accord with internationally accepted standards.

Foreign investments must provide audited statements to the government on a yearly basis to include information on assets, liabilities, profits, losses, earnings, and expenses.

■ CURRENCY CONTROLS

The Bank of the Ukraine is the central bank and is responsible for all matters concerning foreign exchange.

Foreign businesses and individuals are not permitted to open or maintain bank accounts in any foreign currency.

■ TAXATION

The primary taxes in the Ukraine are those levied on association and personal income. Other taxes include those assessed on documents and transfers (sales).

Various deductions and allowances are permitted to include legitimate business expenses. Tax incentives available to investors include special tax concessions and accelerated depreciation of fixed assets.

Special tax concessions are also available where exports exceed imports; where exports are less than 5 percent of total profits in any fiscal year; or where science or technology, related products exported are less than 30 percent of total exports of an investment activity.

Tax exemptions and concessions can be extended by action of the Ministry of External Economic Relations.

■ LEGAL SYSTEM

The judicial system includes local courts thath hear petty criminal and civil cases, and the district courts that function at the trial level for more important cases. Appeals are taken to the Supreme Court, which sits at Kiev.

■ CUSTOMS AND DUTIES

Licenses are required to import and export to and from the Ukraine. The Ministry of External Economic Relations is the licensing authority.

Associations that are established in special economic zones may import goods and materials on the basis of either reduced customs duties or under exemptions from such duties.

■ PROTECTION OF INTELLECTUAL PROPERTY

Ukraine is a member of the World Intellectual Property Organization and supports internationally accepted standards for the protection of copyrights, trademarks, patents, and technology transfer.

■ IMMIGRATION AND RESIDENCE

Visas may be required to enter the country. Potential foreign investors are advised to contact the Ministry of External Economic Relations for complete and current information regarding the issuance of visas, work permits, and residence permits.

■ FOREIGN INVESTMENT ASSISTANCE DIRECTORY

Sources that can provide further information about foreign investment in Ukraine include:

Ministry of External Economic Relations and Trade
vul. Pushkinska 4
Kiev, Ukraine
Telephone: (44) 2122951
Fax: (44) 2125271

Ministry for the Protection of the Environment
vul. Kirova 7
Kiev, Ukraine
Telephone: (44) 2262205

National Bank of Ukraine
Zhovtnevoji Revolyutsiji 9
Kiev, Ukraine
Telephone: (44) 2934264
Fax: (44) 2931698

Chamber of Commerce and Industry
vul. Bolshaya Zhitomarskaya 33
Kiev, Ukraine
Telephone: (44) 2122911
Telex: 131379
Fax: (44) 2123353

Persons interested in obtaining additional information about foreign investment in Ukraine are advised to contact the country's closest embassy or consular office.

Ukraine maintains diplomatic relations with Algeria, Canada, Finland, France, Germany, Greece, Hungary, Iran, Italy, Poland, Russia, United Kingdom, and United States.

United Arab Emirates, The

■ POLITICAL ENVIRONMENT

While, over the years, ruling monarchs have been replaced by other members of the royal family, these generally non-violent overthrows have not affected the stability of the government or the day-to-day activities of the people.

Economically, the country enjoys enormous revenues from its exports of petroleum and natural gas. Despite this, the government has shown a determination to escape from complete dependence on these exports for national revenues. Import substitution is receiving considerable attention in order to relieve, to some extent, the nation's level of imports.

The standard of living in the United Arab Emirates is generally high although some areas of the nation are underdeveloped.

Inflation is low to moderate. Unemployment is negligible. There is no measurable external public debt.

■ SUMMARY OF FOREIGN INVESTMENT POLICY

The two government offices that are generally considered to be the most responsible with regard to foreign investments in the nation are the Ministry of Economy and Commerce and the Ministry of Finance and Industry. The General Industry Corporation is responsible for the development of non-oil foreign and domestic investment activities.

There is no specific law dealing with foreign investment.

The government is interested in foreign investment with regard to the development of light industry and import substitution. Incentives principally are in the form of long-term, low-interest loans from development banks.

Foreign investments are limited to specific areas of the nation's economy. Investments in areas dealing with national security and defense, mass communications, transportation, and telecommunications are among those that are prohibited to foreign interests.

■ FORMATION AND TYPES OF PERMITTED BUSINESS ORGANIZATIONS

Regardless of the form of business organization that may be permitted by the government, to include the creation of a corporation, foreign ownership is limited to no more than 49 percent of any enterprise.

■ ENVIRONMENTAL PROTECTION

There is no specific government ministry or department that has been created to deal with the problem of environmental protection, although some activities in this area appear to be handled by the Ministry of Health, the Ministry of Petroleum and Mineral Resources, and the Ministry of the Interior.

Potential foreign investors are advised to contact those ministries or the Ministry of Economy and Commerce for information on environmental protection laws and regulations.

UNITED ARAB EMIRATES

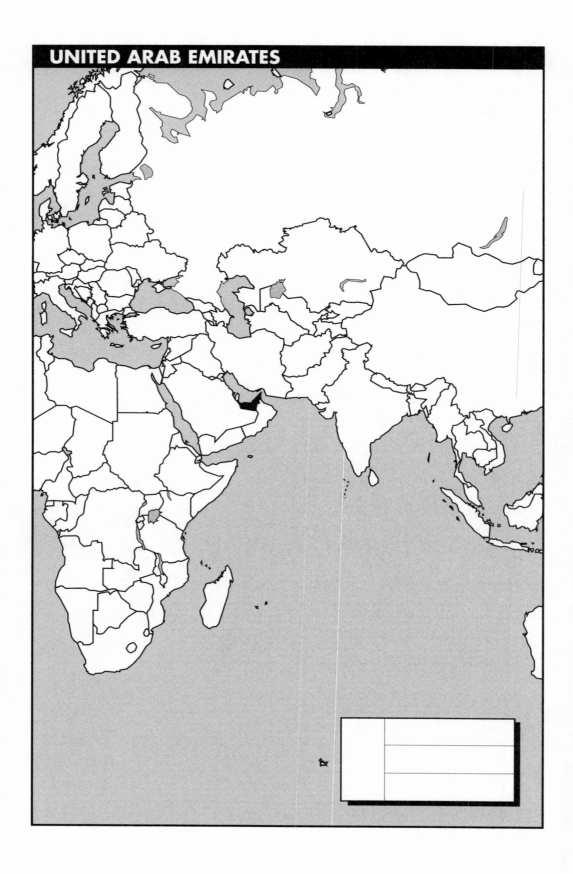

■ RIGHTS AND OBLIGATIONS OF FOREIGN INVESTORS

There are no guarantees with regard to nationalization or expropriation.

Foreign investments and all income derived from such investments may be freely repatriated or remitted abroad.

■ LABOR

There is a complete and extensive body of laws in existence with regard to the subjects of working conditions and employment.

All foreign personnel must possess work permits that are subject to periodic renewal.

■ ACCOUNTING REQUIREMENTS

All companies established in the country are required to maintain accurate accounting and other records, the former in accordance with internationally accepted standards.

■ CURRENCY CONTROLS

The Central Bank of the United Arab Emirates is the nation's official bank.

Currency controls are generally liberal.

Foreign investors may obtain financing from commercial banks or from several development banks to include the Emirates Industrial Bank, United Arab Emirates Development Bank, and the Sharjah Economic Development Corporation.

■ TAXATION

Potential foreign investors are advised to contact the Ministry of Economy and Commerce, the Ministry of Finance and Industry, or the General Industry Corporation for complete and current information regarding taxation as it relates to foreign investment.

■ LEGAL SYSTEM

All courts in the United Arab Emirates are part of the federal system. The Union Primary Tribunals (or local courts) have authority to hear and decide all criminal and civil cases. Appeals are taken to the Union Supreme Court, which sits at Abu Dhabi.

■ CUSTOMS AND DUTIES

There are no import licensing requirements and no import taxes are levied.

Tariffs are low and are based on an ad valorem percentage.

■ PROTECTION OF INTELLECTUAL PROPERTY

The United Arab Emirates is a member of the World Intellectual Property Organization and thus subscribes to accepted international standards with regard to the protection of copyrights, patents, trademarks, and technology transfer.

■ IMMIGRATION AND RESIDENCE

Visas are generally required to enter the country. Potential foreign investors are advised to contact the Ministry of Economy and Commerce, the General Industry Corporation, or the Federate of UAE Chambers of Commerce and Industry for complete and current information on the requirements for visas, work permits, and residence permits.

■ FOREIGN INVESTMENT ASSISTANCE DIRECTORY

Sources that can provide additional information about foreign investment in the United Arab Emirates include:

Ministry of Economy and Commerce
P.O. Box 901
Abu Dhabi, United Arab Emirates
Telephone: (971) (2) 215455
Telex: 22897
Fax: (971) (2) 215339

Ministry of Finance and Industry
P.O. Box 433
Abu Dhabi, United Arab Emirates
Telephone: (971) (2) 726000
Telex: 22937
Fax: (971) (2) 773301

Ministry of Health
P.O. Box 848
Abu Dhabi, United Arab Emirates
Telephone: (971) (2) 214100
Telex: 22678
Fax: (971) (2) 215422

Ministry of Petroleum and Mineral Resources
P.O. Box 59
Abu Dhabi, United Arab Emirates
Telephone: (971) (2) 651810
Telex: 22544
Fax: (971) (2) 663414

Central Bank of the United Arab Emirates
P.O. Box 854
Abu Dhabi, United Arab Emirates
Telephone: (971) (2) 368200
Telex: 22330
Fax: (971) (2) 668483

Federation of UAE Chambers of Commerce and Industry
P.O. Box 3014
Abu Dhabi, United Arab Emirates
Telephone: (971) (2) 214144
Telex: 23883
Fax: (971) (2) 339210

Persons interested in obtaining further information about foreign investment in the United Arab Emirates are advised to contact the country's closest embassy or consular office.

United Arab Emirates maintains diplomatic relations with Algeria, Argentina, Austria, Bangladesh, Belgium, Brazil, People's Republic of China, Czechoslovakia, Denmark, Egypt, Finland, France, Germany, Greece, Hungary, India, Indonesia, Iran, Iraq, Italy, Japan, Jordan, Kenya, Republic of Korea, Kuwait, Lebanon, Malaysia, Mali, Mauritania, Morocco, Netherlands, Pakistan, Philippines, Poland, Qatar, Romania, Russia, Saudi Arabia, Somalia, Spain, Sri Lanka, Sudan, Sweden, Switzerland, Syria, Tunisia, Turkey, United Kingdom, United States, and Yemen.

United Kingdom of Great Britain and Northern Ireland, The

■ POLITICAL ENVIRONMENT

The government is democratically elected and stable.

There is a highly developed and modern national infrastructure.

Inflation, as measured over the past several years, has been low to moderate. The level of unemployment is moderate but rising. The nation's external public debt is low.

The United Kingdom is a member of the European Community (EC).

Government economic planning includes the continuing privatization of many previously owned and operated state enterprises and a commitment to the acquisition of increased foreign investment.

■ SUMMARY OF FOREIGN INVESTMENT POLICY

There are various laws that have been enacted by the government that are relevant to the subject of foreign investment. The principal government department charged with the responsibility for promoting foreign investment in the country is the Invest in Britain Bureau, which is part of the Department of Trade and Industry.

There are few restrictions on the types of economic activity in which foreign investors may be engaged.

Foreign investors may own 100 percent of a domestic company.

There are no requirements for domestic management participation in any firm that is wholly or partially owned by foreign investors.

Among the incentives that are made available to foreign investors are those dealing with taxes, industrial estates, research and development assistance, and support that is provided by local levels of government.

Tax incentives are mainly in the form of allowances to include 100 percent allowances for scientific research and for the construction of industrial and commercial structures in some geographic areas; and 25 percent allowances for plant and necessary equipment.

Direct government support is provided to firms that are engaged in advanced level research and development regardless of the size of the enterprises involved in such research and development activities.

Financial assistance and expert guidance are provided by the government to firms around the nation where economic growth, to include increased labor opportunities, needs to be developed. Grants and government-financed consulting relevant to important management areas will be provided to eligible companies in manufacturing, service industries, and in tourism and related fields.

Numerous industrial estates have been prepared for use by manufacturing companies, many of them available for lease on attractive terms or for sale with low-cost, long-term mortgage arrangements.

In Northern Ireland, grants of up to one-half the cost of necessary plant and equipment are available along with additional grants for training and personnel and for new product development.

Local governments throughout the nation offer financial assistance in the form of grants and low-interest, long-term loans directed toward industrial or other types of

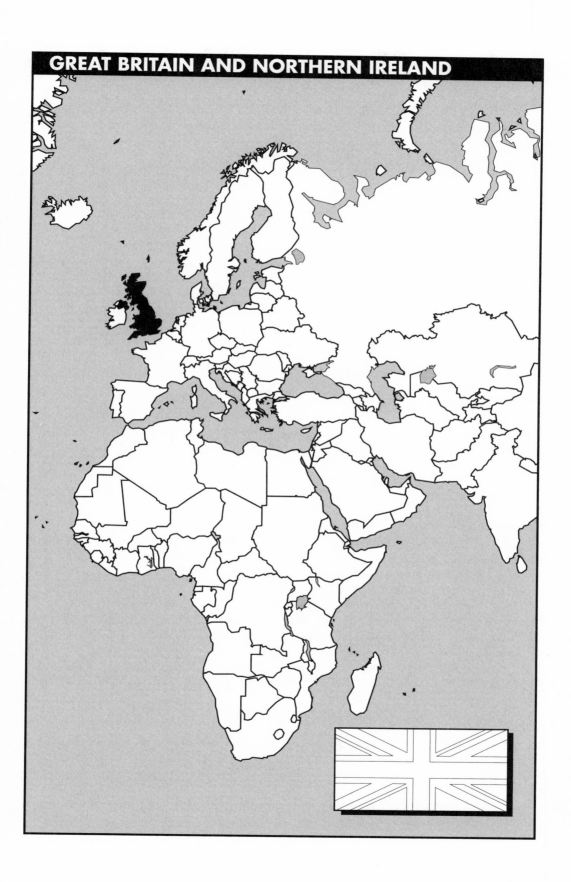

development that are relevant to the geographic area, e.g., tourism.

A number of Enterprise Zones have been developed. Firms that locate in such zones are exempt from local property taxes and planning requirements for periods of up to ten years.

Incentives also are available, generally in the form of grants and convenient locations provided by local governments, in the numerous New Towns and through the Urban Development Corporations that have been created around the country.

Finally, three Free Zones have been established in which materials and goods may be held on a duty free basis prior to reexport outside the EC.

■ FORMATION AND TYPES OF PERMITTED BUSINESS ORGANIZATIONS

Foreign investors may participate in the economy of the country through the formation of a public or private limited company, an unlimited company, a general or limited partnership, or a sole proprietorship.

Joint ventures may be created with domestic investors.

Subsidiaries or branch offices of a foreign corporation may be established.

All limited companies, including subsidiaries of foreign corporations, are considered to be legal entities with juridical person status.

The number of partners in any partnership arrangement is limited to 20.

■ ENVIRONMENTAL PROTECTION

The government has a major and continuing interest in the protection of the environment, which is evidenced at both the central and local government levels. The former is designated as the Department of the Environment that is responsible for environmental issue identification and policy making. Potential foreign investors are advised to contact that department for complete and current information about laws and regulations pertaining to this subject area.

■ RIGHTS AND OBLIGATIONS OF FOREIGN INVESTORS

Foreign and domestic investors are considered to be equal with regard to business opportunities and the application of the laws.

There are no restrictions on repatriation or remittance abroad of foreign investments or any income derived from such investments. In the event of investment liquidation, foreign investors are free to repatriate or remit abroad their rightful share.

Nationalization or expropriation of property is unlawful. Any required taking of private property for reasons of public necessity must be accomplished through specific legal means and must include equitable compensation.

Any disputes between foreign investors and the government may be subject to arbitration. In the event the parties cannot agree, the issue may be resolved by the courts.

■ LABOR

The labor force is large, highly skilled, well educated, and motivated. There is a high level of unionization.

There is a very extensive body of laws that has been developed on the subject of employment and working conditions.

Nationals of EC member countries may work in the United Kingdom for up to six months without the possession of a work permit. Nationals of other nations must obtain work permits, issued by the Department of Employment in the United Kingdom and by the Department of Economic Development in Northern Ireland, subject to meeting various criteria to include the fact that a position exists, that certain skills are required, and that the required skill or expertise is not locally available.

Individuals who will be self employed or who will be acting as the sole representative of a foreign company are not required to possess work permits.

■ ACCOUNTING REQUIREMENTS

Limited companies, whether public or private, must file audited accounts on a yearly basis with the Registrar of Companies. Subsidiaries and branches of foreign corporations must also meet this requirement.

■ CURRENCY CONTROLS

The Bank of England is the nation's central bank.

Currently, there are no foreign exchange controls in existence. There are no restrictions on the amount of money that may be taken into or from the country.

Foreign companies and individuals may maintain bank accounts in any foreign currency.

Local sources of financing are available to foreign investors.

■ TAXATION

The principal taxes imposed are those relating to company profits and individual income. There are other taxes levied to include the value added tax (VAT), local property taxes, and customs charges, in addition to numerous license and registration fees.

The tax year runs from April 6 to April 5 of the subsequent year.

The United Kingdom has entered into a large number of bilateral treaties with other nations on the subject of double taxation.

Deductions and allowances relevant to company profits taxes include those for legitimate business expenses, depreciation, and charitable contributions, among others. Individual taxpayers are entitled to standard deductions and allowances as well as to certain incurred expenses.

■ LEGAL SYSTEM

The court system is extensive. Petty criminal cases are heard by Magistrates' Courts. Minor civil cases are heard by the County Courts. The Crown Court is empowered to hear more serious criminal cases. Major civil cases, to include divorce matters, admiralty cases, and other commercial causes, are heard by one of the three divisions of the High Court of Justice, i.e., Chancery, Family, and Queen's Bench.

Civil appeals from both the County and High Courts and criminal appeals from the Crown Courts are taken to the Court of Appeal. Final appeals are taken to the House of Lords, which sits at London.

■ CUSTOMS AND DUTIES

Historically, the United Kingdom has maintained a high level of interest in foreign trade and that interest continues. There are no trade barriers between the United Kingdom and other members of the European Community (EC). There are low tariffs in existence relevant to trade with non-EC nations.

■ PROTECTION OF INTELLECTUAL PROPERTY

The United Kingdom is a member of the World Intellectual Property Organization and is a signatory to the major conventions and multilateral treaties on intellectual property protection. In addition, the government has enacted extensive protection to copyrights, patents, and trademarks through domestic laws on these subjects.

■ IMMIGRATION AND RESIDENCE

Depending on visitor nationality, visas may be required to enter the country. Potential foreign investors are advised to contact the Invest in Britain Bureau for complete and current information about the requirements and procedures involved to obtain visas, work permits, and residence permits.

■ FOREIGN INVESTMENT ASSISTANCE DIRECTORY

Sources that can provide additional information about foreign investment in the United Kingdom include:

Invest in Britain Bureau
Department of Trade and Industry
Kingsgate House
66-74 Victoria Street
London SW1E 6SW, United Kingdom
Telephone: (44) (71) 21584838 / (44) (71) 2158439
Telex: 8811074
Fax: (44) (71) 2158451

Department of the Environment
2 Marsham Street
London 3EB, United Kingdom
Telephone: (44) (71) 2763000
Telex: 22221
Fax: (44) (71) 2760818

Office of Northern Island
Whitehall
London SW1A 2AZ, United Kingdom
Telephone: (44) (71) 2103000

Department of Employment
Overseas Labor Section
Caxton House, Tothill Street
London SW1H 9NF, United Kingdom
Telephone: (44) (71) 2735336 / (44) (71) 2735337
Telex: 915564

Home Office
Immigration and Nationality Department
Lunar House
Wellesley Road
Croydon CR9 2BY, United Kingdom
Telephone: (44) (81) 6860688

Bank of England
Threadneedle Street
London EC2R 8AH, United Kingdom
Telephone: (44) (71) 6014444
Telex: 885001

Persons interested in obtaining further information about foreign investment in the United Kingdom are advised to contact the closest United Kingdom embassy or consular office.

The United Kingdom maintains diplomatic relations with Afghanistan, Algeria, Angola, Antigua and Barbuda, Argentina, Australia, Austria, Bahamas, Bahrain, Bangladesh, Barbados, Belgium, Belize, Bolivia, Botswana, Brazil, Brunei, Bulgaria, Cameroon, Canada, Chile, People's Republic of China, Colombia, Costa Rica, Côte d'Ivoire, Cuba, Cyprus, Czechoslovakia, Denmark, Ecuador, Egypt, El Salvador, Estonia, Ethiopia, Fiji, Finland, France, Gabon, Gambia, Germany, Ghana, Greece, Grenada, Guatemala, Guyana, Holy See, Honduras, Hungary, Iceland, India, Indonesia, Iran, Iraq, Ireland, Israel, Italy, Jamaica, Japan, Jordan, Kenya, Republic of Korea, Kuwait, Latvia, Lebanon, Lesotho, Liberia, Libya, Lithuania, Luxembourg, Malawi, Malaysia, Malta, Mauritius, Mexico, Mongolia, Morocco, Mozambique, Myanmar, Namibia, Nepal, Netherlands, New Zealand, Nicaragua, Nigeria, Norway, Oman, Pakistan, Panama, Papua New Guinea, Paraguay, Peru, Philippines, Poland, Portugal, Qatar, Romania, Russia, Saint Christopher, Saint Lucia, Saint Vincent and the Grenandines, Saudi Arabia, Senegal, Seychelles, Sierra Leone, Singapore, Somalia, South Africa, Spain, Sri Lanka, Sudan, Swaziland, Sweden, Switzerland, Syria, Tanzania, Thailand, Tonga, Trinidad and Tobago, Tunisia, Turkey, Uganda, United Arab Emirates, United States, Uruguay, Venezuela, Vietnam, Yemen, Zaire, Zambia, and Zimbabwe.

UNITED STATES OF AMERICA

■ POLITICAL ENVIRONMENT

The government is democratically elected and is stable.

Over the period of years that began with the end of World War II, the nation has gradually shifted from being industrially oriented to services oriented. It has, however, remained a world leader in research, development, and high technology applications.

Inflation has remained moderate over the past several years. Unemployment has been rising, both as a result of a stubborn recession and because of corporate downsizing, which began a decade or so ago and will continue to affect white collar employment as firms flatten their organization charts.

The trade deficit is growing and recent economic expansion has been limited to only about 1 percent annually. High levels of federal spending, despite the end of the Cold War and reductions in defense costs, have led to a proposed austerity program that includes increased taxes.

■ SUMMARY OF FOREIGN INVESTMENT POLICY

There is an open door policy with reference to foreign investment. No government approval of foreign investment is required except with regard to foreign purchases of agricultural property, which must be reported to the Secretary of Agriculture.

Except for certain limitations in the defense, telecommunications, and transportation industries there are no restrictions on foreign investment.

Foreign investors may own 100 percent of any enterprise except, as indicated above, in specific industries where foreign ownership percentages are limited and where domestic management is generally required.

No federal tax incentives are offered to potential foreign investors, although some tax benefits are available to both foreign and domestic investors. A large number of incentives are offered by the individual state governments, most of which are interested in obtaining foreign investment that will increase local employment opportunities and generally improve the economy of the state.

The principal federal government contact point for potential foreign investors is the International Trade Administration, which is a part of the Department of Commerce.

Tax incentives available to both foreign and domestic investors include accelerated depreciation on physical assets and depletion allowances on wasting assets, e.g., oil, timber, and mining.

Federal loans and grants are available to states and through banks located in those states. Foreign enterprises established in such areas are generally eligible for such assistance.

Tax incentives are provided by the states in the form of long-term tax holidays, tax reductions, and tax exemptions. Other incentives offered by the states include the provision of advisory services, as well as grants, loans, and other financial assistance, guidance as to location selection, and connections to support activities and organizations.

The creation of any entity, including through a process of acquisition by a foreign investor, that results in a possible restraint by trade through lessening of competition may well be challenged by the Department of Justice or by the Federal Trade Commis-

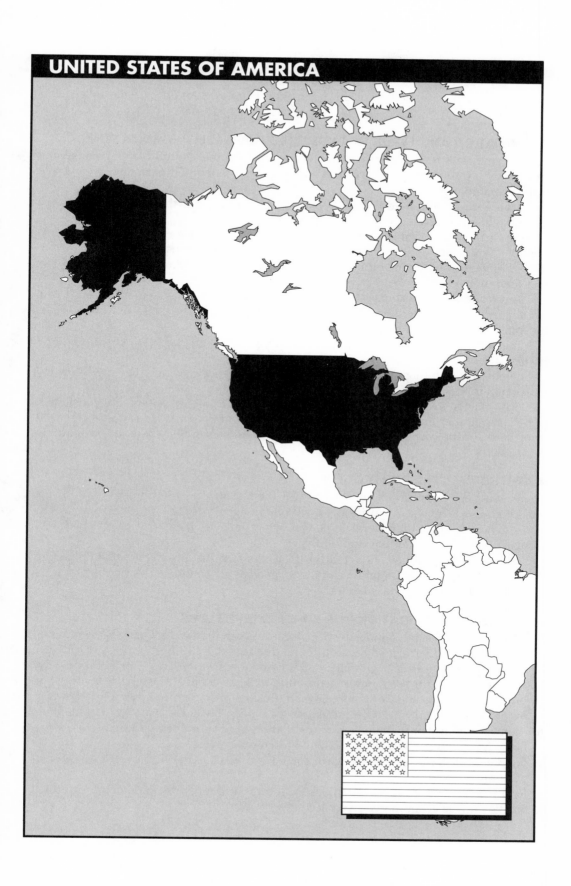

sion following the completion of the acquisition or merger and may force subsequent divestiture.

■ FORMATION AND TYPES OF PERMITTED BUSINESS ORGANIZATIONS

Foreign investors may participate in the economy of the United States through the creation of a public or private corporation; a general or limited partnership; or a sole proprietorship.

Corporations are formed under state laws but may operate throughout the country upon payment of necessary registration fees and taxes.

In an increasing number of states, one-person corporations may be formed. Additionally, many states permit the creation of private corporations that enjoy the corporate advantage of limited liability but where shares are not made available to the public and the number of shareholders is limited.

The creation of both general and limited partnerships is governed by state law usually in conformity with the Uniform Partnership Law or the Uniform Limited Partnership Law as adopted by the individual states.

Joint ventures may be formed between foreign investors or between foreign and domestic investors.

Subsidiaries of foreign corporations may be established and may be wholly owned by foreign investors.

Corporations, including subsidiary corporations of a foreign parent, are considered to be legal entities and to enjoy the status of a juridical person. This status is achieved upon filing of the corporate charter with the proper authorities where the corporation is formed.

■ ENVIRONMENTAL PROTECTION

There is a very high degree of government interest in the environment, both at the federal and state levels. The principal government agency is the Environmental Protection Agency (EPA) at the federal level. State-level agencies have been established with similar responsibilities to that of the EPA.

Potential foreign investors are advised to contact the Environmental Protection Agency and appropriate state development agencies for complete information on laws pertaining to environmental matters.

■ RIGHTS AND OBLIGATIONS OF FOREIGN INVESTORS

Foreign investments and all income derived from such investments may be repatriated or remitted abroad subject to payment of all due taxes.

There is a constitutional guarantee against nationalization and expropriation. Any taking of private property for reasons of public necessity must be accomplished through legal means and fair compensation must be provided to the property holder.

Except with regard to certain industries, as noted above, there are no requirements for domestic equity or management participation in firms owned by foreign investors.

Local financing sources are available to foreign investors.

Foreign and domestic investors are considered to be equal in terms of investment opportunities.

Real property ownership restrictions with regard to foreign companies and foreign nationals may be encountered in some states.

There is no federal law that restricts the sale, lease, or other disposition of real property to foreign companies or nationals.

■ LABOR

There is a large and highly skilled labor force at all levels to include managerial, professional, scientific, technical, clerical, and production personnel.

A comprehensive body of laws exists at both the state and federal levels with regard to employment and working conditions.

There are no laws or regulations that establish a limit on the number or percentage of either foreign or domestic personnel employed by any enterprise.

Foreign nationals who are to be employed in the country must first obtain a special visa that describes the particular classification of employment, business, or professional activity in which they will be engaged.

■ ACCOUNTING REQUIREMENTS

Businesses must maintain accounting and other records as required for tax and various statistical purposes. Independent audits are required of publicly held corporations.

■ CURRENCY CONTROLS

The Federal Reserve System functions as the nation's central bank.

No foreign currency exchange controls exist. There is no requirement to register foreign capital that is taken into the country.

There is no requirement to register foreign loans or to have such loans approved by the government.

■ TAXATION

The principal tax assessed is that on corporate and personal income. Other taxes levied include, but are not limited to, excise taxes, trust, estate and gift taxes, real property taxes, and sales taxes. Income taxes are also assessed by some states and cities.

The tax year is the calendar year, i.e., January 1 to December 31. Taxpayers may select a different, usually their fiscal, year for tax purposes.

Partnerships and joint ventures, unless the latter are incorporated, are not treated as taxable entities. The income generated by partnerships and joint ventures is considered to be that of the partners.

Deductions from corporate taxes include, but are not limited to, legitimate business expenses; depreciation on physical assets; depletion allowances with reference to wasting assets, e.g., mining, timber, and petroleum; insurance premiums; employee compensation; and contributions to charity. Numerous tax credits are also available to eligible corporate taxpayers.

Individual taxpayers may claim deductions for legitimate business expenses; certain personal expenses; mortgage interest on a principal home; and charitable contributions, among others. In addition, taxpayers may claim allowances for dependents.

As noted, gift and estate taxes are also assessed on individuals.

The United States is a party to numerous bilateral treaties with other nations on the subject of double taxation.

■ LEGAL SYSTEM

There are both federal and state court systems. The former, in addition to various specialized courts to include the Tax Court, the Court for Military Appeals, the Court of International Trade, and the Court of Claims, is comprised of U.S. Magistrates' Courts in every federal district, which hear minor federal cases and perform other functions; federal District Courts, which are the trial courts in the federal system for both criminal and civil cases; and the Courts of Appeal, each of which provides an appellate function for the districts within their circuit or area.

State court systems include local courts in virtually every municipality that hear and decide minor criminal matters. District, family, and juvenile courts usually function at the county level. Tax courts and worker's compensation courts are among state-level courts that serve a specialized function. Superior Courts (sometimes otherwise titled) are the trial level courts for more serious criminal and civil cases and are usually empowered to hear appeals from the local courts.

In most states, there is an intermediate appeals court to which appeals from the trial courts are taken. Final state court appeals are taken to the supreme court (sometimes titled court of appeals) of the state where the issue had been heard.

Appeals are taken on certain legal grounds from the state courts to the U.S. Supreme Court, which is also the final appellate authority in the federal court system. The Supreme Court sits at Washington, D.C.

■ CUSTOMS AND DUTIES

The government is interested in increasing international trade and generally pursues a free trade policy that is exemplified with the creation of a free trade agreement with Canada and moves in that direction with Mexico. The United States is a member of the General Agreement on Tariffs and Trade (GATT).

The government may employ quotas, anti-dumping, or countervailing duties to protect domestic industry.

The government has a major interest in developing export trade and has been instrumental in the establishment of many free trade zones across the country. In addition, the government offers tax incentives and other benefits to domestic companies engaged in the exporting of products made in the United States. These other benefits include export credit insurance and financing of exports by the Export-Import Bank, among other government considerations. In addition, the government has entered into numerous bilateral investment treaties that are essentially designed to stimulate trade.

Customs drawbacks are applied to reexported goods and materials.

■ PROTECTION OF INTELLECTUAL PROPERTY

The United States is a member of the World Intellectual Property Organization, and the government has enacted laws that provide protection for copyright, trademark, and patent holders.

■ IMMIGRATION AND RESIDENCE

Visas are generally required to visit the country. There are various visa classifications, including several designed for business use. Potential foreign investors are advised to contact the Immigration and Naturalization Service for current information regarding requirements for visas, work permits, and residence permits.

■ FOREIGN INVESTMENT ASSISTANCE DIRECTORY

Sources that can provide further information about foreign investment in the United States include:

International Trade Administration
Department of Commerce
14th Street and Constitution Avenue, NW
Washington, DC, USA 20230
Telephone: (2) (202) 482-2000

Environmental Protection Agency
401 M Street, SW
Washington, DC, USA 20460
Telephone: (2) (202) 260-2090

Immigration and Naturalization Service
Department of Justice
425 I Street, NW
Washington, DC, USA 20536
Telephone: (2) (202) 514-2530

US Chamber of Commerce
1615 H Street, NW
Washington, DC, USA 20062
Telephone: (2) (202) 566-8195

In addition, potential foreign investors are also reminded that most states, as well as the District of Columbia, Puerto Rico, and the Virgin Islands, maintain industrial development offices in their respective capitals.

Persons interested in obtaining additional information about foreign investment in the United States are advised to contact the closest United States embassy or consular office.

The United States maintains diplomatic relations with Afghanistan, Albania, Algeria, Antigua and Barbuda, Argentina, Armenia, Australia, Austria, Bahamas, Bahrain, Bangladesh, Barbados, Belgium, Belize, Benin, Bolivia, Botswana, Brazil, Brunei, Bulgaria, Burkina Faso, Burundi, Cameroon, Canada, Cape Verde, Central African Republic, Chad, Chile, People's Republic of China, Colombia, Comoros, Congo, Costa Rica, Côte d'Ivoire, Cyprus, Czechoslovakia, Denmark, Djibouti, Dominican Republic, Ecuador, Egypt, El Salvador, Equatorial Guinea, Estonia, Ethiopia, Fiji, Finland, France, Gabon, Gambia, Germany, Ghana, Greece, Grenada, Guatemala, Guinea, Guinea-Bissau, Guyana, Haiti, Holy See, Honduras, Hungary, Iceland, India, Indonesia, Ireland, Israel, Italy, Jamaica, Japan, Jordan, Kenya, Republic of Korea, Kuwait, Laos, Latvia, Lebanon, Lesotho, Liberia, Lithuania, Luxembourg, Madagascar, Malawi, Malaysia, Mali, Malta, Marshall Islands, Mauritania, Mauritius, Mexico, Micronesia, Mongolia, Morocco, Mozambique, Myanmar, Namibia, Nepal, Netherlands, New Zealand, Nicaragua, Niger, Nigeria, Norway, Oman, Pakistan, Panama, Papua New Guinea, Paraguay, Peru, Philippines, Poland, Portugal, Qatar, Romania, Russia, Rwanda, Saint Christopher and Nevis, Saint Lucia, Saint Vincent and the Grenadines, Sao Tome and Principe, Saudi Arabia, Senegal, Seychelles, Sierra Leone, Singapore, Solomon Islands,

South Africa, Spain, Sri Lanka, Sudan, Suriname, Swaziland, Sweden, Switzerland, Syria, Tanzania, Thailand, Togo, Trinidad and Tobago, Tunisia, Turkey, Uganda, Ukraine, United Arab Emirates, United Kingdom, Uruguay, Venezuela, Western Samoa, Yemen, Zambia, and Zimbabwe.

URUGUAY, REPUBLIC OF

■ POLITICAL ENVIRONMENT

Uruguay has been struggling with major economic problems that have included high inflation and a large public debt. Government efforts to curb inflation through austerity measures and programs to privatize the economy have met with resistance in the form of general strikes by the labor unions. Unemployment is relatively high.

■ SUMMARY OF FOREIGN INVESTMENT POLICY

In its efforts to obtain increased levels of foreign investment, the government has enacted the Industrial Promotional Law and has created the Investment Development Committee to assist and advise potential foreign investors.

There is a particular interest in expanding those industries that will increase production of goods for export.

A variety of incentives are available to foreign investors including certain tax incentives and customs exemptions. Duty free zones have been created.

Foreign investments must receive authorization from the Foreign Investment Advisory Unit of the Ministry of Economy and Finance. The application for authorization can be expedited by the Investment Development Committee.

Authorizations will be granted if they are considered to be compatible with the national interest. Specific authorizations are necessary for foreign participation in various areas to include nuclear energy, chemicals, ranching and agriculture, banking, railroads, telecommunications, and mass media enterprises, among others.

■ FORMATION AND TYPES OF PERMITTED BUSINESS ORGANIZATIONS

Foreign investors may form corporations, as well as general and limited partnerships. Foreign companies may establish subsidiaries.

Corporations enjoy juridical person status.

Foreign enterprises may form joint ventures with existing domestic businesses.

■ ENVIRONMENTAL PROTECTION

There is a declared national interest in the protection of the environment generally and, in particular, of the nation's forests. Potential foreign investors are advised to contact the Investment Development Committee for current and complete information on laws and regulations pertaining to the environment.

■ RIGHTS AND OBLIGATIONS OF FOREIGN INVESTORS

Invested capital and the profits derived from such investment may be repatriated or remitted abroad. The conditions for such remittance or repatriation are determined by contract between the investor and the government.

Invested capital may not be remitted or repatriated until the end of the third year of such investment. Realized profits that are not remitted within two years are considered as being capitalized.

Foreign and domestic investors are entitled to equality relevant to investment activities.

Contracts may be drawn showing monetary amounts in any currency.

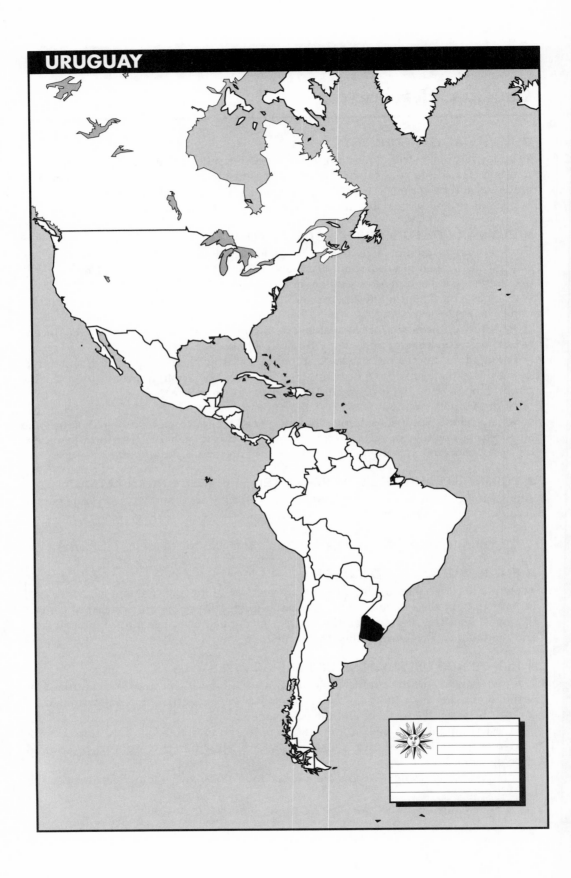

URUGUAY

Foreign investors may be granted short- and long-term financing from the Investment Development Fund upon application and approval of the Ministry of Industry and Energy submitted through the ministry's Industrial Promotion Unit.

Financing for forestry projects may be obtained from the Forestry Fund through the Administrative Committee for Forestry Funding.

■ LABOR

There is an extensive body of laws relating to employment and working conditions including required wage and salary levels, holidays, and other relevant factors.

Generally, Uruguayan workers must be accorded hiring preference. Firms established in the free zones must maintain labor forces that are composed of at least 75 percent local workers.

■ ACCOUNTING REQUIREMENTS

All companies must maintain accurate records for tax and statistical purposes. Financial records must be maintained in accordance with internationally accepted standards.

■ CURRENCY CONTROLS

The Central Bank of Uruguay is responsible for exchange control.

Foreign investors may open and maintain bank accounts in any currency.

■ TAXATION

There is no personal income tax in Uruguay.

There is a tax on industry and commerce, and many exemptions, incentives, and allowances relevant to that tax may be available to eligible companies funded by foreign investment. Exemptions may be applied to machinery, construction, technological research, the development of first class hotels, and forestry projects.

There are minor taxes levied to include those on real property and services, i.e., a value added tax (VAT).

■ LEGAL SYSTEM

There are essentially four court levels. The lowest is that where justices of the peace hear minor criminal and civil issues. The civil and criminal courts are trial level courts. Appeals from these courts are taken to the appellate level and from there to the Supreme Court of Justice, which sits in Montevideo.

■ CUSTOMS AND DUTIES

Any business established in the free zones is exempt from tax.

Goods, machinery and raw materials necessary for manufacturing, finishing, or other registered processing may be received in the free zones without payment of duties.

Uruguay is a member of the Latin American Integration Association, which provides for special trade conditions between the member states.

■ PROTECTION OF INTELLECTUAL PROPERTY

Uruguay, in addition to being a member of the World Intellectual Property Organization, has enacted domestic statutes relevant to copyrights, patents, trademarks, and tradenames, and recognizes the internationally accepted need for the protection of intellectual property.

■ IMMIGRATION AND RESIDENCE

In most cases, visas are required to enter Uruguay. Potential foreign investors are advised to contact the Committee for Investment Development for complete and current information on visa, work permit, and residence permit requirements.

■ FOREIGN INVESTMENT ASSISTANCE DIRECTORY

Sources that can provide further information about foreign investment in Uruguay include:

Committee for Investment Development
Executive Government Office
Edeficio Libertad
Avda Luis Alberto de Herrera 3050
Montevideo, Uruguay
Telephone: (598) (2) 808110
Telex: UY-DICOPRE 22280

Ministry of Economy and Finance
Colonia 1089
Montevideo, Uruguay
Telephone: (598) (2) 919102
Telex: 6269

Ministry of Industry and Energy
Rincón 747
Montevideo, Uruguay
Telephone: (598) (2) 9026000
Telex: 22072

Central Bank of Uruguay
Avda Juan P. Fabini
Montevideo, Uruguay
Telephone: (598) (2) 917117
Telex: 6659

Persons interested in obtaining further information about foreign investment in Uruguay also are advised to contact the closest Uruguayan embassy or consular office.

Uruguay maintains diplomatic relations with Argentina, Belgium, Bolivia, Brazil, Bulgaria, Chile, People's Republic of China, Colombia, Costa Rica, Cuba, Czechoslovakia, Dominican Republic, Ecuador, Egypt, El Salvador, France, Germany, Guatemala, Holy See, Honduras, Hungary, Israel, Italy, Japan, Republic of Korea, Lebanon, Malta, Mexico, Netherlands, Nicaragua, Panama, Paraguay, Peru, Poland, Portugal, Romania, Russia, South Africa, Spain, Switzerland, United Kingdom, United States, and Venezuela.

VENEZUELA, REPUBLIC OF

■ POLITICAL ENVIRONMENT

Venezuela has experienced significant internal unrest to include an attempted coup d'etat in February 1992 and another in November 1992. The stability of the government is questionable given the nation's wide range of problems that include high rates of unemployment, inflation, and a formidable external debt. The nation's economic problems are at least partially created by its dependence on oil as its principal export. Recently, Venezuela suspended payments on both its public and private international debts.

■ SUMMARY OF FOREIGN INVESTMENT POLICY

The government is seeking foreign investment. The Economic Planning •Advisory Board has been given some key responsibilities for promoting foreign investment. Other government departments with responsibilities in this area include the Ministry of Development, the Ministry of Finance, and the Superintendency of Foreign Investment.

There is a specific interest in the development of the country's agricultural sector and in the expansion of the industrial sector of the economy.

In line with the government's interest in obtaining foreign investment, it has adopted tax incentives, established several free trade zones, and generally has acted to lower customs duties.

In most cases, foreign and domestic investors enjoy equality of treatment. However, there are several fields of economic activity in which the percentage of foreign investment is limited, e.g., essential public services, telecommunications, and mass communications.

Foreign participation in the petroleum industry is not permitted in Venezuela.

In most other fields of economic activity, there is no limit to the percentage of foreign investment.

■ FORMATION AND TYPES OF PERMITTED BUSINESS ORGANIZATIONS

There are several types of business organizations that may be formed to include corporations, limited liability companies, general and limited partnerships, joint ventures, and sole proprietorships.

The most prevalent forms of business organization used by foreign investors are the corporation and the joint venture, the latter commonly used to undertake specific projects in cooperation with a local business entity. The limited liability company is sometimes used, but there is a requirement that sets a maximum amount of capital in its formation, and thus it is less flexible than the corporate form.

Wholly owned subsidiaries of foreign corporations and branch offices may also be established.

All businesses must file with the Superintendency of Foreign Investment upon their formation and commencement of operations.

■ ENVIRONMENTAL PROTECTION

There is a major government interest in the protection of the environment. There are several laws that have been enacted to protect the environment and to provide penal-

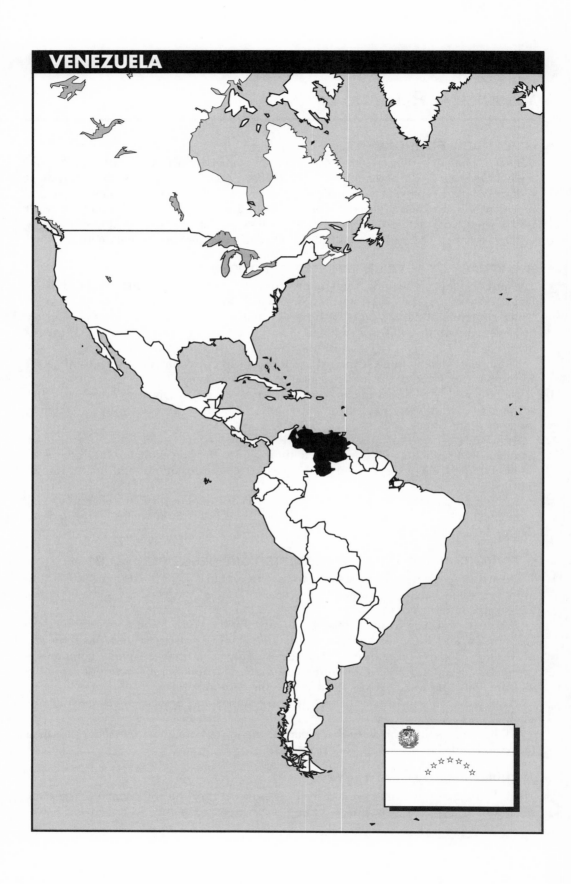

VENEZUELA

ties for causing environmental damage. Potential foreign investors are advised to consult the Ministry of the Environment and Renewable Natural Resources for detailed information about the application of these laws.

■ RIGHTS AND OBLIGATIONS OF FOREIGN INVESTORS

Foreign companies and individuals must file tax returns with the government.

Foreign investors may remit abroad or repatriate profits and other income generated as a result of investments made in Venezuela, without limit, subsequent to the payment of required taxes.

Financing of business activities may be obtained from local Venezuelan sources.

■ LABOR

There is a body of labor law that provides for working conditions, wages, salaries, and fringe benefits. Most businesses are required to provide profit-sharing programs for workers.

The labor pool does not, generally, possess a high level of technical skills.

In most cases Venezuelan workers must be given hiring preference. Venezuelan employees must constitute at least 75 percent of all personnel in most companies. There are also requirements that some line management positions be filled only with Venezuelan personnel.

■ ACCOUNTING REQUIREMENTS

The laws require that all businesses, including proprietorships, maintain accurate accounting books and records. Such records must be maintained in accordance with standard international practices.

■ CURRENCY CONTROLS

There are no present restrictions relevant to foreign currency.

■ TAXATION

Venezuela has not entered into any agreements relevant to the subject of double taxation.

The principal tax is the Venezuelan income tax, which is applied to both corporations and individuals. There are, in addition, a variety of minor taxes at the national level as well as taxes imposed at the local government level.

The tax year for individual taxpayers is the calendar year. Businesses may calculate taxes based on their relevant fiscal year.

There are only a few tax incentives and they include deductions for business expenses and depletion allowances relevant to mining operations. Tax credit bonds are also offered as an incentive to exporters. Firms operating in the free zones may be eligible for a variety of tax incentives.

Tax concessions and tax holidays (or abatements) are available depending on the activities in which a foreign entity is engaged.

■ LEGAL SYSTEM

There is a system of courts throughout the country that hears and decides criminal and civil cases. Appeals from these courts are taken to the Supreme Court of Justice, which sits in Caracas.

■ CUSTOMS AND DUTIES

Raw materials and certain finished products that are imported to a free trade zone are exempt from customs duties or the customs duties will be reduced, depending on the intended use of the imports.

■ PROTECTION OF INTELLECTUAL PROPERTY

Venezuela is a member of the World Intellectual Property Organization and thus subscribes to internationally accepted views on the protection of trademarks, tradenames, patents and copyrights.

■ IMMIGRATION AND RESIDENCE

Potential foreign investors require a visa to enter the country. The visa has a valid duration of 45 days and may be renewed. Resident status may be achieved after two years in Venezuela.

Individuals entering Venezuela as employees must obtain work permits. Visa requirements are the same as for foreign investors.

■ FOREIGN INVESTMENT ASSISTANCE DIRECTORY

The following sources may be contacted to obtain more detailed information about foreign investment in Venezuela:

Economic Planning Advisory Board
Ministry of Development
Edif Sur
Centro Simon Bolivar
Caracas, Venezuela
Telephone: (58) (2) 41-9341
Telex: 22753

Superintendency of Foreign Investment
Esquina Bolsa a Mercaderes
Edif, La Perla
El Silencio
Caracas, Venezuela
Telephone: (58) (2) 483-6666

Persons interested in obtaining further information about investing in Venezuela also are advised to contact the closest Venezuelan embassy or consular office.

Venezuela maintains diplomatic relations with Algeria, Argentina, Australia, Austria, Barbados, Belgium, Bolivia, Brazil, Canada, Chile, People's Republic of China, Colombia, Costa Rica, Cuba, Czechoslovakia, Denmark, Dominican Republic, Ecuador, Egypt, El Salvador, Finland, France, Gabon, Germany, Greece, Grenada, Guatemala, Guyana, Haiti, Holy See, Honduras, Hungary, India, Indonesia, Iran, Iraq, Israel, Italy, Jamaica, Japan, Democratic People's Republic of Korea, Republic of Korea, Lebanon, Libya, Mexico, Netherlands, Nicaragua, Nigeria, Norway, Panama, Paraguay, Peru, Philippines, Poland, Portugal, Romania, Russia, Saudi Arabia, Spain, Suriname, Sweden, Switzerland, Syria, Trinidad and Tobago, Turkey, United Kingdom, United States, and Uruguay.

VIETNAM, SOCIALIST REPUBLIC OF

■ POLITICAL ENVIRONMENT

The government appears to be internally stable. External threats, which have been largely border-related issues involving Cambodia and the People's Republic of China, seem to have been resolved.

There is a marked interest on the part of the government to move from a centrally planned economy to a modified free market system. The nation is also faced with the need to create a modern infrastructure. Essential to that task is the development of substantial foreign investment from the industrialized nations.

■ SUMMARY OF FOREIGN INVESTMENT POLICY

The government enacted an amended Foreign Investment Law on June 30, 1990, which is supplemented by a Decree of the Council of Ministers issued on February 6, 1991, and provides details on the implementation of the law.

The law particularly encourages foreign investment in the following areas:

- Major economic programs to increase export production and import substitution.

- High-tech industries that will employ skilled Vietnamese workers.

- Infrastructure development to include construction of schools; expansion and upgrading of hospitals; construction of stadiums and gymnasiums; construction of museums; theaters, aquariums, information, and exhibit centers; renovation and construction of historic places and monuments; and creation of water and sewage projects including pipe systems, canals, drainage ditches, and reservoirs.

- Large-scale projects that will maximize existing national production.

- Development of labor-intensive industries with the ability to commercially exploit raw materials and resources.

- Programs to increase foreign exchange earnings, e.g., tourism, ship repair, seaport and airport projects.

The State Committee for Cooperation and Investment is the principal government agency responsible for administering the Foreign Investment Law.

■ FORMATION AND TYPES OF PERMITTED BUSINESS ORGANIZATIONS

Foreign investment may be made by several types of business organizations as well as by private individuals. Business organizations include partnerships (referred to as contractual business cooperation ventures), joint ventures, and enterprises 100 percent financed by foreign capitals.

Joint ventures and contractual business cooperation ventures may be totally financed by foreign capital but must be no less than 30 percent so financed.

Contractual business cooperation ventures may be created by two or more partners, one or more being foreign and at least one partner being Vietnamese. A contractual business cooperation venture has general liability and does not acquire the status of a juridical person.

VIETNAM

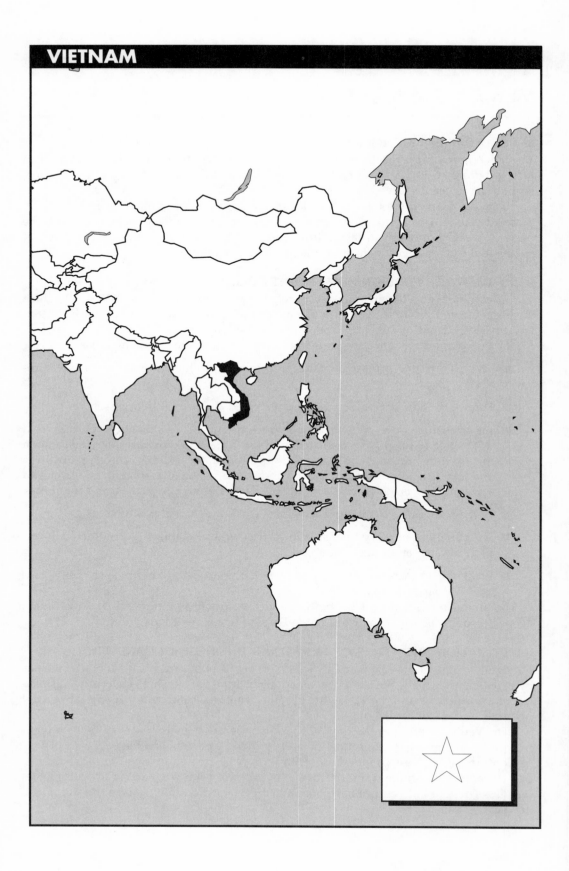

A joint venture is based on a contract between one or more foreign partners and at least one Vietnamese partner, or between a joint venture and a foreign partner. A joint venture may also be created between a foreign government and the government of Vietnam.

Capital contributions by a foreign investor to a joint venture may include foreign currency, plant, equipment, tools, parts, patents, and technology. Capital contributions by a Vietnamese partner may include Vietnamese currency, natural resources, building materials, rights to land and water surfaces, equipment, parts, technology, and patents.

Joint venture assets must be insured either by the Vietnamese Insurance Company or by another carrier agreed upon by the partners.

The minimum capital contribution by a foreign investor to a joint venture is determined in cooperation with government authorities. The value of the contribution is based on international currency levels and must be shown in the joint venture's establishing document either in Vietnamese or foreign currency.

A joint venture is considered to have juridical person status effective on the date the investment license and certificate of registration are issued.

The profits and risks of a joint venture are shared by the partners in proportion to their capital contribution.

A joint venture must appoint a board of managers of which either the general director or the first general director and at least one board member must be Vietnamese.

Enterprises with 100 percent foreign capital invested are granted juridical person status immediately upon the date of charter registration with the State Committee for Cooperation and Investment. Creation, operation, transfer of capital, and dissolution must be accomplished pursuant to the charter and Vietnamese law.

■ ENVIRONMENTAL PROTECTION

The law requires that appropriate action be taken to protect the environment while conducting any enterprise.

■ RIGHTS AND OBLIGATIONS OF FOREIGN INVESTORS

Any enterprise formed with foreign investment must deposit funds with the government to cover social insurance for enterprise employees.

Foreign citizens employed by a business cooperation contract enterprise or by any organization formed with foreign investment have the right, after deduction of income tax, to remit, in foreign currency, any amount of their incomes.

For the duration of the investment, the assets of foreign individuals of business organizations will not be subject to government exploitation or requisition. The law guarantees that foreign investment will not be nationalized.

■ LABOR

There are many qualified Vietnamese workers. When available, they must be given priority in hiring.

Employment contracts must state the rights and obligations of Vietnamese citizens who work for enterprises funded by foreign investment.

Wages, salaries, and benefits provided to Vietnamese workers must be in either Vietnamese or a foreign currency drawn on the bank account of the enterprise funded by foreign capital.

■ ACCOUNTING REQUIREMENTS

Enterprises formed with foreign capital must maintain account(s) in Vietnamese and foreign currency at the Bank of Foreign Trade of Vietnam or at a foreign bank branch approved by the State Bank of Vietnam.

Accounting records must be maintained according to international standards as approved by the Ministry of Finance.

■ CURRENCY CONTROLS

Foreign investors, after payment of applicable taxes, have the right to remit their share of profits and other income abroad.

Upon termination or dissolution of an enterprise funded by foreign investment, the investor has the right, after payment of all debts, to transfer capital or reinvested capital abroad.

■ TAXATION

Enterprises with foreign capital, or the foreign partners of a contractual business cooperation, must pay applicable import duties and other taxes.

All employees of an enterprise financed by foreign investment or by a business cooperation venture must pay income tax to Vietnam.

Tax exemptions and reductions may be granted depending on the type, size, and purpose of a foreign investment.

Royalties must be paid to the government where natural resources are exploited, and rent must be paid for the use of any water or land surface.

In exceptional cases where foreign investment is encouraged, taxes on money remitted abroad may be reduced or exempted.

Patents, technical knowledge, industrial processes, and technical services that are part of capital contribution provided by foreign investors may be exempted from taxation.

Taxable income for any foreign enterprise is the net income in any tax year after deductions of costs and expenses.

The tax year is from January 1 to December 31 unless another 12-month period is selected with the approval of the Ministry of Finance.

■ LEGAL SYSTEM

Arbitration is encouraged as an alternative to the courts.

The People's Courts are located in each province and city. The highest court is the Supreme People's Court, which principally serves an appellate function. In exceptional cases it may be convened as a trial court.

■ CUSTOMS AND DUTIES

Export and import duties on products and services are based on applicable regulations. In specific cases where foreign investment is encouraged, duties may be exempted or reduced by the State Committee for Cooperation and Investment.

Machinery, vehicles, and other items used as part of capital contribution are exempt from import duties.

■ PROTECTION OF INTELLECTUAL PROPERTY

Vietnam is a member of the World Intellectual Property Organization and subscribes to the provisions of international agreements governing copyright and trademark protection. Favorable conditions for the transfer of technology are intended under the provisions of the Decree on the Transfer of Foreign Technology, enacted in 1988.

■ IMMIGRATION AND RESIDENCE

Multiple-entry visas that are valid for three months and for successive three-month extensions may be granted to foreign citizens who are considering investment opportunities.

Foreign citizens engaged in investment projects may be granted one-year multiple-entry visas. They may travel in areas necessary to their investment activities.

Immigration, residence, and travel regulations relevant to foreign investors are equally applicable to all family members and foreign household employees.

■ FOREIGN INVESTMENT ASSISTANCE DIRECTORY

The following offices should be contacted for detailed information concerning investment in Vietnam:

State Committee for Cooperation and Investment
56 Quoc To Giam
Ho Chi Minh City
Telephone: (84) 53666

Chamber of Commerce and Industry of Vietnam
33 Ba Trieu
Hanoi
Telephone: (84) 52961
Telex: 411257
Fax: (84) 56446

Persons interested in obtaining further information about investing in Vietnam are also advised to contact the closest Vietnamese embassy or consular office.

Vietnam maintains diplomatic relations with Afghanistan, Albania, Algeria, Australia, Belgium, Bulgaria, Cambodia, People's Republic of China, Cuba, Czechoslovakia, Egypt, Finland, France, Germany, Hungary, India, Indonesia, Iraq, Italy, Japan, Democratic People's Republic of Korea, Laos, Libya, Malaysia, Myanmar, Philippines, Poland, Romania, Spain, Sweden, Thailand, Russia, United Kingdom, and Yemen.

WESTERN SAMOA, INDEPENDENT STATE OF

■ POLITICAL ENVIRONMENT

The government is stable, and there are no current external threats to its sovereignty.

Most of the country's economic activities are based on agriculture, which makes the nation highly vulnerable to the vagaries of weather and potentially soft markets. There is a major need to develop a modern infrastructure.

The annual rate of inflation has fluctuated but is not chronically high. Unemployment, being related to agriculture, can be considered as relatively high.

■ SUMMARY OF FOREIGN INVESTMENT POLICY

The government is actively seeking increased foreign investment, particularly in the areas of light manufacturing of products for export, development of the tourist industry, improvement of the agricultural sector, and construction of the national infrastructure.

The principal law enacted to assist in the promotion and development of foreign investment is the Enterprises Incentives Act of 1986. The Department of Economic Development is charged with the primary responsibility for working with potential foreign investors.

Priority interests, on the part of the government, are to increase employment opportunities, increase the nation's technological levels and to generally improve the overall quality of life in the country.

A variety of incentives are being offered to foreign investors to include duty free imports of necessary materials and equipment and long-term tax holidays.

An Industrial Free Zone has been established for foreign companies engaged in manufacturing for export. In addition, an offshore financial center is in existence.

All foreign investments must be submitted to the Department of Economic Development for initial screening.

■ FORMATION AND TYPES OF PERMITTED BUSINESS ORGANIZATIONS

Foreign investors may create public or private corporations, partnerships, or sole proprietorships. Firms may also establish branch offices or subsidiaries of corporations that are domiciled in another country. Foreign investors may enter into joint ventures with domestic enterprises or persons.

There is no requirement for domestic participation in the management of any enterprise that is wholly funded by foreign capital.

Any enterprise, including branches and subsidiaries of foreign companies, must obtain a license from the Department of Inland Revenue before conducting operations, and all public companies must register with the Registrar of Companies.

No restrictions exist on the percentage of ownership a foreign investor may acquire in an existing domestic company.

Partnerships are limited in number to 25 natural or juridical persons.

■ ENVIRONMENTAL PROTECTION

Potential foreign investors are advised to contact the Department of Economic Development for full information about laws and regulations on this subject.

WESTERN SAMOA

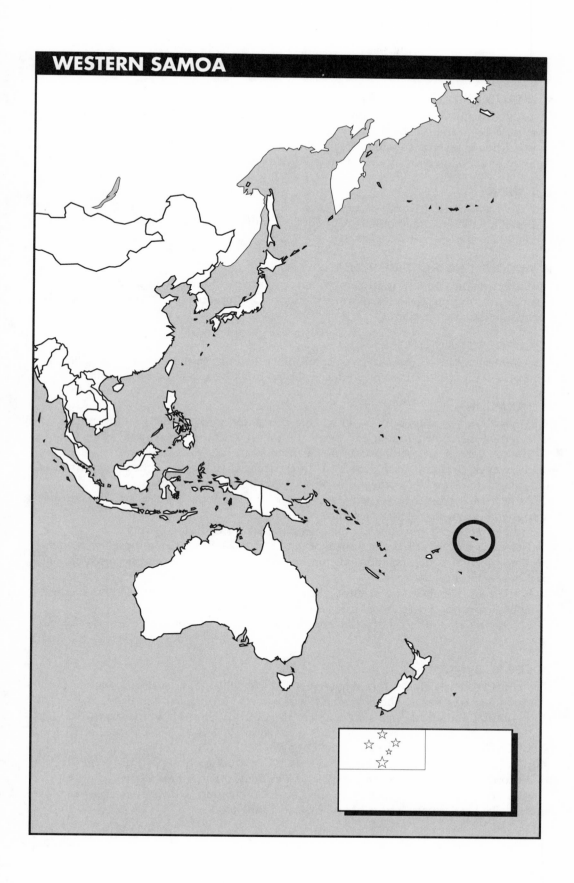

■ RIGHTS AND OBLIGATIONS OF FOREIGN INVESTORS

Investment capital, and all income derived as a result of such investment, may be repatriated or remitted abroad after payment of taxes.

Local financing is available to foreign investors.

Long-term real property leases of up to 40 years may be obtained by foreign investors.

■ LABOR

There is a body of existing laws regarding employment and working conditions.

Foreign nationals must obtain both entry permits and work permits. Entry permits are valid for a period of six months.

■ ACCOUNTING REQUIREMENTS

Public companies operating in Samoa must maintain complete and accurate financial records. Accounting procedures must conform to internationally accepted standards. Annual audits are required.

■ CURRENCY CONTROLS

The Central Bank of Samoa has responsibility for all matters relating to exchange control. All repatriation and remittances abroad must be approved by the bank.

■ TAXATION

The major tax levied on both business enterprises and individuals is on income. A tax is levied on the entertainment and tourism industries. There is no capital gains tax.

The tax year is concurrent with the calendar year, i.e., from January 1 to December 31. However, firms operating under a different fiscal year may, with the approval of the Inland Revenue Department, file on the basis of such fiscal year.

Partnerships are not taxed as entities but must file annual tax returns. The partnership members are liable for taxes due.

Individual taxpayers must use the calendar year for tax filing purposes.

There are a variety of deductions that may be allowed to include those for business expenses incurred, depreciation on buildings and equipment, scientific research, and bad debts, among others.

Individual taxpayers are granted allowances that include reasonable and incurred business expenses. There are no gift or inheritance taxes.

Enterprises operating as offshore companies are exempt from income and other tax laws.

■ LEGAL SYSTEM

The court system includes the Magistrates' Courts, which have jurisdiction over petty criminal and civil cases. The Supreme Court is a trial level court that hears major civil and criminal matters. Appeals are taken to the Court of Appeal, which sits in Apia.

■ CUSTOMS AND DUTIES

Imports on raw materials and equipment used to manufacture exports are received free of customs duties by those firms established in the Industrial Free Zone.

Western Samoa is a signatory to the Lome Convention, which guarantees a minimum price for its cocoa and copra oil exports to the EC.

■ PROTECTION OF INTELLECTUAL PROPERTY

Potential foreign investors are advised to contact the Department of Economic Development regarding the nation's laws and regulations on this subject.

■ IMMIGRATION AND RESIDENCE

Visas are usually required to enter Western Samoa. Potential foreign investors are advised to contact the Department of Economic Development for complete information on visas, work permits, and residence permits.

■ FOREIGN INVESTMENT ASSISTANCE DIRECTORY

Sources that can provide further information about foreign investment in Western Samoa include:

Department of Economic Development
P.O. Box 862
Apia, Western Samoa
Telephone: (685) 24071

Central Bank of Samoa
Private Bag
Apia, Western Samoa
Telephone: (685) 24100
Telex: 200
Fax: (685) 20293

Development Bank of Western Samoa
P.O. Box 1232
Apia, Western Samoa
Telephone: (685) 22861
Telex: 212

Persons interested in obtaining further information about foreign investment in Western Samoa are advised to contact the country's closest embassy or consular office.

Western Samoa maintains diplomatic relations with Australia, People's Republic of China, New Zealand, and United States.

YEMEN, REPUBLIC OF

■ POLITICAL ENVIRONMENT

This is a newly formed national entity created by the unification, in May 1990, of the Yemen Arab Republic (which occupied the northern portion of the present country), and the People's Democratic Republic of Yemen, which occupied the southern part of the nation.

In large measure, the unification was spurred by the rapidly deteriorating economy of the People's Democratic Republic of Yemen, which was closely allied to the former Soviet Union.

The unification was carried out under what appears to have been a dedicated attempt to please all parties. The government bureaucracies were simply merged with no attempt to reduce personnel. Adding to the bureaucratic tangle was the fact that the newly unified Yemen chose to support Iraq during its seizure of Kuwait.

The result of this support was an immediate loss of much needed aid from other Arab states, particularly Saudi Arabia, and the expulsion of Yemeni workers, most of whom returned to Yemen to immediately become a drain on an already struggling economy. Another immediate problem, and directly related to the loss of Yemeni jobs abroad, was the fact that remittances from those Yemeni workers, which constituted a major source of the nation's foreign exchange, immediately terminated.

In a broader financial sense, the new country had agreed, upon unification, to assume the combined debt obligations of both former states.

The net result of these considerations is that the country suffers from a shortage of foreign exchange, a growing level of inflation, high unemployment, and a massive foreign debt.

Yemen's chief resource is oil. However, it is generally considered that oil revenues will not be sufficient to materially improve the nation's economic health in the near term.

In recognition of the need to acquire other revenues, the government has embarked on a major program to acquire investment with the thrust of the effort being directed to foreign interests. Reportedly, some public sector enterprises are being privatized.

■ SUMMARY OF FOREIGN INVESTMENT POLICY

A key element of the government's plan to encourage foreign investment is the Investment Law of 1991, which was enacted with the intent of eliminating much of the bureaucratic red tape that had previously characterized the government's procedures relevant to foreign investment proposals. As part of the program, a new government agency, the General Authority for Investments, has been established that will provide "one stop" approvals for foreign investment proposals. The Authority is responsible to a ministerial board headed by the prime minister.

Among the investment priorities that the government has noted are the need to reduce unemployment, create an economic situation where the private sector is dominant, and to increase exports. Oil revenues, as opposed to other foreign investment revenues, will be used to increase and improve the country's infrastructure.

Foreign investment may be particularly of interest in agriculture, industry, and mining. Oil exploration and exploitation projects will continue to be handled on a separate basis through the Ministry of Oil and Mineral Resources.

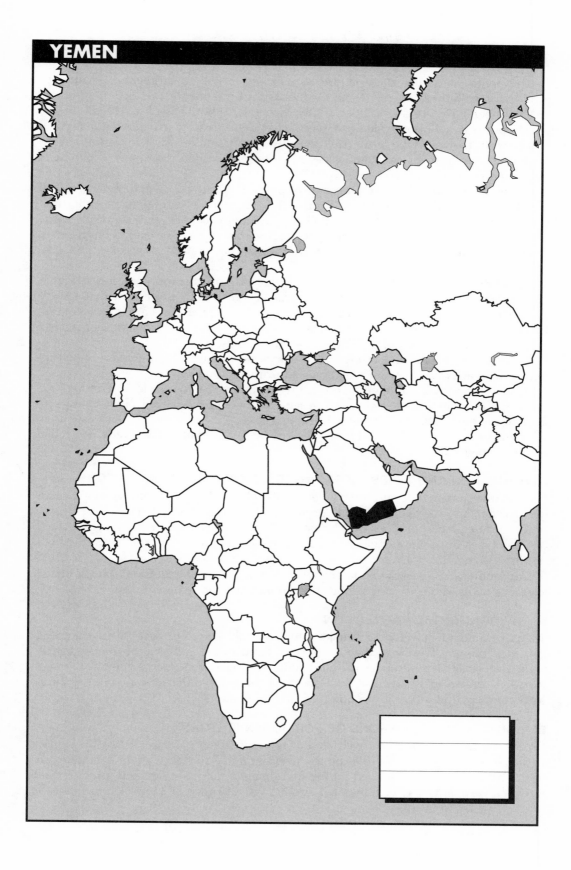

All foreign investment projects must be licensed by the government following approvals received through the General Authority for Investments.

The screening process employed by the General Authority is rather broad. Essentially, approvals will be granted to foreign investment projects that serve the national economy. In more specific terms, that includes investments with fixed assets that exceed 40 million Yemeni riyals and those of at least 20 million riyals, and which meet other criteria for government approval.

Additional criteria for foreign investment proposal approvals include the value that may be added to Yemen's national income; the generation of employment opportunities; the positive impact of the investment on foreign exchange; the use of local raw materials; the potential for increased export trade; the effect of the project on the environment; the introduction of modern technology; and the development of remote geographic areas.

Under the provisions of the law, foreign ownership of a business enterprise operating in Yemen may be either whole or partial. There is no requirement that foreign ownership be reduced over the passage of time. However, there is a requirement that limited liability companies that offer shares to the public in trust companies maintain at least a 55 percent Yemeni holding of the firm's paid-up capital.

The relatively small list of economic areas in which foreign investment is not permitted includes activities relevant to national security and defense.

Among incentives to foreign investors offered under the law are long-term tax holidays that can range from five to ten years, and exemptions from other charges to include customs duties and document (stamp) taxes.

The government is also considering the creation of several foreign trade zones that will encourage export activities.

■ FORMATION AND TYPES OF PERMITTED BUSINESS ORGANIZATIONS

Foreign investors may form publicly held or closely held corporations, general or limited partnerships, or operate in sole proprietorship capacities. Subsidiaries or branch offices of foreign corporations may be established. Foreign investors may, through any of these types of business organizations, form joint ventures with Yemeni individuals or business organizations.

Corporations are considered to acquire juridical person status upon filing of requisite documents under the provisions of the Yemen Company Law.

■ ENVIRONMENTAL PROTECTION

The government is developing a major interest in the need to protect the environment. As noted previously, one of the factors considered in the approval of foreign investment proposals is the impact of the activity on the environment. Potential foreign investors are advised to contact the General Investment Authority for complete information on environmental protection laws and regulations.

■ RIGHTS AND OBLIGATIONS OF FOREIGN INVESTORS

Foreign investments may be repatriated or remitted abroad along with profits subject to the required payment of taxes and to the extent that a sufficient credit balance exists in the bank account maintained by the investment enterprise. The law provides that foreign investments may be liquidated or otherwise disposed of. However, the investor must advise the General Authority for Investments of such action and the project must have been in operation for a period of at least three years.

Nationalization, project seizure (confiscation), or expropriation of foreign enterprises, or freezing, supervision, or sequestration of foreign funds may not occur, nor may real property be taken by the government except by proper legal process. In any such case, fair market value compensation must be provided by the government.

Any disputes arising between foreign investors and the government may be resolved, based on the desires of the investor, pursuant to the provisions of the Arab Investment Guarantee Association Agreement, the International Convention for the Settlement of Investment Disputes Between States and Nationals of Other States, any existing bilateral treaty relevant to investment disputes to which Yemen is a party, the United Nations Commission on International Trade Law, or the arbitration rules and procedures of Yemeni law.

The law provides that foreign investors are guaranteed equality and that there will be no discrimination between such foreign investors and domestic investors relevant to investment opportunities. Concurrently, the government has made a commitment to maintaining a spirit of competition between public and private enterprises and assuring that no preferential treatment will be accorded to the former.

There is no legal restriction on foreign investors seeking financing from local sources. However, the capital markets in Yemen are limited, and foreign investors should be prepared to seek required financing outside of the country.

■ LABOR

The Yemeni labor force is largely unskilled and many of its members are illiterate. A high reliance is placed on the employment of foreign workers in most skilled positions and in virtually all technical and management jobs.

Foreign employers are required by law to provide training to Yemeni workers for the purpose of enabling them to fill jobs at all levels that are currently held by foreign employees. Foreign workers are required to obtain work permits.

■ ACCOUNTING REQUIREMENTS

All enterprises operating in Yemen must maintain accounting and other records for tax and statistical purposes. There is an ongoing movement to require accounting and auditing procedures to fully meet internationally accepted standards.

■ CURRENCY CONTROLS

The Central Bank of Yemen is responsible for the general management of the foreign exchange system. There is a severe foreign exchange shortage. The nation's only real source of foreign exchange is the revenue received from oil exports and oil exploration and exploitation agreements.

There are no current restrictions on the movement of capital from the country.

■ TAXATION

The main Yemeni tax is that levied on business income. Under the new investment law, accelerated depreciation is provided as a tax incentive along with long-term tax holidays that may be increased for an additional two years depending on the economic activity in which an enterprise is engaged. Exemptions from document (stamp) and the business practice tax are also provided as part of the new investment law.

■ LEGAL SYSTEM

The Yemeni judicial system is in a state of reorganization following unification of the two former independent nations that existed. The current system includes local courts that have the authority for deciding a wide range of both petty and more serious criminal and civil cases. Appeals can be taken to the Supreme Court, which sits at San'a.

■ CUSTOMS AND DUTIES

The government, under the provisions of the new investment law, is offering blanket import licenses and numerous customs exemptions to include duty free imports of spare parts and capital goods and a procedure for refunding customs charges paid on the importation of raw materials that are used in manufacturing for export.

A Free Zone Authority has been established for the purpose of creating several free trade zones throughout the country. Companies would receive special incentives to operate as export manufacturers within those zones.

Presently, the Yemen riyal is considered to be overvalued with the result that the nation's negligible exports are considered to be non-competitive. At the same time, the country has employed protective tariffs for the benefit of local industry.

■ PROTECTION OF INTELLECTUAL PROPERTY

Yemen is a member of the World Intellectual Property Organization. There are existing laws on the subject of copyright, trademark, and patent protection. Enforcement of these laws, however, seems to be lax, and registration of property involves both extensive bureaucratic involvement and a major time commitment.

■ IMMIGRATION AND RESIDENCE

Visas are normally required to enter the country. Potential foreign investors are advised to contact the General Authority for Investment for complete and current information on the requirements for visas, work permits, and residence permits.

■ FOREIGN INVESTMENT ASSISTANCE DIRECTORY

Sources that can provide further information about foreign investment in Yemen include:

General Authority for Investment
Office of the Prime Minister
Government Offices
San á, Yemen
Telephone: (967) (2) 247-6900

Central Bank of Yemen
P.O. Box 59
Ali Abd al-Mughni Street
San'a, Yemen
Telephone: (967) (2) 274371
Telex: 2280
Fax: (967) (2) 274131

Federation of Chambers of Commerce of Yemen
P.O. Box 16992
San'a, Yemen
Telephone: (967) (2) 224262
Telex: 2229

Persons interested in obtaining additional information about foreign investment in Yemen are advised to contact the closest Yemeni embassy or consular office.

Yemen maintains diplomatic relations with Albania, Algeria, People's Republic of China, Czechoslovakia, Egypt, Ethiopia, France, Germany, Hungary, India, Iran, Iraq, Italy, Japan, Jordan, Democratic People's Republic of Korea, Kuwait, Lebanon, Libya, Morocco, Netherlands, Oman, Pakistan, Romania, Russia, Saudi Arabia, Somalia, Sudan, Syria, Tunisia, Turkey, United Arab Emirates, United Kingdom, and United States.

ZAIRE, REPUBLIC OF

■ POLITICAL ENVIRONMENT

This nation is beset by a multiplicity of internal political problems along with continuing economic difficulties.

During the past several years there have been many clashes between students and other groups and the police, several of which have resulted in numerous student deaths. The outbreaks of violence were spurred by what appears to be discontent with the government's policies in a wide variety of areas as well as because of rising consumer prices.

Agriculture and mining are the nation's major economic activities. Various forms of produce, together with copper, represent Zaire's principal exports and the country's primary sources of foreign exchange.

Inflation is extremely high, and the external public debt and the accompanying debt service are substantial. The nation has received massive financial assistance both from individual countries and from the International Monetary Fund (IMF). However, the inability or unwillingness of the government to effectively manage the national economy has resulted in a cessation of foreign monetary assistance.

■ SUMMARY OF FOREIGN INVESTMENT POLICY

The government maintains its interest in the acquisition of foreign investment. The principal law relevant to this area is the Investment Code of Zaire of 1986. Under the provisions of this law, a special government agency, the Investment Commission, which functions under the Commission of Plan, was created.

Foreign investment is considered to include technology, assets, or cash that are intended for use by a foreign investor to either continue or establish an enterprise that will provide goods or services.

A foreign investment is one that, whether provided by an individual or a corporation, is at least 51 percent owned by foreign interests.

Three foreign investment regimes have been created, i.e., the General Regime, the Conventional Regime, and the Industrial Free Zone Regime.

All foreign investment proposals must be submitted to the government through the Commissioner of Plan for approval. Among the criteria that are considered as part of the review process are the size of the investment; opportunities that it provides for employment; the use of local raw materials; the level of technologies involved; the possible location of the establishment relevant to underdeveloped geographic areas; and the impact of the investment on balance of payments.

The government has the right, with the agreement of the foreign investors concerned, to take an equity position in investment projects in certain priority areas of the economy, such sectors to be designated in the national development plans.

Proposals under the General Regime are expected to be at a minimum level of 10 million Zaires; 80 percent of the investment must be financed by foreign funds; and the amount of financing required by the investment cannot exceed 70 percent of the total amount of the investment, nor may the loans to be repaid in five years or less be greater than 30 percent of the total investment.

Incentives available to investors include exemptions on taxes relevant to capital

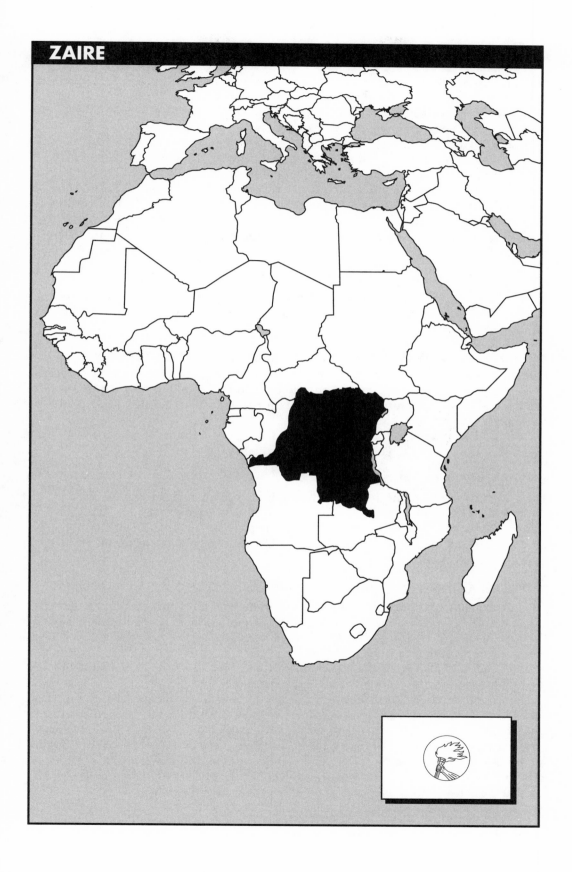

ZAIRE

assets for a period of five years; on import duties with respect to goods required to carry on business; and on the turnover (transactions) tax.

Where investments result in the development of employment opportunities, exemptions are available from the income due on the salaries of permanent employees.

Additional tax incentives are available to firms that become established in geographic regions outside the capital; to firms that provide training for local employees; and for firms that manufacture exclusively for export.

Small and medium-sized investments that do not meet the 10 million Zaire requirement but where the firm is headed personally by the owner, whether in a corporate form or as an individual, are generally eligible for the benefits provided under the General Regime. Special tax and customs incentives are provided to investments established in the Free Zone to include tax-free profits for a period of six years from the date of creation of the investment and substantial tax reductions for a period of up to 30 years from such date.

The government reserves the right of equity participation with firms established in the Free Zone. However, government participation cannot exceed 50 percent of the capital provided.

■ FORMATION AND TYPES OF PERMITTED BUSINESS ORGANIZATIONS

Foreign investors may participate in the economy through the formation of corporations, partnerships, or acting as sole proprietors. Limited liability share companies are eligible for an exemption from the ad valorem tax both when formed and upon any subsequent increase in capital.

Corporations may be publicly or privately held. Corporations, upon filing with the Registry of Commerce, achieve juridical person status.

■ ENVIRONMENTAL PROTECTION

The government maintains an active interest in environmental protection, principally through the Department of the Environment and Nature Conservation. Potential foreign investors are advised to contact that department or the Investment Commission for complete and current guidance regarding laws and regulations pertaining to environmental protection.

■ RIGHTS AND OBLIGATIONS OF FOREIGN INVESTORS

The government guarantees the protection of property rights pursuant to the nation's Constitution. Nationalization or expropriation cannot occur except and unless under the process of law as required by the public interest. In such event, the law provides that fair compensation must be provided.

Dividends and all other income, including proper shares realized from liquidation of the investment, may be remitted abroad or repatriated.

Any conflicts that may arise between the government and a foreign investor must be settled by arbitration. Zaire is a signatory to the Convention for the Settlement of Investment Disputes Between States and the Nationals of Other States. Consent to such arbitration procedures must be provided by a foreign investor as part of the application for admission to the General or Conventional Regimes or for establishment in the Free Zone. Further, any such application must include the provision that the foreign investor shall be considered a "National of another Contracting State."

Any subsequent law that is enacted and that may tend to restrict or eliminate the provisions of the law now in force will not affect firms covered under the provisions of the current law. Any subsequent law that may be enacted that will provide improved benefits will be extended to investments made under the provisions of the present law.

■ LABOR

There is an existing body of laws regarding employment and working conditions. There is a requirement to hire Zaire nationals except in those caes where necessary skills and expertise are not locally available. When foreign companies train and promote local personnel, there is a five-year exemption from the surtax normally assessed on the salaries of foreign personnel.

Foreign personnel must possess work permits.

■ ACCOUNTING REQUIREMENTS

Any enterprise that is admitted under any one of the Regimes contained in the Investment Code must agree to maintain current and complete accounting and other records for tax and other purposes. Accounting records must be maintained in accordance with internationally accepted standards.

■ CURRENCY CONTROLS

The Banque du Zaire is the nation's central bank and has responsibility for the management and operation of the foreign exchange system and related matters.

All transactions made in the Free Zone with regard to payment for electrical energy must be made in foreign currencies.

In the event that foreign currencies are not available in sufficient amounts to meet the requirements of foreign firms that are established in the Free Zone, such firms may be authorized by the government to maintain accounts in foreign currencies as needed. The status of such accounts must be made available, on a periodic basis, to the central bank.

■ TAXATION

Foreign companies and individuals are subject to the tax laws.

In addition to deductions for losses, a tax credit is granted against profits earned during the first five years of operation. Small and medium-sized enterprises may take advantage of an accelerated depreciation rate, which, under the law, is based on 75 percent of equipment value amortized under the equipment's half life expectancy.

Enterprises involved in the construction of public utilities are eligible for customs exemptions on tools, materials, and equipment used in such utility construction or expansion.

■ LEGAL SYSTEM

The County Courts are responsible for deciding criminal and civil matters. Appeals from these courts are taken to the Supreme Court, which sits at Kinshasa.

■ CUSTOMS AND DUTIES

Zaire is interested in expanding its international trade, particularly with regard to exports.

Companies that export all or part of their production are exempt from export taxes.

Any imports received on an import basis for use by firms approved under any of the Regimes cannot be transferred, sold, or used for any other purpose, except after permission is received from the Commissioner of Plan.

■ PROTECTION OF INTELLECTUAL PROPERTY

Zaire is a member of the World Intellectual Property Organization and subscribes to internationally accepted standards concerning the protection of copyrights, patents, and trademarks.

■ IMMIGRATION AND RESIDENCE

Visas are required to enter Zaire. Potential foreign investors are advised to contact the Investment Commission for current information regarding procedures for obtaining visas, work permits, and residence permits.

■ FOREIGN INVESTMENT ASSISTANCE DIRECTORY

Sources that can provide additional information about foreign investment in Zaire include:

Investment Commission
Department of Planning, Resources and Suppliers
P.O. Box 9378
Kinshasa 1, Zaire
Telephone: (0) (0) 313346
Telex: 21781

Department of the Environment and Nature Conservation
P.O. Box 1248
15 Ave de la Clinique
Kinshasa, Zaire
Telephone: (0) (0) 31252

Banque du Zaire
P.O. Box 2697
Boulevard Colonel Tshatshi au nord
Kinshasa, Zaire
Telephone: (0) (0) 20701
Telex: 21127

Persons interested in obtaining further information about foreign investment in Zaire are advised to contact the country's closest embassy or consular office.

Zaire maintains diplomatic relations with Algeria, Angola, Argentina, Austria, Belgium, Benin, Brazil, Burundi, Cameroon, Canada, Central African Republic, Chad, People's Republic of China, Congo, Côte d'Ivoire, Cuba, Czechoslovakia, Egypt, Ethiopia, France, Gabon, Germany, Ghana, Greece, Guinea, Holy See, India, Iran, Israel, Italy, Japan, Kenya, Democratic People's Republic of Korea, Republic of Korea, Kuwait, Lebanon, Liberia, Libya, Mauritania, Morocco, Netherlands, Nigeria, Pakistan, Poland, Portugal, Romania, Russia, Rwanda, Spain, Sudan, Sweden, Switzerland, Tanzania, Togo, Tunisia, Turkey, Uganda, United Kingdom, United States, and Zambia.

ZAMBIA, REPUBLIC OF

■ POLITICAL ENVIRONMENT

This country has been engaged in almost continuous political upheaval since its independence was achieved in 1964. There have been assassinations, revolutions, and widespread rioting.

Economic difficulties have also plagued the country. The government's varied attempts, over the passage of years, and prompted by the World Bank and the International Monetary Fund (IMF), to create a semblance of financial order, often have resulted in popular discontent that has taken the form of major violence and bloodshed. Drought conditions that have affected much of Southern Africa have further exacerbated the economic woes of the country, which is heavily dependent on agriculture.

A substantial portion of the economy is directly controlled by the government, including the copper mining activities that form the principal source of Zambia's economic strength. Copper, along with other mined products, e.g., zinc, lead, and cobalt, are Zambia's major exports.

The national infrastructure, to include rail, road, and communications systems, are both inadequate and obsolete.

In recent years, the currency has been devalued, the external public debt and the debt service have become mountainous, and the annual inflation level has reached triple digits. Unemployment is very high and rising.

The nation was in arrears on its external public debt payments with the result that the World Bank and the International Monetary Fund cut off additional credit.

The government has recently embarked on a new program in an effort to attempt to achieve a viable economy. Among the key program elements are a movement to privatize the economy, tax reductions, and the development of incentives designed to attract foreign investment. Zambia has restructured its debt obligations and has once again been granted access to credit by the International Monetary Fund and the World Bank.

■ SUMMARY OF FOREIGN INVESTMENT POLICY

The government's interest in acquiring foreign investment is exemplified by its enactment of a new law on the subject thath replaces the previous investment act. Under the provisions of the new law, an Investment Board has been established that has responsibilities for both the promotion of foreign investment and initial screening of foreign investment proposals.

All proposals for foreign investment must be submitted to the Investment Board. Decisions are made within a period of 30 days.

The government has determined several priority areas for foreign investment, namely agriculture, the development of rural, undeveloped areas, tourism, and export-oriented or import-substitution manufacturing.

A variety of incentives has been created for foreign investors under the new law. Included among those incentives are opportunities for exporters to retain all hard currency earned from non-mineral exports; tax holidays on dividend income for seven years; a general three-year tax holiday on profits with a 75 percent tax reduction for the

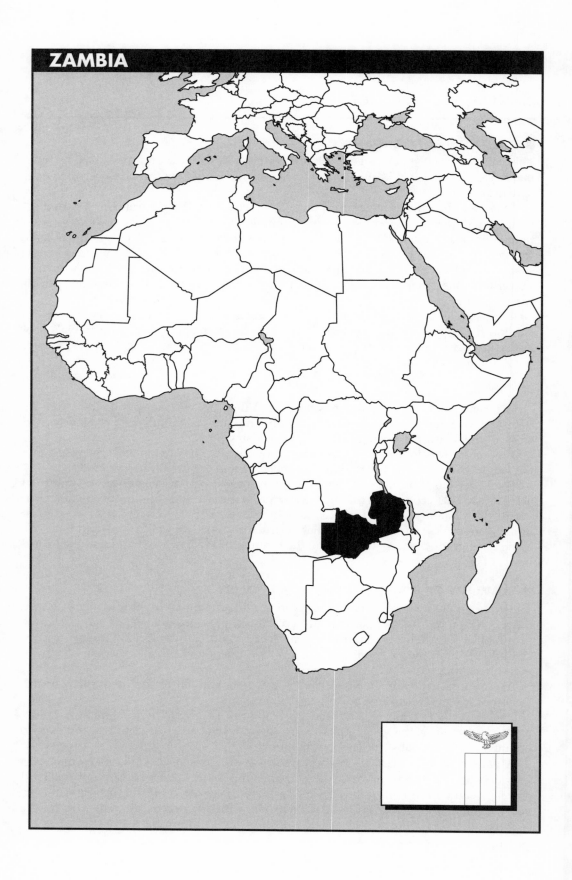

ZAMBIA

subsequent two years; customs duties and sales tax exemptions on imported machinery, equipment and necessary parts; and a seven-year exemption from the employment tax. In addition, the government may act to assist a foreign investor in obtaining land for business purposes.

Incentives are only available to those foreign investors engaged in one of the priority economic areas established by the government. The nation's mining law is currently being revised and will, reportedly, include several industry-specific incentives designed to attract foreign investors.

Approved foreign investments are granted licenses by the government. Operations under that license must commence within one year of the date the license is granted. The Investment Board must be advised when the operations begin.

All businesses must be registered with the government through the offices of the Investment Board. Licensing and registration are completely separate procedures. Licensing is required in order for a foreign investment to become eligible for the incentives provided under the law. If a license is not granted, a firm may still become registered and proceed to operate although it will not be eligible for incentives.

There are no requirements that limit the percentage of ownership in any firm that may be maintained by a foreign investor, or which provide that Zambian nationals participate in the management of any firm that is wholly or partially funded by foreign investment.

■ FORMATION AND TYPES OF PERMITTED BUSINESS ORGANIZATIONS

Foreign investors may participate in the Zambian economy through the formation of publicly or privately held corporations, general or limited partnerships, or as sole investors. Subsidiaries of foreign corporations may be established.

Joint ventures may be created between foreign and Zambian investors.

■ ENVIRONMENTAL PROTECTION

There is a growing interest, on the part of the Zambian government, relevant to the protection of the environment. A high level department, the Ministry of the Environment and Natural Resources, has been created to develop policies and recommend laws pertaining to this subject. Potential foreign investors are advised to contact either the Investment Board or the Ministry of the Environment and Natural Resources for complete and current information on the issue of environmental protection.

■ RIGHTS AND OBLIGATIONS OF FOREIGN INVESTORS

There are no restrictions on the acquisition of Zambian firms, including those state enterprises now being privatized, by foreign investment.

Foreign and Zambian investors are considered to possess equal rights and opportunities with regard to the investment laws.

Foreign investments may be liquidated without government approval. However, transfers of investment licenses require the permission of the Investment Board.

Amounts up to and including 75 percent of after-tax profits on foreign investments may be remitted abroad or repatriated. There are no limits imposed with regard to the repatriation or remittance abroad of principal and interest on foreign loans that are approved by the Bank of Zambia.

A foreign investor's share of an investment that is either liquidated or sold may be repatriated or remitted abroad after payment of all due taxes and other obligations.

Expropriation can only occur through proper legal process and will entitle affected investors to compensation based on fair market value. There is no clear indication as to how such a value will be determined.

Zambia is a party to the Multilateral Investment Guarantee Agency Agreement.

The law provides that disputes arising between the government and foreign investors must first be submitted to domestic dispute settlement procedures before seeking relief through international arbitration.

Local financing is available to foreign investors up to the amount of paid-in-share capital. However, the Zambian capital markets often are unable to provide major financing.

■ LABOR

There is an existing body of laws covering employment and working conditions. The labor force is large and can provide substantial numbers of unskilled personnel. There are few skilled or professional workers. AIDS is considered to be of epidemic proportions in the country and has particularly decimated the skilled worker population.

Foreign personnel can be hired when it is shown that required skills or experience are not locally available. Work permits are required for all foreign workers.

■ ACCOUNTING REQUIREMENTS

All business enterprises in Zambia must maintain complete and accurate financial and accounting records in accordance with internationally accepted standards.

■ CURRENCY CONTROLS

The Bank of Zambia is the nation's central bank, and it has the principal responsibility for management of foreign exchange.

All foreign exchange required for profit repatriation must be generated either from earnings or purchased on the open market.

Generally, restrictions pertaining to the flow of capital from Zambia have been liberalized. However, the movement of capital from the country must be approved by the central bank.

■ TAXATION

The major tax levied is on business and personal income. Deductions include depreciation on assets, business expenses, and losses. Incentives, as previously noted, include long-term tax holidays and exemptions for foreign investments that receive license approvals.

■ LEGAL SYSTEM

Local courts are empowered to hear and decide petty civil and criminal matters. More serious civil and criminal cases are heard by both the Magistrates' Courts and by the High Court. The High Court has an intermediate appellate function. Final appeals are taken to the Supreme Court, which sits at Lusaka.

■ CUSTOMS AND DUTIES

Zambia is a member of the Preferential Trade Areas for Eastern and Southern African

States. Trade between member states of that group can be free of customs duties.

There is a government interest in generating a higher level of international trade, particularly exports. Incentives are now provided to exporters in terms of permitting their retention of hard currency from non-mineral exports.

It is anticipated that in the near future the government will establish free trade zones or free ports that will contribute to an increased level of exports.

■ PROTECTION OF INTELLECTUAL PROPERTY

Zambia is a member of the World Intellectual Property Organization and is a signatory to the Paris Convention on industrial property protection. There are statutes in existence with regard to patent and trademark protection. Copyright protection is narrow in its application.

■ IMMIGRATION AND RESIDENCE

Visas are required to enter Zambia. Potential foreign investors are advised to contact the Investment Board for complete and current information on requirements for visas, work permits, and residence permits.

■ FOREIGN INVESTMENT ASSISTANCE DIRECTORY

Sources that can provide further information about foreign investment in Zambia include:

Investment Board
Office of the Prime Minister
P.O. Box 30208
Lusaka, Zambia
Telephone: (0) 218282
Telex: 42240

Ministry of the Environment and Natural Resources
P.O. Box 30055
Lusaka, Zambia
Telephone: (0) 214988

Bank of Zambia
P.O. Box 30080
Lusaka, Zambia
Telephone: (0) 216529
Telex: 41560

Confederation of Industries and Chambers of Commerce
P.O. Box 30844
Lusaka, Zambia
Telephone: (0) 252369
Telex: 40124
Fax: (0) 252483

Persons interested in obtaining further information about foreign investment in Zambia are advised to contact the closest Zambian embassy or consular office.

Zambia maintains diplomatic relations with Angola, Austria, Belgium, Botswana, Brazil, Bulgaria, Canada, Chile, People's Republic of China, Cuba, Czechoslovakia, Denmark, Egypt, Finland, France, Germany, Ghana, Guyana, Holy See, India, Iran, Iraq, Ireland, Israel, Italy, Japan, Kenya, Malawi, Mozambique, Netherlands, Nigeria, Portugal, Romania, Russia, Saudi Arabia, Somalia, Spain, Sweden, Tanzania, Uganda, United Kingdom, United States, Zaire, and Zimbabwe.

ZIMBABWE, REPUBLIC OF

■ POLITICAL ENVIRONMENT

The country's history is replete with violence, political corruption, and general instability.

Zimbabwe suffers from a lack of foreign exchange. In addition, persistent drought conditions have damaged the country's agricultural production, which is the key element in the nation's foreign trade.

Inflation and unemployment rates are both high and rising.

The government has undertaken an austerity program and, at the same time, has relaxed some previous regulations that tended to hinder foreign investment.

■ SUMMARY OF FOREIGN INVESTMENT POLICY

The government recognizes the need for an infusion of foreign investment. There is a specific desire to increase the nation's industrial base. The plan is to increase export production and thus reduce the nation's dependence on agriculture as the basis for foreign exchange.

Other government desires for foreign investment are directed at the need to create local employment, acquire advanced technology, achieve greater uses of available raw materials, and increase both research and developmen, and overall production levels.

The government's Investment Center has been charged with the responsibility of generating new investment, both foreign and domestic.

In most cases, the government will desire that foreign investors hold a majority interest. Where foreign investors hold a majority or total position in any project, it will be expected that Zimbabwe participation will eventually be in the majority.

Despite the government's desire for foreign investment, no program of incentives to attract such investment is in place. Incentives that exist are offered to both foreign and domestic investors and generally take the form of tax allowances, tariff protection for newly established industries, and tax exemptions.

All foreign investment proposals must be submitted to the Investment Center for review.

Foreign investment is permitted in virtually all of the private industries of the economy. Manufacturing projects are favored for foreign investment. Areas such as telecommunications, rail and air transportation, and similar activities are closed to foreign investment.

Zimbabwe is a party to the Multilateral Investment Guarantee Agency Agreement and, in addition, the government is pledged to protect foreign investment.

■ FORMATION AND TYPES OF PERMITTED BUSINESS ORGANIZATIONS

Foreign investors may participate in the economy of the nation through the creation of public and private companies (i.e., corporations), general partnerships, or as sole proprietorships. Subsidiaries of foreign corporations may also be established. Joint ventures are possible, both with private domestic partners or, on occasion, with the government.

Public companies, other than foreign corporate subsidiaries, must file annual statements with the Registrar of Companies.

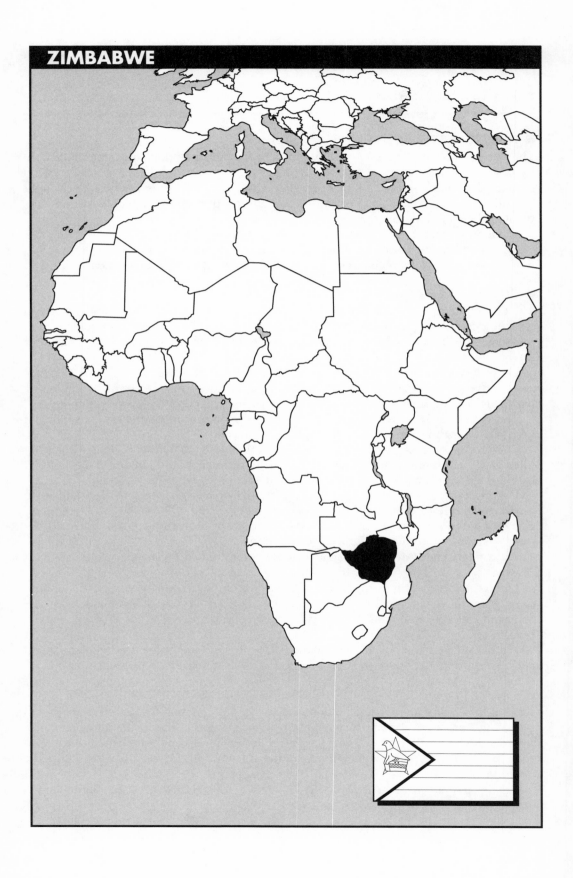

No more than 20 partners are permitted in any partnership. Partnerships, unlike companies, do not enjoy a juridical person status.

■ ENVIRONMENTAL PROTECTION

There is a major and continuing interest, on the part of the government, in the protection of the environment. Potential foreign investors are advised to contact the Investment Center or the Ministry of the Environment and Tourism for complete information on applicable laws and regulations in this area.

■ RIGHTS AND OBLIGATIONS OF FOREIGN INVESTORS

Foreign investors may obtain financing. However, foreign borrowing is subject to a formula that heavily considers the amount of capital that has been invested in the enterprise. Foreign investors may be eligible for financing provided by government institutions to include the Zimbabwe Development Bank and the Zimbabwe Small Business Development Corporation.

There are stringent rules in effect with regard to the right to repatriate or remit abroad foreign investments and income derived from such investments. There is some government activity reported as possible relevant to the current laws on investment remittance. Potential foreign investors are advised to contact the Investment Center or the Reserve Bank of Zimbabwe about the current status of the laws relevant to this subject.

At the present time, foreign remittances must be approved by the central bank.

Foreign employees may generally remit abroad or repatriate up to one-third of their salaries or wages.

The government maintains that it guarantees equality of treatment to both foreign and domestic investors.

Land cannot be acquired through purchase by foreign investors without the approval of the central bank.

■ LABOR

Skilled labor is not plentiful in Zimbabwe. At the other end of the labor spectrum, however, there is a high level of unskilled and unemployed labor. There is a government desire to fill all positions, including managerial ones, with local personnel as quickly as possible. Foreign workers must obtain work permits before beginning employment. Agreements with foreign employers are usually sought that will result in the creation of a training program designed to place local workers in any position held by a foreign national. In general, foreign workers may only be employed where required skills are not locally available. There are no specific percentages that must be maintained as to domestic employees in any enterprise.

Zimbabwe has enacted a comprehensive body of laws regarding employment and working conditions.

■ ACCOUNTING REQUIREMENTS

All companies must maintain complete and accurate financial records for tax and other purposes. Public companies must be audited on a yearly basis.

■ CURRENCY CONTROLS

The Reserve Bank of Zimbabwe is the nation's central bank. It is charged with the responsibility of managing foreign exchange matters pursuant to the Exchange Control Act and the Exchange Control Regulations.

As noted, any foreign investment must be approved by the central bank. This approval is obtained through the offices of the Investment Center.

Foreign currency accounts may not be maintained.

■ TAXATION

Foreign businesses and individuals are subject to the tax laws. The principal tax assessed is that on income. Other taxes that are levied include those on sales, imports, documents, and real estate. A capital gains tax is also in force.

The tax year runs from April 1 to March 31 although companies with a different fiscal year may apply to file on that basis.

Partnerships and non-incorporated joint ventures are not considered to be taxable entities. Participants in such enterprises are taxed individually.

Tax deductions include depreciation of machinery, business expenses incurred, certain special allowances, training allowances and, for mining and forestry activities, depletion allowances. Other deductions available include those for bad debts, travel and entertainment, and research and development costs.

Mining activities are considered to be of special importance to the government and thus certain special tax concessions are provided to enterprises established in this field. A similar situation exists for companies engaged in large-scale agricultural activities.

Individual taxpayers may deduct actual business expenses, medical expenses, and certain other costs from their personal income tax.

Zimbabwe has entered into bilateral treaties on the subject of double taxation with a limited number of nations.

■ LEGAL SYSTEM

The judicial system essentially involves the local or magistrates' courts, which decide petty civil and criminal matters, and the regional courts, which hear only criminal cases. Decisions are appealed to the High Court. Final appeals are taken to the Supreme Court, which sits at Harare.

■ CUSTOMS AND DUTIES

Zimbabwe is associated, for the purposes of trade with the European Community (EC), with the Lome Convention.

Imports are stringently controlled because of the nation's shortage of foreign exchange. Exports are controlled principally to the extent of reporting income on a timely basis to the central bank.

Zimbabwe is a party to the General Agreement on Tariffs and Trade (GATT). Virtually all imports are subject to the imposition of customs duties. Customs duties are refunded in cases where goods or materials are reexported.

■ PROTECTION OF INTELLECTUAL PROPERTY

Zimbabwe is a member of the World Intellectual Property Organization and has enacted domestic statutes covering the protection of property rights relevant to copyrights, patents, and trademarks.

■ IMMIGRATION AND RESIDENCE

Depending on the visitor's nationality, visas may be required to enter Zimbabwe. Potential foreign investors are advised to contact the Investment Center for complete information on visas, work permits, and residence permits.

■ FOREIGN INVESTMENT ASSISTANCE DIRECTORY

Sources that can provide further information about foreign investment in Zimbabwe include:

Investment Center
Ministry of Finance, Economic Planning and Development
Munhumutapa Building
Samora Machel Avenue
Causeway
Harare, Zimbabwe
Telephone: (0) (0) 794571
Telex: 22141

Ministry of the Environment and Tourism
Karigamombe Center
Causeway
Harare, Zimbabwe
Telephone: (0) (0) 794455

Reserve Bank of Zimbabwe
76 Samora Machel Avenue
P.O. Box 1283
Harare, Zimbabwe
Telephone: (0) (0) 790731
Telex: 26075

Persons interested in obtaining further information about foreign investment in Zimbabwe are advised to contact the country's closest embassy or consular office.

Zimbabwe maintains diplomatic relations with Afghanistan, Algeria, Angola, Argentina, Australia, Austria, Bangladesh, Belgium, Botswana, Brazil, Bulgaria, Canada, People's Republic of China, Cuba, Czechoslovakia, Denmark, Egypt, Ethiopia, Finland, France, Germany, Ghana, Greece, Holy See, Hungary, India, Indonesia, Iran, Iraq, Italy, Japan, Kenya, Democratic People's Republic of Korea, Kuwait, Libya, Malawi, Malaysia, Mexico, Mozambique, Netherlands, New Zealand, Nigeria, Norway, Pakistan, Poland, Portugal, Romania, Russia, Senegal, Spain, Sudan, Sweden, Switzerland, Tanzania, Tunisia, United Kingdom, United States, Vietnam, Zaire, and Zambia.

BIBLIOGRAPHY

■ GENERAL

Adler, Nancy J., and Dafna N. Izraeli, eds. *Women in Management Worldwide*. London: M. E. Sharpe, 1988.

This book presents a series of studies of women in management in various regions of the world. These studies vary in content but generally introduce the reader to international views on women managers, as well as the problems and prospects faced by women managers in different parts of the world. Chapters include extensive references, including foreign sources.

Austin, James E. *Managing in Developing Countries*. New York: Free Press, 1990.

A guide to assist corporate managers with the challenges involved in managing operations in developing countries. Issues discussed include finance, production, marketing, firm organization, and relations between business and government. Also included are a large bibliography and four indexes that contain a large amount of data on developing countries.

Ball, Sarah. *The Directory of International Sources of Business Information*. London: Pitman, 1989.

A guide to major data sources for international business. Includes alphabetical country listings, listings organized by industry, and major international associations. Information on major business journals and publications is provided for each country. The volume also contains a listing of international databases.

Burgen, Carl G., editor-in-chief. *Global Finance*. New York: Global Information.

This magazine aims to provide helpful information to assist business managers in their international finance dealings. The publication specializes in presenting major trends in international finance and outlining strategies for corporate financial officers, money managers, and bankers responsible for international transactions.

Chai, Alan, Alta Campbell, and Patrick J. Spain, eds. *Hoover's Handbook of World Business, 1993*. Austin, Tex.: Reference Press, 1993.

This volume provides a wealth of information on world business and includes sections reviewing international business trends, profiling international firms of global importance, offering information on significant economic regions and nations, and containing lists of top companies by country, as well as other useful chapters. Three indexes organize entries by industry, by location of the company headquarters, and by company name.

Coopers and Lybrand, International. *International Accounting Summaries: A Guide for Interpretation and Comparison*. New York: John Wiley & Sons, 1991.

A discussion of accounting and reporting practices for twenty-four countries and for the European Economic Community is presented in this volume. In addition to chapters providing specific information, the authors provide matrices highlighting the differences and the similarities of accounting principles and practices among countries.

Dreifus, Shirley B., ed. *Business International's Global Management Desk Reference.* New York: McGraw-Hill, 1992.

This book covers the major issues facing firms in their international dealings, including planning and investment, trade and supplier relations, marketing, finance, human resources, legal issues, and public policy. The text provides numerous examples of these issues from successful international companies.

Estell, Kenneth. *World Trade Resources Guide: A Guide to Resources on Importing from and Exporting to the Major Trading Nations of the World.* Detroit: Gale Research, 1992.

This directory provides more than 1,000 foreign trade contacts and information for eighty of the largest trading countries of the world. There are three sections to the guide. The first provides information by country, including general economic information about the country, as well as information such as telephone and fax numbers on international trade contacts. The second section contains regional information, while the third is international in scope. There is also a "Keyword and Name" index at the back of the book.

Foster, Dean Allen. *Bargaining Across Borders: How to Negotiate Business Successfully Anywhere in the World.* New York: McGraw-Hill, 1992.

Divided into three parts, this book focuses on cross-cultural communication. Part 1 describes basic principles of cross-cultural communication. Part 2 compares the behavior and expectations of Americans with those of other cultural groups. The third part provides strategies on cross-cultural negotiating. Examples that illustrate points made in the text are provided throughout the book.

Harris, Philip R., and Robert T. Moran. *Managing Cultural Differences: High-Performance Strategies for a New World of Business.* 3d ed. Houston: Gulf, 1991.

The objective of this book is to teach business managers to deal successfully with cultural differences. The first part of the book discusses the role of the manager in influencing organizational culture and in creating cultural change. Chapters also discuss managing for cross-cultural effectiveness, managing human resources, and managing transitions and foreign deployment. The last section of the book features seven chapters on doing business in various regions of the world. The text includes four appendices, references, and subject and author indexes.

Ingo, Walter, and Tracy Murray, eds. *Handbook of International Management.* New York: John Wiley & Sons, 1988.

This volume is designed to provide a broad overview of managerial issues that firms must face when doing business internationally, including international marketing, risk assessment, international finance and accounting, technology transfer, and multinational planning and strategy formulation.

Kaynak, Erdener, editor-in-chief. *Journal of International Consumer Marketing.* Binghamton, N.Y.: Haworth Press.

This is a quarterly journal devoted to topics relevant to firms marketing consumer goods abroad. Articles address topics such as foreign business customs and practices, the behavior of consumers in developing and newly industrialized countries, cross-cultural advertising, and international market segmentation. The journal also publishes reviews of recent books and dissertations on international consumer marketing.

Lamont, Douglas. *Winning Worldwide.* Homewood, Ill.: Business One Irwin, 1991.
Strategies for success in international markets are presented in this text, written by an international business professor and consultant. Examples from the real world are provided to highlight issues in international finance, in marketing, and in managerial organization. Short "executive summaries" are provided at the end of each chapter.

Maggiori, Herman J. *How to Make the World Your Market: The International Sales and Marketing Handbook.* Mission Hills, Calif.: Burning Gate Press, 1992.
This book is particularly oriented toward providing assistance in breaking into foreign markets for small businesses and firms that have no international experience. Topics covered include agents and distributors, export documentation, payment methods, shipping modes, and pricing strategies. The book also provides sources of government assistance available from agencies such as the International Trade Administration.

Moskowitz, Milton. *The Global Marketplace.* New York: Macmillan, 1988.
The history of 102 multinational corporations outside the United States is presented in this volume. Data on sales revenue, profits, sales in the United States, number of employees, year of establishment, and location of headquarters are provided. Case studies are included, as well as appendices with additional statistical information.

Mowery, David C. *International Collaborative Ventures in U.S. Manufacturing.* Cambridge, Mass.: Ballinger, 1988.
This book describes the international collaboration between firms in the United States and abroad in the areas of telecommunications equipment, commercial aircraft, integrated circuits, pharmaceuticals, biotechnology, robotics, steel, and motor vehicles. Eight case studies are presented, illustrating the flow of international technological transfer. These case studies show the range of techniques used in these activities, from research partnerships to agreed marketing of product and from licensing to joint ventures.

Munger, Susan H. *The International Business Communications Desk Reference.* New York: AMACOM, 1993.
This is a basic reference for international business professionals. Information on major countries is provided, including time differences, national holidays, international measures, mail, address formats, fax, telex, and currencies. A bibliography and an index are included.

Nelson, Carl A. *Global Success.* Blue Ridge Summit, Pa.: Liberty Hall Press, 1990.
This is a comprehensive international marketing guide. Information is provided by country concerning local customs, attitudes, and business etiquette. Also, the book describes how to develop an international marketing plan, with information on intermediaries (such as general trading companies, export management companies, brokers, and others), methods of gathering research data, and information on tariffs, laws and

regulations, and licensing agreements. Appendices include data on government and trade organizations supporting international trading activities, an extensive bibliography, and other items providing information pertinent to international business.

Paliwoda, Stanley J., ed. *New Perspectives on International Marketing.* London: Routledge, 1991.

A collection of eighteen articles on international marketing, many from a European perspective. Divided into three sections, the book discusses general international marketing issues and theories, industry-specific empirical studies, and marketing to China and Japan.

Presner, Lewis A. *The International Business Dictionary and Reference.* New York: John Wiley & Sons, 1991.

This volume provides a dictionary of business terms related to international trade and international business. This is also a reference source for information on international associations. Specialized appendices are also provided, along with ten indexes.

Razin, Assaf, and Joel Slemrod, eds. *Taxation in the Global Economy.* Chicago: University of Chicago Press, 1990.

This volume includes eleven scholarly essays analyzing the influence of national tax policy on international trade and competitiveness. The book is divided into four sections. The first section concerns taxation of international income in the United States. The second section looks at the taxation of multinational corporations. The third and fourth sections concern the effects that tax systems have on international trade and capital flows. The economic analysis presented in the book, while excellent, requires a relatively high degree of sophistication from the reader.

Ricks, David A. *Blunders in International Business.* New York: Basil Blackwell, 1993.

Ricks provides an informative discussion of the types of blunders that companies have made in doing business internationally. The examples given include common mistakes in marketing, management, production, and strategy. The book includes a bibliography and indexes organized by company, by country, and by product.

Scherer, F. M. *International High-Technology Competition.* Cambridge, Mass.: Harvard University Press, 1992.

This study focuses on how firms in the United States have responded to foreign competition in high technology industries. The book includes some case studies, as well as some discussion of intra-industry trade and import competition. The author provides recommendations on ways in which the United States can maintain its global leadership in high-technology industries.

Schuller, Frank C. *Venturing Abroad.* New York: Quorum Books, 1988.

This book deals with innovation strategies of multinationals from the United States operating abroad. The author provides an analysis of conditions motivating these companies to innovate, as well as the characteristics of firms that successfully innovate. The book includes extensive references and a bibliography.

Towell, Julie E., and Charles B. Montney, eds. *International Directories in Print.* Detroit: Gale Research, 1988.

An annotated guide to thousands of foreign and international directories from more than one hundred countries. Entries are divided into a number of subject categories, including government, education, the arts, business, and industry. The volume also includes geographic, subject, and keyword/title indexes.

Tuller, Lawrence W. *Going Global.* Homewood, Ill.: Business One Irwin, 1991.

This author provides recommendations as to how firms can compete for opportunities in world markets, based on his thirty years of experience in international operations management and consulting. This text covers major issues related to doing business abroad (including planning, marketing and financing), includes information for every region of the world, and contains thirteen appendices of reference information.

United Nations. *Transnational Corporations: A Selective Bibliography, 1991-92.* New York: Author, 1993.

This bibliography includes references to works on a number of topics related to transnational corporations, including foreign direct investment, legal and policy frameworks, contracts and agreements, and social, political, and environmental issues. This volume includes a technical assistance directory of advisory services and aid programs, an author index, a subject index, and a list of reference sources.

Valentine, Charles F., Ginger Lew, and Roger Poor. *The Ernst and Young Resource Guide to Global Markets, 1991.* New York: John Wiley & Sons, 1991.

This guide is a reference tool for the international businessperson. It includes country-specific information, explanations of key issues relevant to international business, definitions of common international business terms, and directory information on foreign business contacts and international organizations. An annotated bibliography is also provided.

Zuraicki, Leon, and Louis Suichmezian. *Global Countertrade.* Garland Press, 1991.

Countertrade is a growing phenomenon in international trade. This book describes how countertrade is practiced in more than eighty countries around the world. It includes a comprehensive bibliography, as well as author and subject indexes.

■ REGION OR COUNTRY-SPECIFIC

Canada

Laxer, Gordon. *Open for Business.* New York: Oxford University Press, 1989.

A large percentage of Canada's capital stock is owned and controlled by foreign interests. This text examines the reasons why Canada is so dependent on foreign investment and puts forth possible explanations for this dependence.

Central and South America

Grosse, Robert. *Multinationals in Latin America.* London: Routledge, 1989.

This author examines the role that multinational corporations have played in the process of economic development in Latin America. He concludes that these international firms have made positive contributions in many areas, including employment, income, technology transfer, and balance-of-payments. He also concludes, however, that the presence of multinationals has not resulted in improvements in income distribution. The arguments in the text are presented with empirical support, and chapters contain endnotes and bibliographies.

Chile

Kline, John M. *Foreign Investment Strategies in Restructuring Economies: Learning from Corporate Experience in Chile.* New York: Quorum Books, 1992.

Rules governing foreign investment in Chile were substantially liberalized in the 1970s under the Pinochet regime. This volume provides information on the foreign investment that has occurred since then in various sectors of the Chilean economy. Related issues such as technology transfer, export promotion, and labor relations are also discussed. The book relates the Chilean experience to the general topic of foreign investment in the developing countries.

China

Pearson, Margaret M. *Joint Ventures in the People's Republic of China: The Control of Foreign Direct Investment Under Socialism.* Princeton, N.J.: Princeton University Press, 1991.

This text examines China's experience with foreign direct investment from 1979 to 1988. The author describes the conflicting goals of the Chinese government to both control and encourage foreign direct investment. China is seen as a case study of the role of foreign direct investment in a socialist economy.

Eastern Europe

Directory of Foreign Trade Organizations in Eastern Europe. San Francisco: International Trade Press, 1989.

This volume provides a comprehensive compilation of export and import companies in Eastern Europe. Included is information on banks, chambers of commerce, trade ministries, state committees, agencies that trade in manufactured goods, and a list of joint ventures. Addresses and phone numbers of many of these organizations are provided.

Enderlyn, Allyn. *Cracking Eastern Europe: Everything Marketers Must Know to Sell into the World's Newest Emerging Markets.* Chicago: Probus, 1992.

This is a practical guide to doing business in Eastern Europe. Countries (including the former East Germany) are profiled individually, and contacts are provided in organizations that provide assistance to those firms interested in accessing Eastern European markets. A statistical appendix is also included.

Zonis, Marvin, and Dwight Semler. *The East European Opportunity: The Complete Business Guide and Sourcebook.* New York: John Wiley & Sons, 1992.

A reference book that provides basic political and economic information on six Eastern European countries: Poland, Czechoslovakia, Hungary, Romania, Bulgaria, and Yugoslavia. Data in the book are current up to 1990.

India

Encarnation, Dennis. *Dislodging Multinationals.* Ithaca, N.Y.: Cornell University Press, 1989.

The basic thesis of this text is that India's restrictive foreign investment policies have adversely affected the efficiency and growth of India's economy. In addition, these policies have served to dislodge many multinational corporations from the local economy. There is no bibliography in this text.

Indonesia

Dickie, Robert B., and Thomas A. Layman. *Foreign Investment and Government Policy in the Third World.* New York: St. Martin's Press, 1988.

A good source of information on government regulations for foreign ownership in Indonesia. There is a particular focus on Indonesia's capital markets and banking industry. Choices made by government officials in regulating foreign investment in these fields of business are analyzed.

Japan

Balassa, Bela, and Marcus Noland. *Japan in the World Economy.* Washington, D.C.: Institute for International Economics, 1988.

Written by two highly regarded experts on the Japanese economy and economic development, this volume provides an overview of the experience of the Japanese economy. The authors analyze the changing pattern of international specialization, saving and investment policies, and Japanese trade policies. The book includes many statistics on the Japanese economy, as well as numerous references and appendices.

Huddleston, Jackson N. *Gaijin Kaisha.* London: M. E. Sharpe, 1990.

This guide to running a Western business in Japan is based on the author's experience as a general manager in Japan for a major U.S. corporation. The book provides strategies for successful management of Western firms operating in Japan.

Mitsubishi Corporation. *Tatemae and Honne.* New York: Free Press, 1988.

This text contains a glossary of 500 words and phrases used in the Japanese business world. The book explains how these phrases are typically used in business proceedings, and warns against possible misuses in a business context. A pronunciation guide is also included.

Korea

Underwood, Lorraine A., and Shirley G. Sullivan. *International Business Handbook.* Arlington, Va.: Global Quest, 1988.

This volume provides a quick guide to business and trade between the United States and Korea. It includes a directory of 1,000 organizations and individuals concerned with international trade in Korea. The entries are divided into three types: government, nonprofit, and private for-profit. A sixteen-page annotated bibliography is also included.

Mexico

Jenkins, Barbara. *The Paradox of Continental Production: National Investment Policies in North America.* Ithaca, N.Y.: Cornell University Press, 1993.

The passage of the North American Free Trade Agreement will lead to increased international capital flows within North America. This volume describes and compares foreign investment policies and environments in the United States, Canada, and Mexico. The author analyzes the interactions between political forces and economic policies that could result from the NAFTA agreement.

Kent, Kara. *The U.S.-Mexico Trade Pages: Your Single Source for Transborder Business.* Washington, D.C.: The Global Source, 1992.

This directory is divided into seventeen sections, each corresponding to a general source of information for companies engaging in trade with Mexico. These sources include trade associations, law firms, consulting firms, banks, insurance companies, United States and Mexican government resources, transportation specialists, research institutes in the United States and Mexico that specialize in international trade issues, and academic institutions with experts on international trade with Mexico. Contacts, addresses, and phone and fax numbers are included.

Newman, Gray, and Anna Szterenfeld. *Business International's Guide to Doing Business in Mexico.* New York: McGraw-Hill, 1993.

Designed to assist corporate decision makers in taking advantage of opportunities opening up in Mexico, this guide is divided into three sections. The first describes the country's changing environment and gives some perspective on how international firms are planning their strategies for the new Mexican and North American markets. The second part assesses the political outlook for Mexico and discusses changes in business regulations. The third section profiles individual sectors of the Mexican economy.

Whiting, Van R. *The Political Economy of Foreign Investment in Mexico: Nationalism, Liberalism, and Constraints on Choice.* Baltimore: The Johns Hopkins University Press, 1992.

This author provides an analysis of the political economy of foreign investment policies in Mexico. In addition, the text includes case studies on foreign investment in food processing, computers, and the automobile industry. A comprehensive bibliography is also included, along with appendices on the legal foundation of Mexico's foreign investment policy.

Middle East

Fekrat, M. Ali, and James M. Spiegelman, eds. *Impediments to U.S.-Arab Economic Relations.* New York: Praeger, 1989.

Business professionals interested in business ties between Arab nations and the United States will find this book to be informative. It emphasizes the link between economic and political relations between these countries and discusses the diversity of Arab Middle Eastern states.

Presley, John R., ed. *Directory of Islamic Financial Institutions.* London: Croom Helm, 1988.

This text has three parts. The first part explains Islamic banking, including a large bibliography on Islamic economics and banking. The second part contains a country-by-country directory of banking institutions. The third section includes case studies and information on banking laws for Iran, Pakistan, Malaysia, and Turkey.

North America
The Arthur Andersen North American Business Sourcebook: The Most Comprehensive, Authoritative Reference Guide to Expanding Trade in the North American Market. Chicago: Triumph Books, 1994.

This is a source of information for managers interested in international trading within North America. It includes a summary of the North American Free Trade Agreement. It also includes directories to business associations, embassies, consulates, and other business contacts in the United States, Canada, and Mexico.

United States
Feldstein, Martin S., ed. *The United States in the World Economy.* Chicago: University of Chicago Press, 1988.

A conference was held in 1987 under the sponsorship of the National Bureau of Economic Research to explore the consequences of growing interdependence between the United States and its international trading partners. This book presents a selection of papers presented at this conference. The papers contain extensive bibliographies, as well as statistical summaries.

Glickman, Norman J., and Douglas P. Woodward. *The New Competitors.* New York: Basic Books, 1989.

These authors argue that the increase in foreign investment in the United States is the result of a loss in the international competitiveness of the United States. Policy recommendations designed to improve this competitiveness are provided. The book includes useful statistics on foreign investment in the United States.

Western Europe
The Arthur Andersen European Community Sourcebook. Chicago: Triumph Books, 1991.

This is a guide to information resources on doing business in the European Economic Community (EEC). It includes a brief survey of the EEC, country profiles, and directories of information resources organized by topic and by industry category. A bibliography is included that lists relevant publications and online data resources.

Huellmantel, Michael B. *European Business Services Directory.* Detroit: Gale Research, 1993.

A comprehensive reference for business service providers in Europe. The directory contains three parts: a listing of more than 20,000 companies by service type, a geographic listing, and an alphabetical listing. This directory is also available on magnetic tape and floppy disks.

Irvin, Linda, et al., eds. *European Wholesalers and Distributors Directory.* Detroit: Gale Research, 1992.

A comprehensive directory of major wholesalers and distributors of both consumer and producer goods in some forty European countries. Information on companies can be located by SIC code, by product line, and by company name. Addresses and phone, fax, and telex numbers are provided for each entry.

■ COMPUTERIZED DATABASES AND OTHER STATISTICAL SOURCES

International Financial Statistics. Washington, D.C.: International Monetary Fund.

This database provides time-series on basic domestic and international financial statistics for more than 140 countries. Available statistics include exchange rates, money supply, prices, interest rates, government budget, balance-of-payments, GDP, and GDP per capita. The data are published in several forms. Monthly and annual books are published containing the most recent data. In addition, the database is available on CD-ROM. The CD-ROM subscription is put out quarterly, and each CD-ROM disk includes quarterly data back to 1948.

National Trade Database/Foreign Traders Index. Washington, D.C.: U.S. Department of Commerce.

This is a federal document that provides a tremendous amount of information of interest to firms participating in international trade. It includes a collection of 90,000 documents, tables, and time-series published by fifteen federal agencies. The Foreign Trader's Index is a directory including 35,000 overseas importers, agents, and distributors. The index also includes the "Export Yellow Pages," a directory of 12,000 companies in the United States that export or provide export services. These databases are available on CD-ROM with menu-driven software.

Wilson Business Abstracts. New York: H. W. Wilson.

Provides abstracts of articles in 345 business journals published since June of 1990. Information can be accessed using company names or SIC code. The database is available on CD-ROM and includes user-friendly software.

—*Lisa M. Grobar*
California State University, Long Beach

REFERENCE LISTS

■ EUROPEAN COMMUNITY (EC) MEMBERS

Established: April 8, 1965
Effective: July 1, 1967

Belgium, Kingdom of
Denmark, Kingdom of
France (The French Republic)
Germany, The Federal Republic of
Greece
Ireland
Italy (The Italian Republic)
Luxembourg, Grand Duchy of
Netherlands, Kingdom of the
Portugal, Republic of
Spain, Kingdom of
United Kingdom of Great Britain and
    Northern Ireland, The

■ EUROPEAN ECONOMIC COMMUNITY (EEC) MEMBERS

Established: March 25, 1957 (Treaty of Rome)
Effective: January 1, 1958
Also known as: Common Market

Belgium, Kingdom of
France (The French Republic)
Italy (The Italian Republic)
Luxembourg, Grand Duchy of
Netherlands, Kingdom of the
Germany, The Federal Republic of

United Kingdom of Great Britain and
Northern Ireland, The (1973)
Denmark, Kingdom of (1973)
Ireland (1973)
Greece (1981)
Spain, Kingdom of (1986)
Portugal, Republic of (1986)

■ GENERAL AGREEMENT ON TARIFFS AND TRADE (GATT)

Established: October 30, 1947
Effective: January 1, 1948

Antigua and Barbuda
Argentina (The Argentine Republic)
Australia
Austria, Republic
Bangladesh, The People's Republic of
Barbados
Belgium, Kingdom of
Belize
Benin, Republic of
Bolivia, Republic of
Botswana, Republic of
Brazil, The Federative Republic of
Burkina Faso
Burma, Socialist Republic of the Union of
Burundi, Republic of
Cameroon, Republic of
Canada
Central African Republic
Chad, Republic of
Chile, Republic of
Colombia
Congo, Republic of the
Costa Rica, Republic of
Cote d'Ivoire, Republic of
Cuba, Republic of
Cyprus
Czech, Republic of
Denmark, Kingdom of
Dominican Republic, The
Egypt, Arab Republic of
El Salvador, Republic of
Finland, Republic of
France (The French Republic)
Gabonese Republic, The
Gambia, Republic of the
Germany, The Federal Republic of
Ghana, Republic of
Greece
Guatemala, Republic of

Guyana, Cooperative Republic of
Haiti, Republic of
Hong Kong
Hungary, Republic of
Iceland
India, Republic of
Indonesia, Republic of
Ireland
Israel, State of
Italy (The Italian Republic)
Jamaica
Japan
Kenya, Republic of
Korea, Republic of
Kuwait, State of
Lesotho, Kingdom of
Luxembourg, Grand Duchy of
Macau
Madagascar, Democratic Republic of
Malawi, Republic of
Malaysia, Federation of
Maldives, Republic of
Malta, Republic of
Mauritania, Islamic Republic of
Mauritius, Republic
Mexico (United Mexican States)
Morocco, Kingdom of
Netherlands, Kingdom of the
New Zealand, Dominion of
Nicaragua, Republic of
Niger, Republic of
Nigeria, Federal Republic of
Norway, Kingdom of
Pakistan, Islamic Republic of
Peru, Republic of
Philippines, Republic of
Poland, Republic of
Portugal, Republic of
Romania
Rwanda, Republic of
Senegal, Republic of
Sierra Leone, Republic of
Singapore, Republic of
Slovakia (Slovak Socialist Republic)
South Africa, Republic of
Spain, Kingdom of

Sri Lanka, Democratic Socialist Republic
    of
Suriname, Republic of
Sweden, Kingdom of
Switzerland (The Swiss Confederation)
Tanzania, United Republic of
Thailand, Kingdom of
Togo, Republic of
Trinidad and Tobago, Republic of
Tunisia, Republic of
Turkey, Republic of
Uganda, Republic of
United Kingdom of Great Britain and
    Northern Ireland, The
United States of America
Uruguay, Republic of
Venezuela, Republic of
Yugoslavia, Socialist Republic of
Zaire, Republic of
Zambia, Republic of
Zimbabwe, Republic of

■ WORLD INTELLECTUAL PROPERTY ORGANIZATION MEMBERS (WIPO)

Established: July 14, 1967
Effective: April 26, 1970

Albania, Republic of
Algeria, Democratic and Popular Republic of
Angola, People's Republic of
Argentina (The Argentine Republic)
Australia
Austria, Republic
Bahamas, Commonwealth of the
Bangladesh, The People's Republic of
Barbados
Belarus, Republic of
Belgium, Kingdom of
Benin, Republic of
Brazil, The Federative Republic of
Bulgaria, Republic of
Burkina Faso
Burundi, Republic of
Cameroon, Republic of
Canada

Central African Republic
Chad, Republic of
Chile, Republic of
China, The People's Republic of
Colombia
Congo, Republic of the
Costa Rica, Republic of
Cote d'Ivoire, Republic of
Cuba, Republic of
Cyprus
Czech, Republic of
Denmark, Kingdom of
Dominican Republic, The
Ecuador
Egypt, Arab Republic of
El Salvador, Republic of
Fiji, Republic of
Finland, Republic of
France (The French Republic)
Gabonese Republic, The
Gambia, Republic of the
Germany, The Federal Republic of
Ghana, Republic of
Greece
Guatemala, Republic of
Guinea, Republic of
Guinea-Bissau
Haiti, Republic of
Holy See
Honduras, Republic of
Hungary, Republic of
Iceland
India, Republic of
Indonesia, Republic of
Iran, Islamic Republic of
Iraq, Republic of
Ireland
Israel, State of
Italy (The Italian Republic)
Jamaica
Japan
Jordan, Hashemite Kingdom of
Kenya, Republic of
Korea (North), Democratic People's Republic of
Korea (South), Republic of
Lebanon, Republic of

Lesotho, Kingdom of
Liberia, Republic of
Libya (Socialist People's Libyan Arab Jamahiriya)
Liechtenstein, Principality of
Lithuania, Republic of
Luxembourg, Grand Duchy of
Madagascar, Democratic Republic of
Malawi, Republic of
Malaysia, Federation of
Mali, Republic of
Malta, Republic of
Mauritania, Islamic Republic of
Mauritius, Republic
Mexico (United Mexican States)
Monaco, Principality of
Mongolia, People's Republic of
Morocco, Kingdom of
Namibia, Republic of
Netherlands, Kingdom of the
New Zealand, Dominion of
Nicaragua, Republic of
Niger, Republic of
Nigeria, Federal Republic of
Norway, Kingdom of
Pakistan, Islamic Republic of
Panama, Republic of
Paraguay, Republic of
Peru, Republic of
Philippines, Republic of
Poland, Republic of
Portugal, Republic of
Qatar, State of
Romania
Russia
Rwanda, Republic of
Saudi Arabia, Kingdom of
Senegal, Republic of
Sierra Leone, Republic of
Singapore, Republic of
Slovakia (Slovak Socialist Republic)
Somalia, (Somali Democratic Republic)
South Africa, Republic of
Spain, Kingdom of
Sri Lanka, Democratic Socialist Republic of
Sudan, Republic of

Suriname, Republic of
Swaziland, Kingdom of
Sweden, Kingdom of
Switzerland (The Swiss Confederation)
Syrian Arab Republic
Tanzania, United Republic of
Thailand, Kingdom of
Togo, Republic of
Trinidad and Tobago, Republic of
Tunisia, Republic of
Turkey, Republic of
Uganda, Republic of
Ukraine, Republic of

United Arab Emerates, The
United Kingdom of Great Britain and
    Northern Ireland, The
United States of America
Uruguay, Republic of
Venezuela, Republic of
Vietnam, Socialist Republic of
Yemen, Republic of
Yugoslavia, Socialist Republic of
Zaire, Republic of
Zambia, Republic of
Zimbabwe, Republic of

INDEX

A

Accounting requirements. *See individual countries*
Adler, Nancy J., 765
African Caribes Pacific Group, 449
African Organization of Intellectual Property, 250, 445
AG (Public corporations). *See* Austria
Albania, Republic of, 1-6
  accounting requirements, 4
  Albanian State Bank, 4
  Chamber of Commerce of Albania, 6
  Council of Ministers, 1, 3-4
  currency controls, 4
  customs and duties, 5
  diplomatic relations, 6
  District Courts, 5
  environmental protection, 3
  Foreign Investment Act of 1992, 1
  foreign investment assistance directory, 5
  Foreign Investment Law, 3-5
  foreign investment policy, summary of, 1
  foreign investors, rights and obligations, 3
  immigration and residence, 5
  intellectual property, protection of, 5
  labor, 4
  legal system, 5
  Ministry of Trade and Foreign Economic Cooperation, 1, 3-5
  National Privatization Agency, 1
  permitted business organizations, formation and types of, 3
  political environment, 1
  Supreme Court, 5
  taxation, 4
  Territorial Courts, 5
Algeria, Democratic and Popular Republic of, 7-10
  accounting requirements, 9
  Appeals Courts, 9
  Central Bank, 7, 9-10
  Chamber of Commerce and Industry, 10
  Currency and Credit Board of the Bank of Algeria, 7, 9
  currency controls, 9
  customs and duties, 9
  diplomatic relations, 10
  environmental protection, 7
  foreign investment assistance directory, 10
  foreign investment policy, summary of, 7
  foreign investors, rights and obligations, 7
  immigration and residence, 10
  intellectual property, protection of, 9
  labor, 9

  legal system, 9
  Ministry of Industry, 7, 9-10
  Ministry of the Interior, 7
  permitted business organizations, formation and types of, 7
  political environment, 7
  Supreme Court, 9
  taxation, 9
Andersen, Arthur, 773
Angola, People's Republic of, 11-15
  accounting requirements, 14
  Angolan Law on Foreign Investment, 11
  Banco Nacional de Angola, 11, 14-15
  Court of Appeal, 14
  currency controls, 14
  customs and duties, 15
  diplomatic relations, 15
  environmental protection, 13
  foreign investment assistance directory, 15
  Foreign Investment Office, 11, 13-15
  foreign investment policy, summary of, 11
  foreign investors, rights and obligations, 13
  immigration and residence, 15
  intellectual property, protection of, 15
  labor, 14
  legal system, 14
  Ministry of Finance, 13-15
  Ministry of Planning, 11, 15
  permitted business organizations, formation and types of, 13
  political environment, 11
  Supreme Court, 14
  taxation, 14
Anguilla, 16-19
  accounting requirements, 18
  Chamber of Commerce, 16, 19
  currency controls, 18
  customs and duties, 18
  diplomatic relations, 23
  environmental protection, 16
  foreign investment assistance directory, 19
  foreign investment policy, summary of, 16
  foreign investors, rights and obligations, 16
  High Court, 18
  immigration and residence, 19
  intellectual property, protection of, 18
  labor, 18
  legal system, 18
  Magistrates' Courts, 18
  Ministry of Finance and Economic Development, 16, 18-19
  Ministry of Home Affairs, Tourism, Agriculture and Fisheries, 16, 19

G

W

Y

Z